CHINA'S
POST- JIANG
Leadership Succession

CHINA'S
POST- JIANG
Leadership Succession

PROBLEMS AND PERSPECTIVES

edited by

John WONG
ZHENG Yongnian

SINGAPORE UNIVERSITY PRESS
NATIONAL UNIVERSITY OF SINGAPORE

World Scientific
New Jersey • London • Singapore • Hong Kong

Published by

Singapore University Press
Yusof Ishak House, National University of Singapore
31 Lower Kent Ridge Road, Singapore 119078

and

World Scientific Publishing Co. Pte. Ltd.
5 Toh Tuck Link, Singapore 596224
USA office: Suite 202, 1060 Main Street, River Edge, NJ 07661
UK office: 57 Shelton Street, Covent Garden, London WC2H 9HE

British Library Cataloguing-in-Publication Data
A catalogue record for this book is available from the British Library.

CHINA'S POST-JIANG LEADERSHIP SUCCESSION
Problems and Perspectives

ISBN 981-238-187-2

This book is printed on acid-free paper.
Printed in Singapore by Mainland Press

Contents

Acknowledgments

The key mission of the East Asian Institute (EAI) is to promote both academic and policy-oriented research on developments in East Asia, particularly the political, economic, and social developments in contemporary China (including Hong Kong, Macao, and Taiwan) and their impact on the world outside. Towards this end, the Institute organized an international conference on "The Challenges to China's Fourth Generation Leadership" in Singapore in November 2001. The chapters in this collection are derived from the papers presented at the conference.

We are grateful to Mr. Hsuan Owyang and Professor Wang Gungwu for their valuable and insightful comments in their opening addresses and closing remarks. Their comments have been incorporated in the Introduction. We would also like to thank Dr. Lai Hongyi and his rapporteur team for recording many interesting remarks made by the participants during the meeting. Appreciation also goes to Mr. Lye Liang Fook and Ms. Sarah Chan for their research assistance.

John Wong and Zheng Yongnian

The Contributors

Chien-min Chao is Professor of Politics at National Chengchi University, Taipei.

X.L. Ding teaches at Hong Kong University of Science and Technology and is also a Research Associate in the Research School of Pacific and Asian Studies, the Australian National University.

Keith Forster is visiting Senior Research Fellow at the East Asian Institute, National University of Singapore.

He Baogang is Senior Research Fellow of the East Asian Institute, National University of Singapore.

Kong Qingjiang is Associate Professor of the Hangzhou University of Commerce and visiting Research Fellow of the East Asian Institute, National University of Singapore.

Lam Peng Er is Senior Research Fellow at the East Asian Institute, National University of Singapore.

Li Lianjiang is Assistant Professor of Politics at the Hong Kong Baptist University.

Lu Ding is Associate Professor of Economics at National University of Singapore and Research Associate at the East Asian Institute.

Frederick C. Teiwes holds a Personal Chair in Chinese Politics at the University of Sydney, and has been designated an Australian Research Council Special Investigator for the Social Sciences.

Tian Xiaowen is Research Fellow of the East Asian Institute, National University of Singapore.

Ignatius Wibowo is Head of the Center of Chinese Studies, Jakarta, and Lecturer at the University of Indonesia.

John Wong is Research Director of the East Asian Institute, National University of Singapore.

Wang Tongsan is Fellow of the Chinese Academy of Social Sciences, Beijing.

Zhang Tao is Fellow of the Chinese Academy of Social Sciences, Beijing.

Zheng Shiping is Associate Professor of Political Science at the University of Vermont in the United States.

Zheng Yongnian is Senior Research Fellow at the East Asian Institute, National University of Singapore.

Introduction: Succession Problems and Challenges

JOHN WONG AND ZHENG YONGNIAN

SUCCESSION PROBLEMS

As the crucial 16th Congress of the Chinese Communist Party (CCP) (which will officially decide on the transfer of power to the younger and fourth generation leadership) is drawing near, China's succession politics thickens, with scholars and observers all over the world watching closely the developments in Beijing. They are carefully deciphering signs and gestures to find out whether the top leaders are ready to pass on their batons, either completely or partially, to the known successors waiting in the wings. Occasional statements to this effect by Jiang Zemin or Zhu Rongji merely fuel intense speculation both within and outside China on how the final leadership drama will unfold in the months ahead.

Leadership transition is admittedly the single most important political issue in China for 2002. The high level of excitement among China experts is understandable, because leadership transfer under the country's unique political system has been traditionally a "dynamic" process full of uncertainties, especially apparent during Mao's reign. There were also surprises during Deng Xiaoping's period.

How the new leadership will eventually shape up will critically impact China's development in the first decade of this century. Further more, as China is fast emerging as a potential superpower, the pattern of its leadership transition will have significant implications for the Asia–Pacific region, if not for the rest of the world.

While professional China watchers in Washington, Tokyo, and Hong Kong are busy speculating on the final leadership lineup— who among the known successors will get what portfolio, who is in and who is out of the Politburo and the State Council—serious scholars will inevitably find such speculation intellectually futile, for two obvious reasons. First, leadership transition everywhere involves changes in power equations among the contenders or successors. The process is, by its very nature, unpredictable and fraught with uncertainties and last-minute surprises.

Secondly, "China watching" has all along been a very hazardous business. China watchers all over the world, with all their expertise and for all their technical and institutional support in information gathering, had failed to predict the outbreak of the Great Leap Forward, the Cultural Revolution, the fall of the Gang of Four, and the return to power of Deng Xiaoping. Even after the country opened up in 1978, the experts were taken by surprise by the Tiananmen event and the outcome of Deng Xiaoping's *Nanxun*.

It would, therefore, be far more productive and also intellectually more rewarding for us to focus on the potential problems and challenges that China's younger and fourth generation leadership will have to face in the near future. This is essentially what this book is about.

THE CHINESE MODEL OF SUCCESSION

To avoid the danger of being too speculative, our contributors have focused on two key aspects of the leadership transition: first, the changes in the politics of transition, and second, the real and potential problems and challenges that China's fourth generation leadership will have to face in the near future.

Is there a Chinese model of power succession? In dealing with succession, Chinese leaders in fact do not have any existing models to emulate. As a Marxist–Leninist party, the CCP initially looked at the model of the Soviet Union where a unique way of succession could be discerned: Lenin was succeeded by Stalin, then by Khrushchev, then by Brezhnev, and so on, until the demise of the Soviet state under Gorbachev. Certainly, the breakup of the Soviet Union and the collapse of the Soviet Communist Party there in the early 1990s shocked Chinese leaders, who have since been determined to avoid the same fate. The "Communist model" is less useful for China also because of the enormous problems and the socioeconomic chaos arising from leadership transition under a one-party rule. Ever since China's third generation leaders took over the reins of power from Deng Xiaoping, they have tried to cope with succession problems. The third generation leaders under Jiang Zemin have learned from the mistakes of other communist countries and, in the process, created a succession model of their own, which is being institutionalized now. How and to what extent has China's succession process been institutionalized? These are the central questions that will be addressed by individual authors.

The second focus of the contributors is on the enormous domestic and external challenges that the new leadership will have to grapple with. Over the past two decades, China has changed beyond recognition, economically, socially, and even politically. The world outside China is also changing very fast because of globalization and technological progress. The September 11 terrorist strikes in the US have added a new dimension to the ongoing uncertainty worldwide. Nobody can say for sure how the new international order will emerge or how the global economy will fare in the next year. Can China's new leadership grasp such a dynamic "new international situation"? This is on top of the myriads of domestic problems that the new leadership will have to deal with. China is developing, reforming, and building new institutions, all at the same time. There are numerous economic and social problems crying out for attention. How will the leadership cope with them?

The book is organized into two parts. Part one deals with the politics of leadership transition, focusing on how the transition has been institutionalized and how it can affect the other aspects of political life. Part two examines the major problems that will emerge to challenge the new leadership.

LEADERSHIP TRANSITION AND ITS IMPACT

The term "fourth generation leadership" is now widely used inside and outside China. Deng Xiaoping was the first to coin the term "generation." When Deng used this term, he was not only referring to that fact that China had seen different generations of leadership, but was also implicitly suggesting that it had made progress in dealing with leadership transition. It is still too early to talk about institutional succession in China, as a highly institutionalized process of leadership transition has yet to be developed. Liu Shaoqi and Lin Biao both failed to succeed Mao. Deng himself was nobody's successor; in fact, he rose to the top leadership position on his own, or by being simply driven by events. Hu Yaobang and Zhao Ziyang also did not succeed Deng Xiaoping. Hu Jintao, who is supposed to head the fourth generation leadership, was not even chosen by Jiang Zemin, who heads the third generation leadership.

Despite all this, it can be reasonably argued that leadership succession today is getting a bit more transparent. China watchers are now able to predict with greater accuracy which group would comprise the core of the fourth generation leadership. This is something that could not have been possible under Mao Zedong, or even under Deng 10 years ago. The progress towards institutionalization is encouraging, and if this trend persists, it would lead to greater predictability about leadership succession in China.

How did this happen? What new institutional factors have emerged to affect leadership transition? Frederick Teiwes, who has studied politics inside *Zhongnanhai* more closely than any other China scholar, provides a convincing explanation in his paper on power succession. He not only conducts a historical review of succession politics, but also compares the different ways of power succession under Mao Zedong, Deng Xiaoping, and Jiang Zemin. He finds some very important changes over the three generations of leadership. Under Mao, China actually did not have what Teiwes calls succession politics because Mao's power was absolute. No one was able to challenge Mao, and none did. The succession problems lay in Mao's deep sense of insecurity plus his perception of disloyalty among his chosen successors. This was what prompted Mao to remove his two heirs-apparent, Liu Shaoqi and Lin Biao.

After Deng Xiaoping assumed power, the CCP leadership learned from Mao's mistakes in dealing with succession. New factors were introduced into elite politics in general and leadership succession in particular. Whereas Mao acted in accordance with his ideological grand visions and his highly personal judgments of his colleagues and successors, Deng was largely result oriented and measured his successors by their performance and the prevailing political circumstances. The politics of succession thus became more normalized in that conflict was generated by issues rather than by the leader's sense of betrayal. Also, the intensity of conflict reflected the seriousness of the issues rather than the personal differences or ideological campaigns dictated from above.

These changes, however, did not, and could not, eliminate political conflict arising from leadership succession, as was shown in the cases of Hu Yaobang and Zhao Ziyang. Under Deng, China still faced the traditional dilemma of succession resulting from the tension between the old and new generation of leaders. Whereas Hu Yaobang and Zhao Ziyang had worked for the first generation leaders, real power was wielded by the old guards of the first generation. This put Hu and Zhao in a very difficult position vis-à-vis the elders. Both Hu and Zhao were subsequently ousted, not by succession struggles, but through the intervention of the CCP elders who believed them as having stepped out of line. Nevertheless, the criterion for selecting the core of the leadership under Deng was quite rational, with political performance taking precedence over ideology.

Teiwes regards the succession politics under Jiang as "managed institutionalism," meaning that the succession procedure has been partially institutionalized. Owing to his lack of distinguished revolutionary contributions or military experience, Jiang has to turn to institutional factors to deal with succession politics. In the past decade, *Zhongnanhai* is replete with examples of power games being played out, namely, the defeat of Jiang's rivals like the Yang brothers (Yang Shangkun and Yang Baibing in 1992) and the ouster of Chen Xitong in 1996 and Qiao Shi in 1997. But, on the whole, there is almost no evidence of strong challenges to Jiang as the new successor. Unlike Mao and Deng, Jiang has had an easier time in dealing with succession politics. This is largely because, according to Teiwes, the leadership has developed a number of loosely defined, quasi-institutional criteria that governs succession politics; these are:

- Retirement from the Politburo and other top positions at the age of 70.
- A limit of two terms for the top Party and state positions of General Secretary, President, and Premier.
- Younger, better-educated leaders to be brought into the Politburo at each Congress with a view to serving multiple terms and becoming the basis of future "generations" of leadership.
- The Politburo to represent diverse interests of key institutions, functional specialties, and major localities.
- Politburo members to be reelected until retirement age.
- The successor himself to be chosen at least one term ahead of his assuming power so as to reduce uncertainty during the transition process.

Nonetheless, Teiwes' chapter shows that power succession can still be problematic, because China's existing political institutions and rules that regulate succession politics are still weak.

In his chapter, Zheng Shiping goes a step further to show how much political institutionalization has taken place in China's power succession, and highlights some important changes. While personal influence and informal power play still operate in many ways today, institutions and organizational rules also matter, certainly more so than before. Institutional factors, such as distinct career paths, age limits and the successor-designate procedure, have helped in creating a rather smooth transition of power from the old to the new generation.

Nevertheless, succession politics is far from being fully institutionalized. Whether the successor-designate can succeed depends largely on his own initiative and political capability. Zheng observes that before the designated successor can assume power successfully, he needs to:

1. handle the *guanxi* [personal relations] with his political patrons;
2. establish broad supporting networks;
3. build up a skill base, and
4. engage in ideological innovation.

Zheng also highlights the fact that "getting to the top" is actually the first stage in the succession process; the successor-designate will then need to move to the second stage, which is to consolidate his power. Indeed, it took several years for Jiang Zemin to consolidate his power after rising to the top. Hu Jintao will have to do likewise after he assumes the mantle of leadership from Jiang Zemin.

While leadership transition has become progressively "normal," it is but a small aspect of the country's larger succession politics. The more important issue is how leadership transition will affect different aspects of political life in China. Zheng Yongnian discusses the issue of Party transformation, which is probably the most important task that has confronted Jiang Zemin and will continue to challenge the new leadership. Party transformation is at the core of China's overall political reform. How the CCP transforms itself will largely determine the path of China's political development. Zheng examines in detail how the CCP has tried to stay relevant by continuously adjusting itself to the socioeconomic changes in the country. The most important step is Jiang's "Three Representatives" theory aimed at expanding the Party's social base. In his speech on July 1, 2001, Jiang went a step further to declare that private entrepreneurs or capitalists would be admitted into the Party.

Jiang's efforts are politically significant. The CCP under Deng Xiaoping completed the first "great transformation," notably from a primarily revolutionary party to a less ideological and more technocratic one. And, with the admission of capitalists into the Party, the CCP has begun its second "great transformation," from a technocratic party to one that will rule by political means. But this will not be an easy task. Party ideologues have already raised a hue and cry over the admission of the capitalists as members. For the time being, the "Three Representatives" theory will operate to expand the social base of the Party; the momentum of change may eventually transform it into a social democratic party. The main challenge for the new leadership is how to handle such a change.

Ignatius Wibowo examines the impact of leadership transition on the Party's rank and file. Throughout the history of power succession in China, beginning in 1949, an important political phenomenon has been observed. As every new leader brings in his followers to replace those of his predecessor, succession has often been associated with political purges and campaigns. For example, there were two rectification campaigns when power was transferred from Mao to Deng's generation: the campaign against "three classes of people" during 1982–1983 and the one against "leftist deviations" during 1983–1985. Again, during the transition from Zhao Ziyang to Jiang Zemin, the politics of succession came to the forefront in the mid-1980s. There was a clash between the conservatives (headed by Li Peng) and the reformers (led by Zhao Ziyang), which culminated in the Tiananmen incident on June 4, 1989. After the June 4 event, a nationwide rectification campaign was initiated.

Wibowo suggests that different ideological orientations and different political interests among the top leaders often lead to power struggles, resulting in the launching of rectification campaigns against each other's followers. But probably the more important factor is the issue related to Party transformation, as Zheng Yongnian suggests in his chapter. When the CCP was transformed from a revolutionary to a technocratic party, old revolutionaries had to go, and better-educated technocrats had to be ushered in. Similarly, when Jiang's "Three Representatives" theory is adopted and capitalists are allowed to join the party, one can expect great changes in the Party's rank and file. Wibowo is correct in pointing out that the impact of power succession goes beyond the few dozens of senior top leaders. In other words, power succession affects not only a handful of people at the top but also the millions of cadres and government officials below.

Keith Forster focuses on the impact of power succession on central–local relations. One reason why power succession is so critical is that it can easily weaken the power of the central government. Observers inside and outside China have plenty of reasons to worry about such a development. Power struggles between conservatives and reformist leaders in the late 1980s almost paralyzed the government. The succession in the former Soviet Union led to the breakup of the country and the fall of the communist regime. Indeed, Forster points out that there is a wealth of literature on the possibility that China too can break up.

Drawing a different conclusion from these authors, Forster observes that the Jiang Zemin leadership has in fact consolidated central power by implementing new measures. Jiang, with the forceful backing of strong centralists such as Premier Zhu Rongji, has been to a large extent, successful in obtaining the full support of provincial leaders on issues of central concern to Beijing. Foster points out that new institutions have been created to regulate central–local relations. For example, in the past decade, there has been a regular rotation of provincial leaders. Forster argues that the frequent reshuffling of provincial leaders could be a reflection of the weakness of the center, rather than of its strength. He presents two cases that demonstrate how Jiang Zemin has skillfully and successfully consolidated central power: the removal of Chen Xitong in Beijing and the removal of Xie Fei in Guangdong. These two cases, he argues, show that the central government does not like to see a cadre remain in a province for too long for fear that he builds up a power base. They also show that Jiang did not fear localism, because he could easily remove the cadres by citing reasons peculiar to the province from which they came from and problems associated with them.

Through his examination of central–local relations in the post-Mao era, Forster paints a positive picture of how these political relations will evolve under the new leadership. Hu Jintao will assume the top job with impressive credentials reflecting his service at both the local and central levels, credentials that to a large degree outweigh those of Jiang Zemin. While it is likely that the future leadership will continue to rotate and regularly transfer provincial leaders, may be a greater focus on recruiting younger officials and underrepresented groups into the provincial elite.

He Baogang discusses the possible impact of leadership transition on China's national identity problem. China is a multinational country, and the leadership has played a vital role in bringing different minorities under one united state. Indeed, national unity has been the highest priority for the Chinese leadership. He's major concern is whether the coming leadership will use democracy as a tool to deal with the issue of national identity. Through a historical approach, He finds that although the Chinese leaders differed over the resolution of the minority issue, they all emphasized the importance of racial equality and harmony. From early revolutionaries like Sun Yet-sen to later leaders like Chiang Kai-shek, Mao Zedong, Deng Xiaoping, and Jiang Zemin, the policy on the issue of national identity has remained the same. Though both the Kuomintang and the CCP once advocated democracy as a way to deal with the national identity issue, in the course of their respective power struggles, they all abandoned the idea once they came to power.

On the basis of this general trend, He concludes that the forthcoming leadership is unlikely to come up with great initiatives in this regard. One thing is clear: the new leadership will face increasing difficulty in dealing with the national identity issue, and challenges will come from both inside and outside. Although the Chinese leadership is more technocratic than before, it remains to be seen whether it will appeal to democracy as a means to cope with the national identity question.

SOCIAL PROBLEMS AND POLITICAL INEFFICIENCY

Two decades of reform and development have given rise to a host of social problems in China, ranging from a widening in the income disparity and worsening unemployment to outright peasant discontent. All these issues are in pressing need for attention. In fact, social problems in recent years, including the threat of social instability, have particularly troubled the Chinese political elites. Jiang and his followers have repeatedly stressed the importance of maintaining stability. Although the old sources of social instability such as *Falun Gong* activities have been neutralized, new elements have surfaced, as witnessed by the increased number of bombings in several Chinese provinces, such as Shaanxi, Guangdong, Guangxi, Jiangsu, Henan, Shandong, Zhejiang, and Liaoning. The new leadership will have to address seriously the social grievances behind these acts of civil disobedience in order to maintain social stability.

X.L. Ding singles out four big social problems which he believes can pose serious political troubles for the new leadership:

unemployment, income disparities, rising crimes, and official corruption. He highlights how serious each of these problems has become. For example, Ding observes that criminal activities have deepened and expanded, and can be classified under four major leads: syndication, modernization, internationalization, and politicization. Similarly, he asserts that corruption has become highly institutionalized and has become "official organizational behavior." In some provinces, corruption has become the enterprise of an entire regional state (comprising a number of provinces).

After reviewing all these social problems, Ding goes further to show us why and how these issues have become so serious. He points out that the roots of these worsening problems are institutional in nature. For instance, he argues that China's political system encourages people to lie in order to safeguard their political careers. Although China's leaders have taken many measures to cope with these social problems, they have not succeeded. Their attempt to depoliticize these problems has been futile. According to Ding, if no changes are introduced in the governing process, the fourth generation leadership may have to confront a society which appears to be under control but has many intractable problems simmering below, waiting to explode.

In their chapter, Wang Tongsan and Zhang Tao focus on one of the most important issues facing the Chinese leadership: *sannong wenti* [three dimensions of China's rural problems]. *Sannong wenti* [agriculture, rural areas, and farmers] refers to three interrelated problems: how to increase farmers' income, how to make agricultural adjustments, and how to deal with industrialization and urbanization of the countryside. Indeed, the term *sannong wenti* has become so sensitive that it frequently stirs up the leaders' emotions.

Wang and Zhang observe that having experienced rapid growth from 1978 to 2000, China's rural economy is now showning evidence of a slowdown in the growth of farmers' income, lackluster performances of the township and village enterprises (TVEs), and wider urban–rural disparity at the turn of the century. They use time series, cross section, and structure data analysis to show the decrease in farmers' income and to discuss the causes of the three dimensional issue. Many factors, such as the decline in prices of agricultural products, the heavy burden on farmers, and a decrease in the growth rates of farmers' rewards from the TVEs, have had a direct negative impact on rural development. But more serious reasons for the three-dimensional issue can be found in the distorted structure of the national income distribution pattern under the "dualistic structure" of the urban and rural areas.

On the basis of a merit–demerit analysis, the authors also highlight the implications China's membership to the World Trade Organization (WTO) will bring, on the country's agriculture. China's agriculture and rural economy will benefit from adjustments to the domestic agriculture and import–export structure, introduction of new technology, and improvements in the quality of agricultural products. With improved resource allocation, rural labor will be channeled into nonagricultural sectors. However, trade liberalization will also bring about negative effects on the rural economy, including an increase in the cost of agriculture production, higher imports of some key agricultural products, and greater difficulty for the central government in macroeconomic adjustment and in resolving economic and social conflicts in rural areas.

While Wang and Zhang explore the economics behind the rural problem, Li Lianjiang focuses on the political aspect of rural governance. After the collapse of the Maoist style of the commune system in the early 1980s, the Chinese leadership searched for a new form of rural governance. Village elections were introduced in 1987, and rural democracy has sinced worked rather impressively. With the increased occurances of rural instability, the leadership has once again focused on rural governance. Some Chinese policy analysts have argued that introducing direct election of township heads will help improve cadre–mass relationships and prevent rural unrest. In some places, provincial leaders have already pioneered township electoral reforms. To what degree do rural residents demand township elections?

On the basis of his survey data, Li examines how the peasants view the direct election of township heads. He arrives at some complicated but significant conclusions. First, the majority of rural residents held the "liberal" view that township heads should be directly elected and that such elections could be held immediately. Second, respondents who were less satisfied with the performance of township officials were most likely to hold the "liberal" position. Third, respondents who said that there were many or some local policies that the peasants disliked were more likely than those who found no such policies to take the "liberal" view instead of adopting the "conservative" position. In addition, respondents with higher annual household per capita income were more likely to subscribe to the "liberal" view.

Li's study not only contributes valuable findings to the subject of rural democracy, but also carries significant political implications on how the new leadership can strengthen rural governance. Nevertheless, what kind of new governance systems can be established depends not only on the political demands from below, as Li has shown, but also on the willingness of the central leadership to cede ground on this issue. While new institutions have been introduced in the post-Deng era, the highest priority is accorded to improving the existing governance systems. Indeed, many top leaders believe that only by improving the existing governance systems can political stability be realized.

UNFINISHED ECONOMIC REFORM

Since China began its economic reform in the late 1970s, it has achieved the most impressive economic performance in human history, although the pace of reform varied according to the prevailing political circumstances. Deng Xiaoping's speeches during his southern tour *Nanxun* in 1992 justified the ideological legitimacy of capitalism as a way of promoting the country's economic development. After the tour, the leadership, especially under Zhu Rongji, introduced some radical reform measures. Nevertheless, in recent years China's economic reform seems to have been losing steam. It is expected that China's membership of the WTO will exert greater external pressure on the leadership to accelerate the pace of economic reform.

On the other hand, China's further integration into the global economy poses huge risks for the world's most populated country. It is uncertain whether the fourth generation leaders are competent enough to use international capitalism to spur economic growth while ameliorating its negative impacts.

In his chapter, Tian Xiaowen discusses one of the most important and difficult issues facing the Chinese leadership: how to promote the development of the private sector and how to deal with the relationship between this sector and the state sector. Private economy was much neglected during the period of socialist planning, particularly at the height of the Cultural Revolution. This changed with the market-oriented reforms after 1978, the status of the private economy rose as the government began encouraging the growth of individual-owned enterprises. After two decades of reform, the leadership has justified the existence of the private sector ideologically.

However, Tian finds that the private sector is still facing serious policy constraints and remains discriminated. The most significant discrimination is at the legislative level. China's Constitution declares that socialist public property, not private property, is sacred and inviolable. At the policy level, private enterprises can obtain only limited loans from banks and other financial institutions owned by the state. Private enterprises are still denied access to the two stockmarkets in Shanghai and Shenzhen, and they do not enjoy the preferential taxation granted to foreign firms. To make matters worse, they are subject to "arbitrary fines, arbitrary charges, and arbitrary financial levies" imposed by government departments at various levels. Furthermore, private enterprises are also denied access to key industry sectors under state monopoly as well as a wide range of other industries, such as banking, airline, electricity, telecommunications and post, tobacco, steel, petrol, army uniform, and publishing. Other forms of discrimination include difficulty in the requisition of land, higher fees for use of public goods and services, and being barred from joining the Party and working in the government.

All these policy constraints and discriminations have prevented the transformation of China's private sector from an "ugly duckling" to a full-grown swan. Though the Party has shown some commitment in moving towards a market-oriented economy, the fourth generation leadership will have to overcome these constraints and discriminations to move the economy to a higher plane.

The difficulties in reforming the old economic system probably provide the best justification for China's membership to the WTO. Kong Qingjiang and Lu Ding show how China's economic sectors will be affected by the entry into the WTO. Kong discusses how the country will adapt to the WTO dispute settlement mechanism. After its entry into the WTO, China has to conform to the stipulations and rules of this rule-based, multilateral trading body. Its current laws and regulations on trading rights, business operations, intellectual property rights, and antidumping, for instance, need to be drastically revamped in accordance with its WTO agreements. China also needs to amend its administrative and legal systems to bring them in line with the rule of law.

China, however, is still ill-prepared in adapting to the WTO rules. There are huge gaps between the Chinese legal system and the general legal requirements of the world trade body. Further, law enforcement is also a major problem. Administrative and legal mandates from the central authority are often ignored at local levels. In his three case studies of trade friction between China and its trading partners, Kong shows the country's lack of experience in dealing with its negotiating partners at the multilateral forum. But these case studies also provide China with valuable learning experience, and it will gradually become accustomed to the adjudicating procedures of the WTO dispute settlement mechanism.

Lu Ding's chapter discusses China's growth strategy adjustment after its entry into the WTO. Lu points out that China's accession to WTO will bring about two immediate changes. One is a significant reduction of its trade barriers for a wide range of goods and services, and the other is the opening up of a series of domestic sectors to foreign companies. Both will compel China's policymakers to adjust the country's growth strategy accordingly.

According to Lu, China has to redefine its macroeconomic management framework and long-term growth strategy. He examines the implications of WTO membership on the country's macroeconomic environment and growth strategy. By analyzing macroeconomic data, Lu predicts a tendency in the Chinese economy to move towards a deficit trade balance in the coming years. After its shift from an export-oriented growth model to a trade deficit-based, internal demand-driven growth model, China's macroeconomic management should also be adjusted accordingly. In the long run, China must adjust its current exportoriented strategy and brace itself for a strategic shift towards an America-type, trade deficit-based growth model.

CHINA, TAIWAN, AND THE REGION

The new leadership will not only have to face serious domestic challenges as outlined above but will also have to contend with serious external challenges. Such challenges arise not only from the impact of China's growing economic strength in the international arena, but also from the reaction of the outside world to its development.

Here the immediate challenge comes from the Taiwan Strait. National reunification has been the topmost item on the foreign policy agenda for all political leaders since Deng Xiaoping. China's leaders have adhered to the basic principle of "peaceful reunification, one country, two systems" to resolve the Taiwan issue. But the process has not been smooth, and indeed, after Chen Shui-bian came to power, reunification seems to have become more difficult. The chapter by Chao Chien-min deals with the opportunities and challenges confronting the new leadership on the Taiwan issue.

Chao first identifies three major forces working towards integrating the two sides of the Taiwan Strait. First, a common culture is conducive to integration, especially as old ideology and power alignment have given way to the cultural factor in shaping the new world order. Second, economic integration can generate positive spillover effects. The expanding economic exchanges between the mainland and Taiwan can lead to a more integrated economic community. Third, as China is becoming a dominant regional power, Taiwan can be "sucked" into China's orbit.

While theoretically all these forces can bring the two sides of the Taiwan Strait together, in reality they can have contrary effects. Chao points out that while economic and cultural exchanges have been increasing, the two sides are not necessarily moving closer. For example, a decade ago, the majority of the Taiwanese people supported the "one China" policy, but now only a small proportion supports it. Chao argues that the main reason for this is the emergence of divergent cultures and identities on the two sides of the Taiwan Strait after a period of long separation. While the capitalist development strategy in Taiwan has laid the foundation for the growth of individualism, the socialist development strategy on the mainland has produced a "despotic and collective mentality" in China. Furthermore, political differences have divided the two sides for a long time, and mainland China's heavy-handed policies towards Taiwan have aggravated the alienation of the Taiwanese people. It is increasingly clear that the two sides need to tackle these obstacles from the cultural perspective and work on a more congruous interpretation of various political issues. But in the total absence of a consensus between the leaderships in China and Taiwan, no one is sure when and how this process will begin.

External challenges are not confined to the reunification issue; they also arise from China's growing economic might. In his chapter on the impact of a rising China on the ASEAN economies, John Wong discusses how China's domestic development can affect the outside world. Wong examines the changes in China's export structure. In 1978, when China first opened its doors to the outside world, half of its exports were made up of primary commodities like mineral and agriculture products. Indeed, before 1995, traditional labor-intensive items like textiles, clothing, and footwear dominated China's export structure. But today manufactured products constitute about 90% of China's exports. In recent years, the composition of manufactured exports has changed significantly, marked by the increase in nontraditional items like machinery, electronics, and other high-tech products.

The change in China's export structure has huge implications for the ASEAN economies. China's rapid expansion of such nontraditional exports poses serious challenges for the ASEAN countries competing directly with China in third-country markets. China has several advantages vis-à-vis the ASEAN countries. It has by far a much larger pool of skilled as well as nonskilled labor. It has also a large domestic market for all sorts of products, from hightech to low-tech ones, to take advantage of the economies of scale effect. This in turn means lower average cost for the Chinese products vis-à-vis the ASEAN products.

Barring any unforeseen circumstances, China's economy will continue to grow on its own momentum. All Asian countries have to accept the rise of China as a new political and economic entity. They will have to step up the reform and restructuring of their economies so as to find new niches or new opportunities in the expanding Chinese market.

Sino–Japanese relations also seem troublesome. What are the prospects for Sino–Japanese relations in the epoch of terrorism? This is the question Lam Peng Er addresses. The events of September 11 and their aftermath will have a profound impact on the post-Cold War era, the central structure of international relations, and concomitantly, Sino–US relations. This, in turn, will frame Sino–Japan relations especially when the latter is a close ally of the US. A relaxation of tension between Washington and Beijing is likely to facilitate better ties between Beijing and Tokyo. However, the US focus on wiping out global terrorism in the next few years does not mean that Washington will no longer regard China as the potential long-term challenger to US interests in East Asia. In this regard, any deterioration in relations between the US and China may well spill over to Sino–Japanese relations.

After analyzing some major conceivable challenges posed by Japan to the new Chinese leadership, Lam argues that while a military conflict between China and Japan is highly unlikely in the foreseeable future, the phenomenon of "China rising, Japan passing" may generate tension in bilateral relations. Fortunately, there are also areas of common interests between China and Japan that may mitigate historical animosity and differences over geo-strategic outlooks and economics. For example, a more stable and predictable regional environment and greater economic interdependence will benefit both countries. Lam further points to an extremely important issue, that is, how Japan's economic recovery will help strengthen relations between the two. Therefore, a situation of "China rising, Japan recovering" will probably lead to less fear and greater confidence among the Japanese elites towards China. In short, a renaissance enjoyed by both China and Japan may well be a positive sum rather than a zero-sum game.

CONCLUDING REMARKS

The challenges to China's fourth generation leadership can be broadly categorized into two. The first group of challenges can be dealt with by technocrats and bureaucrats, or they can be resolved through continuing economic growth and social development. As the new leadership is admittedly more technocrat-oriented than the third generation, it is competent enough to tackle these problems.

Even then, some of these challenges may require a much longer time to resolve. For example, those challenges that are the result of membership in the WTO, such as restructuring of the economy and increased unemployment, cannot be tackled in a few years. Other problems that require much time and effort to resolve include worsening corruption, crime, and social instability.

The second group of challenges refers to those of a structural nature, and it calls for a totally different set of skills. It is in this area that doubts remain over whether the existing technocrats will be able to meet such obstacles. One example of a structural problem is Party reform, which demands that leaders possess attributes that go beyond mere technocratic skills—attributes like political imagination and courage. What is also uncertain is the level of preparedness of the fourth generation leadership to deal with this set of problems. In contrast, the first and second generations of revolutionary leaders like Mao Zedong and Deng Xiaoping had the necessary determination and the political will to handle issues of a structural nature. These leaders were "trained" in a different way given the prevailing circumstances, and they overcame seemingly insurmountable difficulties. They survived the Long March, expanded their power bases at the expense of the Kuomintang, and went on to assume power. Their boldness and ability to make tough decisions are qualities that do not come naturally to the fourth generation leaders. It will therefore be harder, if not almost impossible, for the new leaders to deal with structural issues.

Moreover, some issues, such as Taiwan, terrorism, and relations with US and its allies, are simply beyond the control of the Chinese leadership. These are nontechnocratic issues which the fourth generation leaders will have to deal with.

As some chapters in this book show, the main composition of China's political leaders since Deng Xiaoping is technocratic in nature. To be fair, the technocratic leadership has been very efficient and skillful in coping with emerging problems. This is because the technocratic leadership is not ideologically oriented and can focus objectively on a problem and resolve it pragmatically. Nevertheless, it is also true that some structural problems, especially those that are beyond the control of the leadership, have persisted for different generations of leadership. When new leaders assume power, they are likely to focus more on problems of a technocratic nature but delay those of a structural nature. However, given the drastic socioeconomic transformation taking place in the country, it is no longer possible for the new leadership to postpone indefinitely the resolution of these structural problems. Doing so will eventually weaken their legitimacy and erode the Party's monopolistic hold on power. As with the Jiang Zemin leadership, only time will tell whether the fourth generation leaders are up to the mark in coping with structural problems.

Chapter 1

The Politics of Succession: Previous Patterns and a New Process*

FREDERICK C. TEIWES

The leadership succession scheduled for the 16th Party Congress in fall 2002, notwithstanding the related trends for the past 20 years, will involve a process unlike anything seen previously. The very fact that, despite various doubts particularly over how complete the transition will be, it is almost universally expected to happen on schedule, indicates a new degree of quasi-institutionalism in leadership politics. Another largely novel aspect is that the succession is widely recognized as embodying a generational transition from the "third" to the "fourth" generation of the Chinese Communist Party (CCP) leaders rather than simply as the designation of a new top leader.[1] Nevertheless, as the time draws closer, many observers fall back on notions of "power struggle" or "succession struggle" to conceptualize the elite politics of the undeniable maneuvers taking place in the run-up to the Congress.

Such interpretive tendencies should not be exaggerated since various analysts argue for a much more orderly transition[2] and the

---

* I am indebted to Warren Sun and Chris Buckley for many insights and much information reflected in this paper.

[1] On the concept of Party generations and their link to a representative leader, see Frederick C. Teiwes, "Politics at the 'Core': The Political Circumstances of Mao Zedong, Deng Xiaoping, and Jiang Zemin," *China Information*, Vol. XV, No. 1 (2001), pp. 1–4.

[2] In addition to this author's writings cited below, see Li Cheng, "Mystery Behind the Myths," *South China Morning Post*, June 11, 2001.

overall tone falls well short of that applied to the often vicious elite politics of the Mao period, or even assessments of the conflicts of the Deng era, "power/succession struggle" remains a recurrent theme. According to some, such struggles are inherent in the system with dire consequences for it: "[the communist system produces] a state of chronic succession crisis"[3] that would be "very costly, entailing potential instability, conflicts, and breakdowns."[4] Less apocalyptic assessments still see the coming succession as a time of potential divisions and enhanced systemic vulnerability, where open leadership splits are likely to occur as significant systemic change takes place alongside leadership succession. And at the level of presumed ongoing leadership conflict, a typical view in fall 2001 argued that "the power struggle at the top is still very intense and there is still one year to go."[5]

The above views are flawed in a number of senses. First, in terms of the ongoing leadership maneuvering, they claim too much. Politics at the top today takes place in a black box that can be penetrated only at the margins, if at all, and confident claims about the progress of the "struggle" are typically no more than dubious deduction or rumor.[6] The fact is that we can only guess at the degree of interpersonal tension among

---

[3] Andrew J. Nathan and Robert S. Ross, *The Great Wall and the Empty Fortress: China's Search for Security* (New York: W.W. Norton, 1997), p. 136.

[4] Peter Nan-shong Lee, "The Informal Politics of Leadership Succession in Post-Mao China," in Lowell Dittmer, Haruhiro Fukui and Peter N.S. Lee (eds.), *Informal Politics in East Asia* (Cambridge: Cambridge University Press, 2000), p. 182.

[5] According to Lau Siukai of the University of Hong Kong, as reported in *China News Digest*, September 27, 2001.

[6] A case in point is the alleged failed effort of Jiang Zemin to get his protégé Zeng Qinghong promoted to full Politburo status at either the fall 2000 or fall 2001 Central Committee plenums. See Willy Wo Lap Lam in *South China Morning Post*, October 25, 2000, and Peter Harmsen's AFP report from Beijing, September 27, 2001, in FBIS-CHI-2001-0927, respectively. Some reliable sources in Beijing question this view, arguing that the issue was never on the agenda of either meeting. The point is not that the story of Jiang's failed effort is unquestionably false, but that there is no way of knowing whether or not it is true. The disappointing feature of the matter is the degree to which leading scholars in the West have accepted Jiang's "failure" as gospel.

top leaders and the parameters of acceptable conflict open to them in the run-up to the Party Congress. Second, the overlay of "succession struggle" assumptions from the People's Republic of China's (PRC) past is based on a misreading of that past. And finally, the emphasis on "struggle" underestimates the long-term trend toward institutionalization and the post-Mao elite's preoccupation with "stability and unity." In what follows, I will first examine the sources of some of the misperceptions concerning CCP succession politics, and construct a model of what must be present for a genuine "succession struggle." The following sections will in turn examine the relevant developments of the Mao, Deng, and Jiang eras. The final section will relate the principles shaping the coming succession to the problems affecting possible outcomes.

"SUCCESSION STRUGGLE" OR SUCCESSION POLITICS?

The tendency to see recurrent "succession struggles" has a number of roots. The first is the undeniable place of such struggles in the history of China's "big brother" and the founding communist state, the Soviet Union, which created a powerful political culture referent for the CCP. The emergence of Stalin and Khrushchev in the post-Lenin and post-Stalin periods indisputably involved sharp struggles against other leaders and often dire results for losers—as particularly seen in Stalin's bloody purges of the 1930s.[7] The history of the PRC under Mao, moreover, also saw harsh political verdicts against, and sometimes physical destruction of, Mao's alleged opponents—notably his chosen successors, Liu Shaoqi and Lin Biao.[8] Conceptually, in the case of Mao's long-term rule, struggle

---

[7] The consequences for losers in the post-Stalin struggle were normally much less drastic, although Beria was shot in 1953 during the first phase of the conflict. The work of Myron Rush, *The Rise of Khrushchev* (Washington: Public Affairs Press, 1958), and *Political Succession in the USSR* (New York: Columbia University Press, 1968), did much to chronicle the politics of these cases and present a model of inevitable "succession struggles."

[8] This basically occurred starting in the late 1950s in the context of the Great Leap Forward with the severe criticism of Zhou Enlai and others at the start of 1958, and the

allegedly involved attacks on his policies and ultimate authority, although not necessarily on his position as Party Chairman, by his notional successors, the Chairman's fear of ceding real power to his successors and repeated actions against those he believed were threatening his predominance, and conflict among potential claimants to his mantle.[9] Even in the less threatening environment of the Deng period, the potential conflict of the leader and his successor has been seen to open the way to struggles against that successor by other claimants. Finally, a key consideration for the PRC as for other communist systems has been, at least before now, the absence of institutionalized methods for the transfer of power.[10] Against this structural background, and the seeming lessons of communist history, an ongoing and substantially unfettered struggle, whether before or after the death of the established leader, appears to be the norm to many if not most observers.

At yet another level, struggle over succession is a logical projection of elite behavior across political systems. Politics, after all, is about conflict and power, and the prize of leadership or the succession to

---

dismissal of Peng Dehuai in 1959; see Frederick C. Teiwes with Warren Sun, *China's Road to Disaster: Mao, Central Politicians, and Provincial Leaders in the Unfolding of the Great Leap Forward, 1955–1959* (Armonk: M.E. Sharpe, 1999), pp. 73ff., 202–212. Physical abuse and death came with the Cultural Revolution, involving, *inter alia*, Politburo members Liu Shaoqi, Peng Dehuai, and He Long. While there is no evidence that Mao ordered the death of any of his colleagues, it is clear that he was aware of their plight and did nothing to protect them. See Michael Schoenhals, "The Central Case Examination Group, 1966–1979," *The China Quarterly* (hereafter *CQ*), No. 145 (1996). Lin Biao, of course, died while fleeing China to avoid a clash with Mao in 1971.

[9] Cf. the patterns discussed by Lowell Dittmer for the mid-1970s in *China's Continuous Revolution: The Post-Liberation Epoch 1949–1981* (Berkeley: University of California Press, 1987), ch. 5. A more recent study adopting the perspective of a "vicious cycle of succession struggles" during the Mao period, which also assertedly extended deep into the reform era, is Huang Jing, *Factionalism in Chinese Communist Politics* (Cambridge: Cambridge University Press, 2000).

[10] Formally speaking, institutions such as Central Committees or Party Congresses did confer successor status (whether premortem as in the designation of Lin Biao in the 1969 Party Constitution) or postmortem (as in the 1977 Party Congress' election of Hua Guofeng). In fact, such actions merely endorsed arrangements made by handfuls of leaders, and there was no binding expectation that they would last.

the leader will stimulate competing ambitions in virtually any context. The issue is two-fold: to what degree do constraints operate to limit the intensity of competition; and to what extent do regularized procedures guarantee stable outcomes. While succession politics in institutionalized systems allows a healthy degree of conflict, it also involves constraints and relatively stable outcomes; in contrast, "succession struggle" implies a lack of restraint in the contest and the ongoing vulnerability of the "victors." But there is a paradox here. In nearly all cases, whether during some of the most vicious periods of the Maoist era or under Deng and Jiang, succession politics fell short of a "succession struggle." Yet in certain respects it has also involved *more* constraints on conflict than those operating in more institutionalized polities.

A first step to understanding the paradox is to construct a model of the characteristics of a "succession struggle" against which previous events can be assessed. These characteristics are:[11]

1. In Tang Tsou's memorable phrase, it is a "game to win all."[12] That is, those who lose are forever finished, although not necessarily physically or in being totally denied a future political career. But they have no future as major political figures.
2. As suggested above, even if the victor "wins all," s/he can never be secure. There may be a lull in the conflict, but sooner or later new challengers will emerge and the struggle will be on again. Conversely, the leader must always be on guard, especially from designated successors.[13]

[11] The following is based on how such "struggles" have been treated in the literature, combined with a commonsense view of what deep political conflict over succession would involve. It does not rigorously reflect the views of any single writer.

[12] See Tang Tsou, "Chinese Politics at the Top: Factionalism or Informal Politics? Balance-of-Power Politics or a Game to Win All?," *The China Journal* (hereafter *CJ*), No. 34 (July 1995).

[13] Cf. David Bachman, "Emerging Patterns of Political Conflict in Post-Deng China," in Hung-mao Tien and Yun-han Chu (eds), *China under Jiang Zemin* (London: Lynne Rienner Publishers, 2000), pp. 57–60. Bachman analyzes post-15th Congress politics in

3. Also, as suggested above, there are no rules for the struggle. In extremis, as during the Cultural Revolution, extra-Party forces and violence were employed, while even in the reform era formal rules were cast aside, particularly by Party elders, overruling the legally responsible bodies.

4. There must be at least two hostile groupings, led by a representative figure, competing for the prize—Maoist revolutionaries versus Liuist revisionists, Zhou/Deng modernizers versus Jiang Qing radicals, Hua Guofeng's "neo Maoists" versus Deng's reformers, reformers (e.g., Hu Yaobang, Zhao Ziyang) versus conservatives (e.g., Li Peng) throughout the reform era. Each side actively pursues the struggle against the other.

5. The competing forces organize around distinctive programs. These in turn are designed to appeal to major interests in the polity. Given the lack of binding rules and the regime's ultimate reliance on force, the military is a particularly sought after ally in any struggle.

With these criteria in mind, I will begin my historical review of succession politics with the Maoist era.

SUCCESSION POLITICS UNDER MAO: INTENSE CONFLICT BUT FEW CLASSIC STRUGGLES

Several basic considerations must be kept in mind in assessing the Maoist period. The first and most fundamental—as demonstrated most clearly by recent scholarship—was that Mao's authority was

---

terms of possible combinations among the top three leaders (Jiang Zemin, Li Peng and Zhu Rongji) from the perspective that Jiang's role as the successor was potentially under threat from a combination of the other two. The point here is that this gives little legitimacy to the newly reelected leader, but instead depicts him as immediately vulnerable to threats. The difference of this situation from more institutionalized settings is that, while hardly invulnerable to political pressures, the leader of such systems will normally be secure, barring significant failures or regularized contests.

absolute in the post-1949 period till his death in 1976.[14] There was not, and never could be, any struggle against Mao—either direct or subterranean.[15] This did not mean, however, that Mao did not perceive inadequacy or disloyalty and act against the successors he came to question. As one PRC scholar put it concerning the background to the Cultural Revolution, "There was no opposition but Mao may have believed there was—and that's another matter."[16] A second consideration was the value Mao and the leadership generally placed on Party unity. A central part of the program Mao put together in the 1940s was a rejection of the "ruthless struggles and merciless blows" of earlier CCP history. This was married to a political method of recognizing the contributions of all constituencies or "mountain tops" within the Party; the aim was give each constituency a stake in the revolutionary cause.[17] The resultant unity contributed mightily to CCP success, and as a consequence became a valued part of Party traditions for both the organization as a whole and for Mao himself. That Mao grievously damaged Party unity through his subsequent action (even though he ineffectually returned to the unity theme in the years immediately preceding his death) could not eliminate its importance in CCP political culture.

---

[14] See the Introduction to the 2nd edition of Frederick C. Teiwes, *Politics and Purges in China: Rectification and the Decline of Party Norms 1950–1965* (Armonk: M.E. Sharpe, 1993), for an overview of this argument. Roderick MacFarquhar's *The Origins of the Cultural Revolution 3: The Coming of the Cataclysm 1961–1966* (New York: Columbia University Press, 1997), the definitive chronicle of the early 1960s, a period often viewed as one of Mao's weakness, comes to the same basic conclusion. That contrary views nevertheless still exist is seen most systematically in Huang Jing's book cited in n. 9, above.

[15] This is distinct from different policy views which, before the Great Leap, could be expressed relatively openly. See "Editors' Introduction" to Frederick C. Teiwes and Warren Sun (eds), *The Politics of Agricultural Cooperativization in China: Mao, Deng Zihui, and the "High Tide" of 1955* (Armonk: M.E. Sharpe, 1993); and Teiwes with Sun, *China's Road to Disaster*, pp. 27–29.

[16] Cf. Teiwes, *Politics and Purges*, pp. xxxvi–xliv.

[17] On these aspects of Mao's pre-1949 program, see *ibid.*, pp. 48–51; and Frederick C. Teiwes with Warren Sun, *The Formation of the Maoist Leadership: From the Return of*

The first major leadership purge of the PRC period, the Gao Gang case of 1953–1954, was quintessentially about succession. Yet it fell short of the criteria for a succession struggle.[18] Briefly, Mao had become critical of Liu Shaoqi, who had been the accepted successor since at least the 7th Party Congress in 1945,[19] and made his disenchantment known to Gao, another Politburo member and a personal favorite. Mao's motives are inherently unknowable,[20] but the result was that Gao launched an effort to undermine Liu with the clear aim that he would become the new successor. While there were policy differences between the two men, Gao's effort did not involve any distinctive program distinguishing himself from Liu. Gao did attempt to attract key "mountain tops" from the revolutionary period, notably the main armies of the struggle. The main way in which the affair fell short of a "succession struggle" was that it was entirely one-sided. There is no evidence of Liu, or for that matter Zhou Enlai who was also attacked by Gao, doing anything to defend themselves, much less counterattack. The affair involved two factors which, on the one hand, made succession a potentially explosive issue, but on the other, at least for the time being, kept it within limits. Mao's unquestioned power meant that the issue quickly came to a head and virtually paralyzed the leadership for months simply because of the belief, fed by Gao's rumors and his approaches to other leaders, that the Chairman was indeed considering a change of successor. But constraints were applied by Mao's commitment to

---

Wang Ming to the Seventh Party Congress (London: Contemporary China Institute Research Notes and Studies No. 10, 1994), especially pp. 40–52, 66–67.

[18] The following is based on Frederick C. Teiwes, *Politics at Mao's Court: Gao Gang and Party Factionalism in the Early 1950s* (Armonk: M.E. Sharpe, 1990). A different interpretation is Huang Jing, *Factionalism*, pp. 173–197.

[19] See the discussion in Teiwes with Sun, *Formation of the Maoist Leadership*, pp. 34–40.

[20] They conceivably range from, at the benign end of the spectrum, a mere private airing of frustration without larger political intent, to an attempt to have Liu removed without getting directly involved himself. My view opts for a middle ground, that is, an attempt to give Liu a warning without altering his status; see *Politics at Mao's Court*, pp. 37–38. For an argument that Mao was indeed seeking to oust Liu, see MacFarquhar, *Origins 3*, pp. 639–640.

the Party unity that had contributed so vitally to revolutionary victory. Whatever Mao's initial calculations in complaining to Gao, by the end of 1953, as he became aware of the damage to unity that Gao's actions were causing, he turned decisively against his favorite. The net result was to solidify further Liu's status as the successor.

The succession matter remained settled well into the first half of the 1960s when Mao, *circa* 1962, began to have doubts concerning Liu. Before this, the main structural development concerning succession bolstered Liu's status, and that of his top colleagues more broadly, through the gradual implementation of the "two fronts" of leadership whereby Mao retreated to the "second front" to consider large questions of policy and direction, while Liu and others ran the day-to-day affairs of the Party and state on the "first front." A second development was the positioning of Deng Xiaoping, arguably Mao's greatest leadership favorite of all, as the successor to Liu.[21] This latter arrangement is relevant to future developments in that "generational" factors were introduced—a recognition of the need to prepare younger leaders for an ongoing staged succession process.[22] The main problem, of course, was that by 1965 Mao had completely lost confidence in Liu and decided he had to go, while his more complicated attitude toward Deng called for "striking him down for

[21] On the "two fronts," see Teiwes, *Politics at Mao's Court*, pp. 32, 116–117; and Roderick MacFarquhar, *The Origins of the Cultural Revolution 1: Contradictions among the People 1956–1957* (New York: Columbia University Press, 1974), pp. 152–156. On Deng as a future successor, see Teiwes with Sun, *China's Road to Disaster*, pp. 148–149; Frederick C. Teiwes and Warren Sun, *The Tragedy of Lin Biao: Riding the Tiger during the Cultural Revolution, 1966–1971* (London: C. Hurst & Co., 1996), p. 20; and MacFarquhar, *Origins 3*, pp. 433, 640–641. By the early 1960s Lin Biao was also mentioned as a possible future successor, but initially this did not appear to have had the same degree of seriousness as in Deng's case.

[22] Of course, in a fundamental sense this was different from preparing younger generations for future leadership in the late Mao or post-Mao periods in that Deng (and Lin Biao) were heroes of the revolution and extremely well-known to the leader. Also, the age differences were narrower than what applied later; see n. 42, below.

a year, two at most."[23] In turning to Lin Biao as the new successor in 1966, Mao not only relied on another personal favorite whom he seemingly regarded as totally loyal, but, as the "succession struggle" model would suggest, in doing so he sought to secure the support of the army for the unprecedentedly disruptive Cultural Revolution. But again, developments fall well outside crucial aspects of the model. Most significantly, the "struggle" was again one-sided. The most striking fact about the emergence of the Cultural Revolution is that virtually *everyone* was caught by surprise.[24] Leaders at the top and throughout the system were astonished to discover that they had "opposed Chairman Mao," and, despite stratagems to refute such claims, accepted passively decisions from above, ending—at least in the short run—their careers. At the highest level, the new successor, Lin Biao, while not completely uninvolved in the unpredictable events of late 1965–early 1966, was in poor health and lacked political ambition, and even sought to avoid the position but could not deflect Mao's demand.[25]

Once reluctantly installed as the successor, Lin essentially adopted the passive tactic of echoing whatever positions Mao adopted.[26] This,

---

[23] Wang Li's memoirs of his conversations with Mao, cited in Xue Qingchao, *Lishi zhuanzhe guantou de Deng Xiaoping* [Deng Xiaoping at the Turning Point of History] (Zhengzhou: Zhongyuan nongmin chubanshe, 1996), p. 220. This 1967 statement, which also observed that "If Lin Biao's health does not hold out, it's Deng Xiaoping who will have to come forward," was another albeit odd indication of Mao's favoritism towards Deng, and a pointer to the Chairman's intention to bring Deng back at some point.

[24] Not only were the victims of the Cultural Revolution completely dumbfounded at developments, but even Kang Sheng, a key radical, showed no sign of realizing that leading figures of the Party establishment were in trouble until Mao's attitude became clear in March 1966. See Teiwes, *Politics and Purges*, p. lxi.

[25] The following is based on Teiwes and Sun, *Tragedy of Lin Biao*, especially ch. 2 and pp. 57–65, 127–160. One of the more recent statements of the traditional view of Lin is Roderick MacFarquhar, "The Succession to Mao and the End of Maoism, 1969–1982," in idem (ed.), *The Politics of China, Second Edition: The Eras of Mao and Deng* (New York: Cambridge University Press, 1997), pp. 254–275.

[26] Cf. Lin's advice to Tao Zhu to be "passive, passive and again passive," along with other statements in this vein cited in Teiwes and Sun, *Tragedy of Lin Biao*, p. 1.

of course, involved fulsome praise of the Cultural Revolution, but no more—and arguably less—than that offered by Zhou Enlai. Crucially, there is little evidence of concrete action by Lin with the exception of a few initiatives involving military affairs or, ironically, on the side of moderation. Moreover, the notion of a struggle between Lin and Zhou in anticipation of a post-Mao succession is without basis. All the evidence points to mutual respect and an underlying preference for moderate policies by both men. Nevertheless, by 1970–1971 Mao had come to doubt and take precautionary measures against his successor, and conflicts involving turf warfare and petty personal frictions unfolded between civilian radicals led by Mme Mao, Jiang Qing, and a group involving Lin's household—particularly his wife and son, and top central military officials from his revolutionary "mountain top." In bizarre circumstances, and probably influenced by a sense that the military had gathered too much power, Mao sided with his wife at the 1970 Lushan plenum, demanded self-criticisms from Lin's group but found them inadequate, and eventually foreshadowed a showdown with Lin that led to the latter's fateful fleeing from China in September 1971. That the succession issue was involved is clear—Mao had been toying with Jiang's associate Zhang Chunqiao as a successor (whether following Lin or as an alternative to him is unclear), and Lin's camp saw Zhang as a threat. Nevertheless, during late 1970 and 1971 when the "struggle," whether between Mao and Lin or between Jiang's group and Lin's followers, should have been most severe, Lin's key army supporters believed they had finally satisfied the Chairman's demands for self-criticism (and later offered no resistance to their own purge); Lin basically continued his passive role,[27] albeit with signs of resentment toward Mao; Zhou sought to

---

[27] This, of course, is directly contrary to official claims that Lin planned a military coup and an attempt to assassinate Mao. I believe Lin was ignorant of any such plots, and to the extent they existed they were little more than loose, desperate talk by Lin's son, Lin Liguo, and other young military officers rather than serious plans. See *ibid.*, pp. 152ff.; and Jin Qiu, *The Culture of Power: The Lin Biao Incident in the Cultural Revolution* (Stanford: Stanford University Press, 1999), ch. 7.

smooth tensions between the Chairman and his successor; Jiang proclaimed loyalty to Lin on the day preceding his flight; and after Lin's death Mao slipped into deep depression[28]—hardly the response of someone who had just emerged victorious from a struggle with a dangerous enemy.

Of all the succession politics of the Maoist era, the case coming closest to a classic "succession struggle" was the post-Lin Biao conflict of the radicals around Jiang Qing against the remaining pre-Cultural Revolution elite represented by Zhou Enlai and, after his 1973 rehabilitation, by Deng Xiaoping.[29] Clearly, in broad terms, there were two camps, and the game between them in the final analysis was one to "win all." The struggle had few if any rules involving harsh criticism—particularly of Zhou Enlai, purges, and bitter memories of the late 1960s when lives were literally on the line. Distinct policy preferences were apparent, although ultimately the conflict is better seen as pitting those who made major contributions to the pre-1949 revolution, and/or were part of the pre-Cultural Revolution establishment, against those with few historical achievements who suddenly came to prominence from the margins of the system in 1966.[30] Yet even this conflict had Mao-driven peculiarities at odds with what one would expect from a no-holds barred struggle. First of all, there were constraints: both sides, particularly the Party veterans in view of Mao's abiding commitment to the Cultural Revolution, often had to restrict their attacks, as

---

[28] See Barbara Barnouin and Yu Changgen, *Ten Years of Turbulence: The Chinese Cultural Revolution* (London: Kegan Paul International, 1993), pp. 245–246.

[29] The following draws on research being currently conducted by Warren Sun and myself.

[30] Conventional views picturing a third group, sometimes termed "moderate beneficiaries" of the Cultural Revolution (see Barnouin and Yu, *Ten Years*, pp. 292–293), as standing between the radicals and old revolutionaries and susceptible to the blandishments of both sides, fundamentally misperceive the situation. While the situation was fluid and groups did not cohere into well-organized camps largely because of the variability of Mao's positions, the underlying predilections—and in key cases established personal loyalties—of the "moderate beneficiaries" were firmly with the senior revolutionaries whose revolutionary status they deeply respected.

the Chairman repeatedly insisted on Party unity.[31] Relatedly, the People's Liberation Army (PLA), despite its deep hostility to the radicals and latent power, was basically a passive actor in the conflict as long as Mao lived, accepting harsh attacks on its leaders by Jiang Qing and company without protest. Another factor was that the issue of succession itself was complex, with generational succession now firmly on the agenda in an unprecedented fashion. Thus Zhou or Deng were never designated successors, although had Mao died in either 1972 or 1975 they surely would have assumed that role, while Mao considered a range of younger leaders as eventual successors, particularly the radical Wang Hongwen, and eventually Hua Guofeng, who also had support from veteran revolutionaries for such a role.[32] Still another consideration is that there were contradictions within each "camp:" notwithstanding a shared antipathy to the radicals, the fact that Mao was "good to Comrade Xiaoping and bad to the Premier"[33] forced Deng's participation in criticism of

Another indication of the importance of revolutionary status is the fact that Kang Sheng, a radical by inclination and Cultural Revolution villain by deed, was deeply antipathetic to the Jiang Qing radicals and supportive of Zhou Enlai and Deng Xiaoping to the extent allowed by Mao's attitudes. Mao Mao [Deng Rong], *Wode fuqin Deng Xiaoping, shangce* [My Father Deng Xiaoping], Vol. 1 (Beijing: Zhongyang wenxian chubanshe, 1993), pp. 179–181; idem, *Wode fuqin Deng Xiaoping: "wenge" suiyue* [My Father Deng Xiaoping: The "Cultural Revolution" Years] (Beijing: Zhongyang wenxian chubanshe, 2000), pp. 433–434; and interviews with Party history specialists on the period.

[31] Thus Deng curbed criticism of the Gang of Four at Politburo meetings in May–June 1975. He had concluded that the Mao-stipulated criticism could not go too far, something he understood in his bones since Mao made "not opposing Jiang Qing" one of the conditions for his return to the leadership. See Yao Jin (ed.), *Yao Yilin baixitan* [One Hundred Evenings' Talks with Yao Yilin] (Beijing: Zhongguo shangye chubanshe, 1998), p. 189.

[32] According to Party historians, Mao also considered Li Desheng, Wu De, and Ji Dengkui. Concerning the old revolutionaries, consideration of younger officials as future successors involved Ji Dengkui in addition to Hua. See *Deng Liqun guoshi jiangtan, disance* [Deng Liqun's Speeches and Talks on National History], Vol. 3 (Beijing: Zhonghua Renmin Gongheguo shigao bianweihui, 2000), pp. 102, 347.

[33] *Ibid.*, p. 323. The comment, made by Li Xiannian, actually referred to Mao's niece, Wang Hairong, and his interpreter, Tang Wensheng. My argument is that Wang and

Zhou, while Wang's designation as eventual successor was not fully accepted within the "gang."[34] While the underlying conflict quickly led to decisive action against the radicals after Mao's death, while he lived the struggle could not be pursued to its conclusion.

Several lessons can be learned from this review of succession politics under Mao. First, the Chairman's dominance was such that there were no premortem challenges to his authority, from successors or anyone else. This did not, however, prevent Mao from turning on successors based on *perceptions* of their ideological weakness or personal disloyalty.[35] The oft-noted problem of the supreme leader providing sufficient clout to his chosen successor without feeling threatened, in terms of policy vision or the loss of power, had become a central part of the equation by the mid-1960s. Before this time, however, with the brief exception of the Gao Gang affair, succession arrangements were stable. Had Mao died at any point before 1965, Liu Shaoqi would have become the new leader without any significant challenge, although clearly his authority would have fallen well short of Mao's. Intense competition for the postmortem succession emerged only during the Cultural Revolution decade, precisely because Mao placed incompatible forces on the Politburo. Ironically, given that the Chairman had done so much damage to Party unity from 1966, by the mid-1970s he was again emphasizing unity, and for a time during 1974–1975 seemingly envisioned an

---

Tang were basically reflecting Mao's attitude in 1973–1975, which was repeatedly disapproving of Zhou, while still highly partial to Deng.

[34] As a poorly educated factory worker, Wang was looked down upon by the intellectual Zhang Chunqiao and Yao Wenyuan, while Mao commented that on several occasions Jiang Qing complained to him about Wang. A telling indication that the Gang of Four was less cohesive than subsequently assumed is that the leaders who discussed the coup of October 1976 were initially uncertain over whether to include all of the four in the arrests; Wu De, "Guanyu fensui sirenbang de douzheng" [On the Struggle to Smash the Gang of Four], manuscript, 1995, p.10.

[35] For a discussion of the factors causing Mao to veer in radical policy directions, doubt his successor and other colleagues, and thus damage Party unity from the time of the Great Leap Forward, see Teiwes, "Politics at the 'Core,'" pp. 14–22.

improbable succession where Deng Xiaoping would provide immediate-term guidance and Wang Hongwen long-term leadership.[36] In any case, he was able to contain the underlying conflict between deeply hostile forces while he lived. In sum, the conflict surrounding succession issues was always Mao-initiated, and it intensified or relaxed according to his actions. Conversely, without the "later Mao," succession issues would undoubtedly have been handled relatively smoothly, given the elite's commitment to Party unity and the deep respect for revolutionary status.

DENG XIAOPING AND SUCCESSION POLITICS AFTER MAO: "NORMAL" CONFLICT WHILE PURSUING "STABILITY AND UNITY"[37]

The very disruptiveness of the late Mao period meant that, once the Gang of Four had been arrested, "stability and unity" became an overarching theme of the post-Mao period down to the present. This did not, and could not, eliminate political conflict affecting succession issues as well as a plethora of other matters. Indeed, the passing of leadership from Mao to Deng meant a profoundly different approach to elite politics in general and succession in particular. Whereas the late Chairman acted in accordance with vast visions and deeply personal judgments of colleagues and successors, Deng was result-oriented and measured his successors by their performance and political circumstances.[38] Politics had also become more "normal" in that conflict was generated by issues rather than the leader's sense

[36] The politics was complex and shifting, but Mao emphasized the need for Wang and the radicals more generally to cooperate with Deng and the old revolutionaries. The situation was organizationally reflected in Deng having responsibility for the State Council from January 1975 while Wang, until that June, was in charge of the daily affairs of the Party.

[37] This section draws heavily on Frederick C. Teiwes, "The Paradoxical Post-Mao Transition: From Obeying the Leader to 'Normal Politics,'" *CJ*, No. 34 (1995); and idem, "Normal Politics with Chinese Characteristics," *CJ*, No. 45 (2001).

[38] On the contrasting approach of Mao and Deng to successors, see Teiwes, "Politics at the 'Core,'" pp. 22–26, 38–43.

of betrayal, and the intensity of conflict reflected the seriousness of the issues rather than obscure personal differences or ideological campaigns dictated from above. In any case, the conflicts which did occur all fell short of a "succession struggle."

Before Deng unambiguously assumed the position of paramount leader, however, the conventional view holds that the elite politics of the period from the purge of the radicals in October 1976 to the Third Plenum in December 1978 was driven by a "succession struggle" between him and Mao's last successor, Hua Guofeng. In this interpretation, the power struggle was linked to pronounced ideological and policy divisions between "neo-Maoists" around Hua and Deng's reform coalition, with Deng emerging victorious at the Third Plenum owing to a combination of failures in Hua's policy program, the construction of an attractive alternative program by Deng, and Deng's skill in building a broad anti-Hua coalition. New materials, both documentary and oral, now provide the basis for a radically different picture:[39] after the purge of the radicals Deng's return to work quickly became a consensus position with Hua's full support;[40] Hua's policies were based on the measures implemented by Deng in 1975, and there is little evidence of policy conflict between the two men; Deng's authority, based on his high revolutionary status including vast military prestige, was never challenged by Hua;[41] developments at the pre 1978 plenum work conference which weakened Hua were not orchestrated by Deng but caught both men by surprise; and at the work conference and on other occasions during the period Deng

---

[39] These conclusions are based on current research jointly conducted with Warren Sun.

[40] According to Wu De, "Guanyu fensui sirenbang," pp. 21–22, by late October 1976 Deng had already been told that he would be restored to "at least your previous positions." It is likely that this dates the decision slightly too early, but the balance of evidence is that a Politburo consensus on Deng's return had been formally endorsed by December. The delay in effecting his return to July 1977 was due to the need to manage the process in a manner protecting Mao's prestige and preventing attacks on the new leadership from the left.

[41] Deng's authority was such that immediately upon his return in 1977 he took charge of key areas such as foreign policy and, most crucially, military affairs. On Deng's military prestige, see Teiwes, "Paradoxical Post-Mao Transition," pp. 67–68.

emphasized "stability and unity" rather than pressing for a decisive outcome that would "win all."

These complicated developments reflected the disorder Mao had brought to succession arrangements during his last decade. In contrast to his earlier planned sequence of Liu Shaoqi and Deng Xiaoping—both revolutionary heroes and logical candidates in "generational" terms,[42] by the post-Lin Biao period Mao in effect named no immediate successor, but in Wang Hongwen a long-term candidate who lacked any revolutionary prestige or pre-1966 establishment role. Even if Hua Guofeng was a more acceptable choice as immediate and future successor for the elite as a whole after Deng's 1976 purge, proper status relationships had still been stood on their head. This is not to say that after Mao's death Hua's legitimacy was questioned by the veteran revolutionaries; for the time being, at least, he was widely accepted.[43] This, however, was accompanied by a view that Hua lacked the experience to run the ship of state, that Deng would be required to provide a guiding hand until Hua was ready. The potential for tension in such an arrangement, particularly when linked to the fact that Deng was a decisive, often abrasive personality while Hua was more cautious and diffident, was obvious, although it appears to have been contained for most of the 1977–1978 period.[44] When Hua was undermined at the late 1978 Party meetings, the impetus came from, as it were, the wings where Chen Yun in particular raised another aspect of how revolutionary status

---

[42] Mao was born in 1893, Liu in 1898, and Deng in 1904. Lin Biao, also considered a possible successor by Mao from about 1960, was born in 1907. While the age differences were too narrow to be considered true generations, there at least was a logical progression.

[43] This view was strongly put forth by one of China's most senior and respected Party historians in an interview. As for Deng, while there are some differences among Party historians concerning his possible attitude towards Hua upon his return, the general view is that there is no solid evidence indicating that he did not accept Hua as the successor.

[44] The glaring exception concerned the spring 1978 incident when, after Deng criticized navy leader Su Zhenhua over a naval accident, Su approached Hua for backing, Hua indicated he would make an inspection of naval units as a show of support, and Deng abruptly canceled the inspection. The episode brutally revealed the real power equation well before the Third Plenum. See Tan Zongji's 1984 inner-Party report, "The Third

had been perverted during the Cultural Revolution—the need to reverse verdicts on old revolutionaries who had been unjustly dealt with during the movement. That Hua was now vulnerable to the slowness of verdict reversals, as well as for losses caused by economic overexpansion, only underlined the importance of revolutionary status, because Deng had been as cautiously deliberate as Hua in dealing with rehabilitations and at least as reckless in pushing through economic expansion. In short, no clearly opposing factions or programs had emerged. Deng and Hua did not confront or organize against each other, and the issue of succession was not even raised on the occasion usually identified as Deng's decisive victory over Hua.

What the Third Plenum did achieve was to make clearer the real state of power relations at the top, begin—without "struggle"—the process of marginalizing Hua, which would not include open attacks before fall 1980, and reestablish a sense of proper generational succession. With Deng now obviously the de facto leader and Chen Yun back on the Politburo Standing Committee as an ally who then and thereafter recognized Deng's preeminence,[45] the older generation of revolutionaries now assumed their rightful role of guiding China's course. Figures from the younger generation, Hu Yaobang and Zhao Ziyang (both of whom ironically had good personal relations and some policy compatibilities with Hua[46]) soon effectively displaced Hua in the Party and government, respectively, and although each

Plenum of the Eleventh Central Committee is a Major Turning Point in the History of the Party Since the Founding of the People's Republic of China," trans. in *Chinese Law and Government* (May–June 1995), pp. 44–47.

[45] Much of the literature, mistakenly in my view, sees the Deng–Chen relationship as a conflictual one where the relative balance shifted according to events. See, for example, Richard Baum, *Burying Mao: Chinese Politics in the Age of Deng Xiaoping* (Princeton: Princeton University Press, 1994). For a concise statement of Deng's dominant power and the nature of the complex Deng–Chen relationship, see Teiwes, "Paradoxical Post-Mao Transition," pp. 62–78.

[46] Hu had cordial relations with Hua dating from his 1962 posting to Hunan, had in all likelihood been placed in his crucial Party School position by Hua in 1977, and had been deeply impressed with Hua's commitment to modernization in the early post-Mao

formally outranked Deng as the putative successor at different stages, they were unambiguously his subordinates. In this sense, the dilemma of Mao's successors had been re-created—in their responsibilities for running the Party–state they ran the risk of displeasing the leader and suffering the consequences. In one regard their situation was worse: the "second front" was not simply occupied by the leader himself, but by a number of extremely prestigious Party elders who could and did interfere in the affairs of the "first front."[47] In another sense they were much better off. While, in Deng's words, "if we find we've chosen the wrong people we can still change them for others,"[48] the criteria would be largely rational and related to political performance. In the event, both Hu and Zhao fell, not because of "succession struggles," but because of a combination of their political deficiencies and the events they could not control.

While moves against Hu Yaobang in 1986 involved people, notably Party elders,[49] who had concluded that Hu was no longer an acceptable successor, they did not involve an attempt by any other leaders or factions to seize the successor position for themselves. As suggested, Hu's fall is best understood as a product of his own shortcomings as a politician. Although his position had been significantly compromised by a factor beyond his control, the late 1986 student demonstrations, Hu had already alienated virtually every key constituency within the Party leadership. By the latter part of 1986, the relationship with the most critical "constituency"—Deng himself—was clearly under strain. Whether this was largely due to

---

period. Zhao and Hua had been Party secretaries responsible for agriculture in Central–South provinces before the Cultural Revolution and had worked smoothly in that capacity, and their views on agriculture in the late 1970s overlapped in important respects.

[47] On the role of the Party elders, see Teiwes, "Paradoxical Post-Mao Transition," pp. 78–82.

[48] *Selected Works of Deng Xiaoping (1975–1982)*, Vol. 2 (Beijing: Foreign Languages Press, 1984), p. 198.

[49] Ironically, these included many of the same people who supported Hu as the replacement for Hua. Hu's positives, in their earlier view, included more (if still limited) revolutionary prestige than anyone else from his generation given his significant, if junior, military

differences over "bourgeois liberalization" as officially claimed, it does appear that Hu had let the relationship wither through insufficient cultivation. Similarly, Hu alienated Chen Yun, who initially had also been favorably disposed, but who frowned upon Hu's habit of touring the country and giving repeated on-the-spot directives without undertaking in-depth surveys. Hu also alienated the Party elders as a group by pursuing some of their children during the anticorruption drive in 1986.

But Hu Yaobang's difficulties were not limited to the "second front." Apart from his inevitable conflict with conservatives in the propaganda apparatus (who might have been isolated in other circumstances), Hu's penchant for issuing directives on a wide variety of matters offended the responsible bureaucracies and their leaders. This was nowhere more important than in the economic realm where the state rather than the Party organs were supposed to take the lead, with Song Ping, head of the powerful State Planning Commission, openly criticizing Hu. But Hu's interference in economic matters caused problems with an even more important figure—and a key reformist leader—Zhao Ziyang, a tension that led Zhao to complain to Deng. Yet, despite being cast in some studies as Hu's challenger for the succession,[50] Zhao had little interest in toppling a fellow reformer. In fact, he vainly sought to avoid taking on the Party position after Hu fell, preferring to concentrate on economic reform as Premier. Hu, although still highly popular among intellectuals and Party reformers, had created opposition and lost support on a wide basis; in the words of one of Hu's Politburo colleagues, his essential shortcoming was an inability "to unite the Party." This, rather than a concerted attack from competitors for the succession or the dark suspicions of the leader was the cause of

---

credentials earned on the Long March and subsequently during the revolution; his role in advocating and implementing the reversals of verdicts on Cultural Revolution victims; and his credentials as a Party generalist with experience at both the local and central levels.

[50] See Susan L. Shirk, *The Political Logic of Economic Reform in China* (Berkeley: University of California Press, 1993), p. 14.

Hu's demise. In the end, Deng came to the cold-blooded decision that Hu had reached his use-by date.[51]

The decline and fall of Zhao Ziyang during 1988–1989 was similar, although harder to assess, in that key aspects of the process are less accessible in the black box of leadership politics. The uncertain part of the equation concerns Zhao's standing after the shift in economic policy in the summer of 1988, a shift which also saw the bolstering of the authority of Premier Li Peng in this area. While Zhao was a more savvy politician than Hu, this setback was due to a policy failure—the overheated economy which had produced unprecedented inflation. Although this could be blamed to some degree on Deng's radical price reform initiative, in fact a great deal of the culpability lay with Zhao's expansionary policies, and those with more cautious views like Li Peng and Yao Yilin benefited as a result in the following policy debates.[52] While Zhao had suffered a setback, and in the view of some these developments and what followed can only be explained as a new "game to win all,"[53] it is in fact still unclear whether or to what degree his position was under threat when the crisis of spring 1989 began.

In any case, during the crucial first two weeks of May, Zhao acted as the "first front" leader in charge, presumably with Deng's blessing.[54] But differences had appeared early on between Zhao, who

---

[51] For greater detail on Hu's political inadequacies, see Teiwes, "Paradoxical Post-Mao Transition," pp. 87–88. The observation of the Politburo member, which was originally made *well before* Hu came under heavy pressure in 1986, was related by an oral source who heard it first hand.

[52] See Joseph Fewsmith, *Dilemmas of Reform in China: Political Conflict and Economic Debate* (Armonk: M.E. Sharpe, 1994), ch. 7; and You Ji, "Zhao Ziyang and the Politics of Inflation," *The Australian Journal of Chinese Affairs*, No. 25 (1991). See also Shirk, *Political Logic*, p. 14, for a view of Zhao and Li contesting the succession.

[53] See Joseph Fewsmith, "Elite Politics," in Merle Goldman and Roderick MacFarquhar (eds.), *The Paradox of China's Post-Mao Reforms* (Cambridge: Harvard University Press, 1999), pp. 64–65.

[54] This is my supposition. None of the available evidence, including *The Tiananmen Papers*, gives much indication of Deng's views in this crucial period. I cannot imagine Deng not being involved, or Zhao daring to act without at least the "paramount

pursued a conciliatory approach towards the students occupying Tiananmen Square, and Li Peng and others who advocated a harder line, and as the crisis escalated, divisions within the leadership intensified. With Zhao's approach failing to produce acceptable results, Deng decided to declare martial law, setting in train the events which culminated in the tragedy of June 4. Zhao had again failed in policy, and he guaranteed his removal by declining to back Deng's position on martial law. Yet it was only as Deng came down decisively on the side of martial law that Li Peng and others directly attacked Zhao.[55] If, notwithstanding the absence of any evidence, seizing Zhao's position for himself was part of Li Peng's objective, it was not realized. Instead, Deng selected a relative outsider, Jiang Zemin, as the new successor and the "core" of a "third generation," notionally in the tradition of Mao and himself.

leader's" tacit support. Such support is implied in an account of a purported meeting of Deng, Zhao, and Yang Shangkun on May 13 in *ibid.*, pp. 147–152

The highly publicized *Tiananmen Papers*, compiled by Zhang Liang, edited by Andrew J. Nathan and Perry Link (New York: Public Affairs, 2001), do not provide any fundamentally new insights into the elite politics of the 1989 events; I have tentatively cited them in support of points already indicated by other sources. Indeed, the *Papers* are credible in large part because they confirm what was already known, but any judgment concerning their authenticity is premature. This much can be said at present: many of the bureaucratic documents, which were available fairly widely, are clearly genuine. But the crucial documents purporting to convey the content of high-level meetings and personal conversations between Deng, Zhao, Yang Shangkun, and Jiang Zemin are suspect. They may indeed represent the meaning of the exchanges depicted, assuming such exchanges actually took place, but they are not credible as verbatim records. Whether they were edited and polished by official organs, or fabricated by the Chinese compiler of the documents on the basis of widely held understandings within Party circles, is uncertain.

[55] The first evidence of Li departing from disagreement over tactics to criticism of Zhao was at a May 17 meeting where Deng made his intentions known; see *Tiananmen Papers*, pp. 185–186. This timing is consistent with the previous careful review of developments by Tang Tsou, "The Tiananmen Tragedy: The State–Society Relationship, Choices, and Mechanisms in Historical Perspective," in Brantly Womack (ed.), *Contemporary Chinese Politics in Historical Perspective* (Cambridge: Cambridge University Press, 1991), especially pp. 303ff. The dynamics suggested here, that is, policy differences escalating into political polarization under

Like Zhao before him, and also like individuals as diverse as Lin Biao and Hua Guofeng,[56] Jiang neither expected nor sought elevation.[57] In Mao-like fashion, although in consultation with other Party elders,[58] Deng had decided and Jiang had no choice but to serve. But unlike Mao, Deng was not obsessed with either considerations of personal loyalty or ideological purity, and he seemingly had less personal experience of Jiang than Mao had with almost any of his successor candidates.[59] In the same cold-blooded manner that Deng discarded failed successors, he now chose Jiang in view of Jiang's political assets and the needs of the current situation. Jiang's assets were considerable despite his nearly total lack of revolutionary contributions or military experience:[60] he was not, like Li Peng, tarred with responsibility for the Tiananmen crackdown

---

conditions of crisis, has also been noted by Lowell Dittmer, "The Tiananmen Papers," CQ, No. 166 (2001), pp. 481–482.

[56] While, in the wake of the purge of the Gang of Four, Hua clearly sought to retain the position of new CCP Chairman, in early 1976 when Deng had been removed and the situation was extremely fluid, he and other younger leaders recommended to Mao that Li Xiannian take over responsibility for the State Council; Mao Mao, "Wenge" suiyue, p. 449.

[57] See Bruce Gilley, Tiger on the Brink: Jiang Zemin and China's New Elite (Berkeley: University of California Press, 1998), pp. 134–135, on Jiang's surprise and hesitation when he learned of his selection. In Zhao's case, notwithstanding his efforts to avoid elevation so that he could remain Premier and focus on economic reform, once Hu fell, his position as the clear number two on the "first front" made promotion virtually inevitable.

[58] Deng consulted Li Xiannian and Chen Yun on the new successor, and it is likely one or the other first suggested Jiang. See Selected Works of Deng Xiaoping, Volume III (1982–1992) (Beijing: Foreign Languages Press, 1994), p. 288. However, as Deng noted shortly thereafter, he had appointed both Hu and Zhao (ibid., p. 300), and there is no reason to believe the situation was any different on this occasion. Cf. Tiananmen Papers, pp. 143, 260, 279.

[59] Arguably, the exception would be Wang Hongwen who seemingly attracted Mao in large part because of his background as a worker from a peasant family who had also served in the army, as well as because of his role as a Cultural Revolution activist. There appears to have been minimal personal contact, however, before Wang was brought to Beijing and groomed as the future successor.

[60] For a fuller discussion, see Teiwes, "Politics at the 'Core,'" pp. 46–49.

and bloodshed; his centrist policy stance combining a consistent proeconomic reform stance with sensitivity to challenges to political control placed him in a position to build consensus and reduce his vulnerabilities, in contrast to Zhao Ziyang and especially Hu Yaobang who suffered from being too exposed on the cutting edge of reform; he had displayed both flexibility and firmness in dealing with demonstrations in Shanghai in 1986 and 1989; he fitted the profile for future generations of leaders that had been repeatedly emphasized throughout the 1980s—a younger, tertiary-educated technocrat; he had experience in leading political and bureaucratic roles at both the center and in the localities; and he possessed a personal moderation that would not overly threaten his Politburo colleagues. Yet, as important as these qualities were, without the intervention of the leader from above, Jiang would not have become the successor. Equally important, and notwithstanding some dissatisfaction with Jiang's performance, Deng stood by his choice, which allowed him gradually to consolidate and extend his power throughout the first half of the 1990s.[61] Even then, however, the politics of succession was entering a new phase that would accelerate with Deng's terminal illness and death.

SUCCESSION IN THE 1990S: FEAR OF INSTABILITY AND MANAGED INSTITUTIONALISM

If "stability and unity" was a preoccupation of the post-Mao leadership before the Tiananmen crisis, it became an obsession afterwards. This can be seen in policy, particularly the concern that too rapid changes might damage social stability, and in extreme nervousness about the loss of political control. In terms of elite politics generally, it has been manifested in an effort to contain leadership tensions, to avoid splits that would jeopardize not only losers in "games to win

---

[61] See *ibid.*, pp. 49–52, for a brief overview of this process. Deng's major disappointment with Jiang and the "third generation" generally was with the cautious pace of reform in the early 1990s. While he reacted to this boldly in his early 1992 "southern tour," he

all" but CCP rule itself. And with regard to succession, the aim has also been to minimize and contain conflict and to develop a quasi institutionalized process to manage future transitions. In part, this simply reflects the passing of the last great leader who could enforce choices from above, but it also epitomizes a deep commitment to a more rational and predictable process, and a deep dread of potential instability.

As implied, the lesson of Tiananmen stood at the center of this mindset. Previously, with an eye to the ravages of the Cultural Revolution, "stability and unity" had been repeatedly emphasized, and had in fact served to contain leadership conflict,[62] but significant policy differences produced sharp—and for attentive audiences visible—contention which, together with unanticipated crises, had contributed to the fall of two successors. In assessing the reasons for the unprecedented challenge to the regime represented by the Tiananmen crisis, the leadership quickly concluded that the root cause had been a "Party split," a division at the Party center which prevented decisive action and encouraged the CCP's enemies. While somewhat dubious when applied to the 1989 events, Party leaders seemingly agreed with Andrew Walder's argument that political instability arises when elite conflicts "are revealed outside the circle of top leaders,"[63] and they have been determined not to repeat the mistake. Future differences would have to be contained, and conflicts kept hidden ever more deeply in the black box of elite politics. To put the lesson another way, the post-Tiananmen leaders concluded that "we all hang together or we hang separately."

---

never indicated an intention to change the leadership, and, with Jiang having quickly adapted to Deng's position, strongly supported Jiang's reelection at the 14th Party Congress later in the year.

[62] Constraints could be seen in the "soft landings" for "losers" (e.g., Hua Guofeng continues to hold a Central Committee place, Hu Yaobang remained on the Politburo, and even Zhao Ziyang retained his Party membership), and even more significantly in efforts to achieve consensus. See Teiwes, "Paradoxical Post-Mao Transition," pp. 82ff.

[63] See Andrew G. Walder, "Does China Face an Unstable Future? On the Political Impact of Rapid Growth," in Maurice Brosseau, Kuan Hsin-chi and Y.Y. Kueh (eds), *China Review 1997* (Hong Kong: The Chinese University Press, 1997), p. 341. The

This, together with the support of Deng Xiaoping, goes a long way towards explaining why there is virtually no persuasive evidence of challenges to Jiang as the new successor. This is not for want of trying by outside observers to peer into the increasingly opaque world of leadership politics to discover evidence of struggle. Nevertheless, the three cases commonly cited—the Yang brothers in 1992, Chen Xitong in 1995, and Qiao Shi in 1997—all come up well short. The first case, involving President Yang Shangkun and his half brother, army political department head Yang Baibing, was clearly the most important, not only because Jiang's position was not fully consolidated, and Deng Xiaoping's "southern tour" at the start of the year amounted to a rebuke of Jiang's stewardship, but because the case did pose a significant challenge. The challenge, however, apparently related to military affairs rather than representing a threat to Jiang's status as Party leader. According to well-connected oral sources, the affair was a result of Yang Baibing's attempt to freeze Jiang out of military affairs on the ground that he was a novice. It was, they reported, settled when Jiang appealed to Deng on the basis that he could not function as Chairman of the Central Military Commission (CMC) under such circumstances, and Deng intervened decisively on his behalf. If true, this indicates another political skill of Jiang apart from his well-known centrism: the willingness to act boldly when significant matters are at issue. In the event, the affair was settled by Yang Baibing's dismissal from his military post (but not the Politburo), and Yang Shangkun's retirement with less influence than a long-time supporter of Deng could have expected.[64]

In comparison, the Chen Xitong and Qiao Shi cases posed little threat to Jiang and were relatively easily dealt with. Chen, of course,

problem with this formulation in the context of 1989 is that while the elite differences which became apparent after May 4 (but which, if the above analysis is correct, fell well short of a Party split before the 17th) may have exacerbated the crisis, political instability had arrived by late April, and it would have been difficult, although hardly impossible, for even a unified leadership to bring the unprecedented situation to a satisfactory conclusion.

[64] This interpretation is a case of trusting one's sources on the basis of past reliability and general compatibility with one's own sense of things; it by no means represents a

was removed from his position on the Politburo and as Beijing municipal Party chief on corruption charges, finally winding up as a convicted felon in 1998. A man with a conservative reputation because of his prominent role in the 1989 crackdown but someone who had spoken out for reform measures on various occasions, Chen, as some sources suggest, may have had low regard for Jiang, but there is little to indicate major policy differences or any effort to launch a "game" against Jiang. Chen's quite spectacular corruption may simply have given Jiang the opportunity to get rid of an annoyance and win, in the process, some points with a public fed up with official corruption. In the event, Jiang acted with great sensitivity in handling the case in order to avoid charges of factional bias, apparently gained the acquiescence of Li Peng in the removal of Li's 1989 ally, and acted well within formal procedures. Even if Chen wound up losing almost all, there is no indication of a hard fought game leading to his demise.[65]

As for Qiao Shi, despite persistent efforts of outside analysts to paint him as Jiang's "rival," there is again little persuasive evidence to suggest that Qiao imagined he could challenge Jiang after the latter was named the "core" of the "third generation" leadership in 1989. This is not to claim that there were no differences or tensions between the two—as in collective settings elsewhere (e.g., Cabinet government in Westminster systems) clashing egos and policies could coexist as long as restraint was observed. Apart from questions of evidence, the context does not seem right for an attempt to oust Jiang. The window of opportunity would have been in 1992, given Deng's dissatisfaction with the slow pace of reform under Jiang's leadership, and indeed this has been suggested in some accounts

claim of absolute validity. For an account of the affair claiming an effort in conjunction with Qiao Shi to unseat Jiang, see Joseph Fewsmith, "Institution Building and Democratization in China," in Howard Handelman and Mark Tessler (eds), *Democracy and Its Limits: Lessons from Asia, Latin America, and the Middle East* (Notre Dame: University of Notre Dame Press, 1999), p. 100.

[65] See You Ji, "Jiang Zemin: In Quest of Post-Deng Supremacy," in Maurice Brosseau, Suzanne Pepper and Tsang Shu-ki (eds), *China Review 1996* (Hong Kong: The

linking Qiao to the Yang brothers. This, however, would have been an exceptionally bold and dangerous move in a situation where not only was "stability and unity" the regime's top goal, but where the only man with the clout to upset the apple cart—Deng—had made a substantial investment in Jiang. In short, making a move was a recipe for "losing all," sitting tight guaranteed another comfortable term on the Politburo Standing Committee. Whatever the problems between Jiang and Qiao five years later, they would not have encouraged a bid for the top job by the 73-year-old Qiao. Again using existing, if loosely defined, procedures, Jiang apparently maneuvered Qiao into retirement. Moreover, as Joseph Fewsmith has observed, Jiang then moved towards the positions Qiao had advocated, a phenomenon quite different from the ritual denunciation of losers of "succession struggles." The indications are that Qiao did not appreciate the outcome, but it was more a golden handshake than the result of a no-holds-barred struggle.[66]

The retirement measure used by Jiang against Qiao was part of a broader set of loosely defined, quasi-institutional procedures governing selection to the Politburo generally and the management of succession—both of the number one leader and of entire "generations" of leaders. While the procedures are also to a significant extent in black box territory,[67] a number of principles can reasonably be deduced from the practice of the late Deng period and afterwards. These include retirement from the Politburo and other top positions at age 70, although this rule was relaxed for the 71-year-old Jiang at the 15th Congress;[68] a limit of two terms in the top Party and

Chinese University Press, 1996), pp. 14–17; and Fewsmith, "Institution Building," pp. 100–101.

[66] See Fewsmith, "Institution Building," pp. 101–102; and idem, *Elite Politics in Contemporary China* (Armonk: M.E. Sharpe, 2001), n. 33 to the "Introduction." For a summary of varying Hong Kong accounts of the maneuvers surrounding Qiao's retirement, see Richard Baum, "Jiang Takes Command: The Fifteenth National Party Congress and Beyond," in Tien and Chu, *China Under Jiang*, pp. 23–25.

[67] See the discussion in Teiwes, "Normal Politics with Chinese Characteristics," p. 76.

[68] The exception for Jiang, I would argue, had less to do with the office than the political situation. As the "core," and a "core" only marginally older than his senior

state positions of General Secretary, President and Premier;[69] appointing younger, better-educated leaders to the Politburo at each Congress with a view to serving multiple terms and becoming the basis of future "generations" of leadership;[70] guaranteed representation for the regime's key institutions, functional specialties, and major localities on the Politburo;[71] emphasizing stability by reelecting Politburo members short of extreme circumstances, until retirement age is reached;[72] and chosing the successor himself at least one term ahead of assuming the role in order to eliminate as much uncertainty as possible from the transition.

By unquestionably designating Hu Jintao successor and "core" of the "fourth generation," the CCP is fulfilling this last "principle." Hu, who had already served one term on the Standing Committee, was all but treated as the "core in waiting" in the official biography issued at the 15th Congress. The following year he was made PRC Vice President with the right of automatic succession should anything happen to Jiang, and in 1999 he was named CMC Vice Chairman. Moreover, given the age structure of the Standing Committee, there is little chance of anyone on that body, presumably a must for

---

peers, Jiang was crucial to the system at that juncture less because of his skills than because competition for the succession (real succession competition if not necessarily "struggle") would have been deemed a threat to stability. The 70 age limit was generally observed by the time of the 14th Congress, with the exception of military leaders. See Frederick C. Teiwes, "The Problematic Quest for Stability: Reflections on Succession, Institutionalization, Governability, and Legitimacy in Post-Deng China," in Tien and Chu, *China Under Jiang*, pp. 76–77, p. 79.

[69] The state positions of President and Premier are constitutionally limited to two terms. Although not legally so limited, the fact that, as of late 2001, there has been no suggestion that Jiang would stay on as General Secretary after the 16th Congress indicates that a similar understanding applies for the top Party post.

[70] Hu Jintao (see below) can be regarded as an archetype in this regard, while various others first elected to the Politburo in 1997 can expect two to four terms before reaching 70.

[71] While this is hardly new, it became increasingly regularized as the Deng period proceeded.

[72] See Teiwes, "Paradoxical Post-Mao Transition," pp. 88–89; and idem, "Problematic Quest for Stability," p. 78.

aspiring to be the "core," mounting an effective challenge.[73] And at 59 in 2002, Hu will be poised for two terms as "core."[74] Politically, moreover, Hu's profile contains many of the same qualities that made Jiang attractive in 1989: no involvement in the Tiananmen events, an image as a reformer, and acceptability to both the "conservative" and "reform" wings of the CCP.[75]

In terms of succession politics, however, Hu Jintao can be regarded a transitional figure. On the one hand, his elevation is a product of the quasi-regularized process discussed above; moreover, Hu's confirmation as "core in waiting" came in the absence of a great leader, and he arguably would not have been Jiang Zemin's preference if the choice had been left entirely to the General Secretary.[76] But it is even clearer that Hu owes his position to Deng Xiaoping. Hu's initial elevation to the Standing Committee at the age of 49 came at the 14th Congress, a time when Deng was indisputably calling the shots on personnel. While it must again be emphasized that this is black box territory, according to the most credible account of Hu's selection in 1992, Deng had instructed the "first front" leaders to propose some younger candidates for the

---

[73] Jiang, Li Peng and Zhu Rongji, who will all be well past 70, would be expected to retire, under the above under standings, while Li Ruihuan's position appears anomalous. As Li was added to the Standing Committee in the crisis days of 1989 at the age of 55, he will be 68 in 2002, but his power can be regarded as suspect. The newly appointed Standing Committee members in 1997, Wei Jianxing and Li Lanqing, will have passed 70 when the 16th Congress meets.

[74] Hu will be two months short of his 70th birthday when the 18th Congress meets in 2012, thus under current age limits still eligible for another term. It is likely, however, that a two-term limit will by then be firmly in place.

[75] I am indebted to Warren Sun concerning the similarity of Hu's and Jiang's political assets as they would have been seen by both Deng and the broader political elite. Regarding Hu's acceptability to both Party "factions," note that he had worked under the more conservative Song Ping in Gansu in the late 1970s and early 1980s, and that he was promoted by Hu Yaobang to be Youth League secretary in 1982, and then in 1985 to become Party secretary in Guizhou.

[76] This is not to suggest that Hu was imposed on Jiang against his wishes, and available evidence suggests the Jiang–Hu relationship has been a smooth one. But their relationship was in effect determined by Deng, and Jiang had no known career links to Hu before

Standing Committee. When, shortly before the Congress, Jiang, Song Ping, a representative "conservative" figure who had been Hu's boss in the late 1970s and early 1980s, and the purportedly "reformist" Qiao Shi approached Deng with a draft list of candidates, they raised Hu's name. Deng reportedly responded with "Hu Jintao is a fine person," an interjection which settled the matter.[77] Hu's elevation, then, came without struggle and, on the available information, without any effort on his part to advance his candidacy. Given the absence of a leader who can dictate an outcome and the ongoing preoccupation with stability, future succession will most likely be managed to limit struggle, but in a more "normal" environment where succession competition will evolve.

PROBLEMS OF THE COMING SUCCESSION

Few of the principles discussed above are as clear-cut as the term limits on top state positions. Nevertheless, if we take the apparent age limit at face value, we could expect at least 11 Politburo places (or over 45%) to be vacant at the 16th Congress, including five (over 71%) on the Standing Committee. This will not only allow filling the "fourth generation's" top leadership posts (particularly the presumptive Premier) under Hu Jintao—undoubtedly largely if not entirely through orderly promotions of current Politburo members[78]— but also a blooding in of prospective leaders of the "fifth generation."

1992. Regardless of the reliability of reports concerning Jiang's alleged efforts to promote Zeng Qinghong (see n. 6, above), Jiang's long close relationship with Zeng makes plausible that he would prefer Zeng as his successor.

[77] See Yang Zhongmei, *Hu Jintao—Zhonggong kua shiji jiebanren* [Hu Jintao—the CCP's successor for the new century] (Taipei: China Times Publishing, 1999), pp. 160–164.

[78] While not wishing to make predictions about individuals, it is plausible that Zeng Qinghong has a good chance of being promoted from alternate Politburo status to the Standing Committee, even though this would represent a jump over full Politburo status. If so, it would demonstrate that the speculation about Zeng being denied promotion in 2000–2001 (cf. n. 6) was ill-conceived, that the dynamic was to avoid changes in the leadership outside of Party Congresses which might suggest instability, rather than

Of course, the precise outcome of this process, not simply in individual terms but in terms of the overall pattern, is unknowable. But the new Politburo lineup will include leaders who simply have not reached retirement—most probably Li Ruihuan on the Standing Committee[79] and perhaps several other Politburo members who will be in their late 60s,[80] leaders settling in for multiple terms, and possibly—in selected cases—officials appointed for single terms at their respective levels.[81] Clearly, the specific outcomes will reflect a range of particularistic factors, but the overall result will embody the recruitment of younger, better-educated and professionally competent leaders.[82]

With the "core" of the "fourth generation" already determined, one of the key decisions facing the next Congress will concern the successor for the "fifth generation," someone who will have to come

to rebuff Jiang in an ongoing power struggle. I am indebted to Chris Buckley for this observation.

[79] It is, of course, possible that Li will retire at the 16th Congress while still two years short of his 70th birthday, but the impulse to avoid signs of instability, not to mention Li's purported enjoyment of the perks of power, suggests that he will continue for another term.

[80] However, it may not simply be a matter of age, but of political significance as well. See the discussion of Li Tieying's dubious qualifications, below. In contrast, Luo Gan, although 67 in fall 2002, is significant enough to continue on the Politburo regardless, and perhaps receive a promotion to the Standing Committee on the Wei Jianxing/Li Lanqing pattern (see n. 81).

[81] Using the 15th Congress as a benchmark, the two new Standing Committee members, Wei Jianxing and Li Lanqing, both promoted from full Politburo status, will only have a single term if age limits are strictly adhered to. Regarding Li Lanqing, however, see below. In addition, the two new military representatives on the Politburo, Zhang Wannian and Chi Haotian, clearly are eligible for only a single term. On the pattern of PLA Politburo representatives being older, see Teiwes, "Problematic Quest for Stability," p. 79.

[82] Cf. Li Cheng's observation that while nepotism and favoritism may play a pivotal role in the choice of individuals for the Politburo and other influential posts, wide administrative experience and other "objective" criteria are also essential; "China in 1999: Seeking Common Ground at a Time of Tension and Conflict," *Asian Survey*, Vol. 40, No. 1 (January/February 2000), pp. 116–117. For an overview of the background of the "fourth generation," see idem, "Jiang Zemin's Successors: The Rise of the Fourth Generation of Leaders in the PRC," *CQ*, No. 161 (2000).

from outside the current Politburo.[83] As suggested above, this will surely not be an authoritative decision by a single leader as was the case with Deng for both Jiang Zemin and Hu Jintao. It will still be from above, but will involve a collective process seeking consensus. Presumably, leaders of both the "third" and "fourth generations" will have their preferences; it is less certain how or to what degree potential candidates can position themselves for selection. Successors have always previously been determined from above essentially by an individual's decision, even though Deng clearly consulted other Party elders. While impressing the leader was obviously essential, too much ambition could be a negative in a system that has frowned on the expression of individual goals.[84] One would expect, though, that under conditions of "normal politics," there would be more scope for presenting one's case. Be that as it may, there are larger uncertainties as to how the issue will be approached. A Hu Jintao type solution would be to designate a potential "core in waiting" and promote him directly to the Standing Committee. This would have the advantage of clarity, but also the drawback of placing too many eggs in one untried basket. An alternative approach might be to promote two or three possible "fifth generation" successors to full Politburo membership, observe their performances, and make a definitive choice at the 17th Congress in 2007. The aim would still be an orderly process with the matter settled well in advance of the next transition, but with a realistic view to making a decision based on the demonstration of abilities at the highest level.[85]

[83] Assuming two terms for the "core," no present Politburo member would be eligible for one term, much less two, after Hu's expected retirement in 2012. In fact, at 59 Hu is the youngest of all present Politburo members.

[84] Mao noted Hua Guofeng's modesty when determining his promotion to acting Premier; Mao Mao, *"Wenge" suiyue*, p. 449. Note also Li Peng's awkward performance at a 1991 press conference, when he could only say that he would stay at his post as Premier for the remainder of the government's present term in the interests of political stability; *Beijing Review*, No. 16 (1991), p. 18. In cases where leaders clearly did campaign for the succession, Gao Gang and the Gang of Four, they did not come to a good end.

[85] This pattern would be close to the Mexican system which worked effectively for 70 years. With a presidential term limit of one six-year term, the incumbent president

The problems of selecting a new "core in waiting" are further reflected in the politics of selecting a new Politburo as a whole and the broader generational succession. Quite clearly, there is considerable jockeying for position as the 16th Congress approaches, with various retiring leaders touting their protégés, different institutions seeking suitable representation and deciding on their respective candidates, and representative figures of various policy and ideological tendencies trying to ensure that their views will be included in the new power structure. Given the preoccupation with stability, such maneuvering will not produce a recognizable "succession struggle." Tension and conflict there is and will be, but the overall objective is a balance that can garner broad elite support. In terms of institutional representation and functional specialties, new candidates from the PLA, the Central Discipline Inspection Committee (CDIC), and the foreign affairs system will be required, because all the sitting Politburo members from these organizations face retirement.[86] On the other hand, the existing representation of local Party leaders may be sufficient, with reelection of the four sitting provincial and municipal secretaries considered enough.[87] If this pattern is followed, there will still be at least six seats to be filled, most probably from State Council and Party center organs, and there will undoubtedly be pushing and hauling within and between these bodies as to who gains selection; the result will almost certainly involve representatives of the propaganda, organization, political and legal, and several economic bureaucracies. As implied, there will also be a range of policy and ideological preferences,

designated his successor during the last third of a presidential term from a member of his cabinet, the only source of possible candidates, after consulting widely within the government and ruling party.

[86] Zhang Wannian and Chi Haotian from the military, Wei Jianxing from the CDIC, and Qian Qichen from the foreign affairs system.

[87] Jia Qinglin of Beijing, Huang Ju of Shanghai, Wu Guanzheng of Shandong, and Li Changchun of Guangdong, all of whom would qualify for at least two more terms on strict age criteria. Of course, one or more of these officials could be transferred to the Center, thus creating possible vacancies for new local officials. Since the 13th Congress in 1987, key localities have been represented on the Politburo by three to five leading

although it is unlikely that any views too far from the current consensus will be incorporated. This will not prevent vigorous discussion within high Party councils,[88] but in all likelihood it will exclude "extreme" views that could potentially threaten leadership stability.

In the inevitable jockeying for precious positions in the leadership, a conflict may emerge between the principle of an orderly infusion of new talent, and the practice of no removals from the Politburo short of retirement apart from exceptional cases. Might not space be created for a talented representative of the "fifth generation" by "prematurely" retiring an ineffectual sitting member? A case in point is Li Tieying, the son of Li Weihan, the highest-ranking "Party prince" after Li Peng, and one of the longest serving Politburo members who first joined the body in 1987. For all that, Li will still be only 66 in 2002 and will therefore be entitled to another term. Yet Li has been unpopular within the elite, and according to one account his seat was saved by Jiang Zemin's intervention at the 1997 Congress not only on the stability argument, but also by emphasizing that Deng himself had approved Li's appointment.[89] Currently, Li holds the hardly prepossessing position of President of the Chinese Academy of Social Sciences, seemingly a post which gives him something to do without interfering in the serious business of the regime. Arguably, a much more significant case is Li Ruihuan, whose portfolio as head the of Chinese People's Political Consultative Committee is marginal to the CCP's tasks— although in his case his position as a Standing Committee member,

---

Party secretaries at any given time. Shanghai has been continuously represented, and Beijing virtually so with the exception caused by Chen Xitong's removal for corruption. Guangdong and Shandong have been represented since 1992, while Tianjin and Sichuan have had more limited representation.

[88] See the report of C. Fred Bergsten, "A Glimpse of the Other China," *The Washington Post*, September 3, 2001. While obviously not a Politburo meeting, Bergsten reports on a Shanghai conference where senior Chinese officials including ministers sharply criticized one another while discussing aspects of economic policy.

[89] This specific oral report cannot be verified, but there is little doubt concerning the low regard in which Li is held.

and his (exaggerated) reputation as a reformer, suggests that any early retirement would be rejected as providing the impression of disunity.[90] In any case, a tradeoff exists between maximizing new, talented blood and adhering rigidly to the right to Politburo membership until retirement age, however it is played out in the selection of the new leadership.

Another possible conflict of principles, one pushing in the opposite direction of that discussed in the previous paragraph, concerns balancing the enforcement of strict age limits against the need for continuity, for the "stability" in "stability and unity." Speculatively, this could affect the position of Li Lanqing on the Politburo Standing Committee. Li, who will reach his 70th birthday four months before the 16th Congress convenes, may stay on to provide such continuity. It would be quite a different situation from that created if Jiang Zemin were to stay on as CMC Chair (see below), in that Li, an experienced and competent leader, would have no higher personal ambitions for the future, and certainly would be in no position to dictate policy from "above." But he could provide ballast for the transition period. If Li did retire "on schedule," however, a turnover of five of the seven members of the Standing Committee could be seen as too disruptive of leadership stability and continuity.[91]

Of all the questions facing analysts concerning the upcoming transition, none has been more extensively canvassed than the issue of the role of the "third generation" leaders after the 16th Congress. While there has been some speculation on possible positions that might be assumed by "new Party elders" Li Peng and Zhu Rongji, the overwhelming focus has been on the future of Jiang Zemin— specifically on whether he will stay on as CMC Chairman in a Deng

---

[90] Cf. n. 73 and 79, above. Another indication of senior Politburo members being placed in less vital positions is that several (Tian Jiyun, Jiang Chunyun) assumed NPC duties in recent years before their expected retirement at the 16th Congress. Consider also the case of NPC Vice Chairman Xie Fei, who moved from Party secretary in Guangdong to his NPC post in 1998 and would have been 69 in 2002, but died in 1999.

[91] This discussion is based on an exchange of views with Chris Buckley.

Xiaoping-type role on the "second front" hovering over the Hu Jintao leadership on the "first front." This issue remains deep in the black box, but the very fact that it has not been clearly dealt with, suggests it has been a matter of contention. As Susan Shirk has argued, the "fourth generation" will not look kindly on a limitation of its authority.[92] Apart from the interests of this generation, for Jiang to hold on to the military role would run against both the entire post-Mao emphasis on more regularized procedures, create confusion over the key principle of "the Party controls the gun," and potentially revive one of the destabilizing features of the 1980s—the clashing authority of the "first" and "second fronts." However, whatever the outcome concerning the CMC post,[93] the situation would be very different for Jiang than it was for Deng. Deng was a PLA hero, the virtual 11th marshal,[94] and the unquestioned leader of his generation who could still determine state policies and future successors in his 88th year while holding no official post. Similarly, the "new Party elders" can hardly be considered equivalent to the Party elders of the 1980s who combined revolutionary prestige with major roles in the Party–state since 1949. To be sure, Jiang, Li, Zhu, and others will retain prestige and some influence whatever the circumstances,

---

[92] Susan L. Shirk, "Will the Institutionalization of Party Leadership Survive the 2002–2003 Succession?" *CJ*, No. 45 (2001), argues that such tension is likely given the probable unwillingness of Jiang, Li, and Zhu to retire gracefully.

[93] On balance, the existing evidence as of late 2001 suggests that Jiang will not continue to hold the post, but it is far from being clear-cut. Perhaps most indicative was Zeng Qinghong's remark during an inspection tour in Shenzhen in early 2001 that such an outcome was "not likely"; *Asia Times* online report, March 8, 2001. More recently, but unverifiable, an informed source claimed that at the fall 2001 Central Committee plenum, Jiang declared he would give up the CMC post, noting that he originally did not have much experience in military affairs, took up the post at Deng's behest, and that Deng had set a good example of retiring from the office, which he should follow. Nevertheless, Jiang has sidestepped the issue in public comments, and various sources in Beijing believe he will continue in the CMC position.

[94] When military ranks were granted in 1955, it had originally been planned to name Deng a marshal, a proposal that was dropped because it was decided no "civilian" leader would hold the rank. See Teiwes, "Paradoxical Post-Mao Transition," p. 68.

but even if Jiang holds on to the CMC Chair in some messy compromise,[95] it will once again be clear that he is no Deng.

All of the above is according to a premise that is not necessarily so—that the CCP will be relatively successful, develop a tolerable relationship with society, and avoid a regime-shaking crisis. This is not to predict such an outcome, even if I have spoken in terms of a similar succession process extending to the 18th Party Congress in 2012.[96] It is definitely within the realm of possibility that such a crisis, or a combination of major problems and a recognition by a significant segment of the elite that systemic political change can no longer be put off, will produce a major change. In either case, the likelihood of a centrist consensus necessary to maintain leadership stability would be seriously undermined. What has been outlined in this analysis is, in a sense, the ideal world for the existing Party elite—a world that protects the elite from the divisive and un predictable internal conflicts of the past, upholds the valued principle of Party unity, provides orderly successions, and as a result helps underpin stability in the wider polity. In a context where the relations of regime and society fall far short of the degree of institutionalization the CCP has gradually created for itself, it remains to be seen how long this ideal succession politics can be maintained.

[95] One possible basis for such a compromise suggested by Chris Buckley is that, in contrast to the paramount leader role Deng continued to exercise until his health gave out, Jiang might be limited to overseeing military affairs. In sharp contrast to Deng, this would not involve any deep respect or automatic obedience based on war accomplishments, but it could reflect the army's comfort with Jiang's sympathetic handling of its affairs over the past decade. On Jiang–PLA relations, see You Ji, "Jiang Zemin's Command of the Military," *CJ*, No. 45 (2001).

[96] Carol Lee Hamrin in "Inching Toward Open Politics," *CJ*, No. 45 (2001), p. 123, mistakenly concluded that I was arguing that the regime had achieved "an equilibrium that will last" in my earlier discussion, "Normal Politics with Chinese Characteristics." As indicated here, my argument concerns a pattern of leadership politics that is "stable" in the sense that the Party elite has a deep commitment to it and will not lightly depart from it. In this sense, I am reasonably confident that the 16th Congress transition will largely uphold the trend to institutionalization, notwithstanding Shirk's thoughtful canvassing of the alternative (see n. 92). But whether these comfortable elite arrangements can withstand evolving state–society relations over a longer run is quite another matter.

Chapter 2

Crossing the Political Minefields of Succession: From Jiang Zemin to Hu Jintao

ZHENG SHIPING

POLITICAL SUCCESSION AS A PROBLEM

As the Chinese leaders are busy preparing for the handover of power from the third generation headed by Jiang Zemin to the fourth generation to be headed by Hu Jintao, political succession has again become the concern of many political analysts.[1] This is because political succession in China is neither institutionalized as in some Western democracies nor does it follow the lineage as in some traditional monarchies. From the cases of failed succession by Liu Shaoqi, Lin Biao, and Hua Guofeng in the Mao Zedong era and by Hu Yaobang and Zhao Ziyang in the Deng Xiaoping era, there is sufficient evidence to suggest that political succession in China can be unpredictable and even dangerous.

The problem of political succession is of course not exclusive to China. In the biological sense, aging leaders need to be replaced by younger leaders. In the political sense, paramount leaders may want

---

[1] For some recent studies of China's political succession, see Li Cheng, "Jiang Zemin's Successors: The Rise of the Fourth Generation of Leaders in the PRC," *The China Quarterly*, Vol. 161 (March 2000), pp. 1–40; Zheng Yongnian, "The Politics of Power Succession," in Wang Gungwu and Zheng Yongnian (eds), *Reform, Legitimacy* and

to pick their own successors. And in case of emergency when something unexpected and devastating happens to the occupant of the highest political office (and often the commander-in-chief as well), it is in the best interest of the nation in general and the regime in particular to have someone who can legitimately take over the reins from the incapacitated leader.[2]

Nevertheless, there are some fundamental differences between China and other countries on the issue of political succession. First of all, in Western democracies, leadership changes are generally completed through popular elections. When the leader of either of the two major political parties alternatively takes over the highest political office, it is hard to say that one party's leader "succeeds" the other. It is true that in parliamentary democracies based on the Westminster model, leadership changes sometimes also happen to the ruling party without a new general election. The outgoing prime minister, therefore, may play a role in picking his or her successor to be the new leader of the party and concurrently the new prime minister. But even here the successor-designate has to win a majority of votes from the party members and ultimately win the next general election in order to hold on to the office of prime minister.

In the US presidential system, succession has also somewhat different meanings. Presidential succession may mean that the Vice President shall become the President "in the case of the removal of the President from office, or of his death, resignation, or inability to discharge the powers and duties of the office of the Presidency." For presidential succession beyond the Vice President, the Presidential Succession Act passed by the US Congress in 1947 has established a clear line of succession.[3]

Dilemmas: China's Politics and Society (Singapore: Singapore University Press, 2000), pp. 23–49; and the special issue of *The China Journal*, No. 45 (January 2001).

[2] For comparative studies of political succession, see Peter Calvert (ed.), *The Process of Political Succession* (New York: St. Martin's Press, 1987).

[3] According to *the Presidential Succession Act of 1947*, the line of succession to the US President is as follows: The Vice President, Speaker of the House, President *pro tempore* of the Senate, Secretary of the State, Secretary of the Treasury, Secretary of Defense, Attorney General, Secretary of the Interior, Secretary of Agriculture, Secretary of

In imperial China of the past and in some monarchies and North Korea of today, political succession basically follows the lineage when the son succeeds the dying or deceased father as the next ruler of the land. In post-1949 China, however, although some of the sons and daughters of the revolutionary veterans, the so-called "princelings," have "succeeded" their parents in a general sense by assuming high-ranking political offices, there has not been a precedent in which the paramount leader (Mao Zedong or Deng Xiaoping) designated his child to be his successor.

What is more relevant to China is perhaps the case of political succession in the former Soviet Union and Eastern European countries under communist rule. All of them have failed to institutionalize the process of political succession and have, therefore, suffered both the intended and unintended consequences, whether in the form of sudden policy changes shaking the political system or in the form of bloody power struggle costing thousands of lives.[4] Lowell Dittmer thus points out, "Succession is both important and problematic in all Communist Party states."[5] Or as Michel Oksenberg suggests, "There is nothing in a Leninist system short of a coup to prevent the preeminent leader from remaining in power after his mental and physical capabilities have eroded."[6]

Commerce, Secretary of Labor, Secretary of Health and Human Services, Secretary of Housing and Urban Development, Secretary of Transportation, Secretary of Energy, and Secretary of Education.

[4] For the classic study of political succession in the Soviet Union, see Myron Rush, *Political Succession in the USSR* (New York: Columbia University Press, 1968). See also Anthony D'Agostino, *Soviet Succession Struggles: Kremlinology and the Russian Question from Lenin to Gorbachev* (Boston: Allen & Unwin, 1988) and R. Judson Mitchell, *Getting to the Top in the USSR: Cyclical Patterns in the Leadership Succession Process* (Stanford, CA: Hoover Institution Press, 1990). For studies of political succession in Eastern European Communist regimes, see Carl Beck, William A. Jarzabek and Paul Ernandez, *Political Succession in Eastern Europe: Fourteen Case Studies* (Pittsburgh: University Center for International Studies, 1976) and Martin McCauley and Stephen Carter (eds), *Leadership and Succession in the Soviet Union, Eastern Europe and China* (Armonk, New York: M.E. Sharpe, 1986).

[5] Lowell Dittmer, "The Changing Shape of Elite Power Politics," *The China Journal*, No. 45 (January 2001), p. 61.

[6] Michel Oksenberg, "China's Political System: Challenges of the Twenty-First Century," *The China Journal*, No. 45 (January 2001), p. 29.

Nevertheless, students of comparative politics in the Soviet Union and China have also observed the difference in "postmortem succession" struggle in the former and "premortem succession" problem in the latter.[7] In the Soviet Union, there was no clear successor-designate when Lenin, Stalin, or Brezhnev died, whereas in China a successor was often designated when the paramount leader was still alive. In the Soviet Union, therefore, political succession basically meant power struggle among peers; in China, political succession often meant changing power relations between the successor-designate and the paramount leader. The process of political succession in China has consequently followed somewhat different rules.

In this chapter, I am not focusing on the thousands upon thousands of officials of the younger generation who are working their way up on the ladder of political power. Political succession in a generational sense is inevitable and unstoppable. Every regime, democratic or otherwise, needs young talents and fresh blood. China is no exception. Since the late 1970s, China has witnessed enormous and successful generational changes in its leadership. Political succession in the plural form—a group or a generation of successors—has been well institutionalized. Through the regular process of recruiting, training, evaluation, and promotion, the regime in China does not face the problem of lack of qualified candidates to fill various political offices vacated by aging officials.

The main concern in this chapter is political succession in the singular form—one person who is chosen to succeed the current predominant leader to take over the highest political office(s) in due time. Of course, much more is at stake than just the political career of one person whether the successor-designate succeeds or not. In the Soviet Union and during the Mao Zedong era in China, failed succession attempts were often followed by purges, persecution, and sometimes loss of lives. During the Deng Xiaoping era, political succession is no longer a "life and death" struggle, but is still intrinsically connected with the political careers or fortunes of hundreds of thousands of Party and government officials.

---

[7] For an analysis of the difference between these two patterns, see Lowell Dittmer, "The Changing Shape of Elite Power Politics," pp. 61–64.

CHANGING POLITICAL RULES IN POST-MAO CHINA

Many, if not all, students of comparative and Chinese politics recognize that political succession is a problem in communist party states or Leninist systems. However, what exactly is the succession problem in China needs more clarification. Political succession to Mao Zedong has never succeeded. While we are all too familiar with the cases of "failed succession," ranging from Liu Shaoqi to Lin Biao and, to a lesser extent, Hua Guofeng, we simply do not have one single case of successful succession in the Mao Zedong era. If succession to Mao was doomed to fail, then succession was not a problem; it was a certainty—failure is just as certain as death. Thus one can hardly study political succession in the Mao era as a problem, because it can neither be handled successfully nor produce a different result. It is only in the Deng Xiaoping era that political succession has become a problem, because political succession to a paramount leader like Deng can either fail or succeed. It is this uncertainty that makes the issue of succession in post-Mao China problematic and interesting.

Since the post-Mao reforms began in the late 1970s, China has been undergoing a profound economic and social transformation. While it is true that China's political reforms lag behind economic reforms and social changes, the political environment has also witnessed several significant changes that affect the rules of the game of political succession. Although personal influence and informal power-play still works in many ways, institutions and organizational rules also matter, and certainly matter more than before. In other words, political institutionalization has become a meaningful factor of restraint.

Distinctive Career Paths

Modernization and economic development have led not only to specialization of professional skills but also to different political career paths. Although the Party committee secretary and the head of government are still interchangeable at the provincial and local level, many other political career paths are reasonably distinct and not easily interchangeable. A paramount leader like Mao could pick his political successors at will, regardless of different career paths. First it was Liu Shaoqi, a Party theoretician and a veteran political organizer. Then it was Lin Biao, a strategically superb but physically frail military leader, followed by Wang Hongwen, a young and politically inexperienced factory worker, and finally by Hua Guofeng, a parochial provincial official.

In post-Mao China, although it is impossible to say which career path will be the most direct route to becoming the "core" of the new leadership, it is likely that the candidate for becoming the "core" of the new leadership will have some work experience in both the Party organization and government institutions at both the central and provincial level. It is also possible to suggest that certain career paths are unlikely to help someone become the "core" of the new leadership. For instance, if someone has spent most time of his career as an expert in one special area of work, it is unlikely that he will become the "core" of the new leadership. If someone intends to pursue a career in the military, it is almost impossible for him to become the "core." The best that he can hope for is to become a member of the Politburo and a vice chairman of the Party's Central Military Commission (CMC). The CMC chairmanship, the most important of the top three offices that define the status of "core," has to be assumed by a civilian leader.

Other careers like business, diplomatic service, intelligence, public security, and law enforcement also greatly reduce one's chances of becoming the "core" of the new leadership. The "core" status, therefore, is not something that every young and ambitious Chinese official can hope to contend for; nor should we assume that it is something that the many of China's rising political stars are interested in.

Age Limits

Out of all the rules, what matters the most for political succession is perhaps the increasingly institutionalized age limits for officials. For instance, the set retirement age for central ministers, provincial governors, commanders of major military regions, and armed services is 65. Upon approaching this age, one has to assess his or her chance of "going up" above the level of central minister/provincial governor or accept the reality of "going out."

At the 15th Party Congress, a gentleman's agreement seemed to have been reached between Jiang Zemin and the rest of the Politburo Standing Committee. Subsequently, Qiao Shi, who was 72 years old and one year older than Jiang, retired from the Central Committee in exchange for Jiang's promise to serve only one more term as the Party general secretary.[8] Qiao Shi has thus set a precedent for members of China's highest decision-making body—the Politburo Standing Committee—to retire after the age of 70. To put this precedent of age limit in perspective, when Mao launched the Cultural Revolution in 1966, he was already 73 years old. When Deng Xiaoping came back to the power center in 1978, he was already 75 years old. Many observers are anxious to see if Jiang will honor this agreement at the 16th Party Congress. It seems, though, that opposition to Jiang is fierce whenever Jiang wants to contest this informal agreement.

The informal rule of retirement after the age of 70 for China's top leaders can be a significant factor for political succession. For one thing, the age limit will shrink the pool of potential contenders for the "core" status of the new generation. If someone, on his 65th birthday, has not yet climbed the ladder of political power higher than that of the central minister/provincial governor, there is no chance he will become a candidate for becoming the "core" of the new leadership.

Moreover, this age limit would undoubtedly shorten the expected tenure of the "core" leader. For instance, Mao Zedong as the paramount leader had stayed in power for 27 years from 1949 until he died in 1976. Deng Xiaoping's political tenure in post-Mao China may be counted in two different ways. The longer version began in

---

[8] For an analysis of this agreement, see Richard Baum, "The Fifteenth National Party Congress: Jiang Takes Command?" *The China Quarterly*, No. 155 (March 1998), pp. 141–156; Joseph Fewsmith, "The New Shape of Elite Politics," *The China Journal*, No. 45 (January 2001), p. 91.

1978 when Deng came back to the power center, and it ended with his death in February 1997. This was a total of 18 years in power. The shorter version began in 1981 when Hua Guofeng was forced to resign from his Party chairmanship, and it ended in 1994 when Deng lost his effective control, if not influence, because of his declining physical condition. This was a total of 14 years in power.

Jiang Zemin as the "core" of the third generation obviously can no longer hope to have a political tenure as long as that of Mao or of Deng. Between 1989 when Jiang went to Beijing and the 16th Party Congress in 2002, this would be a total of 13 years. If we begin with 1994, when Jiang was able to walk out of the political shadow of Deng Xiaoping, this would be a total of only eight years running up to 2002. Hu Jintao (born in 1942) can realistically expect a political tenure of no longer than 10 years as the "core" of the fourth generation.

When it comes to characterizing different generations of China's leaders, there are such terms as the "the Long March generation" referring to those who were born before the late 1910s; "the Anti-Japanese War generation" referring to those born between the 1920s and the early 1930s; the "Socialist Transformation generation" referring to those born in the late 1930s and the early 1940s; "the Cultural Revolution generation" referring to those born between the late 1940s and early 1950s; and "the Economic Reform generation" referring those born in the late 1950s and early 1960s.[9] These generational divisions can sometimes become arbitrary and confusing, however. For instance, Deng Xiaoping invented the term "core" and characterized Mao Zedong as the "core" of the first generation and himself as the "core" of the second generation of Chinese leadership. But the so-called second generation included members of the "Long March generation" as well as of the "Anti-Japanese War generation." Insofar as political succession is concerned, however, an age gap of 10 years will perhaps distinguish the "core" of the current generation and the "core" of the new generation of leadership.

[9] Li Cheng, "Jiang Zemin's Successor: The Rise of the Fourth Generation of Leaders in the PRC," p. 7.

SUCCESSOR-DESIGNATE AS ACTIVE AGENT

Many studies of China's political succession have traditionally framed the research question in terms of power struggle, political purges, or failed arrangements. In these studies, the designated successor was often viewed either as a helpless victim or as a passive follower. To understand the intriguing and complex politics of political succession in China, I suggest that we conceptualize the successor-designate as an active player who tries to maximize his chance of succession or minimize the danger to his career in a political environment.

The successor-designate is not a puppet of his patrons but an active agent. He is not merely a product of the political process; he himself is a key player in politics, which ultimately affects his power and political fate. He knows what his mission is and what challenges are after he is designated the successor. The process of selecting a political successor is most likely a secret one, and therefore the final result is often surprising, even for the one who is chosen. Yet, once the official word is out, the successor-designate, willingly or reluctantly, must quickly learn to play the succession game to his advantage.

Moreover, the successor-designate acts in an organizational environment where there are certain rules and norms he must follow. Violation of these organizational rules and norms would make him vulnerable to his opponents and jeopardize his chance of a smooth political succession. Specifically, he must learn to deal with two major challenges, namely, managing relations with the patron and building a broad network of support. In the Chinese political environment, these challenges constitute two political minefields. It is almost unthinkable that one could hope to establish oneself as the top leader of China without trying to walk through these political minefields. Yet any major misstep in any of these minefields could cause serious damage to one's political career and chance of success.

Finally, political succession has to mean more than just "getting to the top" of the power structure. If "getting to the top" means a smooth succession, then Hua Guofeng certainly succeeded in 1978 when he held the three highest political offices in the country, being the central committee Chairman of the Chinese Communist Party (CCP), the Premier of the State Council, and the Chairman of the Party's CMC. Jiang Zemin had also succeeded by 1993 when he was concurrently the Party General Secretary, the Chairman of the CMC, and the state President. But if "getting to the top" means the first stage in the succession process, we may assume that the successor-designate will need to move on to the second stage of the succession process—"consolidating power," for want of a better term. The successor-designate therefore will have to continue to walk through the political minefields even after he gets to the top.

MANAGING PATRON–PROTÉGÉ RELATIONSHIPS

It is no exaggeration that Chinese officials cannot hope to advance their political careers without the support of one or more political patrons. The significance of being a member of the "princelings" (children of high-ranking officials) or of the *mishu* (personal secretaries to high-ranking officials) is that one's parents or one's former boss would be the most natural political patrons.

By the same token, the significance of patron–protégé relations in political succession simply cannot be overstated. In most cases, a patron's support is the most important source of power for the favored successor. This is especially true for the younger and junior leaders, because it can greatly compensate for one's lack of seniority and prestige. The patron's support is initially informal and personal, for it exists only in the personal relationship between the patron and his protégé. But this informal power can interact with the formal organizational processes. A casual but positive comment about a young official, a personal recommendation to the organizational department, an offer in political horse-trading among senior leaders, or a nomination in the recruitment process can all raise the political status of the protégé.

After the protégé becomes the officially designated successor, however, his special relationship with his patron becomes a political minefield. To be a leader of his own, the successor-designate must consolidate his formal authority and expand his organizational power base, because as long as the main source of his power comes from the support of his patron, the protégé is not stable in his position; his political power is little more than the extension of the personal influence of his patron. When the patron dies, the power of the protégé can easily collapse. Any successor-designate, therefore, must try to consolidate his own power base while his patron is still alive. To make moves towards building his own power base, however, runs the risk of losing the trust of the patron, leading possibly to withdrawal of support. This is the classic "Catch-22" problem facing the successor-designate: he is damned if he is totally dependent on his patron and is damned if he tries to become independent.

Analysts have long noticed this problem in political succession. Shortly after Mao died, Lowell Dittmer characterized the "successor's dilemma" in the Mao era in the following way:

"the favorite is sooner or later inclined to seek a secondary base in addition to his personal one, for otherwise he will perish when his patron does. In turn, the patron, originally attracted by the prospect of a personal servitor, without competing organizational vested interests, tends to view a favorite's attempt to build his own power base as a relapse or a betrayal."[10]

This "successor's dilemma" is also referred to as the dilemma of being "No. 2" in Chinese politics.[11]

Ironically, points of comparison with China's "successor's dilemma" must be made not with other communist regimes, but with the US. In the US, on other hand, there does exist a "vice presidential dilemma"—how can a sitting vice president acquire a separate sphere of influence to enhance his chance of being elected president while in most instances his political future is linked to the

[10] Lowell Dittmer, "Bases of Power in Chinese Politics: A Theory and an Analysis of the Fall of the 'Gang of Four'," *World Politics*, Vol. 31, No. 1 (October 1978).

[11] Zheng Yongnian, "The Politics of Power Succession," pp. 45–46.

sitting president?[12] In some sense, this vice presidential dilemma resembles what a successor-designate in China faces in his relationship with his patron.

In the more than 200 years since the US was formed, many vice presidents have faced this dilemma: Al Gore's awkward and troublesome relationship with Bill Clinton is just the most recent example. Since there was only one vice president who succeeded in being elected president in the 19th century (Martin Van Buren in 1836) and only one vice president who succeeded in being elected president in the 20th century (George Bush in 1988), the cases of success are few and far between.

As mentioned earlier, political succession to Mao Zedong never succeeded. If Mao's chosen successor, Liu Shaoqi, and later Lin Biao initially thought of succeeding Mao, they soon realized that they were mistaken. Until he died, Mao was the only political patron who mattered for the successor-designate, because Mao was the ultimate source of all political power in China. A nomination by Mao would immediately enhance one's status, and conversely a withdrawal of support by Mao could immediately render a successor-designate powerless. Political succession therefore meant, above everything else, gaining trust and support from Mao, which was in essence a mission impossible.

As for Hua Guofeng, it remains a mystery whether Mao had actually designated him to be the official successor. At any rate, no matter how much or how little Hua Guofeng had thought about his chance of surviving Mao and defeating the challenge from Deng Xiaoping, he managed to "get to the top" after Mao died only to be removed within five years. To be sure, Deng also managed to come back to power after Mao died, and finally succeeded in establishing himself as the new predominant leader in post-Mao China. But Deng was nobody's successor.

Political succession in the Deng Xiaoping era has shown some interesting and hopeful changes. Deng was a complicated figure,

---

[12] Vance R. Kincade Jr., *Heirs Apparent: Solving the Vice Presidential Dilemma* (Westport, CT: Praeger, 2000), p. 6.

having demonstrated both the tendency to be a strongman and a willingness to compromise under pressure from his senior colleagues. More than 10 years ago, when Harry Harding used Hu Yaobang's relationship with his patron, Deng Xiaoping, to analyze the "successor's dilemma" inherent in China's succession process, he observed:

> "If Hu were to succeed to Deng's position as China's preeminent political leader, he would have to build his own power bases within the Party by staffing the Party bureaucracy with trusted followers and by defining his own position on significant policy issues. In doing so, Hu ran the risk of alienating the senior generation of Party leaders, including Deng, whom he hoped to succeed."[13]

Here Harding already noticed that other Party elders mattered just as much as Deng.

Today we know well that Deng had a rather ambivalent attitude towards Hu Yaobang and Zhao Ziyang, two of his most trusted supporters during the reforms in the late 1970s and 1980s. Although Deng had his disappointments with Hu in 1985–1986 and with Zhao in 1988–1989, it was the concerted efforts by the members of the "senior generation of Party leaders" that persuaded or forced Deng Xiaoping to sacrifice his two protégés. As far as patron–protégé relationships are concerned, it is perhaps useful to make a distinction between the era of paramount leader and the times when the top leader is only the first among equals or at best the so-called "core" of his generation.

If one's political downfall is no longer determined by one patron–protégé relationship, then one's political rise also requires having good relationships with more than one patron. The nomination of Jiang Zemin to be the "core" of the third generation in 1989 was not exactly Deng's idea. Jiang was the first choice for Party elders like Li Xiannian and Chen Yun, but a choice of no choice for Deng.

---

[13] Harry Harding, *China's Second Revolution: Reform After Mao* (Washington, DC: Brookings Institute, 1990), p. 235.

Deng could have withdrawn his support for Jiang even after Jiang was already designated the "core" of the third generation. Indeed, during his "southern tour" in 1992, Deng openly expressed his dissatisfaction with the Party central leadership with Jiang as the "core" and warned that "those who do not follow the line of the 13th Party Congress will have to step down." The first few months of 1992 were indeed the most difficult time for Jiang as he faced overwhelming political pressure from Deng.

We do not know for certain how Jiang managed to survive this succession crisis. It is perhaps one of the following factors or a combination of them that saved Jiang's political career:

1. Deng might have never intended to replace Jiang, but to put pressure on Jiang in order to shape the direction and agenda of the upcoming 14th Party Congress;
2. Deng might have realized that it was already too late for him to replace Jiang Zemin as his successor, having removed Hu Yaobang and Zhao Ziyang before;
3. As suggested earlier, the choice of Jiang as the "core" of the third generation was the result of a collective bargaining among the Party elders during the crisis in 1989. Deng did not want to upset the political balance painstakingly reestablished after the crackdown; and
4. Jiang quickly got the message and worked hard to win back Deng's confidence and support.

At any rate, by the time the 14th Party Congress convened and when Deng decided to intervene in Jiang's favor by agreeing to remove the Yang brothers from power,[14] the message should have been clear to all: Jiang was here to stay. Meanwhile, Deng maneuvered to have his protégé, Admiral Liu Huaqing, elected as one of the seven members of the Politburo Standing Committee. He also

---

[14] The "Yang brothers" refer to CMC Vice Chairman Yang Shangkun and his half-brother Yang Baibing, Director of the PLA General Political Department. Both were Deng's followers.

promoted his personal secretary Wang Ruilin as deputy director of the General Political Department of the People's Liberation Army (PLA). Moreover, with the recommendation from other Party elders like Song Ping, Deng endorsed the promotion of Hu Jintao as one of the seven members of the new Politburo Standing Committee, thus paving the way for Hu to succeed Jiang Zemin in the future.

Today, Deng is dead, Admiral Liu Huaqing is retired, and General Wang Ruilin is expected to step down soon because of his advanced age. But Hu Jintao as the "core" of the fourth generation is waiting only to take over power from Jiang Zemin. Perhaps nothing upsets Jiang more than the fact that Hu is simply not his chosen successor. Indeed, there are unconfirmed reports that Jiang has complained about being deprived of his chance to pick his political successor.

This has put Hu in an awkward position. Hu's biggest political asset is Deng Xiaoping's endorsement. Moreover, since the 14th Party Congress in 1992, a general consensus has emerged that Hu is the expected successor to Jiang Zemin. Jiang's political opponents will certainly make sure that this remains so up to the 16th Party Congress in November 2002. In addition to these advantages, Hu's age makes him the youngest among the most powerful leaders in China today. Despite all this, however, Hu Jintao still cannot afford to lose Jiang's de facto, albeit reluctant, acceptance of him as the successor-designate.

During the decade since 1992, Hu seems to have handled his relationship with Jiang remarkably well. Although Hu is not exactly Jiang's protégé, Jiang can always count on Hu's support in the Standing Committee of the Politburo. Hu is also willing to take up difficult assignments from Jiang. The most noteworthy examples are Hu heading the task force to persuade the military establishment to get delinked from business activities in 1998 and appearing on China's national television in 1999 to urge people to keep calm in the wake of the US bombing of the Chinese embassy in Belgrade and the ensuing explosive demonstrations in several Chinese cities. Hu has thus survived the death of his patron, Deng Xiaoping, and has not invited any opposition from Jiang.

BUILDING A BROAD NETWORK OF SUPPORT

A network of political support may imply both formal and informal dimensions. On the formal side, one's institutional affiliations or organizational power bases can certainly make a difference. As Myron Rush argued many years ago, a political succession struggle in the former Soviet Union involved the mobilization by contending leaders of various institutions and organizations.[15] The more institutional affiliations one has in the Party organization, the government, and the military, the better it is for the political succession.

On the informal side, personal connections or *guanxi* are said to be one of the most important assets in Chinese life, political or otherwise. In the eyes of many China specialists, personal connections are almost emblematic of Chinese political culture. It is generally held that one cannot possibly understand Chinese politics unless one understands the importance of personal connections in China.[16] In the Chinese organizational environment, however, personal connections cannot automatically be translated into one's power base in political institutions.

Here is the second political minefield a successor-designate has to walk through. To expand or consolidate his power, he has to turn his personal connections into institution-based networks of support by appointing his followers to key positions. By doing so, however, he runs the risk of being accused of engaging in factionalism, which opens a window of vulnerability to his political opponents. Moreover, to make him acceptable to most of the ruling elites, he must also go beyond his personal connections to build broad political coalitions. Thus the successor-designate is facing a second dilemma: he is damned if he does not have strong organizational power bases and is damned if he promotes too many of his followers and stands accused of engaging in factionalism.

---

[15] Myron Rush, *Political Succession in the USSR*, p. 32.

[16] Lucian Pye, *The Dynamics of Chinese Politics* (Cambridge, MA: Oelgeschlager, Gunn and Hain Publishers, Inc., 1981), p. 14.

Jiang's "Shanghai Clique" and Hu's Connections

In 1989 when he went to Beijing to take over the job of Party general secretary, Jiang brought no one with him from Shanghai. Trying to find his way around in the Zhongnanhai Compound, Jiang soon realized that he had to place his men in key positions, especially in control of the General Office of the Central Committee, the Central Bodyguard Bureau, and the capital city of Beijing. Moreover, he needed to build a network of support in the Politburo and among the provincial Party secretaries. Jiang's first move was to put his deputy from Shanghai, Zeng Qinghong, in charge of the General Office of the Central Committee. He then put another protégé from Shanghai, You Xigui, in charge of the Central Bodyguard Bureau. In 1992, he promoted Wu Bangguo, Party secretary of Shanghai, as a full member of the Politburo, followed by the promotion of Huang Ju, another protégé from Shanghai, as a full member of the Politburo in 1994. In 1995, in the name of anticorruption, Jiang finally succeeded in bringing down the powerful "Beijing Gang" headed by the Politburo member Chen Xitong, who had until then frequently challenged Jiang's power. With the appointment of his protégé, Jia Qinglin, as Party secretary of Beijing, Jiang now has Beijing under his control.

A decade after he got to the top and after several years of consolidating power, Jiang today looks very safe in the Politburo Standing Committee. Besides Li Lanqing, Jiang can almost always count on two other members of the Standing Committee, namely Zhu Rongji and Hu Jintao. Zhu Rongji is not exactly a member of Jiang's "Shanghai Clique," and he has recently tried to distance himself from that association. But Zhu has never intended to challenge Jiang's "core" status and appears willing to support Jiang's position even at the expense of his own reputation. As suggested earlier, Hu Jintao, as the successor-designate, has always been willing to support Jiang. Plus Jiang himself, this alliance means four votes in the Standing Committee. Even though Jiang needs to bargain with the other three members, Li Peng, Li Ruihuan, and Wei Jiangxing, on various issues, he seems to have a comfortable majority in the Standing Committee as far as voting is concerned.

Among the remaining 14 members of the Politburo, Jiang's network of support is even stronger, for he can count on unqualified support from Huang Ju, Jia Qinglin, Li Changchun, Wu Bangguo, and Wu Guanzheng, and expect support from Chi Haotian, Ding Guangen, Jiang Chunyun, Li Tieying, Luo Gan, and Zhang Wannian. At the apex of the political power in China, Jiang has successfully consolidated his power base.

The biggest victory for Jiang at the 15th Party Congress in 1997 was the promotion of Zeng Qinghong as not only a full member of the Central Committee, but also as an alternate member of the Politburo and a member of the Secretariat of the Central Committee. Zeng jumped three steps on the ladder of political power, as he was not even an alternate member of the 14th Central Committee five years earlier. Zeng's rise is particularly unusual because, out of the 24 members of the new Politburo and the seven members of the new Secretariat of the 15th Central Committee, he was the only one who had not served on the Central Committee before.

Such bold moves in promoting one's protégés were not risk-free. Although Jiang has fended off most of the accusations of factionalism, he has not walked through this political minefield unscathed. It was in forming the 15th Central Committee that Jiang faced strong opposition to promoting members of his "Shanghai Clique." In the end, he managed to promote Chen Zhili, deputy Party secretary of Shanghai (now Minister of Education), as a full member. With the promotion to full membership of two of Jiang's protégés not from Shanghai, Zeng Peiyan, Minister of the State Development and Planning Commission, and Teng Wensheng, head of the Policy Research Office of the Central Committee, this is a net gain of three seats in the new committee. Jiang's other protégés from Shanghai managed to enter the new Central Committee only as alternate members who have no voting right. The list includes Chen Liangyu, deputy Party secretary and now mayor of Shanghai; Meng Jianzhu, former vice mayor of Shanghai and now Party secretary of Jiangxi; and You Xigui, director of the Central Bodyguard Bureau.

Zeng Qinghong's promotion in 1997 was extraordinary. Since then, however, his political career seems to have stagnated. Despite his intention to see Zeng sharing the "core" status with Hu Jintao in the fourth generation, Jiang has so far not succeeded in promoting Zeng Qinghong to be a full member of the Politburo. Months before the 16th Party Congress, when Jiang is expected to retire from the position of Party general secretary, his network of support in the central committee is strong, but not politically overwhelming.

Hu Jintao's network of support is expected to be based on three major sources: those who have been associated with the Communist Youth League (the "Communist Youth League connection"); those who are graduates of Qinghua University (the "Qinghua connection"); and those who have been trained at the Central Party School (the "Central Party School connection").[17] This is because Hu studied at Qinghua University in 1959–1965, was in charge of the Communist Youth League in 1980–1985, and has served as the president of the Central Party School since 1993. These connections should constitute an enormous reservoir of political capital.

However, because all the political promotions so far have been controlled by Jiang Zemin and his associate Zeng Qinghong, Director of the Organizational Department of the Central Committee, it is difficult to know how effectively Hu Jintao has turned his extensive personal connections into his organizational power bases. Among the incumbent provincial Party and government leaders, though, the list of those who have either the "Qinghua connection" or the "Communist Youth League connection" is relatively short: three are known to have graduated from Qinghua University (Tian Chengping, provincial Party secretary of Shanxi; Xi Jinping, governor of Fujian; and Xu Rongkai, governor of Yunnan) and four have connections with the Communist Youth League (Wang Xuedong, provincial Party secretary of Hebei; Song Defu, provincial Party secretary of Fujian; Li Keqiang, governor of Henan; and Zhao Leji, governor of Qinghai). We of course must also caution against adding anyone to Hu's network of support simply

---

[17] Li Cheng, *China's Leaders: The New Generation* (Lanham, MD: Rowman & Littlefield Publishers, Inc., 2001), pp. 116–119.

because he or she was a graduate of Qinghua University or because he or she once worked in the Communist Youth League.

What does play to Hu's strength is his relatively young age and his seniority in the Party organization. Twenty years ago (1982), at age of 39, Hu became a full member and indeed the youngest member of the 12th Central Committee. In 1985, at the age of 42, Hu became the youngest provincial Party secretary. Ten years ago (1992), at the age of 50, Hu became the youngest member of the Standing Committee of the Politburo. These factors should serve Hu very well, especially among the new generation of China's leaders.

Since 2000, many months before the 16th Party Congress convenes, a new round of leadership changes has been already taking place. A close look at the 64 newly appointed or reappointed provincial Party secretaries and provincial governors suggests that most of them as well as Hu Jintao belong to the same generation (see Table 1). These new provincial leaders are likely to turn to Hu even if they do not have the "Qinghua" or the "Communist Youth League" connection. What is specially significant is that we may very well look at a partial list of the 16th Central Committee, since the newly appointed or reappointed provincial Party secretary and provincial

Table 1. Newly Appointed/Reappointed Provincial Leaders before the 16th Party Congress

Province/city	Name	Position	Age
Anhui	Wang Taihua	Party secretary	57
	Xu Zhonglin	Governor	59
Fujian	Song Defu	Party secretary	56
	Xi Jinping	Governor	49
Gansu	Song Zhaosu	Party secretary	61
	Lu Hao	Governor	55
Guizhou	Qian Yunlu	Party secretary	58
	Shi Xiushi	Governor	60
Hainan	Bai Kemin	Party secretary	59
Hebei	Wang Xuedong	Party secretary	56
	Niu Maosheng	Governor	63

Table 1. (*Continued*)

Province/city	Name	Position	Age
Heilongjiang	Song Fatang	Governor	62
Henan	Chen Kuiyuan	Party secretary	61
	Li Keqiang	Governor	47
Hubei	Yu Zhensheng	Party secretary	57
	Zhang Guoguang	Governor	57
Hunan	Yang Zhengwu	Party secretary	61
	Zhang Yunchuan	Governor	56
Inner Mongolia	Chu Bo	Party secretary	58
	Uyunqing	Governor	60
Jiangsu	Hui Liangyu	Party secretary	58
	Ji Yunshi	Governor	57
Jiangxi	Meng Jianzhu	Party secretary	55
	Huang Zhiquan	Governor	60
Liaoning	Wen Shizhen	Party secretary	62
	Bo Xilai	Governor	53
Qinghai	Su Rong	Party secretary	54
	Zhao Leji	Governor	45
Shandong	Zhang Gaoli	Governor	56
Shanghai	Chen Liangyu	Mayor	56
Shanxi	Tian Chengping	Party secretary	57
	Liu Zhenhua	Governor	62
Sichuan	Zhou Yongkang	Party secretary	60
	Zhang Zhongwei	Governor	60
Tibet	Guo Jinlong	Party secretary	55
	Legqog	Governor	58
Xinjiang	Wang Lequan	Party secretary	58
	Abulahat Abdurixit	Governor	60
Yunnan	Bai Enpei	Party secretary	56
	Xu Rongkai	Governor	60

Source: *China Directory 2001* (Japan: Radiopress, Inc., 2000); *Zhonggong Yanjiu* [Study of Chinese Communist Problems] (Taipei: The Institute for the Study of Chinese Communist Problems), various issues of 2000–2001.

governor before the Party Congress is almost guaranteed a seat on the Central Committee.

Relationship with the Military

Of the many networks of support, the successor-designate's relationship with the military is undoubtedly the most important. In the previous failed succession attempts, Liu Shaoqi and Hua Guofeng never gained an effective control over the military. Only Marshal Lin Biao partially controlled the military and, therefore, posed the most serious threat to Mao. After Mao, Deng firmly controlled the military. Hu Yaobang, on the other hand, never made himself acceptable to the military generals. During his tenure first as chairman and later as general secretary of the Party, Hu Yaobang never managed to get a permanent seat on the powerful CMC. Zhao Ziyang was indeed appointed the first vice chairman of the CMC in 1987, but perhaps because there was Deng as the CMC chairman and Yang Shangkun as the executive vice chairman of the CMC, Zhao either never tried or failed to build his power base in the military.

In 1990, Jiang Zemin became the first civilian leader to be the CMC chairman. An engineer by training, Jiang had never served in the army, nor did he have his own network of supporters in the military before taking over the reins of the CMC. It is no surprise that he has spared no effort to establish himself as the actual commander-in-chief. Jiang soon faced his first serious challenge from the Yang brothers: CMC Vice Chairman Yang Shangkun and his half-brother Yang Baibing who controlled the PLA General Political Department and thus the power of promotion in the military. It was Deng Xiaoping's intervention in Jiang's favor in 1992 that helped Jiang consolidate his leadership in the military.

After the removal of the Yang brothers, Jiang faced the new challenge of having to listen to two senior military leaders, Admiral Liu Huaqing and General Zhang Zhen, whom Deng Xiaoping put in the CMC. It was not until 1995 that Jiang was able to change the CMC membership to reflect his choice. In August of that year, he expanded the membership of the CMC from six to nine and promoted General Zhang Wannian and General Chi Haotian as the new vice chairmen of the CMC.

At the 15th Party Congress in 1997, Jiang succeeded in having General Liu and General Zhang retired from the CMC. The retirement of Liu Huaqing from the Politburo Standing Committee in 1997 was conspicuously not followed by the appointment of another military general. For the first time, there is no military representative in the party's highest decision-making body—the Politburo Standing Committee. Whether this change represents a significant decrease of the military involvement in party politics is open to different interpretations. It does, however, make Jiang the only one to represent the Politburo Standing Committee at the CMC meetings and to represent the military at the meetings of the Politburo Standing Committee.[18]

Jiang has also succeeded in changing the military leadership below the CMC level by enforcing the military retirement system. Between 1995 and 1997, through the enforcement of the military retirement system, Jiang removed 14 generals from active duty. Meanwhile, Jiang has wasted no time in promoting younger military leaders to high military ranks in the hope of winning their support. Between 1994, a crucial year in Jiang's succession process, and 2002, a total of 57 military leaders have been promoted to the rank of general, the highest military rank in the PLA.

In September 1999, with Jiang's support, Hu Jintao became the second civilian leader to sit on the powerful CMC, despite the initial resistance from the military. Like Jiang, Hu was an engineer by training and has never served in the army. Hu therefore had no connections with the military before his appointment. Becoming the vice chairman of the CMC then becomes crucial in Hu's political succession, because it gives Hu the legitimacy to court new relationships with military leaders.

---

[18] This situation slightly changed when Hu Jintao, another member of the Politburo Standing Committee, was appointed vice chairman of the CMC in September 1999. This change, however, was designed to help Hu succeed Jiang, not to counterbalance Jiang's power in the party and the military.

A careful look at the top brass of the PLA suggests that many of the top military leaders currently serving in the PLA are above the retirement age of 65. Some will be in their early 70s when the new CCP CMC is formed in November 2002 (see Table 2). The two most senior military leaders, CMC Vice Chairmen Zhang Wannian and Chi Haotian, are expected to retire, but who will succeed them is unclear. The current PLA Chief of Staff, Fu Quanyou, and Director of PLA General Department, Yu Yongbo, would seem to be the natural candidates, but their age works against them. Born in 1930 and 1931 respectively, Fu and Yu are 72 and 71 years old,

Table 2. China's Top Military Leadership (as of 2002)

Military unit	Name	Post	Age
Central Military Commission	Jiang Zemin	Chairman	76
	Hu Jintao	Vice Chairman	60
	Zhang Wannian	Vice Chairman	74
	Chi Haotian	Vice Chairman	73
	Fu Quanyou	Member	72
	Yu Yongbo	Member	71
	Wang Ke	Member	71
	Wang Ruilin	Member	73
	Cao Ganchuan	Member	67
	Guo Boxiong	Member	60
	Xu Caihou	Member	59
General Staff Department	Fu Quanyou	Chief of Staff	72
	Guo Boxiong	Deputy Chief	60
	Kui Fulin	Deputy Chief	64
	Wu Quanxu	Deputy Chief	63
	Qian Shugen	Deputy Chief	63
	Xiong Guangkai	Deputy Chief	63
	Zhang Li	Deputy Chief	NA
General Political Department	Yu Yongbo	Director	71
	Xu Caihou	Deputy Director	59
	Wang Ruilin	Deputy Director	73
	Zhou Ziyu	Deputy Director	67
	Tang Tianbiao	Deputy Director	62
	Yuan Shoufang	Deputy Director	63
	Zhang Shutian	Deputy Director	67

Table 2. (*Continued*)

Military unit	Name	Post	Age
General Logistics Department	Wang Ke	Director	71
	Zhou Kunren	Commissar	65
	Wang Tailan	Deputy Director	63
	Zhou Youliang	Deputy Director	NA
	Zuo Jianchang	Deputy Director	NA
	Wen Guangchun	Deputy Director	NA
	Sun Zhiqiang	Deputy Director	NA
	Su Shuyan	Deputy Director	NA
General Armaments Department	Cao Ganchuan	Director	67
	Li Jinai	Commissar	58
	Li Yuanzheng	Deputy Director	62
	Chen Dazhi	Deputy Director	NA
	Hu Shixiang	Deputy Director	NA
	Xiao Zhentang	Deputy Director	NA
	Zhu Zenquan	Deputy Commissar	NA

Sources: Zhongguo Renwu Nianjian 2000 [China's Who's Who Yearbook 2000] (Beijing: China's Who's Who Yearbook Press, 2000), pp. 121–123, 132–140; *Zhonghua Renmin Guoheguo Nianjian 2000* [PRC Yearbook 2000] (Beijing: PRC Yearbook Press, 2000), p. 436; *China Directory 2001* (Japan: Radiopress, Inc., 2000), pp. 158–207; *Zhonggong Yanjiu* [Study of Chinese Communist Problems] (Taipei: The Institute for the Study of Chinese Communist Problems), various issues of 2000–2001.

respectively, in 2002, beyond the age limit for appointment for another term. Another candidate for the vice chairmanship of the CMC is General Cao Ganchuan, Director of the PLA General Armaments Department. General Cao is a protégé of Jiang Zemin and may be expected to move up in the military hierarchy, but his age (67) could also become an issue.

This may offer an opportunity for General Guo Boxiong (aged 60), the executive Deputy PLA Chief of Staff, and General Xu Caihou (aged 59), the executive Deputy Director of PLA General Political Department, to move two ladders up in the military hierarchy to become the vice chairmen of the CMC at the 16th Party Congress. If that is the case, Hu Jintao will deal mainly with the PLA generals of the same generation and does not have to live in the shadow of more senior and older military generals as Jiang did between 1990 and 1997.

BEYOND THE FOURTH GENERATION

By now Hu Jintao seems to have become too entrenched to be removed from the "core" status by anyone, and therefore "getting to the top" is only a matter of time. But whether he will be able to consolidate his power at and after the 16th Party Congress remains to be seen. Since Hu's political tenure as the "core" of the fourth generation is expected to be no longer than 10 years (two terms), there is not much time left for him. Hu can no longer afford to live in the political shadow of Jiang Zemin or, worse still, to serve as an extension of Jiang's power. Hu Jintao, as an active agent in playing the succession game, must have been contemplating ways and opportunities to overcome the "successor's dilemma" and to begin to turn his extensive connections into valuable organizational power bases.

Hu Jintao will also need to look for supporters among those who were born in the 1950s—the fifth generation of China's leadership. This is where Hu's "Communist Youth League connection" and the "Central Party School connection" can become extremely valuable, because it is most likely that members of the fifth generation either have had prior work experience in the Youth League or have been trained in the Central Party School. Most members of the fifth generation are still junior officials in their agencies, but some have moved up to the level of provincial governor or were already in the 15th Central Committee as alternate members. We can reasonably expect some of these younger alternate members of the 15th Central Committee to be promoted as full members in the 16th Central Committee.

If at the 16th Party Congress in November 2002, Hu Jintao, at the age of 60, will finally be confirmed as the "core" of the fourth generation, then the candidates for the "core" of the fifth generation can be expected to come from those younger officials who will be no older than 60 years by the 18th Party Congress in 2012. Although "dark horses" and surprises are common in China's political succession process, it will be difficult to believe that candidates for the "core" position of the fifth generation will not be among the members of the new Central Committee headed by Hu Jintao. Therefore, the leadership changes at the 16th Party Congress in 2002 should not only tell us who the key members of the fourth generation are, but also define the pool of potential candidates for the "core" position of the fifth generation of China's leadership.

Chapter 3

Technocratic Leadership, Private Entrepreneurship, and Party Transformation in the Post-Deng Era

ZHENG YONGNIAN

Conventional wisdom tell us that the transition from the communist system involves two interrelated and interdependent processes—the transition from a command economy to a market economy and the transition from communist party dictatorship to democracy. Therefore, economic development and democratization must go hand in hand; if economic development encounters difficulties, democratization becomes necessary.[1] But once political democratization takes place, the communist party is likely to lose its political monopoly, and even go out of the political scene. Political developments in Russia and other East European countries seem to confirm this argument. It is widely believed that in China, the difficulty of this dual transition is almost insurmountable, because the command economy and the Communist Party system are the very foundation of its political system. Yet both the market economy

---

[1] Ysuyoshi Hasegawa, "The Connection Between Political and Economic Reform in Communist Regimes," in Gilbert Rozman (ed.), *Dismantling Communism* (The Woodrow Wilson Center Press & The Johns Hopkins University Press, 1992), pp. 59–117; Barrett L. McCormick, *Political Reform in Post-Mao China: Democracy and Bureaucracy in a Leninist State* (Berkeley, CA: University of California Press, 1990); Minxin Pei, "Is China Democratizing?" *Foreign Affairs*, Vol. 77, No. 1 (January–February 1998), pp. 68–82; George Schopflin, "Postcommunism: The Problems of Democratic Construction,"

and democracy are in opposition to this system. Consequently, China's reform has been regarded as a model of "economic reform without political reform."[2]

Nevertheless, China's experience in the past two decades has shown that the reformist leadership has not only endorsed and supported capitalism but has also made enormous efforts to recruit capitalists into the ruling party, the Chinese Communist Party (CCP). In this, China's political system has demonstrated its great flexibility. Without suddenly changing the overall system, the leadership has implemented political incrementalism, aimed at continuously adjusting its institutional framework to guarantee capitalist economic development and political stability, as well as to accommodate drastic changes resulting from socioeconomic progress. Therefore, capitalism is not necessarily antagonistic to the party's authoritarian rule, and a rising capitalist class is not necessarily a political threat to the party leadership.

How could this happen? Studies on the linkage between the market transition and the Party–state in China and Eastern Europe have focused on the impact of the market transition on the Party–state, especially on individual party members and government officials. Scholars have debated on whether party members and government officials have more advantages than ordinary people during the market transition. Many studies have shown how party members and government officials become entrepreneurs and gain more benefits from the market than other social classes.[3] This literature has enabled us to see who gets what and how during the

Deadalus, Vol. 123, No. 3 (Summer 1994), pp. 127–141; and John T. Ishiyama, "Communist Parties in Transition: Structure, Leaders, and Processes of Democratization in Eastern Europe," *Comparative Politics*, Vol. 27, No. 2 (January 1995), pp. 147–166.

[2] For example, Susan Shirk, *The Political Logic of Economic Reform in China* (Berkeley, CA: University of California Press, 1993).

[3] For example, Ivan Szelenyi and Eric Kostello, "The Market Transition Debate: Toward a Synthesis," *American Journal of Sociology*, Vol. 101 (1996), pp. 1082–1096; Ivan Szelenyi, *Socialist Entrepreneurship: Embourgeoisement in Rural Hungary* (Madison, Wisconsin: University of Wisconsin Press, 1988); Victor Nee, "A Theory of Market Transition: From Redistribution to Markets in State Socialism," *American Sociological*

process of market transition. In this chapter, we will try to go one step further to demonstrate how the interplay between the Party–state and private entrepreneurs helps not only the market transition but also the Party–state transformation in China.

The dual transition has been leadership-driven. In the initial stages of reform, the Communist leadership provided strong political support for the private sector in order to achieve economic growth, and in the later stages, rapid development of the private sector influenced the Party's transformation. Deng Xiaoping's southern tour in 1992 legitimized a capitalist economy, and thereafter China experienced a long wave of rapid economic growth. Economic growth enabled the leadership to deliver economic goods to its people and increase its political legitimacy, but the rise of a private entrepreneur class also generated dynamics for Party transformation. The CCP under Deng Xiaoping's leadership finished the first grand transformation—from a revolutionary party to an administrative party. Now with the rise of capitalists, the CCP has begun its second grand transformation—from an administrative party to one that rules the country by political means.

CAPITALIST CLASS VERSUS COMMUNIST LEADERSHIP

Without denying the dual transition assumption stated above, we argue that the two transitions, especially the democratic transition, are far more complicated than what had happened in advanced Western countries. While in the West, capitalism and capitalists

---

Review, Vol. 54 (1989), pp. 663–681; Nee, "Social Inequalities in Reforming State Socialism: Between Redistribution and Markets in State Socialism," *American Sociological Review*, Vol. 56 (1991), pp. 267–282; Andrew G. Walder, "Markets and Inequality in Transitional Economies: Toward Testable Theories," *American Journal of Sociology*, Vol. 101 (1996), pp. 1060–1073; and Walder, "Rural Cadres and the Market Economy in the Deng Era: Evidence from a National Survey," in John Wong and Zheng Yongnian (eds), *The Nanxun Legacy and China's Development in the Post-Deng Era* (Singapore and London: Singapore University Press and World Scientific, 2001), pp. 95–120.

played an important role in these transitions, in China, it is the reformist leadership that has promoted these transitions.

Scholars have shown that democracy is most likely to take firm hold in wealthy capitalist countries with traditions of proto-democracy.[4] The rising business classes successfully tamed the monarchical state. Capitalists successfully challenged the aristocratic claim of government as a prerogative of birth and gradually replaced it with the principle that government is a natural domain of wealthy commoners. Nevertheless, the bourgeoisie also created an organized working class, and under pressure from this class, legitimacy in Western democracies came to rest on the notion that governmental representatives have to be elected by a legally equal citizenry.

Why is capitalism so important for democracy? Capitalism, first of all, is an economic system based on private property and thus provides a fundamental check on state power. It separates the private space of social and economic activity from the public sphere, and this separation becomes an initial and necessary condition for the evolution of democracy as a form of limited government. Capitalism generates economic wealth, which in turn helps to ease both intra-elite and elite-mass political strains. In Western capitalist economies, prolonged periods of steady economic growth laid the basis for welfare states. The welfare state, in turn, helped ease and tame class conflict in early industrial capitalism. Wealthy capitalism also helps alleviate the intensity of intra-elite conflict. The stakes of the political game are lower when the losers have other channels of social and economic mobility. Under these conditions, access to the state is not necessarily viewed as the only route for upward mobility. The struggle for power is also not viewed as a zero-sum game. Losers in the power game in these circumstances are less likely to attempt to destabilize political mobilization, such as the organization of mass demonstrations, riots, or participation in underground terrorist activities. In other words, wealth helps to create boundaries within

---

[4] Barrington Moore Jr., *Social Origins of Dictatorship and Democracy: Lord and Peasant in the Making of the Modern World* (Boston, MA: Beacon Press, 1966); Charles Lindbloom, *Politics and Markets: The World's Political–Economic System* (New York: Basic Books,

which elites choose to fight. Disruption of these boundaries damages the system that creates the wealth and thus curtails the opportunities for advancement.[5]

As will be discussed later, some connections between capitalism and political changes embedded in Western democracies have already taken shape in China. While it is still too early to say whether nascent Chinese capitalists will be able to initiate democratization like what their Western counterparts did previously, the leadership has played a crucial role in leading China's transition from a command economy to a market one, and from a proletariat political system to one in which capitalists assume an increasing political role.

Scholars have found that policy initiatives in Third World countries can be fully understood by giving due attention to the perception, motivation, values, skills, and opportunities of the decision makers and to the impact that the characteristics of the decision-making process have on the choices that are made.[6] In China, the decision to first legitimize capitalism as a way of pursuing economic growth, and to later allow capitalists to play a role in the Communist regime, was initiated and implemented by the technocratic leadership.

Technocratic Leadership and the Embrace of Capitalism in China

The legitimation of capitalism in China was mainly due to Deng Xiaoping's leadership. From the late 1970s, when reform was initiated until the CCP's 14th Congress in 1992, when the market economy was formally justified, Deng Xiaoping repeatedly emphasized that there was no contradiction between China's socialist system and the market economy. The issue is how Deng Xiaoping's ideas on

---

1977); Samuel Huntington, *The Third Wave: Democratization in the Late Twentieth Century* (Norman: University of Oklahoma Press, 1991).

[5] This description is based on Atul Kohli, "Democracy and Development," in John P. Lewis and Valeriana Kallab (eds), *Development Strategies Reconsidered* (New Brunswick: Transition Books, 1986), pp. 153–182.

[6] *Ibid.*, p. 19.

capitalism have taken root and become the mindset of the leadership. We argue that what has embraced and supported capitalism is the technocratic leadership. If we define China's political system in terms of who rules, we can say that it is now a truly technocratic state.[7]

China's technocratic movement was initiated after Deng Xiaoping came to power in the late 1970s. The movement has spread to government and CCP organizations at different levels and has introduced drastic changes in the composition of the Chinese leadership.[8] In 1982, the CCP held its first post-Mao congress, symbolizing the establishment of the Deng leadership. During this congress, many technocrats such as Li Peng, Hu Qili, and Jiang Zemin, among others, were recruited into the Central Committee (CC). Since then, major leaders have risen and fallen owing to bitter power politics, but the momentum of the technocratic movement remains. The movement reached its peak at the 15th Party Congress in 1997. In this congress, all seven members of the Standing Committee of the CC's Political Bureau and 18 of the 24 Political Bureau members are technocrats. This new leadership has thus been called a "full-fledged technocratic leadership."[9] Table 1 reflects the progress of China's technocratic movement.

[7] For discussion on the technocratic nature of the Chinese state in the post-Mao era, see Hong Yong Lee, *From Revolutionary Cadres to Party Technocrats in Socialist China* (Berkeley, CA: University of California Press, 1991); Cheng Li, *China's Leaders: The New Generation* (Lanham: Rowman & Littlefield Publishers, Inc., 2001); and Cheng Li and Lynn White, "The Fifteenth Central Committee of the Chinese Communist Party: Full-Fledged Technocratic Leadership with Partial Control by Jiang Zemin," *Asian Survey*, Vol. 38, No. 3 (March 1998).

[8] Hong Yung Lee, *From Revolutionary Cadres to Party Technocrats in Socialist China*; and Cheng Li and David Bachman, "Localism, Elitism, and Immobilism: Elite Formation and Social Change in Post-Mao China," *World Politics*, Vol. 42, No. 1 (October 1989), pp. 64–94.

[9] Li Cheng and Lynn White, "The Fifteenth Central Committee of the Chinese Communist Party: Full-Fledged Technocratic Leadership with Partial Control by Jiang Zemin," *Asian Survey*, Vol. xxxviii, No. 3 (March 1998), pp. 231–264; David Shambaugh, "The CCP's Fifteenth Congress: Technocrats in Command," *Issues and Studies*, Vol. 34, No. 1 (January 1998), pp. 1–37.

Table 1. Technocratic Representation in High-Level Leadership (1982–1997)

	1982		1987		1997	
	No.	% of total	No.	% of total	No.	% of total
Political Bureau members	0	0	9	50	18	75
Full members of the CCP CC	4	2	34	26	98	51
Ministers of the State Council	1	2	17	45	19	66
Provincial party secretaries	0	0	7	25	19	61
Provincial governors	0	0	8	33	23	74
The fourth generation of leadership	–	–	–	–	180	60

Source: Cheng Li, "Jiang Zemin's Successors: The Rise of the Fourth Generation of Leaders in the PRC," *The China Quarterly*, Vol. 161 (2000), p. 22.

Table 2. Changes in Average Age of the Members of the
CCP Leadership (1982–1997)

	12th (1982)	13th (1987)	14th (1992)	15th (1997)
Member of CC	62	55.2	56.3	55.9
Member of Standing Committee	73.75	63.6	63.4	65.1
Member of Political Bureau	71.8	64	61.9	62.9
Member of Secretariat	63.7	56.2	59.3	62.9

In China, the technocratic movement meant recruiting younger and better-educated party cadres and government officials into the leadership. Table 2 shows the trend of the rejuvenation. The average age of the CC members has dropped from 62 in the 12th Party Congress in 1982, where most members were still revolutionaries, to less than 60 in the 15th Party Congress in 1997.

The average age of a member in the most powerful institutions— Standing Committee, Political Bureau and Secretariat of the 15th CC—are much younger than those of the 12th CC but older than those of the 13th and the 14th CC. The reversal is largely due to the post-Deng power succession. Both the 13th and 14th Party Congresses were still dominated by Deng Xiaoping. With Deng standing behind the scene of power politics, the Party was able to introduce rather radical changes in the personnel arrangement. By contrast, the 15th Party Congress was the first Party gathering in the post-Deng era, and leadership stability became the most important theme of the Party. Although, aged leaders such as Qiao Shi and Liu Huaqing exited gracefully from power politics, many senior leaders (those who were still within the "legitimate" age range) remained in their positions and were even promoted. Hence, the average age of these power institutions did not decline.

Changes have also occurred in major leaders' educational levels and background. Table 3 shows a dramatic increase in the number of the CC members with college degrees, from 55.4% in 1982 to 92.4% in 1997. The same also happened to the Political Bureau (Table 4). Indeed, recruiting elites with college degrees has been a consistent norm in China's technocratic movement. The CCP's *nomenklatura* system, under which all major public positions are filled by Party appointees, has enabled the Party to achieve this goal.[10]

Table 3. Percentage of College-Educated in the
CC (1982–1997)

CC	Percentage
12th (1982)	55.4
13th (1987)	73.3
14th (1992)	83.7
15th (1997)	92.4

Source: Li Cheng and Lynn White, "The Fifteenth Central Committee of the Chinese Communist Party: Full-Fledged Technocratic Leadership with Partial Control by Jiang Zemin," *Asian Survey*, Vol. xxxviii, No. 3 (March 1998), p. 248.

---

[10] For a discussion of the CCP's nomenklatura, see John P. Burns, *The Chinese Communist Party's Nomenklatura System: A Documentary Study of Party Control of Leadership Selection, 1979–1984* (Armonk, NY: M.E. Sharpe, Inc., 1989).

Table 4. Change in Educational Level of Political Bureau Members (1982–1997)

	12th (%)	13th (%)	14th (%)	15th (%)
No education	3 (10.7)	0	0	0
Primary school	10 (35.7)	0	0	0
Middle school	3 (10.7)	5 (27.7)	3 (13.6)	2 (8.3)
Military school	3 (10.7)	1 (5.6)	1 (4.5)	2 (8.3)
College	9 (32.2)	12 (66.6)	17 (77.2)	18 (7.5)
Postgraduate	0	0	1 (4.5)	2 (8.3)
Total	28	18	22	24

Source: Adopted from Li Cheng and Lynn White, the same as Table 3.

More importantly, most of the elite had their professional training in engineering and other fields of science and technology. From Table 5, we can see the distribution of the educational background of the 15th CC members. Among 177 full CC members with college degrees, 44% (78) majored in engineering and 11.3% (20) in geology, agricultural, biology, physics, chemistry, medicine, economics, and management, and 10% (18) in military science and engineering.

In the technocratic state, technically trained political leaders rule by virtue of their specialized knowledge and position in dominant political and economic institutions. Why is China's technocratic leadership able to embrace capitalism? Why is this technocratic leadership able to depart, to a great degree, from the predatory Leviathan state which preys on its citizens for the economic benefit of an autocracy, policy elite, bureaucracy, or factional state which only serves factional interests within the state?

The embrace of capitalism and capitalists by the party is due to the technocratic nature of the political leadership. The rise of the technocratic leadership is a reaction to the Maoist elite recruitment policy. One major theme in Maoist China was the conflict between "red" and "expert." Mao initiated waves of campaigns against intellectuals and professionals in the first three decades of the People's Republic, particularly during the Cultural Revolution. Since the previous policy had been disastrous, this elite recruitment policy was reversed after Deng Xiaoping came to power. The leadership

Table 5. Academic Majors of Full Members of the 14th and 15th CC Possessing College Degrees

	14th CC (N = 158)	%	15th CC (N = 177)	%
Engineering	46	29.1	78	44.1
Geology	3	1.9	3	1.7
Agriculture	2	1.3	3	1.7
Biology	1	0.6	0	0
Physics	3	1.9	4	2.3
Chemistry	2	1.3	1	0.6
Medical Science	2	1.3	0	0
Economics and Finance	3	1.9	7	4.0
Management	1	0.6	2	1.1
Statistics	1	0.6	0	0
Military Science and Engineering	17	10.8	18	10.2
Politics and Party History	9	5.7	7	4.0
Political Economy	1	0.6	3	1.7
Law	1	0.6	3	1.7
Philosophy	0	0	2	1.1
History	2	1.3	0	0
Education	1	0.6	1	0.6
Chinese Language and Literature	3	1.9	4	2.3
Foreign Language	2	1.3	2	1.1
Unknown	58	36.7	39	22
Total	158	100.0	177	100.0

Sources: Zang Xiaowei, "The Fourteenth Central Committee of the CCP," *Asian Survey*, Vol. xxxiii, No. 8 (August 1993), p. 797, and Li Cheng and Lynn White, "The Fifteenth Central Committee of the Chinese Communist Party," *Asian Survey*, Vol. xxxviii, No. 3 (March 1998), p. 250.

to appreciate the role of the "expert" and downplayed that of the "red." To promote economic development, the "expert" had to be placed in the center of the whole system.

The rise of the technocratic leadership is also the outcome of depoliticization. Political chaos during the prereform period resulted from Mao's political campaigns and mass mobilization. Mobilization in turn led to the politicization of social life. Recruiting technocrats into the Party and government would undoubtedly depoliticize the decision-making process because, unlike politicians whose aims are power and interests, technocrats are more concerned with rational thinking, task orientation, and problem solving.[11] Therefore, technocratic leadership helps reduce the role of ideology in policy making. With generational changes in the leadership, the basis of authority needed to be redefined. The old revolutionaries could appeal to their charisma and ideology for mass mobilization, but new leaders did not have such power resources and had to turn to more secular and pragmatic forms of political authority. For technocrats, ideology cannot be taken as a dogma that provides specific and infallible solutions to immediate political as well as economic issues. Even though it had to reduce politics to technical solutions, technocrats do have a pragmatic attitude towards reality.

Because of this pragmatism, technocrats are able to overcome difficulties to reach a consensus.[12] They can

"evaluate even political decisions in terms of actual outcome rather than ideological value. In developing a range of policy options, each of which carries only different costs, benefits, and feasibility, this way of thinking inclines the bureaucratic technocrats toward compromise and bargaining."[13]

While the technocratic leadership provides an institutional support for capitalism, it was Deng Xiaoping's leadership that formally legitimized capitalism. During his southern tour in 1992, he decided to end the lasting debate on whether China's development should be socialist or capitalist. He repeatedly called for Party leaders to open their minds further so that they could learn from capitalism to promote the country's development. The southern tour talks immediately resulted in unprecedented changes, generating not only a new and strong reform momentum, but also pointing to a new direction for reform and development. After the tour, there was no

---

[11] For a discussion of this point, see Ernst B. Hass, *Beyond the Nation-State: Functionalism and International Organization* (Stanford, CA: Stanford University Press, 1964).

[12] For a discussion of this point, see Erza Suleiman, *Politics, Power, and Bureaucracy in France: The Administrative Elite* (Princeton, NJ: Princeton University Press, 1974), 380 p.

[13] Lee, *From Revolutionary Cadres to Party Technocratics*, 404 p.

more official debate on socialism and capitalism,[14] and capitalism as a means of economic expansion was no longer regarded as antagonistic to Party ideology.

For the Party leadership, this was the only way out. In the early 1990s, a serious political legitimacy crisis hit the CCP, following the crackdown of the 1989 pro-democracy movement and the breakdown of communism in the Soviet Union and Eastern European countries. Deng Xiaoping realized that the fall of the Soviet Union and the collapse of communism was mainly due to the failure of economic development there; thus the CCP needed to achieve radical economic growth if it wanted to avoid such a misfortune and restrengthen its political legitimacy. Therefore, Deng Xiaoping chose to continue to tighten political control while radically liberalizing the economic system.[15]

While the leadership, especially Deng Xiaoping, decided to implement radical economic reform, it also began to build a new social order in accordance with capitalist economic changes. In the prereform era, China was an ideologically organized society. As Franz Schurmann correctly pointed out in the 1960s, "Communist China is like a vast building made of different kinds of brick and stone. However when put together, it stands. What holds it together is ideology and organization."[16] The leadership under Mao Zedong initiated various political experiments, especially during the Cultural Revolution from 1966 to 1976, to reorganize China basically according to Mao's own utopian ideal of society. Whatever Mao did, his aim was to destroy all possible private space and politicize the Chinese society. Totalitarian state power penetrated every corner

---

[14] It is worth noting that there have heated debates in intellectual circles about socialism and capitalism. For a collection of the articles on the debates, see Zhang Wenmin et al. (eds), *Zhongguo jingji da lunzhan* [Debating about China's Economy], 3 volumes (Beijing: Jingji guanli chubanshe, 1996, 1997, and 1998). What is important is that Deng's *Nanxun* speeches legitimized capitalistic development.

[15] Deng, "Zai Wuchang, Shenzhen, Zhuhai, Shanghai dengdi de tanhua yaodian," 379 p.

[16] Franz Schurmann, *Ideology and Organization in Communist China* (Berkeley, CA: University of California Press, 1968), p. 1.

of the society, and coercive institutional mechanisms were used to eliminate private space and manage public space.[17]

Only after Deng Xiaoping regained power in the late 1970s did the leadership begin to shift its emphasis to economics as a way of reorganizing the country. Capitalist economic expansion since the southern tour has generated enormous political benefits for the Party. It has increased the Party's political legitimacy, because rapid development has enabled the Party to continuously deliver economic goods to people. It has also changed the class structure in the country where an interest-based social order has emerged.[18]

THE RISE OF PRIVATE ENTREPRENEURS

The rapid expansion of the private sector is reflected in the decline of the state sector and the development of the non-state sector, as shown in Tables 6 and 7. From Table 6, we can see that the gross industrial output by the state-owned enterprises declined from 55% in 1990 to 27% in 1998, while that by individually owned enterprises increased from 5 to 16% during the same period. The non-state sector has overwhelmingly surpassed the state sector.

Table 8 also shows the economic significance of the private sector. The private sector consumed 4% of the total retail sales in 1996 and increased its consumption to 13.5% in 1999. During the same period, the industrial and commercial taxes paid by the

[17] For example, Tang Tsou, *The Cultural Revolution and Post-Mao Reforms: A Historical Perspective* (Chicago: The University of Chicago Press, 1986).

[18] This is not the place for a full discussion of this rising interest-based social order. But it is worth noting that terms associated with economic interests such "interest" (or "interests") and "class" have been increasingly used by scholars in China to analyze the Chinese society since Deng's *Nanxun*. See Zhu Guanglei et al., *Dangdai Zhongguo shehui ge jieceng fenxi* [An Analysis of Social Strata in Contemporary China] (Tianjin: Tianjin renmin chubanshe, 1998); Liang Xiaosheng, *Zhongguo shehui ge jieceng fenxi* [An Analysis of Social Strata in China] (Beijing: Jingji ribao chubanshe, 1998); Lu Xueyi and Jing Tiankuai (eds), *Zhuanxing zhong de Zhongguo shehui* [Chinese Society in Transition] (Ha'erbin: Heilongjiang renmin chubanshe, 1994); Qin Shaoxiang and Jia Ting, *Shehui*

Table 6. Gross Industrial Output in China (1980–1998)

Year	State-owned enterprises (%)	Collective-owned enterprises (%)	Individually owned enterprises (%)	Other types of enterprises (%)
1980	76.0	23.5	0	0.5
1985	64.9	32.1	1.9	1.2
1990	54.6	35.6	5.4	4.4
1991	56.2	33.0	4.8	6.0
1992	51.5	35.1	5.8	7.6
1993	47.0	34.0	8.0	11.1
1994	37.3	37.7	10.1	14.8
1995	34.0	36.6	12.9	16.6
1996	33.7	36.5	14.4	15.4
1997	29.8	35.9	16.9	17.4
1998	26.5	36.0	16.0	21.5

Source: Figures calculated from data in Zhongguo tongji nianjian 1999 [China Statistical Yearbook 1999] (Beijing: Zhongguo tongji chubanshe, 1999), p. 423.

private sector in the national total increased from 1 to 2.6%. The private sector has become even more important in revenue contribution at local levels. According to a calculation, as of the mid-1990s, the private sector had contributed about 10% of the total tax revenue at the provincial level, 20% at the prefectural level, and 30% at the county level.[19] Overall, local governments are more dependent on the revenue from the private sector than the central government. For instance, in 1996, the private sector in Zhejiang contributed 4.4 billion yuan in industrial and commercial taxes, or 13.4% of the total industrial and commercial taxes in that province. In some rich areas, the private sector contributes township revenue as high as 60%.[20]

xin qunti tanmi: Zhongguo siying qiyezhu jieceng [A Study of a New Social Group: China's Private Enterprise Class] (Beijing: Zhongguo fazhan chubanshe, 1993).

[19] Li Qiang, "Guanyu siyingjingji de ruogan ziliao" [Data on the Private Economy], Zhenli de Zhuiqiu [The Seeking of Truth], No. 5 (2001), pp. 18–19.

[20] Ibid., p. 19.

Table 7. The Development of the Private Sector in China (1989–1997)

	Private enterprises*				Individually owned and operated enterprises†			
	Number	Change (%)	Employees (million)	Change (%)	Number (million)	Change (%)	Employees (10,000)	Change (%)
1989	90,581		1.6		12.5		19.4	
1990	98,141	8.3	1.7	3.7	13.3	6.5	20.9	7.8
1991	107,843	9.9	1.8	8.2	14.2	6.7	22.6	7.9
1992	139,633	29.5	2.3	26.1	15.3	8.3	24.7	9.3
1993	237,919	70.4	3.7	60.8	17.7	15.2	29.4	19.1
1994	432,240	81.7	6.5	73.3	21.9	23.8	37.8	28.5
1995	654,531	51.4	9.6	47.5	25.3	15.6	46.2	22.2
1996	819,252	25.2	11.7	22.2	27.1	7.0	50.2	8.7
1997	960,726	17.3	13.5	15.2	28.5	5.4	54.4	8.5
1998	1,200,978	25.0	1709	26.7	N/A	N/A	N/A	N/A
1999	1,508,857	25.6	2022	18.8	N/A	N/A	N/A	N/A

Note:
* Refer to those with more than eight employees.
† Refer to those with less than eight employees.
Annual percentage change in number of employees may not be exact due to rounding off of figures of number of employees.

Sources: Adopted from Zhang Houyi and Ming Zhili (eds), *Zhongguo siying qiye fazhan baogao 1978–1998* [A Report on the Development of Private Enterprises in China, 1978–1998] (Beijing: Shehui kexue wenxuan chubanshe, 1999), p. 60, 66; *Zhongguo siying jingji nianjian* [The Yearbook of Private Businesses in China, 2000], p. 402.

Table 8. The Economic Significance of the Private Sector in China

	1996	1997	1998	1999
Percentage of goods consumed by the private sector in total retail sales (%)	4.1	6.8	10.5	13.5
Percentage of industrial and commercial taxes by the private sector in total industrial and commercial taxes (%)	1.11	1.31	2.14	2.63

Sources: Zhongguo siyingjingji nianjian (2000); and *Zhongguo shuiwu nianjian* (1994–1997).

HOW POLITICAL ORDER WAS AFFECTED

The rise of an interest-based social order has gradually undermined the existing political order and has thus created pressure for political reform for the leadership. With rapid economic expansion, the private arena has become more profitable than the public arena. The nascent interest-based social order has attracted not only social members, but Party cadres and government officials. This is especially true in the period after Deng Xiaoping's southern tour. Party cadres and government officials were allowed, even encouraged, to turn to business. This soon resulted in a nationwide wave of *xiahai* [literally "plunging into the sea"].[21] As shown in Table 9, in 1992, Party cadres and government officials were the second largest group (25.5%) who established private businesses, following household-business owners (38.2%). But by the mid-1990s, they had become the largest group among private entrepreneurs, as shown in Table 10.

By doing so, the reformist leadership aimed to reduce Party cadres' political resistance to radical economic reforms. It provides them with

Table 9. Background of Owners of Private Enterprises in China (%)

Original position	Business established before 1988	Business established between 1989 and 1992	Business established in 1992	Total
Professionals	1.9	4.3	4.9	4.6
Party cadres	19.8	16.0	25.5	25.5
Workers	13.2	8.6	10.8	10.7
Peasants	20.8	17.9	15.8	16.7
Household-business owners	35.8	46.3	36.9	38.2
Others	8.5	6.8	6.1	6.5
Total	100	100	100	100

Source: as Table 7, p. 153.

[21] For a description, see John Wong, "The *Xia Hai* Phenomenon in China," *Ritsumeikan Journal of International Relations and Area Studies*, Vol. 6 (March 1994), pp. 1–10.

Table 10. Background of Owners of Private Enterprises in China (%)

	1993 Survey			1995 Survey		
	Urban areas	Rural areas	Total	Urban areas	Rural areas	Total
Professionals	3.9	1.6	3.3	4.1	2.3	3.3
Cadres in urban state and collective sectors	43.2	16.6	36.3	33.2	11.8	24.0
Rural cadres	4.1	16.9	7.5	3.5	11.2	6.8
Cadres in the non-state sectors	11.2	17.9	13.0	11.0	17.9	14.0
Peasants	4.4	16.3	7.5	6.3	17.3	11.0
Workers	22.9	11.4	19.7	21.7	17.5	19.9
Small-scale individual business owners	8.8	18.2	11.2	15.8	18.1	16.8
No occupation	1.5	1.0	1.4	4.5	3.8	4.2

Source: Lau Siu-kai et al. (eds), *Shichang, jieji yu zhengzhi* [Market, Class and Politics] (Hong Kong: Hong Kong Institute of Asian–Pacific Studies, The Chinese University of Hong Kong, 2000), p. 328.

an "exit" from the political arenas. Without such an "exit," Party cadres would have to struggle for their power via various political means. To a great degree, this goal was realized. But it was achieved with great costs. Party cadres and government officials were given opportunities to use their public power to gain private economic benefits. For example, Party cadres and government officials have attempted to build up their connections [*guanxi*] with the private sector. In a survey conducted in 1993, when private entrepreneurs were asked to name their closet friends, the distribution was as follows: professionals (16.6%), cadres in the government sector (24.4%); cadres in SOEs (18%), workers (1.3%), farmers (3.7%), specialized artisans (6.4%), staff in the service sector (9.5%), and small enterprise owners (8.9%), and others (2.9%).[22] According to the study, to build their connections with the private sector, Party cadres and government officials aimed to

[22] Li Qiang, "Guanyu siyingjingji," p. 23.

1. gain economic benefits for themselves and their family members;
2. search for opportunities to *xiahai*, that is, leave the government sector and engage in businesses; and
3. seek political support from the private sector due to its increasing political importance.[23]

When public power is used for economic benefits, corruption becomes inevitable and exggravates the problem. While in the old days, political loyalty was the most important standard used to evaluate the political achievements of Party cadres and government officials, "money" now replaces political loyalty. Corruption has undermined not only the effectiveness of the government but also popular confidence in the government. Political legitimacy thus once again poses a serious challenge for the Party and the government.

The rise of an interest-based social order has also rendered ideological decline irreversible. An interest-based social order means that the official ideology no longer plays an important part in regulating the daily life of Party cadres and government officials, let alone social members. Indeed, in order to promote rapid economic development, the leadership had to downplay the role of ideology. The official ideology has shifted from an offensive position to a defensive one, that is, from being a means to control Party cadres and government officials and to guide decision making, to providing justification for Party and government policies. There have been unexpected consequences resulting from this transformation, the most notable being the inevitable decay of the Party itself.

The most serious threat is that the Party is increasingly facing pressure to incorporate newly rising social forces into its political order. The nascent social order has had great incentive to ask for political relevance, because government policies have an inevitable impact on its rise and fall. Table 11 shows the results of two nationwide surveys conducted in 1995 and 1997,

---

[23] Cited in Li Qiang, *ibid.*, pp. 23–24.

Table 11. Key Political Factors Affecting Private Businesses

	1995 (%)	1997 (%)
Legal protection of property rights	5.1	4.1
Government propaganda	5.0	6.0
Taxation policy	18.8	N/A
Credit policy	31.8	27.2
Government macroeconomic adjustment	23.6	17.9
Industrial and commercial management	2.6	31.9
Household system	0.6	5.2
Ownership	5.0	0.4
Others	7.5	7.2
Total	100	100

Source: as Table 7, p. 150.

respectively. We can see that taxation policy, credit policy, government macroeconomic adjustment, and industrial and commercial management, among others, have been the most important political factors affecting business activities. More and more, private businesspersons expect to participate in policy making or at least have some input in policy making. Moreover, the private sector has been affected not only by relevant government policies, but also by various forms of social and political practices prevalent in China. As shown in Table 12, "exchange between power and money," "worsening public order"

Table 12. Social Problems with Most Serious Negative Impact on Private Businesses

	1995 (%)	1997 (%)
Unjust income distribution	5.1	9.9
Exchange between power and money	37.3	37.6
Worsening public order	20.6	41.1
Arbitrary fees, arbitrary fines, and arbitrary levies	31.4	6.3
Business involvement of government and military in businesses	2.6	3.9
Others	8.1	1.3
Total	100	100

Source: as Table 7, p. 148.

and "arbitrary collection of fees, fines and levies" have been regarded as the factors that have had the most serious impact on private businesses. Changing such social and political practices is certainly a political task that calls for political participation by private businesspersons.

Indeed, private entrepreneurs have been making great efforts to participate in the political process, especially in local politics. No systematic national statistics is available to show the degree of political participation by private businesspersons. But as shown in Table 13, a rapid expansion of their political involvement in local politics took place in the early 1990s. According to a survey conducted in 1993, on average, each private entrepreneur was a member of 2.75 organizations, such as private enterprise associations, guilds, different democratic parties, Youth League, and even the CCP. Almost 84% of private entrepreneurs argued that it was imperative to establish their own organizations.[24] Joining the CCP is another way for private entrepreneurs to influence China's political process. According to various surveys, more and more private entrepreneurs have joined the Party. In 1993, among all private entrepreneurs, 13% were CCP members. This figure increased to 17% in 1995,

Table 13. Representatives from the Private Sector in Political Organizations

Year	Representatives in the People's Congress at the county level and above	Representatives in the CPPCC at the county level and above*	Representatives in mass organizations[†]
1990	5114	7238	4603
1994	7296	11,721	7671
Change (%)	42	62	67

* CPPCC: The Chinese People's Political Consultative Conference.
† Such as the Communist Youth League, and the Women's Federation.
Source: Zhonghua gongshang shibao [China Industrial and Commercial Daily], April 29, 1996.

[24] Cited in Li Qiang, "Guanyu siyingjingji," p. 27.

Table 14. Self-Evaluation by Private Businesspersons of Their Economic, Social, and Political Status

	Economic status	Social status	Political status
1993	4.5	4.0	4.6
1995	4.5	4.2	5.1
1997	4.7	4.6	5.7

The highest score: 1.0.
The lowest score: 10.0.
Source: as Table 2, p. 163.

16.6% in 1997, and rose to almost 20% in 2000, far higher than other social groups such as workers and farmers.[25]

Political participation by private entrepreneurs is still extremely limited at the national level. For example, only 46 out of more than 2000 representatives of the Ninth Chinese People's Political Consultative Conference in 1998 were private businesspersons.[26] A low degree of political participation indeed has caused dissatisfaction among private businesspersons. As shown in Table 14, whereas self-evaluation by private businesspersons of their economic and social status has been consistent, that of their political status has deteriorated. It is worthwhile to note that their self-evaluation for political status was the lowest in 1997, the year the private sector was formally legalized by China's Constitution.[27]

LEFTISTS' VOICE AGAINST PARTY PLURALISM

Strong demands for political participation from private entrepreneurs and their actual penetration into China's political process, especially

---

[25] *Ibid.*, p. 26.

[26] Jiang Nanyang, "Lun siying qiyezhu de zhengzhi canyu" [Political Participation by the Owners of Private Businesses], in Zhang Houyi and Ming Zhili (eds), *Zhongguo siying qiye fazhan baogao 1978–1998* [A Report of the Development of Private Enterprises in China, 1978–1998] (Beijing: Shehui kexue wenxuan chubanshe, 1999), pp. 103–117.

[27] Keyuan Zou and Yongnian Zheng, "China's Third Constitutional Amendment: An Assessment," in A.J. De Roo and R.W. Jagtenberg (eds), *Yearbook Law and Legal*

at the local levels, have worried China leftists such as Deng Liqun and other old-style ideologues. They are afraid that such a development will change the socialist nature of the regime, with the bourgeoisie and its representatives taking over political power.

In 1997, the Party's Congress legitimized the private sector, and a constitutional amendment in the following year formally provided constitutional protection for private ownership. Once private ownership was legitimized and given constitutional protection, the next logical question was how private entrepreneurs should join the Party and share political power with other traditional ruling classes such as workers and farmers.

Before the Party's 16th Congress in 2002, the leftists are now again initiating a campaign, opposing the entry of private entrepreneurs into the Party. Among other vocal opponents, Lin Yanzhi, Deputy Secretary of the Jilin Provincial Committee of the CCP, published a long paper in *Zhenli de Zhuiqiu*, a Beijing-based leftist journal.[28] Like other leftists, Lin argued that a new bourgeoisie has formed in China and is seriously challenging the political power of the CCP. According to Lin, though the new bourgeoisie had grown out of China's communist system, the exploitative nature of this new class did not change. Many new capitalists were formerly CCP cadres and government officials who had lost their party identity after they entered the business world. It is still as exploitative as its predecessors in old China and in the world that Marx described.[29] What is worse, the new bourgeoisie class is undermining the very foundation of the socialist system. In the old days, the bourgeoisie supported the socialist system, because the Chinese capitalists then were also exploited by foreign capitalists. This gave the CCP an opportunity to form an ally with this class in its struggle for a socialist system. However, nowadays, the newly rising

---

Practice in East Asia, Vol. 4, 1999 (The Hague, London and Boston: Kluwer Law International, 2000), pp. 29–42.

[28] Lin Yanzhi, "Gongchandang yao lingdao he jiaoyu xin zichan jieji" [The CCP Must Lead and Control the New Bourgeoisie], *Zhenli de zhuiqiu* [The Seeking of Truth], No. 5 (2001), pp. 2–11.

[29] *Ibid.*, pp. 5–6.

bourgeoisie class does not have the experience of being exploited by foreign capitalists. Many of them, who try to lead China to capitalism, view the socialist system as a barrier to their further development. Therefore, it is imperative for the CCP to "lead and control" [*lingdao he jiaoyu*] this new class.

So how can the CCP lead and control this emerging new class? To "lead and control" the new bourgeoisie is to make it "voluntarily to accept the CCP's leadership and be coordinative to socialist modernization within the framework of the socialist system."[30] According to Lin,

> *"The key to control socialist market economy is to control bourgeoisie and its capitalist component; the key to control the bourgeoisie is that there is no capitalist within the party; and the key to no-existence of capitalists in the party is to see clearly their true colors"* (emphasis original).[31]

More concretely, two main measures should be taken to enable the Party to "lead and control" the bourgeoisie. First of all, the Party must consolidate "the dominant position of the state economy, and enable the state sector to lead and control the whole national economy. *The bottom line is that the private economy cannot be larger than the state economy*" (emphasis original).[32] Second, the party must maintain its purity. Lin argued that

> *"the CCP cannot recruit capitalists, and there cannot be any representatives of the bourgeoisie within the party.* Only organizational purity will enable the party to recognize [the bourgeoisie] thoroughly, to unify its guiding principle, to empower its cohesiveness and fighting capacity, and to lead socialist market economy" (emphasis original).[33]

According to Lin, the recruitment of capitalists in the Party will generate enormous negative consequences for it, threatening its

---

[30] *Ibid.*, p. 5.
[31] *Ibid.*, p. 7.
[32] *Ibidem.*
[33] *Ibidem.*

survival. It will have to face three main threats. First, the recruitment of capitalists will lead to pluralism within the Party. Lin contended,

> "The pluralization [*duoyuanhua*] of classes within the party means to provide an organizational foundation for political pluralism and thought pluralism. *A pluralist party will inevitably lead to dissensions.* [And] only a unified CCP will be capable of leading pluralist economies and pluralist classes in China" (emphasis original).[34]

Second, the recruitment of capitalists implies that the CCP endorses the legitimacy of the exploitative classes. Lin believed that the CCP has aimed at eliminating the exploitative system; and once such a system becomes legitimate, the CCP has to change itself completely. According to him, "*once these capitalists enter the party, they will first devote all their energy to struggle for leadership of and change the nature of the party. And, such changes are irreversible*" (emphasis original).[35] Third, the party will become alien to workers and peasants. The last two traditionally leading classes have been the very foundation of the CCP leadership. Given the capitalists' strong economic power, once they enter the Party, members who are workers and peasants will inevitably become subordinate to the capitalists. Consequently, the CCP has no choice but to give up its leadership.[36]

Similarly, Zhang Dejiang, Party Secretary of Zhejiang Provincial Committee of the CCP, also strongly argued that private entrepreneurs should not be allowed to join the CCP.[37] Zhejiang is among a few provinces where the private sector has developed rapidly and played an increasingly important role in the local economy and even politics. Generally, local officials from rich areas

---

[34] *Ibid.*, p. 8.

[35] *Ibid.*, p. 9.

[36] *Ibidem.*

[37] Zhang Dejiang, "Yao mingque siying qiyezhu buneng rudang" [To Make Clear that Private Entrepreneurs Cannot Join the Party], *Zhengli de zhuiqiu*, No. 5 (2001), p. 28. Zhang's original paper was published in *Dang de jianshe* [Party Constructing], No. 4 (2000).

were expected to provide political support to the rising private sector. Zhang's strong opposition clearly suggested that there was no consensus within the Party leadership on the political role of the private sector. Indeed, such arguments presented by Lin and Zhang are very representative and popular among old-style leftists.

The issue of whether private entrepreneurs should be allowed into the Party has been controversial. The private sector played an important role in the pro-democracy movement in 1989, and many private entrepreneurs not only contributed financial resources to the movement, but also played a leadership role.[38] In the aftermath of the 1989 crackdown, the CC of the CCP issued a regulation on August 28, 1989, entitled "A Notice on Strengthening Party Building" (Document No. 9, 1989). The regulation stated, "Our party is the vanguard of the working class. Since it is an exploitative relationship between private entrepreneurs and workers, private entrepreneurs cannot be recruited into the party."[39] Jiang Zemin, then summoned to Beijing to replace Zhao Ziyang as Party Secretary of the CCP, who was among the major political force behind this regulation. At the national conference for directors of Party organizational departments on August 21, 1989, Jiang argued,

> "The state needs to protect the legal rights of private entrepreneurs. I completely agree to the regulation that private entrepreneurs cannot join our party. Our party is the vanguard of the working class. If we allow those who do not want to give up exploitation and those who live on exploitation, what kind of party are we going to build?"[40]

Deng Xiaoping's southern tour created the impetus for the rapid development of the private sector. More importantly, the *xiahai*

---

[38] This is especially true in the case of Wan Runnan, the former head of the Stone Group. See Merle Goldman, *Sowing the Seeds of Democracy in China: Political Reform in the Deng Xiaoping Era* (Cambridge, MA: Harvard University Press, 1994).

[39] The Office of the Documentary Research of the Central Committee of the CCP (ed.), *Xinshiqi dang de jianshe wenjian xuanbian* [Selected Documents of Party Building in the New Era] (Beijing: Renmin chubanshe, 1991), p. 456.

[40] *Ibid.*, p. 442.

movement pushed many Party cadres and government officials to turn to businesses and become capitalists, and more and more private entrepreneurs joined the Party throughout the 1990s. Liberals within the Party proposed that private entrepreneurs should be allowed to join and thus expand the Party's social bases. For example, Guo Shichang, Vice Governor of Hebei province, argued in a conference on economic reforms that "the dynamics of economic development in our province lies in the private economy in the future. All departments concerned must provide support and protection to the development of the private economy."[41] Li Junru, a well-known theorist of the CCP, argued that the Party should legitimize private entrepreneurs' membership.[42] Such liberal arguments triggered strong reactions from the leftists.

BUILDING A NEW POLITICAL ORDER

Despite the controversies and the sensitivity of the issue, the leadership under Jiang Zemin decided to go one step further to formally allow private entrepreneurs to join the Party. In his speech celebrating the Party's 80th anniversary on July 1, 2001, Jiang Zemin declared that the CCP would recruit its members from various non-state sectors such as professionals and private entrepreneurs. According to Jiang, all these people have been a positive force in rebuilding China's socialism; therefore, they should not be excluded from the Party because whether they are politically advanced [*xianjin*] or backward [*luohou*] they cannot be judged by class structure and how much property they possess. Moreover, changes in the component of classes had become a reality in China, and only by recruiting elites among these social groups could the Party be revived.[43]

---

[41] Cited in *Zhenli de zhuiqiu*, No. 5 (2001), pp. 35–39.

[42] *Ibid.*, pp. 29–31.

[43] Jiang Zemin, "Jiang Zemin zai qingzhu Zhongguo gongchandang chenli bashi zhounian dahui shang de jianghua" [Jiang Zemin's Speech at the Conference Celebrating the 80th Anniversary of the Chinese Communist Party, July 1, 2001], *People's Daily*, July 2, 2001.

As a matter of fact, since the southern tour, the Jiang Zemin leadership has made great efforts not only to legitimize and institutionalize this interest-based social order, but also to search for a proper political order compatible with this emerging social order. While the Party–state has tried, albeit without success, to incorporate some social groups into the regime, it simply cannot tolerate any direct democratic challenge which became apparent towards the end of the 1990s. Within a few months towards the end of 1998, the preparatory committees of China's Democracy Party were established in 23 out of China's 31 provinces and major cities. Applications to register the new party were made in 14 provinces and cities.[44] The CCP leadership was intolerant of political challenges from social groups, but this does not mean that it had declined to accommodate the newly rising social forces. The Party leadership has consciously adjusted China's political system to accommodate such drastic socioeconomic changes. This can be exemplified by changes introduced in the Constitution.

Constitutional changes in China means, firstly, the change of the Constitution itself (1954–1982), and second, the amendment to the Constitution (1982–1999). When there is a change in the political situation, the old Constitution is likely to be replaced by a new one. Thus the 1975 Constitution is called the "Cultural Revolution Constitution," the 1978 Constitution the "Four-Modernization Constitution," and the 1982 Constitution the "Reform and Open-Door Constitution." Needless to say, each revision of the Constitution had strong political motivations and was heavily influenced by the attempt of the leadership to adjust the political system to changing situations. It is worthwhile to examine briefly the constitutional changes due to the emergence of the private sector.

According to the 1954 Constitution, the first in the history of the People's Republic, China's political system was based on the working class as its leading class and the worker–peasant alliance as

---

[44] John Pomfret, "Why 'Beijing Spring' Cooled: Dissidents Overstepped," *International Herald Tribune*, January 4, 1999, p. 1, 7.

its foundation (Art. 1). With regard to the economic system, the Constitution stated that the state would aim at eliminating the exploitative system and building a socialist system. While the state sector should be in a dominant position, other sectors, such as collective cooperatives, individually owned enterprises, private capitalist economy, and state capitalism, were allowed to coexist (Art. 5 and 10). Furthermore, the Constitution also provided protection to citizens' ownership of legal income, savings, properties and other forms of productive materials (Art. 11), and protection to the right of inheritance of private properties (Art. 12). Meanwhile, the state would collect and even confiscate land and other forms of productive materials in accordance with laws and regulations in order to meet the needs of public interests (Art. 13), and everyone was prohibited from using his/her private properties to undermine public interests (Art. 14). The Constitution also declared that public properties were sacred and inviolable, and it was every citizen's duty to protect them (Art. 101).

Many waves of political movements such as the Anti-Rightist Movement and the Cultural Revolution almost completely nullified the 1954 Constitution. In 1975, the party leadership under the Gang of Four made a major constitutional revision. The 1975 Constitution formally nullified many articles regarding citizens' rights in the 1954 Constitution and added some articles to meet the political needs then. To support the Party became the citizens' right, and of course, citizens were also given the right to rebel. The revised Constitution was reduced to 30 articles from the original 106.

After the demise of Mao Zedong and the smashing of the Gang of Four in 1976, the CCP leadership under Hua Guofeng decided to make another constitutional revision in 1978. Though the Constitution was expanded to 60 articles by restoring some articles of the 1954 Constitution, it was still based on the 1975 Constitution. In accordance with political changes then, the use of material incentive to promote the four-modernizations was legalized.

After Deng Xiaoping returned to power, the CCP leadership passed a new constitution, that is, the 1982 Constitution. The new Constitution restored almost all articles in the 1954

Constitution. New articles were added (from 106 articles in 1954 to 138) to meet the new political and economic needs. Though the 1982 Constitution still emphasized that the state sector had to be dominant, it recognized that individual economic activities in both rural and urban areas were complementary to the state sector (Art. 11). What was later called the private enterprise—those which employed more than eight workers—was not legalized.

In 1988, the first constitutional amendment was made. Two significant changes were made in the economic system. First, one paragraph to be added to Article 11 stated:

"The state allows the private economy to exist and develop within the legal boundary. The private economy is a complement to the socialist public economy. The state protects legal rights and interests of the private economy, provides it with leadership, supervision and management" (Art. 11, para. 3).

Second, para. 4 of Article 10 was revised: The state recognized "land use right can be transferred in accordance with legal regulations." This change was significant, because it meant that the state legalized employment, capital accumulation, land commercialization, and other newly rising economic activities. Five years later, in 1993, the second constitutional amendment was made. The 1993 amendment gave up the planned economic system and formally declared that socialist market economy was to be established.

The official confirmation of the market economy led to serious criticism of the capitalistic development, by the leftists, both the old and the new, in the mid-1990s. Despite all the controversy, the leadership decided to proceed with its own plan. The 15th Party Congress in 1997 further pointed to how a market economy could take root in China and declared a program of partial privatization of state-owned enterprises. Further, based on the 1993 amendment, the Second Session of the Ninth National People's Congress (NPC) in 1999 made a constitutional amendment which, for the first time since the establishment of the People's

Republic, provides constitutional protection for the private economy.[45]

While it will take a long time for the CCP to establish an interest-based political order, all these constitutional changes in the 1990s show that the Party leadership has made great efforts to adjust China's political system, not only to promote further economic development but also to accommodate capitalist economic institutions. In February 2000, Jiang Zemin brought in a new concept, *san ge dai biao* [literally meaning "Three Representatives"]. According to this concept, the CCP represents the "most advanced mode of productive force, the most advanced culture, and the interests of the majority of the population."[46] The "Three Representatives" theory is undoubtedly the CCP's affirmation of the non-state sector in the economy. More importantly, it also shows that the CCP has begun to consider how the interests of the newly rising classes or social groups can be represented. As mentioned above, the CCP leadership has also legitimized Party membership of private entrepreneurs. All these changes have been warmly received and are widely regarded as a symbol of the CCP's transformation from a communist party to one containing some social democratic elements.

TOWARDS A SOCIAL DEMOCRATIC PARTY?

Previously, private entrepreneurs were formally prohibited from joining the Party. The liberalization immediately generated a great incentive for private entrepreneurs to join the Party. According to a Hong Kong source, immediately after Jiang's speech, more than 100,000 private entrepreneurs submitted their applications for Party membership; and the Department of Organization of the CCP, headed

---

[45] For a discussion of this constitutional amendment, see Zou and Zheng, "China's Third Constitutional Amendment: An Assessment."

[46] The Xinhua News Agency, "Jiang Zemin tongzhi zai quanguo dangxiao gongzuo huiyi shan de jianghua" (June 9, 2000) [Comrade Jiang Zemin's Talk in National Party Schools Working Conference], *People's Daily*, July 17, 2000.

by Zeng Qinghong, has planned to recruit 200,000 private entrepreneurs into the Party before the Party's 16th Congress next September.[47]

Traditionally, the CCP had claimed that it represented the interests of five major groups—workers, peasants, intellectuals, PLA, party cadres, and government officials. The majority of its members were also recruited from these groups. What, then, is the underlying implication of the CCP's opening its door to private entrepreneurs whom the Party had tried to eliminate for so many years, especially under Mao Zedong?

The CCP has been transformed over time. During Mao Zedong's era, it was a genuine revolutionary party with its members consisting overwhelmingly of workers and peasants. For example, in 1956, Party members from these two groups were 83%. The figure still remained high, at 64% in 1981. When Deng Xiaoping came to power, he initiated a so-called technocratic movement, replacing workers and peasant members with technocrats. Party members from among workers and peasants were reduced from 64% in 1981 to 48% in 1994.[48]

The Jiang Zemin leadership is pragmatic enough to accommodate a rising entrepreneur class. The leadership has its reasons for recruiting private entrepreneurs into the Party. First, the decision implies that the Party is adjusting itself to China's changing political reality. As mentioned above, an essential portion of private entrepreneurs have already joined the Party. What the Party leadership does is to formally legitimize their membership. Second, by doing so, the leadership tries to expand the Party's social bases. Capitalist economic development has rapidly changed China's class structure. When the traditional ruling classes such as workers and peasants decline, the role of the entrepreneur class becomes increasingly important. Embracing such new social classes will certainly enable the Party to

---

[47] *Ming Pao*, July 23, 2001.

[48] Ignatius Wibowo, "Party Recruitment and the Future of the Chinese Communist Party," Unpublished manuscript, East Asian Institute, National University of Singapore, 2001.

expand its social bases. Third, the decision also shows that the Party is developing a new way to rule the country. When class struggle was used by Mao Zedong to govern the country, political mobilization became important and inevitable. To mobilize social forces, the Party leadership then had to rely on the so-called ruling classes: workers and peasants. But now the Party is the only ruling party, and it has to represent as many social interests as possible. Whether the Party can succeed in governing an increasingly diversified society depends, to a great degree, on whether it can stand above all social forces and coordinate these different and even conflicting interests.

Jiang Zemin's decision helps the Party to solve some major political problems resulting from a rising private entrepreneur class. But it also creates as many political problems as it solves. The Party leadership will soon face two major political tasks. One is how the Party will represent the interests of all these social forces, and the other is how it coordinates these interests. The solution really depends on whether the Party can develop a sound set of democratic institutions. As widely expected among China's liberals, both the theory of "Three Representatives" and the decision to recruit private entrepreneurs will help the Party transform itself into a social democratic or socialist party. Although it is a difficult task to make this transformation a reality in a country without any democratic tradition, once the CCP opens its door to private entrepreneurs whom the Party had tried to eliminate for so many years (especially under Mao Zedong), genuine dynamism will be introduced into the CCP to democratize itself.

Chapter 4

Leadership Succession and Its Impact on the Party's Rank and File

IGNATIUS WIBOWO*

Leadership succession in China since 1949 has always been marked by power struggle among the top leadership at the Politburo level. Studies on this subject abound, with each author bringing his or her distinct perspective.[1] One question that has been left out is: what is the impact of leadership succession on the Party? Has the power struggle at the Politburo been contained at the top level? Or, has it spilled over and affected the rank and file?

This chapter seeks to address such questions. It will argue that leadership succession since the death of Mao (1976) has made an impact on the rank and file in the form of purges and campaigns. The central thesis is that any new leader will bring in his followers and purge those of his predecessor. Leadership succession, therefore, has inevitably caused big commotion both within the Party and in society at large, because many old members are purged and many new members are brought in. This understanding, it is expected, will help us to predict the political consequences of the coming leadership succession in 2002.

The first part of this article will provide a theoretical framework, and it will be followed by a summary of the past events, focusing

---

* The author thanks Benny Hari Juliawan for reading the early manuscript and the participants of the seminar for their comments and criticisms.
[1] There is a huge literature on the subject, the latest being the collection of articles published in *China Journal*, No. 45 (January 2001).

on the purges and recruitments after the death of Mao Zedong in 1976 until the fall of Zhao Ziyang in 1989. I will draw some conclusions and connect them with the coming leadership succession in which Jiang Zemin will pass on the baton to Hu Jintao.

THEORETICAL FRAMEWORK

Struggles between the old leaders and the new aspirants in a party have long been known. In his meticulous study of political parties, Robert Michels, for instance, observes: "Every oligarchy is full of suspicion towards those who aspire to enter its ranks, regarding them not simply as eventual heirs but as successors who are ready to supplant them without waiting for a natural death."[2] The reason for this struggle differs from case to case: age, region, ideology, class background. It also includes personal reasons such as antipathy, envy, and jealousy. As such, one can expect that the succession process will not be easy and will be marked by fear and hatred. All parties, surely, will mobilize all available resources to beat their opponents.

Michels further observes that the crucial factor in this struggle is the masses. Democratic parties consist of deputies elected by the masses. In times of crisis, as happens during the leadership succession, these deputies must be able to win the support of the masses. He writes: "Democratic deputies endeavor to disarm their adversaries within the party, and at the same time to acquire a new prestige in the eyes of the masses, by displaying in parliament 'a formidable activity on behalf of the common cause.'"[3] In other words, they are required to employ sophisticated tactics, often by appealing to loftier motives.

Leadership succession in a democratic party, according to Michels, does involve political struggle, but such a struggle does not affect its rank and file. This may have to do with the fact that democratic

---

[2] Robert Michels, *Political Parties* (New York: Free Press, 1962), p. 176.
[3] *Ibid.*, p. 174.

parties belong to the category of mass parties. The electorates have the final say on who is going to be the leader. In what Duverger terms "devotee parties," the struggle for succession takes a different form.[4]

The distinguishing factor of a "devotee party" is its strict selection of membership; only selected people can join it. This type of party, therefore, needs some time to test a prospective member's loyalty and ideological orthodoxy. In communist party parlance it is called the "probationary period," in which the candidate for membership is put under close scrutiny over his/her allegiance to the ideology. Thus, for example, the Chinese Communist Party (CCP) requires that before admitting a candidate

> "the Party branch committee must canvass the opinions of persons concerned, inside and outside the Party, about an applicant for Party membership and, after establishing the latter's qualifications following a rigorous examination, submit the application to a general membership meeting for discussion." (Art. 5, Party Constitution of 1982)

The party meanwhile undergoes fluctuation of ideology, which occurs during the leaders' struggle for the top job. Although the party sticks to the ideology of Marxism and Leninism, during a struggle for power, leaders could actually produce different interpretations of the ideology to support their particular cause. Since early times, leaders of communist movements have been bitterly engaged in the correct interpretation of ideology, resulting in the split of communist movements, each with its own claim to orthodoxy. The violent struggle of Stalin and Trotsky for leadership in the 1930s is a case in point.

Thus a new leader means a new ideology, and accordingly, demands a change of allegiance of the party members. After one faction wins, there are only two options for the rank and file: either switch their allegiance or be purged. This is certainly not an easy

---

[4] Maurice Duverger, *Political Parties* (New York: Wiley, 1963).

task. In a rapidly changing political situation, a simple party member may become confused and take a wrong decision and accidentally get purged. The Party Constitution (1982) indeed stipulates a lengthy and complicated process of disciplining (Art. 40). Yet, in chaotic circumstances, measures such as purge or expulsion can be carried out quite easily.

In this chapter, I will show how this pattern holds good for the CCP. Leadership succession in the CCP is always accompanied by a power struggle, which produces a new leader who takes action against Party members who fail to express allegiance to his new ideology. Thus the power struggle among the elite determines the fate of the rank and file. The fiercer the power struggle, the more severe the impact on the rank and file. Ideology here is the criterion for purging the undesirable members.

Ever since the CCP came to power in 1949, there have been two occasions of leadership succession: transition from Mao to Deng, and from Zhao Ziyang to Jiang Zemin. On both occasions, the Party rank and file encountered various policies that adversely affected their lives. Will this pattern be repeated during the transition from Jiang Zemin to his successor? I will discuss this in the fourth section of this chapter.

FROM MAO TO DENG

With Zhou Enlai lying incapacitated in hospital and Mao debilitated by Parkinson's disease in 1976, the problem of leadership succession came to the fore. Mao's position as Party Chairman was at stake: who was going to replace him? There were, according to MacFarquhar, three potential contenders to the throne: Mao's wife Jiang Qing, Hua Guofeng, the appointed heir, and a group of military generals around Deng Xiaoping.[5] The first contender, however, was easily defeated by the alliance of the second and the

---

[5] Roderick Macfarquhar (ed.), *The Politics of China, 1949–1989* (Cambridge: Cambridge University Press, 1993), p. 278. He terms the three groups as: radicals, survivors, and beneficiaries of the Cultural Revolution. Jiang Qing and the Gang of Four belonged to the radicals, the generals to the survivors, and Hua Guofeng to the beneficiaries.

third contenders. Jiang Qing and other members of the Gang of Four were arrested on October 6, 1976, less than a month after Mao's death.

The struggle, then, became one between Hua Guofeng and the generals. Supported by the words of Mao "With you in charge, I'm at ease," Hua Guofeng emerged as Party Chairman, the legitimate successor to Mao. His position was further strengthened by the fact that he was also the Prime Minister. It was surprising, however, how he was outmaneuvered by the generals. MacFarquhar remarks: "Yet, in the relatively short period between the Third Plenum of the Tenth CC, in July 1977, and the Third Plenum of the Eleventh CC, in December 1978, those power relations had been turned around."[6] Hua was not immediately relieved from his office, but he was by all means defeated by the generals. It took the generals another three and a half years (September 1982) to reduce Hua Guofeng to a mere member of the Central Committee.

The end result of this struggle was the emergence of Deng Xiaoping as the undisputed leader. Soon after he assumed this position in the late 1970s, Deng got down to tackling those who had been the supporters of either the Gang of Four or Hua Guofeng. In his speech at the end of July 1979, Deng was fully aware that, although the followers of his rivals had been removed from offices at the higher levels, a substantial number of Party members were still problematic. "We must take note of the fact that a fair number of people are still opposed to the Party's current political and ideological lines."[7] Deng clearly pointed out that they were followers of Lin Biao and the Gang of Four, and were following "the principle of the 'two whatevers.'" He wanted to eradicate them. "If we entrust power to those who have not changed, how can we expect them to listen to the Party? They will stir trouble whenever there is a chance."

[6] *Ibid.*, p. 317.
[7] Deng's speech of June 2, 1978, in *Deng Xiaoping Wenxuan* [Selected Works of Deng Xiaoping], Vol. 2 (Beijing: Renmin chubanshe, 1983), p. 176 (thereafter: DXPWX).

Deng even vowed that not a single one of these elements

"should ever be allowed to enter the leadership on any level, and those already in the leadership must be dismissed. If we do not increase our vigilance, and if we allow them to hold leadership positions, then they will renew their two-faced intrigues, plant their roots, and conceal their identities."[8]

This idea was translated into a numbter of policies, two of which stand out: rectification campaign and cadre retirement policy.

Rectification Campaign

The rectification campaign was clearly intended to weed out the recalcitrant members. There were two rectification campaigns between 1978 and 1987. The first one was against "three types of people." First, those who had gained by engaging in rebellious acts during the Cultural Revolution. They had followed closely Lin Biao and the Gang of Four, had engaged in factional strife, and had since been promoted as leading cadres. Second, there were those who had espoused the ideological line of Lin Biao and the Gang of Four, and who continued to oppose the party's line after 1978. Third, there were those who had committed serious acts of "beating" (and torturing people to cause injury or death), "smashing" (official organizations), and "looting" (government documents and properties).

The campaign against the "three types of people" lasted for one year, 1982–1983. By December 1984, Bo Yibo was able to report that some 50% of people identified as the "three types" had been dealt with.[9] However, the leaders continued their efforts to eradicate the "three types." Throughout 1985, official publications stressed the need for their total elimination. Party organs in many places declared their commitment to devoting the year 1985 to conducting yet another thorough exposure of the crimes of the "three types." In late

---

[8] Deng's speeches of January 16 and August 28, 1980, in DXPWX, Vol. 2, p. 232, 283.
[9] *People's Daily*, December 23, 1984, p. 1.

1985, Bo Yibo made a second report that good results had been achieved.[10]

The task of exposing and removing the "three types" was done thoroughly. Once people were identified as the "three types," they were immediately dismissed from office or expelled from the Party. Mercy was rarely shown, and thus the campaign created panic among the members at the local level.

The campaign against the "three types" coincided with the "rectification campaign," which started in 1982. At the 12th Party Congress on September 1, 1982, Hu Yaobang announced the decision to launch a three-year rectification campaign, commencing sometime in late 1983.[11] The report, in arguing against his rivals, was replete with condemnation of Lin Biao and the Gang of Four, and more significantly, of "leftist mistakes." The new regime, clearly, was determined to eradicate its rivals who held diverse allegiances and ideologies.

This was made even clearer in a special document on rectification. The Party, the document says, wanted to direct the rectification campaign at the whole Party. "The Party now has 40 million members, of which 9 million are cadres. It had 2.5 million Party organizations at the grassroot level and above. From this winter, for three years, the campaign will be conducted in two steps."[12] Its first and main objective was to rectify "those who held the view of anti Four Basic Principles, and those who held the incorrect tendency of both 'left' and 'right' which contravened the decision of the Third Plenum of the Eleventh CC."[13] The new leaders, evidently, did not want to take a chance: the Party was to be cleared of its potential rivals and opponents as soon as possible.

---

[10] *Hongqi*, No. 20 (1985), p. 5.
[11] Hu Yaobang's report to 12th Party Congress, September 1, 1982, in *Zhonggong zhongyang wenjian xuanbian* [Selected Important Documents from the Central Committee of the CCP] (Beijing: Zhonggong zhongyang dangxiao chubanshe, 1992), pp. 253–254 (thereafter: ZZWX).
[12] *Ibid.*, p. 271.
[13] *Ibid.*, p. 264.

The campaign was carried out in three phases. In the first phase, which lasted more than a year, 388,000 members from the national and provincial levels were affected. In the second phase, which lasted six months, about 13.5 million members at the district and county levels had to go through rectification. Finally, 28 million members, in a shorter period, had to rectify themselves.[14] On May 27, 1987, Bo Yibo reported that the campaign had accomplished much and that the overall results were positive.[15] Bo, however, did not release any figures of those who had been expelled, punished, or suspended. At the 13th Party Congress (1987), Zhao Ziyang gave a very conservative number, claiming that during 1982–1986, the Party had taken disciplinary action against 650,141 members, of whom 151,935 had been expelled.[16]

Complementary Policies

Meanwhile, other policies were made to complement the two rectification campaigns: the policy of cadre retirement and the policy of rejuvenation of Party members. The policy of cadre retirement was targetted at older members or veterans. Deng might well have been aware that he could not simply expel or dismiss them, because they enjoyed a high degree of respect both within and outside the Party. Nevertheless, he knew quite well that many of them were either apathetic to or non-supportive to his program of "reform and openness." "They were the opportunists who temporarily made peace with Deng but who might side with the die-hard radicals if the latter attempted a comeback."[17]

The best way to get rid of them was to provide them a graceful exit, namely retirement. Deng did not express his deepest thought openly, but argued from the point of objective law of nature: "The old cadres are now mostly over sixty years of age ... Their energy

---

[14] Hsi-sheng Ch'i, *Politics of Disillusionment* (New York: M.E. Sharpe, 1991), p. 185.
[15] *People's Daily*, May 28, 1987, p. 1.
[16] See, Ch'i, *op. cit.*, p. 207.
[17] *Ibid.*, p. 53.

level has declined. Otherwise, why are many cadres holding offices at home? Why can't they tough it out in the office for eight straight hours?"[18] Old people have to, according to nature, make way for the young because they do not have enough energy to carry out the duties imposed on them, Deng suggests.

Thus, in February 1980, the Fifth Plenum of the 11th Party Congress formally abolished the practice of guaranteed lifetime tenure for regular Party cadres. In April 1980, the ban was extended to the leadership level, not allowing old leaders in poor health to become members of the Central Committee of the 12th Party Congress. In September 1980, several aging leaders resigned as vice-premiers, and in June 1981, at the Sixth Plenum, Deng Xiaoping declined to take up the topmost post of the CCP. Finally, in February 1982, the Party formally adopted the resolution to introduce a "system of retirement for old cadres."

The resistance of Party cadres to this policy is reflected in the introduction of two types of retirement: *tuixiu* and *lixiu*. The former is intended for ordinary cadres, and the latter to the "old cadres." Party cadres, in general, refused to retire for many reasons, all of which had to do with the privileges they had been enjoying for decades. This partly explains the slow progress of the retirement program. For instance, a year after its announcement, only 423,000 "old cadres" had accepted *lixiu*.[19] Dissatisfied with this progress, the Party stepped up its efforts. Consequently, by the spring of 1984, the number of provincial governors, deputy governors, and party secretaries was reduced by 34% and the subprovincial and municipal leadership by 36%.[20] By November 1984, a total of 1.3 million old cadres had left state agencies and enterprises.[21] The year 1986 saw an even faster pace in the program, and by June, some 1.8 million old cadres had retired.[22] Since China probably had some 2.6

---

[18] Deng's speech on November 2, 1979, in DXPWX, p. 193.

[19] *People's Daily*, July 6, 1983, p. 4.

[20] *People's Daily*, January 24, 1984, p. 1.

[21] *People's Daily*, February 11, 1985, p. 1.

[22] *Hongqi*, No. 19 (1985) p. 8.

million "old cadres" as of mid-1980s,[23] this meant that 70% of them had retired by then.[24]

The policy of rejuvenation complemented the policy of retirement. There was an urgent need to replace the old cadres. Indeed, it was this rejuvenation policy which became the main reason for retiring the old cadres. Young people, who were more educated, more professional, and more revolutionary, were expected to play important role in modernizing China. This policy was summed up in "Four Processes" [si hua]: nianqinghua [rejuvenation], geminghua [revolutionization], zhuanyehua [specialization], zhishihua [intellectualization].[25]

The policy of rejuvenation meant recruiting new members who were more in line with the new ideology. The more there were who supported the program of "reform and openness," the more confident the Party felt in pursuing its agenda. Roberta Martin argued that the recruitment of new and young members under Deng Xiaoping was closely linked with his attempt to revamp the Party.[26]

What was the general situation of Party membership in the turbulent years of the 1980s? There was clearly a fluctuation in the number of members. Thus, although the period between 1980 and 1982 showed an increase in membership, there was a fall in the gross increase of members—from one million to slightly more than 700,000 (Table 1). In the following year, membership jumped to more than one million, to be followed by a marginal rise of 50,000 in 1984. The small increase may have to do with the severity of the two campaigns (the campaigns to weed out "three types of persons" and the three-year Party rectification campaign) as well as the retirement of old cadres. Apparently, the expulsion of members might have exceeded the intake of new members.

[23] Bo Yibo's statement as quoted in People's Daily, January 26, 1984, p. 1.

[24] For further discussion, see Melanie Manion, Retirement of Revolutionary Cadres in China: Public Policies, Social Norms, Private Interests (Princeton: Princeton University Press, 1993).

[25] Hu Yaobang's report to the 12th Party Congress, September 1, 1982, in ZZWX, pp. 248–250.

[26] Roberta Martin, Party Recruitment in China: Patterns and Prospects, Occasional Papers (New York: East Asian Institute, Columbia University, 1981), pp. 75–77.

Table 1. Annual Growth of the CCP (1979–1989)

Year	Total membership	Gross increase	% Increase
1979	37,000,000	NA	NA
1980	38,000,000	1,000,000	2.7
1981	38,923,569	923,569	2.4
1982	39,657,212	733,643	1.9
1983	40,950,000	1,292,788	3.3
1984	41,000,000	50,000	0.1
1985	42,000,000	1,000,000	2.4
1986	44,000,000	2,000,000	4.8
1987	46,011,951	2,011,951	4.6
1988	48,000,000	1,988,049	4.3
1989	49,000,000	1,000,000	2.1

Source: Zheng Shiping, *Party versus State in Post-1949 China. The Institutional Dilemma* (Cambridge: Cambridge University Press, 1997), p. 268.

How did the members experience the turbulence? We do not know for sure. Taking into consideration the fierce resistance to all the policies, we may be able to feel their resentment and anger. Being rectified and retired is like being punished without going to jail. As they were only low-ranking Party members, they just had to accept it as their fate. The new regime under Deng Xiaoping was interested only in ensuring the success of its agenda.

FROM ZHAO TO JIANG

The issue of succession came to the surface in the mid-1980s. In September 1986, in an interview with CBS correspondent Mike Wallace, Deng reiterated his wish to retire during the 13th Party Congress the following year.[27] This was actually one of the many occasions in which Deng had expressed his wish to retire. Indeed, Deng decided to resign from the Central Committee at the 13th Party

---

[27] Chu-yuan Cheng, *Behind the Tiananmen Massacre* (Boulder, CO: Westview Press, 1990), p. 59.

Congress, a move which was usually interpreted as one aimed at forcing other octogenarians also to resign. (Deng was born in 1904).

Thus, the question, "Who is going to replace Deng Xiaoping," in the late 1980s, was a real issue—first among the people, and then among the two contending forces within the Party elite: the conservatives and the reformers.[28] Deng himself looked indecisive. Just several months before the 13th Congress, he suddenly decided to remove his appointed successor, Hu Yaobang, from the post of General Secretary of the Party. Deng seemed to indicate that he was in favor of the conservatives. But the appointment of Zhao Ziyang as the new General Secretary proved that this was not so, because Zhao was not less radical than Hu Yaobang.

The clash between the conservatives (headed by Li Peng) and the reformers (headed by Zhao Ziyang) intensified in 1988. In early February 1988, Zhao published an article titled "Further Emancipate the Mind and Further Liberate the Productive Forces," to attract popular support and to refute the arguments of the conservatives, who contended that economic stability rather than bold strategies should be the key objective of economic reform. Li Peng fought back by taking the stage at the Seventh National People's Congress. On March 20, 1989, delivering his report, Li Peng implicitly accused Zhao of seeking quick results in economic and social development and overlooking the country's vast population.[29]

The death of Hu Yaobang on April 15, 1989, and the ensuing large-scale student demonstrations both occurred at this critical time. Zhao Ziyang and the reformers who might have been desperate to win popular support considered the demonstrations a golden opportunity to keep their program alive. The conservatives and Li Peng might have seen the demonstrations as an excuse to uproot Zhao and his group. One month earlier, Deng Xiaoping had

---

[28] There were many different factions within the CCP at that time; though the terms, *reformers* and *conservatives*, are not quite appropriate, they nonetheless point to important conceptual differences among leaders throughout the period of Deng Xiaoping.

[29] Li Peng's report to the National People's Congress, March 20, 1989 in ZZWX, pp. 242–469.

announced that he was seriously considering complete retirement after the Beijing summit with Soviet President Mikhail Gorbachev.[30]

The student demonstrations in the Tiananmen Square which lasted for about 40 days were, in my view, an arena of power struggle within the top elite of the Party. A fight between Zhao and Li took place behind the walls of Zhongnanhai as the students demonstrated in favor of democracy in Tiananmen Square. The recent publication of classified documents confirms this.[31] Their fight was no longer over economic policy; it spilled over into the question of how to deal with the students. Li was in no mood to negotiate with the students, whereas Zhao was willing to. This difference in approach was skillfully manipulated by Li to his advantage, and it was, in the end, Li who won. Deng gave his final verdict: "In the recent turmoil Zhao Ziyang has exposed his position completely. He obviously stands on the side of the turmoil, and in practical terms he has been fomenting division, splitting the Party, and defending turmoil."[32] Deng ceased supporting Zhao.

In the report delivered by Beijing Mayor, Chen Xitong, to the Standing Committee of the National People's Congress (June 30, 1989), similar arguments were put forward. He argued that the demonstrations and hunger strikes were part of a conspiracy planned by a small group which was under the protection of Zhao Ziyang. In his view, the student movement was "exploited by organizers of the turmoil from the very beginning," and Zhao was the one who "supported the turmoil and split the Party."[33]

As we know, Zhao was stripped of all his positions, but he still retained his Party membership. There was a big surprise, however. Although Li Peng won the battle, he did not win the war. Deng Xiaoping, instead of appointing Li as General Secretary to replace

---

[30] Cheng, *op. cit.*, p. 61.

[31] Andrew Nathan and Perry Link (eds), Zhang Liang (compiler), *Tiananmen Papers* (London: Little, Brown and Company, 2001).

[32] *Ibid.*, p. 260.

[33] Chen Xitong's report "Putting Down Anti-government Riots," in *China Daily*, July 7, 1989, p. 4.

Zhao, asked Jiang Zemin to come from Shanghai to Beijing and take up the post left vacant by Zhao. Apparently, Deng did not have trust in Li Peng to become General Secretary or to be his successor.

What was the impact of this struggle for leadership? The student demonstrations were quelled by using military force, at the dawn of June 4, 1989. The conservatives continued to hunt down the supporters of the student demonstrations. On June 8, Public Notice No. 11 of the Beijing municipal government and the Martial Enforcement Troops Command called on citizens to report on the "criminal activists of the counter-revolutionary rioters," stressing that "each and every citizen" in Beijing had the "right and obligation" to report and expose the rioters.[34] By June 20, more than 1500 people were officially reported to have been arrested throughout China. By the middle of September, it was estimated that 5000 to 10,000 people had been arrested in Beijing and at least as many in other parts of the country.[35]

There were no detailed figures as to how many of those arrested were Party members. Since the arrests were done indiscriminately, there was a big possibility that Party members were among those arrested or even executed. Against the Party members who were not arrested, the Central Discipline Investigation Commission (CDIC) launched a rectification campaign. During the campaign, all Party members in Beijing and other cities were required to undergo investigation and re-registration in connection with their attitudes and behavior during the event.[36] By April 1991, 72,000 Party members were expelled, and 256,000 more were subjected to lesser forms of punishment.[37]

Interestingly enough, right after the crackdown on the student demonstrations, the government put into full gear the campaign against corruption. On July 10, 1989, the *People's Daily* announced the expulsions of hundreds of corrupt Party members. This was accompanied by an announcement of cases of corruption against high ranking cadres. Although this anticorruption campaign was meant to

[34] Cheng, *op. cit.*, p. 140.
[35] *Ibidem.*
[36] Macfarquhar, *op. cit.*, p. 466.
[37] *China News Digest*, April 18, 1991, quoted in *ibid.*, p. 468.

satisfy the demands of the students, it was also used as a pretext to carry out purges of the supporters of Zhao Ziyang both inside and outside the Party. The anticorruption campaign was, actually the most convenient way of putting down rival political groups.

We do not know the exact number of Party members punished by the leaders for their support of Zhao Ziyang. At the end of 1989, there was a slight decline in recruitment to the Party. The number of recruitments dropped in 1987 and picked up again in 1988 (by almost two million). But in the following year, 1989, only one million new members were added, owing most probably to the crackdown on members who had taken part in the Tiananmen demonstration in June 1989 (Table 1).

FROM JIANG TO HU?

It was very difficult for Jiang, at the beginning of his term, to consolidate support in the capital city. As a newcomer to Beijing, he was in a desperate situation where, except for Deng Xiaoping, no one seemed eager to support him and his cause. For example, he had to deal with two rivals as well as opponents, Chen Xitong, the mayor of Beijing, and General Yang Baibing, who worked in tandem with General Yang Shangkun. Perhaps, Jiang himself was fully aware that he was only a transitional figure who would soon be replaced.

But observers agree that Jiang was eventually able to consolidate his power after 1992. Thanks to Deng's intervention, the Yang brothers were sidelined in autumn 1992, and Jiang's position in the Central Military Commission (CMC) was made secure. Since then, Jiang has been accepted as undisputed chairman of the CMC; the two deputy chairmen of the CMC, Liu Huaqing and Zhang Zhen, were on good terms with him.[38] Also, with the support of Deng Xiaoping in 1995, another rival of Jiang, Chen Xitong, was removed

[38] You Ji, "Jiang Zemin's Command of the Military," *China Journal*, No. 45 (January 2001), pp. 131–142.

on corruption charges from his post in the Politburo and as Beijing municipal party chief.[39]

Meanwhile, Jiang was also able to draw support from people whom he had known well since the time he was in Shanghai. These people included Premier Zhu Rongji, Vice-Premier Wu Bangguo, Huang Ju (a Politburo member), and Zeng Qinghong, an alternate Politburo member and head of the powerful Party's Organization Department. At the local level, in just two years, from March 1994 to March 1996, Jiang changed the leadership of 19 provinces out of 30, either of governors or Party secretaries.[40]

Jiang put his stamp on the ideology too. Although, in the past two decades, Chinese society had undergone de-ideologization, a true supreme leader was supposed to define an ideology for the whole population. True to this tradition, Jiang produced in 2000 a new teaching called "Three Representatives" (i.e., that the Party represents the broad mass of the population, an advanced culture, and the most advanced production). This new ideology could be viewed as a breakthrough because it symbolized the "inclusionary orientation" instead of an "exclusionary one," by which the Party was willing to incorporate societal forces other than workers and peasants.[41] A massive campaign had been carried out throughout 2000 till mid-2001 to implement the ideology.[42]

---

[39] You Ji, "Jiang Zemin: In Quest of Post-Deng Supremacy," in Maurice Brosseau, Suzanne Pepper and Tsang Shu-ki (eds.), China Review 1996 (Hong Kong: The Chinese University Press, 1996), pp. 14–17.

[40] Hongwu Ouyang, "The PRC's New Elite Politics: The New Institutionalism Perspective," Issues and Studies, Vol. 34, No. 5 (May 1998), p. 8.

[41] Joseph Fewsmith, "The New Shape of Elite Politics," China Journal, No. 45 (January 2001), pp. 88–89.

[42] From February to mid-November 2000, the People's Daily (the CCP's mouthpiece) alone published more than 300 papers on the "Three Representatives" and various reports on how the concept had spread throughout the country. See Zheng Yongnian, "China's Politics in 2000: Preparing the Ground for Power Transition," EAI Background Brief, No. 79, Singapore, December 26, 2000, p. 6.

It is now widely accepted that Jiang is in full command of China, especially after the 15th Party Congress (1997).[43] As the issue of leadership succession is looming large, the question is whether he will relinquish his position. More importantly, whether the leadership succession will take place in a peaceful manner. Jiang, evidently, is credited with institutionalizing the political system.[44] As such, he is expected to pass on the baton to his successor (whoever he is), because he has completed his term twice and reached the age of retirement (70 years).

One is curious to know who will replace Jiang as General Secretary. All political commentators agree that Hu Jintao will be the next boss of the CCP. This prediction apparently ignores the other contenders such as Zeng Qinghong or Li Ruihuan. The latter has been a member of the Standing Committee since 1987, and in terms of age, is still qualified for the job.[45] The former is the confidant of Jiang, currently in charge of the powerful Organization Department. There may be a "dark horse" which eludes outside observers. The contest, therefore, will not necessarily be between Jiang Zemin and his successor, but also between Hu Jintao and other potential candidates. Such a power struggle will surface only during the Congress, and it will be nothing less than a life-and-death struggle.

If that is so, we could expect purges to follow. Like in the previous two cases, the winner will take full advantage of his new position to clear up the followers of the loser. If the winner is on Jiang's side, the purge or "rectification campaign" will be limited and not massive, just enough to eradicate those who are loyal to

---

[43] This does not negate the fact that during the Congress Jiang's speech received only lukewarm praise. See, Richard Baum, "The Fifteenth National Party Congress: Jiang Takes Command?" *China Quarterly*, No. 153 (March 1998), pp. 141–156.

[44] Frederick C. Teiwes, "Normal Politics with Chinese Characteristics," *China Journal*, No. 45 (January 2001), pp. 69–82; David Shambaugh, "The Dynamics of Elite Politics During the Jiang Era," *Ibid.*, pp. 101–111.

[45] Susan Shirk writes: "This may be the reason why some people in China are quietly discussing the possibility of Li Ruihuan challenging Hu Jintao for the position of Party general secretary." Susan L. Shirk, "Will the Institutionalization of Party Leadership Survive the 2002–2003 Succession?" *China Journal*, No. 45 (January 2002), p. 141.

the loser. If the winner is critical of Jiang, or even anti-Jiang, the rank and file, who so far have expressed their loyalty to the "Three Representatives," will surely suffer a lot. Yet, the new leader could well be someone who stands in the middle, trying to balance the two opposing forces. This is certainly in the best interest of the majority of the rank and file.

THE FATE OF BEING RANK AND FILE

In a communist party system, there is a stark contrast between the party leaders and the rank and file. The leaders or the "cadres" enjoy many privileges, whereas the rank and file have almost none. This is because communist parties adhere to the principle of elitism: the lower you are in the hierarchy, the fewer privileges you have.

One of the privileges, for instance, is the access to information that is distributed to the recipient's official rank (e.g., province–army, district–division, or county–regiment levels). Only the leading cadres have the privilege of reading certain types of internal documents and "reference materials," or listening to tape recordings of secret speeches by important national leaders. They are constantly informed about major policies and events in the country. Information like this gives them both psychological gratification and political power.

The leading cadres also enjoy material benefits that cover nearly every aspect of life: the houses they live in, schools for their children, medical service, even the restaurants they dine in, the kind of entertainment they have, and the special class of train they travel by. For these reasons, it was very difficult for Deng, in the 1980s, to carry out his program of retiring old cadres because they were quite accustomed to the privileges.

The special privileges covered even the punishment meted out to the cadres. The Party Constitution states: "Any decision to remove a member or alternate member of the Central Committee or a local committee at any level from posts within the Party, to place such person on probation within the Party or to expel him from the Party must be taken by a two-thirds majority vote at a plenary meeting of the Party committee to which he belongs. Such a disciplinary measure against a member or alternate member of a local Party committee is subject to approval by the higher Party committees" (Art. 40). This provision obviously makes it difficult to punish the cadres. First, it needs a two-thirds majority vote, and secondly, it also needs approval by the higher Party committee.

Thus, when a rectification campaign takes place, the rank and file are the first target. This is because (1) unlike cadres who have access to inside information, they do not know it in advance; (2) having no connection [*guanxi*] they are rendered powerless against an imminent campaign. The cadres might also face disciplinary measures, but they would have found ways to avoid or circumvent them. The rank and file normally have to brace themselves and accept their fate.

CONCLUSION

In this chapter, I have tried to describe the causal relationship between leadership succession and the suffering of the rank and file. On both occasions (from Mao to Deng, and from Zhao to Jiang) leadership successions were accompanied by upheaval at the rank-and-file level. As the old leader goes and the new leader comes, the rank and file also come and go, following the downfall of their leader. After Mao died, and after a period of power struggle with the Gang of Four and Hua Guofeng, Deng Xiaoping carried out a series of policies to purge the rival groups. It took almost a decade to do that: 1978–1987.

The same pattern was repeated when the issue of leadership succession was imminent as Deng Xiaoping expressed slowly his desire to retire. Zhao Ziyang and Li Peng were the two strong candidates to assume the mantle of leadership, but they belonged to two different schools of economic and political thought. The student demonstrations following the death of Hu Yaobang, a reformist himself, became the immediate factor of clash between Zhao and Li. Zhao was defeated, but Li did not get the coveted seat; Jiang

Zemin got it. After the crackdown on the student demonstrations, the Party leadership carried out a massive purge of the Party for at least one year (1989–1990).

As Party members are required to adhere to one particular ideology at the time of their entry, it is understandable that when leadership succession takes place, the new leader finds it necessary to get rid of those who support a different ideology. In communist parties, which is a devotee party, a new leader always comes out with a new ideology, because this could serve as a legitimizing instrument of his regime's program. So the struggle over leadership is, at the same time, a struggle over ideology, and accordingly a struggle to control the rank and file.

We can expect this pattern to be repeated during the coming leadership transition from Jiang Zemin to Hu Jintao (or anybody). At the moment, Jiang seems to be in full control of the Party, not giving any opening for rival ideologies. The situation, however, is a fierce, life-and-death struggle for power. As far as we know, there is no indication of such power struggle between Jiang Zemin and Hu Jintao, who is most likely to replace Jiang. Under these circumstances, its impact on the Party's rank and file may be almost nil. If a fierce struggle takes place between Hu Jintao and other candidates, then we will see an impact on the rank and file at a scale similar to that of the previous period.

Chapter 5

Central–Provincial Relations and the Fourth Generation Leadership: The Political Dimension*

KEITH FORSTER

This chapter will focus on the political dimension of central–local relations over the past decade in order to make some educated predictions about where this crucial relationship is heading when the new generation of leadership assumes the reins of power at the 16th Party Congress in 2002. In this chapter I will examine the following questions: What have been the main features of central–local relations over the past decade and more during Jiang Zemin's stewardship of the Chinese Communist Party (CCP)? How has the center been able to retain control over provincial politicians in an environment of increased economic decentralization and provincial autonomy? What new mechanisms, in addition to the traditional ones of the power of appointment, promotion, and dismissal, has Beijing added to its arsenal to discipline and keep in check the provincial leaders many of whom rule over large areas, populations, and economies? The chapter concludes by tying this review of the past decade to a prognostication of how central–provincial relations may evolve in the immediate future.

* Thanks are due to my colleague at EAI, Zheng Shiping, for kindly sharing his insights into some of the issues discussed in this chapter. Naturally, I take full responsibility for the chapter's content and argument. The term "province" is used in this chapter as shorthand for the 31 provinces, centrally administered cities, and autonomous regions that comprise the first subnational level of administration in China.

First, mainly for reasons of space and focus, I will not discuss directly the issue of the local military establishment and its role in central–local relations. Second, I will limit myself mainly to the political, organizational, and disciplinary aspects of the topic, and confine the bulk of my discussion to the two key figures at the apex of the provincial political structure— the party secretary and governor. I will omit any detailed discussion of the economic dimensions of the topic. This issue has been covered extensively over the past two decades, in particular the crucial fiscal dimension of central–local relations.[1] Third, my main points apply most directly to the majority Han people provinces of China proper and do not encompass issues of nationality, separatism, and security, related to the border regions of China occupied by Tibetans, Mongols, Uighurs, and other nationalities. And finally, I leave aside the interesting issue of the subprovincial level of Chinese politics, in particular the increasingly important role that cities of various types (deputy-provincial cities, central economic cities, open coastal cities, and special economic zones) now play in central–local relations and in inter- and intra-provincial affairs.

CHANGE AND CONTINUITY IN APPROACHES TO CENTRAL–LOCAL RELATIONS

It has been argued that central–provincial relations should not be seen as a zero-sum game where, for example, measures to increase provincial autonomy axiomatically result in a weakening of central power.[2] The tendency for such an approach to predominate is seen to emanate from the undue focus on fiscal relations as a barometer for the state of central–provincial relations, ignoring other important dimensions to what is now a complex, interactive and interdependent relationship. What was in the Maoist years largely a relationship of

---

[1] For my recently completed paper on taxation reform, see Keith Forster, "Taxation reform in China: The Proof of the Pudding...," *EAI Background Brief*, No. 106, East Asian Institute, National University of Singapore, November 2001.

[2] See, Jae Ho Chung, "Studies of Central–Provincial Relations in the People's Republic of China: A Mid-Term Appraisal," *The China Quarterly* (1995), pp. 501–503; Linda

compliance and dependence has, since the launching of economic reform in the late 1970s, become a more complicated and sophisticated relationship involving bargaining, compromise, cooperation, and mutual dependence. However, these changes do not, in my opinion, change the essential and fundamental nature of central–provincial relations as one between a superior and subordinate where, in a unitary state that makes no constitutional provision for the separate and distinct powers of subnational administrations, the center, in many ways, represents and personifies the state.

When we talk about the relationship between center and periphery in China, we are not referring to the degrees of autonomy and decision-making powers that pertain to subnational administrations in a federal political system. Rather, we are analyzing "how to differentiate the nature of variation in provincial compliance according to policy type."[3] Jae Ho Chung has tabulated an ideal situation whereby the degree of local discretion is viewed in terms of the scope, type, and nature of the policy concerned. He asserts that the scope of policy may be either encompassing or selective, that the type of policy may be seen functionally as allocative or nonallocative, and that the nature of the policy may be viewed as radical or routinized in terms of how much it departs from the status quo. While Chung acknowledges that "a majority of policies fall somewhere between these two extremes," and that the combination of selective, allocative, and radical policy which normally, in his view, results in a high level of local discretion, neither invariably occurs in tandem nor results in such an outcome.[4]

Although a useful heuristic device, the correlation of this typology with reality does not appear very strong, and even the basis of the distinctions could be questioned. For example, while allocative

Chelan Li, "Central–Provincial Relations: Beyond Compliance Analysis," *China Review* 1998 (Hong Kong: Chinese University of Hong Kong Press, 1998), pp. 159–164.

[3] Chung, "Studies of Central–Provincial Relations," p. 504.

[4] *Ibid.*, pp. 504–506. If exceptions outweigh the rule, the value of such distinctions is clearly devalued.

policies may be dictated by an economic rationale, and nonallocative policies by political values, as argued by Chung, the pressures for provincial compliance may have more to do with the overall importance of the policy concerned to the center than with the category of policies into which they slot. While there may have been a lengthy process of bargaining between the center and provinces over the introduction of the 1994 taxation reform (a policy characterized by Chung as allocative but encompassing), once the center made up its mind to go ahead, provincial objections were largely brushed aside. And while the streamlining and restructuring of provincial administrations in 1999 was carried out under central supervision and direction (a policy that fits Chung's categorization as both nonallocative and selective), it appears that certain supposedly important goals were not met, or were met more in outward appearances than in reality.

Whatever the inadequacies of Chung's policy compliance variation model in post-Mao China, his analysis alerts us to some important changes that have occurred in central–provincial relations over the past 20 years. However, there are also important continuities in central–provincial relations from the Maoist era. It remains largely true, as Frederick Teiwes argued 30 years ago in a detailed paper on provincial politics during the pre-Cultural Revolution period, that the provincial politician "is the spokesman and the representative of provincial interests before the central authorities, and at the same time he is the arm of those authorities in dealing with the people and the functionaries of his province."[5] The provincial politician continues to be the classic "middleman" of the political system.[6] However, the contemporary provincial leader suffers less than his

---

[5] Frederick C. Teiwes, "Provincial Politics in China: Themes and Variations," in John M.H. Lindbeck (ed.), *China: Management of a Revolutionary Society* (Seattle: University of Washington Press, 1971), pp. 129–130. See also David S.G. Goodman, "The Provincial First Party Secretary in the People's Republic of China, 1949–1978: A Profile," *British Journal of Political Science*, Vol. 10 (1980), pp. 39–74.

[6] Sexist language is hardly avoidable given the staggering extent of the underrepresentation of women in leading provincial posts since 1949.

Maoist predecessors from being forced to carry out an unending series of political campaigns that directly damage the national economy and injure the interests and standard of living of the people over whom he rules. The contradiction that Teiwes pointed out as applying to a provincial politician, whereby "While success in provincial politics demands responsiveness to the visions and goals of the center, it also requires respect for the concrete realities of the local scene"[7] is not as acute today, when the interests of the center and province in developing the economy and raising the people's standard of living coincide much more closely than they did in the past.

Teiwes' argument that "there is evidence that outstanding displays of political activism do not in the long run benefit the career of provincial leaders and in fact may be detrimental", and "a more appropriate strategy for political survival is a steady and lasting performance"[8] certainly ring true today. Nevertheless, the pressures on provincial leaders to provide the conditions and environment for rapid economic growth and to meet centrally imposed growth targets are now considerable. All politicians, whether in the center or province, are today judged largely by the performance of the economy, and the basis of legitimacy for the continued rule of the CCP rests largely on this single variable.

BACKGROUND

In recent years, it has been clear that the central authorities, under the leadership of Jiang Zemin and with the forceful backing of strong centralists such as Premier Zhu Rongji, have been to a large extent successful in obtaining the full (if not always enthusiastic) support of provincial leaders for issues of central concern to Beijing. When Jiang Zemin gave a speech about the "Three Representatives," the propaganda apparatus of the CCP moved into top gear across the

---

[7] Teiwes, "Provincial Politics in China," pp. 173–174.
[8] *Ibidem.*

country to ensure that the localities studied and tried to apply the lessons of the speech to their own realities. The same process has occurred since Jiang's July 1, 2001 speech on the 80th anniversary of the CCP, where he indirectly proposed that the Party admit members from sectors of society (such as the burgeoning private entrepreneurial class) that had never been targeted for recruitment (see other chapters in this volume). While ideology as a legitimating and cohesive force has lost much of its impact since the death of Mao Zedong, it would be foolish to ignore completely its continuing presence and influence as a tool of integration and power. Mao Zedong Thought, as the expression of modern Chinese nationalism, always contained a strong anti-imperialist flavor that, gutted of its revolutionary and subversive content, could be adapted to the contemporary demands of patriotism and xenophobia. While various provinces and interest groups have expressed doubt and fear over China's application to join the World Trade Organization (WTO), the central government, while trying to allay these concerns, has not let their apprehensions prevent the country's entry into the organization.

It appears that as Jiang Zemin consolidated his power into the 1990s, and with the appointment of Zhu Rongji as Premier in early 1998, earlier fears, that the devolution of economic power in China could possibly lead to the breakup of the country under a leader who did not possess the undisputed authority enjoyed by his predecessors Mao and Deng, have not only proven unfounded but a recentralization of authority has occurred over the past few years. In a recent article, the veteran China watcher, Willy Lam, cited unnamed colleagues in the field as arguing that "the tradition of strong, independently minded provincial cadres pretty much ended with the late 1980s."[9] The evidence suggests that this assertion contains a great deal of truth. If so, it is necessary to explain why such a change has occurred, given that Jiang Zemin's prestige and

---

[9] Willy Wo-lap Lam, "Beijing: Taming the Regional 'Warlords'," CNN, July 17, 2001, at http://asia.cnn.com/2001/WORLD/asiapcf/east/07/17/china.willy.column/index.html.

stature as the "core" of the central leadership are of an entirely different nature from those of the core leader of the 1980s, Deng Xiaoping.

During the Maoist period (1949–1976), there was very little evidence of recalcitrance or localism among provincial or subprovincial officials. In the Anti-Rightist Struggle of 1957, some provincial officials were accused of such deviations, but the evidence was either nonexistent or was manufactured. Rather, these officials were purged mainly as the result of factional tensions within local leaderships, with the winning side (often with the open support of the supreme leader) using such charges to provide ideological justification for the removal of their political opponents from power.[10] The Cultural Revolution provided the opportunity for different social strata and groups to take advantage of the chaos and temporary breakdown in the authority of the state to pursue all kinds of localist grievances, vendettas, and ambitions. Evidence from the county level of administration suggests that there was a marked increase in the number of native cadres (many of them rebels and Red Guards) in the new local organizations of power. However, the reconstituted Party state quickly reined in and quashed all activities that threatened central power and authority, and by the time Mao Zedong died in 1976, the unitary power of the Chinese state remained fundamentally intact.

During the reform period since 1979, scholars and observers have regularly sounded the alarm about the centralized Chinese state coming under threat from various localist and splittist tendencies. However, despite the major devolution of economic power over the past 20 years and manifestations of internal market protectionism

---

[10] See Frederick C. Teiwes, "The Purge of Provincial Leaders 1957–1958," *The China Quarterly*, Vol. 27 (July–September 1966), pp. 14–32; Keith Forster, "Localism, Central Policy and the Provincial Purges of 1957–1958: The Case of Zhejiang," in Tim Cheek and Tony Saich (eds.), *New Perspectives on State Socialism in China* (New York: M.E. Sharpe, Inc., 1997), pp. 191–233; idem (ed.), "The Purge and Rehabilitation of Sha Wenhan, Governor of Zhejiang," *Chinese Law and Government*, Vol. 31, No. 4 (July–August 1998).

and disputes between various local authorities, reports of the death of China have been, as one scholar has rightly indicated, highly exaggerated.[11] After Jiang Zemin's elevation to the central leadership of the CCP in 1989 following the tragic events in June, his position was initially bolstered by the continuing presence and influence of the master politician Deng Xiaoping. Deng lived long enough to oversee and assist Jiang consolidate his power within the party, and while Jiang may have had his differences with the present Premier Zhu Rongji over the timing and scope of certain policies, Zhu has acted assertively to assist Jiang in consolidating his authority by introducing new measures to bolster and reinforce Beijing's will over the whole country.[12]

Of course the major source of control over the localities that Beijing has possessed since the establishment of the People's Republic of China (PRC) has been its power over the appointment, promotion, and dismissal of all provincial-level leaders. In the 1950s and early 1960s, provinces in south China, which were "liberated" only after troops of the People's Liberation Army (PLA) marched into Beijing in early 1949, were ruled by outside cadres sent in alongside the PLA troops in the later stages of the civil war. Regional party bureaus ensured that Beijing's authority was firmly consolidated in the provinces. During the Cultural Revolution, military control was asserted over many regions, with PLA forces acting in place of paralyzed Party and civilian state authorities. In the early reform period, the stipulation that local officials could not serve in their place of birth was to a great degree relaxed in order to stimulate local economic development. It was recognized that native cadres were more in touch with local problems and with the desires and aspirations of local populations. At the beginning of the 1990s, it

[11] John Fitzgerald, "'Reports of My Death have been Greatly Exaggerated': The History of the Death of China," in David S.G. Goodman and Gerald Segal (eds.), *China Deconstructs: Politics, Trade and Regionalism* (London and NY: Routledge, 1994), pp. 21–58.

[12] Willy Wo-Lap Lam, "Vice-Premier Lashes out at Regionalism," *SCMP*, January 14, 1998.

was alleged that 73% of the current provincial leaders had devoted their entire careers in the provinces where they were serving. The transfer of Wang Zhaoguo from the center to Fujian in 1988 as provincial governor was considered sufficiently unusual to be commented upon.[13]

CENTRAL–PROVINCIAL RELATIONS UNDER JIANG ZEMIN

In the 12 years since Jiang Zemin has held the post of general secretary of the CCP, there has been a regular rotation of provincial leaders. The numbers vary from province to province. Xinjiang and Zhejiang have each been ruled by two party secretaries during this period, while at the other extreme Hainan and Henan have had five. The number of provincial governors has varied from two (Ningxia) to five (Fujian, Gansu, Liaoning and Qinghai).[14] There appears to be no clear correlation between the degree of economic development and the stability of provincial leadership. One scholar, who also objects to the analysis of central–provincial relations in terms of a zero-sum game, believes that the term "compliance" is inadequate to characterize the important area of personnel appointment. She argues that the "frequent reshuffles of provincial leaders could be a reflection of central weakness rather than strength."[15]

Such an argument assumes, first, that under Jiang Zemin's leadership provincial leaders have been changed frequently, and second that the major reason for the rotations is the center's

[13] Xiaowei Zang, "Provincial Elite in Post-Mao China," *Asian Survey*, Vol. XXXI, No. 6 (June 1991), p. 524.

[14] This information is derived from a table that the author has revised and updated from one kindly supplied by Zheng Shiping. By late November 2001, the leadership of 14 provinces had been reshuffled during the year, with the remaining provinces due to go through this process before the 16th Party Congress. See Josephine Ma, "Obey Party Directives, Reshuffled Cadres Told," *SCMP*, November 20, 2001, at http://china.scmp.com/ZZZHE8U81UC.html.

[15] Li, "Central–Provincial Relations," p. 161.

dissatisfaction with the leader's willingness or capacity to carry out central policies. While the first assumption may be correct (although a statistical analysis would be required to compare the turnover of provincial leaders with that under Mao Zedong and Deng Xiaoping), it appears that there are very few instances of provincial leaders having been replaced for the reason Linda Li suggests.

The two outstanding examples of Jiang Zemin removing entrenched provincial leaders, because he allegedly considered them as threats to either his own power or the authority of the center, concern Chen Xitong in Beijing and Xie Fei in Guangdong. Both served concurrently as members of the Politburo and were, therefore, leaders with stature at the central level. In the first case, Jiang's ability to remove Chen Xitong from his posts was greatly facilitated by Chen's personal involvement in corruption on a massive scale.[16] Charges of corruption have always been targeted politically and have served this purpose first and foremost.[17]

The case of Xie Fei and Guangdong goes to the heart of the issue of whether a province can win a test of strength with the center over personnel.[18] If any province has been seen to assert a degree of independence, it has been this economic powerhouse of south China. In early 1998 an article argued that "Guangdong officials seem to take a separatist approach by opposing outsiders to head their provincial government," and that "such examples suggest that regional

[16] Vivien Pik-Kwan Chan, "Party Poised to Kick Out Shamed Boss," SCMP, May 1, 1997; Renmin ribao, September 10, 1997; Agence France-Presse, "The 15th Party Congress: Disgraced Beijing Boss in Detention," SCMP, September 11, 1997.

[17] See Keith Forster, "The 1982 Campaign against Economic Crime in China," Australian Journal of Chinese Affairs, Vol. 14 (July 1985), pp. 1–19.

[18] That provinces or subprovincial administrations can find ways either to avoid policy restrictions on economic development or to advance ahead of the mainstream has long been the case in reformed China. See the comments of the Shenzhen Party secretary at the 15th Party Congress in 1997 where he stated, after listening to Jiang Zemin's political report: "Previously, Shenzhen has experimented with some ideas but we dared not to make them public." "Now the Party Secretary has spoken, we can do them openly." Daniel Kwan, "The 15th Party Congress Report 'Lifts Ideological Shackle' from Province," SCMP, September 15, 1997.

representation increasingly has become a crucial issue in Chinese elite recruitment".[19] It was also asserted at the time of the 15th National Party Congress in 1997 that Guangdong was resisting any suggestion that an outsider be appointed to replace the incumbent Party secretary, Xie Fei, who had reached retirement age.[20] While Xie Fei retained his seat on the Politburo at the Party Congress, early the following year the center appointed the secretary of the Henan provincial committee, Li Changchun, to head the Party administration in Guangdong, after first promoting him to the Politburo at the same Party Congress.[21] Guangdong was forced to accept the appointment as an unpalatable manifestation of the predominance of the center's will, and Li has proved to be a staunch supporter of the general secretary and his "theory" of the "Three Representatives."[22]

Of course it is sometimes difficult to judge whether provincial leaders have been transferred for perceived or actual disobedience to central dictates or in line with the center's policy of circulating elites.[23] In early 1999, Jiang Zemin is alleged to have reiterated the principle of the "five lakes and four seas" to justify the appointment of cadres from different geographical and "factional" backgrounds to

---

[19] Li Cheng and Lynn White, "The Fifteenth Central Committee of the Chinese Communist Party: Full-Fledged Technocratic Leadership with Partial Control by Jiang Zemin" *Asian Survey*, Vol. XXXVIII, No. 3 (March 1998), p. 247.

[20] Willy Wo-Lap Lam, "Guangdong Fights to Keep Politburo Seat," *SCMP* August 28, 1997.

[21] Vivien Pik-Kwan Chan, "1st Plenum of the 15th Central Committee Politburo Promotions Reflect Regional Power," *SCMP*, September 20 1997.

[22] Willy Wo-Lap Lam, "Guangdong crusade for 'Jiang Thought'," *SCMP*, April 12, 2000, in http://www.scmp.com/News/China/Article/FullText_asp_ArticleID-20000412031724294.asp. Recent reports suggest that because of a series of corruption scandals in Guangdong, as well as the provinces of Liaoning and Henan where he previously served, Li's ambition for higher office may well have been thwarted. See Susan V. Lawrence, "Primed for power," *FEER*, February 22, 2001, at http://www.feer.com/_0102_22/p016region.html; Will Wo-Lap Lam, "China's New Star in the Making," *CNN*, April 26, 2001, at http://asia.cnn.com/2001/WORLD/asiapcf/east/04/24/china.willycolumn/index.html.

[23] It is alleged that the 1993 removal of Jiangsu party secretary, Shen Daren, related to his opposition to the imminent tax-sharing reform. See Chung, "Central–Provincial Relations," p. 503, n. 38.

leading positions in the central and provincial apparatus.[24] Li Cheng has argued that the regular reshuffling of both provincial and military leaders will ensure that no region can dominate in the fourth generation leadership."[25] Not only does the center dislike senior provincial officials remaining in one locality for too long because they make take advantage of the longevity of tenure to build up a factional clique, but, relatedly, the longer they stay the greater the possibility that they will become entrapped in the web of business relations that intersect with political power.[26]

A 1998 study showed that provincial party secretaries are likely to stay in their posts longer than provincial governors. Seventeen of the provincial party secretaries in mid-1998 had previously served as governor, 13 in the same province and four in other provinces. Seven provincial party secretaries were serving in the province where they were born, compared to 14 governors. In three provinces both leading officials were natives of the locality in which they were working. Seven party secretaries and 15 governors had spent their whole career locally. "Strong local connections [were] therefore the case for half of the top provincial leadership."[27] This suggests that the Jiang Zemin leadership does not overly fear the threat of localism and that the modern version of the Chinese feudal law of avoidance is applied selectively. Loyalty (and ability), rather than place of birth, has always been the principal criterion for selecting provincial leaders in modern China.

---

[24] Willy Wo-Lap Lam, "Jiang Rotates Cadres to Curtail Fiefdoms," SCMP, February 3, 1999.

[25] Li Cheng, "Mystery Behind the Myths," South China Morning Post, June 11, 2001, http://china.scmp.com/lifestyle/ZZZXXELDPNC.html.

[26] The case of the North-eastern "rust-belt" city of Shenyang is instructive. The center appointed a dynamic city Party secretary to shake the city out of its economic lethargy it had sunk into with the unraveling of the planned economy. However, this official used his power to build a political and economic network of corruption by linking the Party state with local criminal gangs. See Japser Becker, "Struggle Rages to Tame Rogue Province," SCMP, November 19, 2001, at http://china.scmp.com/today/ZZZUE5U81UC.html, and http://china.scmp.com/today/ZZZUE5U81UC_p2.html.

[27] China News Analysis, No. 1613-14, July 1–15, 1998, pp. 14–15.

The whole issue of factional alignments between central and provincial leaders is an issue fraught with guesswork and one that often leads to idle and unproductive speculation. The promotion of provincial leaders to the Politburo, for example, depends on the locality. Beijing and Shanghai are the most important cities in China, and their leaders have to be of stature to deserve a seat on the Politburo. Guangdong's economic might (in particular its preeminent role in China's foreign trade) virtually assures its party secretary a seat, while Shandong's revolutionary past, the size of its population, and its now increasing weight in the national economy mean that its party secretary has a good chance of joining the powerful central body as well. The presence of other provincial party secretaries on this body may well illustrate the power of the provinces in today's reform China, but it does not mean as a consequence that the provinces have gained more political power at the expense of Beijing. It is the center that appoints the local officials who gain the opportunity thereby to hold a seat on the Poliltburo. During the early 1970s, Mao Zedong appointed regional military leaders to this august body, and during the reform period, just as the party secretaries of key cities in a province become ipso facto members of the provincial party committee's standing committee, so do provincial leaders of key areas become Politburo members.

Sometimes the central authorities are forced to transfer provincial leaders for reasons that relate essentially to provincial politics and to the personalities of the individuals concerned. The Chinese political system has been unable to deal successfully with a problem that dates back to the 1950s of the relationship and division of responsibilities between the provincial party secretary and provincial governor (who always holds the second-most senior party post as deputy secretary of the provincial committee). In fact, with provincial leaders now judged by economic performance even more than they were in the past, and with provincial governors supposedly in charge of economic policy, the role that the party secretary cuts out for himself depends to a great extent on his personal background, abilities, and interests. The possibility of both incumbents vying to take credit for economic success and shifting the blame for policy failures is even greater than in the past. Personal chemistry and ambition may determine how well a provincial party secretary and governor get along and share work responsibilities. It appears that in Hainan province this relationship failed in 1993, necessitating the simultaneous transfer of both incumbents out of the province and their replacement by a successor who took on the posts of both party secretary and governor (1993–1998).

At present about one-third of provincial party secretaries double as chairmen of the provincial People's Congress. The implications of this situation for the relationship between the provincial party secretary and governor are difficult to gauge, but it does suggest an augmentation of the role and status of the Party secretary. The additional post also allows him to play an active and open role in the legislative process and perhaps act as a check on the authority and activities of the provincial government. In another three provinces the immediately preceding party secretary, who in all cases had served in the position for between six and nine years, has stayed on as People's Congress chair. This suggests that the post has also become somewhat of a sinecure for retiring provincial leaders who have passed the age limit for tenure in one of the two substantive provincial posts but remain sufficiently active and influential to continue in office. Whether the continued presence of his predecessor undermines in any way the power and status of the incumbent provincial party secretary is also difficult to judge and undoubtedly varies according to local conditions.

For the sake of their careers, all provincial leaders have no choice but to demonstrate loyalty to their patrons in Beijing and unswerving adherence to matters of principle and top policy priority. The secretary of the Zhejiang provincial committee, Zhang Dejiang, has been touted as a rising star among provincial politicians.[28] In 2000, Zhang published an article on Party building in which he argued strongly that there was no place for private entrepreneurs in the

---

[28] Willy Lam, "Beijing: Taming the Regional 'Warlords'."

ranks of the CCP.[29] Since Jiang Zemin's July 2001 speech, Zhang Dejiang has been forced to beat a hasty retreat, and he has been at the forefront among provincial leaders in promoting the wisdom and foresight of his leader's words.[30]

COMPLIANCE MEASURES

Jiang Zemin's predecessor as party general secretary, the hapless Zhao Ziyang, warned at the third plenum of the 13th CCP Central Committee in September 1988 that "if there are instances of violations of the central government's unified guidance on allocation (of resources), the provincial Party secretary and the provincial governor will be held responsible."[31] Whether Zhao had the power and authority to make good on such a threat will remain a matter for speculation. However, over the past few years, provincial and subprovincial leaders have been held responsible for meeting targets for an increasing number of social and economic indices, as well as having their jobs put on the line for the occurrence of major disasters involving the death of citizens living in their jurisdiction, the outbreak of social disturbances, and for their own personal involvement in corruption. Given the continuing highly personalized nature of China's political system, however, the punishment for failure to meet targets and for policy and personal failures is often imposed inconsistently. Whether punishment is enforced and the degree of its severity often depend more on personal and factional ties between provincial and central leaders than on the implementation of a set of standard, formal norms and regulations.

Since Zhu Rongji's ascendancy to the Premiership in 1998, annual projected figures for economic growth have been issued at the

---

[29] See the excerpt from Zhang's article in *Zhenlide zhuiqiu* [The Pursuit of Truth], No. 5 (2001), p. 28.

[30] This assertion is based on a regular reading of *Zhejiang ribao*. Of course Zhang had no alternative except reversing his position as quickly and completely as possible.

[31] Zang, "Provincial Elite," p. 525.

beginning of each year at sessions of the National People's Congress. The political pressures on provincial leaders to meet them are great. It appears that such targets are turned into executive orders and issued to provincial and subprovincial administrations for implementation, leading to reported numbers that may have little relation to reality.[32] In addition, the central authorities, under the continued policy of provincial grain self-sufficiency, set annual targets for the area sown to grain and grain output. In the developed coastal province of Zhejiang, the provincial leadership made extraordinary efforts to demonstrate that it takes this policy seriously. By the mid-1990s continuous falls in grain area and output occurred in Zhejiang. Beginning in 1995, the provincial leadership launched a full-scale propaganda offensive to alert officials to this alarming decline in grain production.[33] It backed this up by issuing a set of detailed targets for subprovincial jurisdictions.

In May 1995, the Zhejiang authorities issued a circular to hold local officials responsible for specified grain targets.[34] In November of the same year, the provincial government issued a circular that contained tables for grain area, output, procurements, and transfers for the following year.[35] Similar detailed targets have been published

---

[32] See Willy Wo-Lap Lam, "Disobedient Cadres Face Jiang's wrath," and "Provincial Cadres Back Zhu Drive," *SCMP*, December 30, 1998, January 8, 1999; "Senior Statisticians Criticize Provinces Exaggerated 98 Growth Rate," *CND*, Global News, No. GL99-021, February 17, 1999; Thomas Rawski, "China's GDP Statistics—A Case of Caveat Lector?," p. 2, from http://www.pitt.edu/~tgrawski/papers2001/caveat.web.pdf.

[33] See *Zhejiang ribao*, January 8, 10, 11, 24; March 4, 21, 23, 25, 30; April 3, 5, 8, 10, 11, 1995.

[34] "Zhonggong Zhejiang shengwei bangongting, Zhejiang sheng renmin zhengfu bangongting guanyu yinfa 'Zhejiang sheng liangshi gongzuo fenji fuzeren zhi kaohe banfa (shixing)' de tongzhi" [Circular of the Offices of the CCP Zhejiang Provincial Committee and Zhejiang People's Government Concerning Printing and Distributing "Trial Assessment Methods for a Division of Responsibility System in Zhejiang's Grain Work"], May 24, 1995, *Zhejiang zhengbao* [Zhejiang Government Gazette], No. 18 (1995), pp. 20–23.

[35] "Zhejiang sheng renmin zhengfu guanyu 1996nian liangshi chanxiao jihuade tongzhi" [Circular of the Zhejiang Provincial People's Government Concerning the Plan for Grain Production and Sales in 1996], November 14, 1995, *Zhejiang zhengbao*, No. 36 (1995), pp. 9–13.

since.[36] However, since the beginning of this offensive in 1995, the key indices of grain output, the value of grain production, and the area sown to grain have continued to fall in Zhejiang. Between 1995 and 2000, the area sown to grain in the province had fallen from 2.8 to 2.3 million hectares, output from 14.3 to 12.2 million tonnes, and the gross value of grain output from RMB23 billion to RMB16 billion.[37] It appears that Zhejiang has neither sought nor obtained exemption from this central policy on the grounds that it is both counterproductive and fundamentally at odds with the overall direction of provincial economic development.

Apart from being expected to meet other centrally dictated targets such as those for population growth and urbanization rates, provincial leaders have now become subject to an unspecified set of accountability criteria. It has been widely reported that since 2000 the central authorities have instituted a policy of holding senior provincial cadres accountable for major disasters or crimes that occur in their jurisdiction.[38] As one reporter commented, "The fact that errant Chinese officials can now be held accountable is no small progress in the People's Republic. But that is no consolation for the hundreds of disaster victims and their families." Xinhua reported that in the first six months of 2001, accidents at mines, factories, and public places killed 47,000 people.[39] In 1999, about 40 children died daily from "poisoned food, drowning, traffic accidents, and school building collapses."[40]

---

[36] See *Zhejiang zhengbao*, No. 12 (1997), pp. 19–22; No. 13 (1998), pp. 19–25; No. 8 (2000), pp. 21–24.

[37] *Zhejiang tongji nianjian*, 1996, p. 203; 2001, p. 216, pp. 234–235.

[38] It has also been reported that the northeast city of Changchun has introduced a policy assigning administrative and criminal responsibility to leaders of enterprises and state utilities in accidents under their jurisdiction where the death toll exceeds two. See *Hangzhou ribao*, October 25, 2001, at http://www.hzrb.com.cn/20010825/ca39186.htm.

[39] Jaime Florcruz, "Deadliest Mines Shame China," *CNN*, August 1, 2000, at http://asia.cnn.com/2001/WORLD/asiapcf/east/08/01/china.mines.florcruz/index.html.

[40] The figure comes from Xinhua news agency, an official Chinese source. See Julia Han, "Accidental Deaths of Children under Official Scrutiny," *SCMP*, March 28, 2001, at http://china.scmp.com/today/ZZZJM4PZRKC.html.

While the existence of such a policy of accountability is unprecedented, it is clear that it has been implemented arbitrarily and haphazardly. For example, the governor of Henan continues to hold his post despite the outbreak in 2000 of two major fires that killed at least 400 people in city buildings.[41] Nevertheless, while the city authorities in Luoyang, the site of the conflagration that engulfed a discotheque, may have contributed to the disaster by their oversight of building fire regulations, and treated the relatives of the dead with great cruelty, in a new twist for Chinese public officials they were forced to face the consequences of the tragedy before the local population. It was reported that the mayor of Luoyang appeared on local television to "deliver an emotionally charged speech apologizing for 'oversights and errors' in response to the fire, vowing the city 'could not evade responsibility' for the tragedy. 'We are working very hard and feel very guilty these days,' the mayor said." Such a phenomenon is a striking new development in Chinese politics and shows that Chinese leaders have to take into account public perceptions of their behavior and responses to such tragedies, even if their reaction is dictated more by the need to appease public anger than to accept any responsibility for the disaster.

Nor were the Hebei authorities called to account for the March 2001 explosion that killed over 100 people in the provincial capital of Shijiazhuang.[42] The center may have calculated that, as both the provincial party secretary and governor were relative newcomers to their jobs, they could afford to be lenient. Such an excuse cannot be used by the well-established Shanghai leadership for the wharf accident in

---

[41] Matthew Miller, "Grief Turns to Anger," SCMP, January 5, 2001, at http://china.scmp.com/today/ZZZMX8AVPGC.html; http://china.scmp.com/today/ZZZMX8AVPGC_p2.html.

[42] Josephine Ma and Agencies, "Payouts for Families 'a Tricky Task': Blast Compensation Delayed," SCMP, March 20, 2001, http://china.scmp.com/ZZZ81KNJDKC.html. However, it is reported that the city Party secretary and mayor have been removed from their posts. See Vivien Pik-Kwan Chan, "City Party Chief Steps Down amid Explosion Fallout," SCMP, June 20, 2001, at http://china.scmp.com/today/ZZZTZ1VL5OC.html.

July 2001 that killed over 40 engineers and workers.[43] In this case, political and personal connections to Jiang Zemin and Zhu Rongji would certainly have saved the local officials from any political embarrassment.

When at least 70 miners died in an accident at the privately operated Nandan coal mine in Guangxi in July 2001, the county Party secretary and magistrate were dismissed for their responsibility for the disaster as well as being part of the subsequent coverup, and harassment of investigating journalists. However, their provincial superiors seem to have been spared.[44] Virtually all of the above disasters were initially covered up or their severity downplayed.

One provincial official who may count himself unlucky for being held accountable for accidents of a similar gravity and magnitude is the present governor of Shaanxi, Cheng Andong. In April 2001, he was punished with an administrative demerit as the result of a series of coal-mining accidents that have plagued the province. Additionally, he was held accountable for a stampede among pilgrims to a Daoist temple on Mt. Hua, which led to the death of nearly 20 people. *Xinhua* reported that Cheng was told to learn a lesson from the accidents and hand in an in-depth self-criticism report.[45] According to media reports, Cheng broke down in tears when he made his "self-criticism" before an audience of provincial cadres.[46]

---

[43] "Disasters' Haunt China's Image," *CNN*, July 20, 2001, http://cnn.worldnews.printthis.clickability.com/pt/printThis?clickMap=printThis&fb=Y&url=http%3A//asia.cnn.com/2001/WORLD/asiapcf/east/07/17/china.accidents/index.html&title=CNN.com%20-%20Disasters%20haunt%20China%27s%20image%20-%20July%2017%2C%202001&random=0.13474203873460194&partnerID=2006&expire=-1.

[44] See *China News Digest* (*CND*), August 5, 2001 in http://www.cnd.org/Global/01/08/05/010805-4.html; "China Arrests Mine Boss for Cover-up," *CNN*, August 4, 2001, in http://asia.cnn.com/2001/WORLD/asiapcf/east/08/04/china.mines/index.html. At the October 2001 CCP Congress of the Guangxi Autonomous Region both the Party secretary and governor were reconfirmed in their key Party posts. See *Renmin ribao*, October 26, 2001, at http://www.snweb.com/gb/people_daily/2001/10/26/a1026013.htm.

[45] Clara Li, "Governor Disciplined over Tragic Accidents," *SCMP*, May 18, 2001, http://china.scmp.com/today/ZZZT375UTMC.html.

[46] Daniel Kwan, "Governor could become Political Casualty," *SCMP*, July 18, 2001, http://china.scmp.com/today/ZZZIROXN4PC.html.

But he also defended his administration's record, stating that "we cannot say one's administrative ability is not good because of one fault."[47] Less than two months later, another disaster hit the province when an explosion destroyed a house where illegal explosives were stored, killing scores of people.[48] Cheng continues to hold his post, and has done so for nearly seven years, despite Shaanxi becoming somewhat of a disaster zone.

Perhaps one of the most atrocious and heart-rending tragedies that occurred in China in 2001 took place in a rural school in Jiangxi province. Children had been ordered to make fireworks to raise money for the school. An explosion in March 2001 killed over 40 students and teachers and ultimately led to the removal of the provincial Party secretary and the governor. Initially, Zhu Rongji castigated foreign reports of the disaster and accused them of trying to cast a slur on China, and without any investigation into the matter, denied that the children were engaging in such a dangerous occupation.[49] Shortly afterwards, a fire at a kindergarten in the provincial capital, Nanchang, which killed over 10 children, led to the replacement of the city Party secretary and mayor.[50] Thus, in the space of several months, the two principal leaders of the province and its capital city had been dismissed as a result of major disasters.

[47] Josephine Ma, "Shaanxi Governor Defends Track Record after String of Accidents," SCMP, May 22, 2001, http://china.scmp.com/today/ZZZEQ85UTMC.html.

[48] The Baltimore Sun, March 15, 2001; Reuters, "Zhu Apologises over School Blast," SCMP, March 16, 2001, at http://china.scmp.com/today/ZZZYIMCYBKC.html; Staff Reporter, "Zhu Promise to Widen Blast Probe Welcomed: Villagers Believe Premier but Sceptical about Local Officials," SCMP, March 17, 2001, at http://china.scmp.com/ZZZ0NZNJDKC.html; Fong Tak-Ho, "Top Two Ousted after Deadly Pre-School Fire," SCMP, June 19, 2001, at http://china.scmp.com/ZZZMJAWIWNC.html; "Disasters' Haunt China's Image."

[49] Tom Mitchell, "Scapegoat or Murderer?," SCMP, March 15, 2001, at http://china.scmp.com/lifestyle/ZZZGNP165KC.html; http://china.scmp.com/lifestyle/ZZZGNP165KC_p2.html.

[50] "Zhonggong zhongyang jueding Meng Jianzhu ren Jiangxi shengwei shuji" [The CCP CC Decides to Appoint Meng Jianzhu Secretary of the CCP Jiangxi Provincial Committee]," Sina.com.cn, April 1, 2001, http://dailynews.sina.com.cn/c/220751.html; "Top Two Ousted after Deadly Pre-School Fire."

CORRUPTION

It is clear from the above examples that the strength of political connections between provincial and central leaders can protect the former from the latter's policy of accountability. Likewise, considerations concerning the political dimensions of corruption far outweigh the nature and gravity of the crime per se. The incidence and the scale of corruption have undoubtedly expanded greatly in the brave new world of China's market economy. With systemic and endemic corruption at all levels of the administrative hierarchy and in all areas of social, economic, and political exchange, national leaders lack the institutional capacity and legal means, even if they possess the political will, to root it out. Punishing provincial leaders for involvement in corrupt practices is a difficult and politically sensitive exercise that impinges not only on political matters but also on issues of social status, economic well-being, family ties, and respectability.

That is why the September 2000 execution of the former administrative head of the Guangxi Autonomous Region, Cheng Kejie, for corruption has become somewhat of a cause celebre.[51] The massive Yuan Hua smuggling and corruption case in Xiamen from 1994 to 1999 allegedly involved senior officials in Beijing, perhaps including relatives of the city's present Party secretary, Jia Qinglin.[52]

---

[51] *Xinhua*, September 15, 2000, http://www.snweb.com/gb/people_daily/2000/09/15/ b0915003.htm.

[52] "Sex, Lies and Videotapes as Scandal Threatens Party," *Irish Times*, January 25, 2000; Mark O'Neill, "Lure of the Red Chamber" and "The Wrath of Zhu Rongji," *SCMP*, December 1, 2, 2000, http://www.scmp.com/news/Comment/Article/ FullTextaspArticleID-20001130222441621.asp; http://www.scmp.com/news/Comment/ Article/FullTextaspArticleID-20001201224321014.asp; Susan V. Lawrence, "A City Ruled by Crime," *FEER*, November 30, 2000, in http://www.feer.com/_0011_30/p014.html; Bruce Gilley, "Hooked on Dirty Money," *FEER*, May 31, 2001, in http://www.feer.com/ _0105_31/p028region.html. Similar cases of smuggling, corruption, major accidents, incompetence, and maladministration on a smaller scale have involved the subprovincial administrations of Shantou and Dongguan in Guangdong province. See Tom Mitchell, "Party Axes Top Cadre in Scandal City," *SCMP*, March 26, 2001, in http://

Most recently, the Governor of Yunnan was summoned to Beijing to answer charges of graft and abuse of power. He has been expelled from the CCP and handed over to judicial authorities for criminal investigation.[53] Provincial leaders are probably no more prone to involvement in corrupt practices than leaders on any other echelon of the administrative hierarchy. However, the combination of local economic autonomy and weak legal enforcement in the mixed market economy certainly poses problems in asserting central authority over entrenched and symbiotic political and economic elites in China's provinces.

WHAT LIES AHEAD?

What does the above brief examination of the political dimensions of central–local relations under Jiang Zemin alert us to in terms of how these relations will evolve under the fourth generation central leadership? First, Jiang Zemin's putative successor, Hu Jintao, will come to the job with impressive credentials about his length and depth of service in both locality and center, credentials that to a large degree outweigh those of his predecessor. This will provide him with a basis for the kind of authority and esteem that central leaders require in the Chinese political system. On the other hand, the offstage presence of Jiang Zemin as a would-be advisor may be more of a liability than an asset to Hu, unlike the benefits that Deng Xiaoping's initial guiding hand lent to Jiang in his early years in Beijing. Second, it is clear that the devolution of economic power that has accompanied the reform program will not be reversed, and

china.scmp.com/ZZZZVMLSNKC.html; Fong Tak-Ho, "Official Replaced after Crime Spate: Dongguan Party Boss Steps Down to Take Responsibility for Lawlessness," SCMP, June 12, 2001, in http://china.scmp.com/ZZZDBVEDPNC.html.

[53] Jasper Becker, "Graft Probe on Former Governor: Ex-Official not Seen since Call-Up to Meeting as Investigators Trace 'Missing Millions'" in Yunnan, SCMP, June 22, 2001 http://china.scmp.com/ZZZBHQWL5OC.html; Sina.com.cn, June 26, 27, 2001, in http://dailynews.sina.com.cn/c/286643.html; http://dailynews.sina.com.cn/c/287527.html;

that provinces will be left largely to their own devices on how they develop their local economies. Location, resource base, the pool of skilled personnel, and the degree of comparative advantage and competitiveness will largely determine the future prosperity of China's provinces, although the center may be expected to play a greater role in the redistribution of fiscal resources by implementing an institutionalized transfer payments system and continuing the present investment bias towards the poorer, backward, inland regions of the country under the rubric of the ambitious Great Leap West program. Third, accountability criteria to judge the performance of provincial leaders may continue to be subject to the same factional and noninstitutional considerations that affect and even determine their current implementation. While it is likely that the future leadership will continue to rotate and regularly transfer provincial leaders, there may be a greater focus on recruiting younger officials, and perhaps more women and other underrepresented groups, into top provincial posts.[54] Finally, the ability or resolve of the next generation of leaders to deal, in a determined, resolute, and comprehensive fashion, with corruption must be questioned. They can, however, make a start by introducing an effective legal system that is not subject to the whims and directives of Party leaders to grapple seriously with the problem.

The continued internationalization of the Chinese economy and its further opening to the outside world will mean that Chinese companies and government departments become subject to laws that govern trade and business dealings between domestic and foreign

---

September 26, 2001; in http://news.sina.com.cn/c/2001-09-26/366589.html. It is possible that the Shenyang case of gangsterism and corruption will spill over into the provincial arena. The appointment of Bo Xilai as governor in February 2001 suggests this to be the case. See Reuters, "Chinese City Rocked by Scandal, Hostage Taking," December 22, 2000; Vivien Pik-Kwan Chan, "Criminal Empire Crushed," *SCMP*, January 20, 2001, in http://china.scmp.com/ZZZ2V0UL2IC.html; Fong Tak-Ho, "Former Mayor Investigated in Shenyang Bribery Probe," *SCMP*, June 16, 2001, in http://china.scmp.com/today/ZZZJVGVIWNC.html.

[54] In October 2001 a cadre of 40 was appointed vice-governor of Jiangsu province, making him the youngest person to hold such a post in China. See Ma, "Obey Party Directives."

partners. This may have a flow-on effect into domestic affairs. Provincial courts will find it increasingly difficult to discriminate in favor of local entities in the globalized economy, and if they are found to discriminate against foreign companies, the national, not the provincial, authorities will be held responsible. However, it is entirely possible that the new challenges (as well as the perennial challenges of the Taiwan question and relations with the US) that face China amid the uncertainty and dangers of the post-September 11 world will tend to reinforce even more the centripetal forces that have great historical and cultural force in the long (if punctuated) and impressive history of the unified Chinese state.

Chapter 6

Can Democracy Provide an Answer to the National Identity Question? A Historical Approach

HE BAOGANG

INTRODUCTION

If Hu Jintao succeeds Jiang Zemin smoothly in 2002 as the core of the fourth generation leadership, he and his colleagues, like their predecessors, will continue to face multiple challenges. Two of these concern China's stability and unity. One is the national identity problem; the other is the international pressure on Chinese leaders to adopt a democratic approach to the national identity question. China will remain under political and moral pressure to democratize, or at least behave like a democratic state, for example, by refraining from threatening Taiwan with the use of force.

A democratic approach to the national identity question is a much more serious and significant challenge to the fourth generation leadership than the national identity question itself. The government of Taiwan called for the democratization of China as a precondition for settling the issue of the divided nation.[1] Tien Hung-mao, a distinguished scholar from Taiwan and the former Minister of

---

[1] For example, Su Chi, the Chairperson of the Mainland Affairs Council (MAC), said, on June 7, 1999, that the improvement of cross-Strait relations depends on whether the mainland could embark on a path of democratization, on which the unification of China hinges. MAC *News Briefing*, No. 0128, June 7, 1999, p. 1.

Foreign Affairs of Republic of China (Taiwan), has discussed the peaceful resolution of Mainland–Taiwan conflicts through the promise of democratization.[2] Some members of the Democratic Progressive Party (DPP) in Taiwan appeal to democratic procedures, suggesting that the national identity issue could and should be decided through a referendum. The Dalai Lama, the International Commission of Jurists, and Chinese liberal dissidents, such as Yan Jiaqi, call for referenda and democratic federalism to resolve the question of Tibet.

Various social and political theorists from different perspectives and disciplines have paid some attention in recent years to the various elements of the democratic management of the national identity issue.[3] Empirically, the global experience of democratization reveals multiple possibilities. Elections facilitated the secessionist movements and helped the Baltic states to gain independence, leading to the breakdown of the Soviet Union. By contrast, the democratization of Spain, the Philippines, and South Africa helped to manage the national identity problem and strengthened their national unity through a democratic accommodation of secessionist demands. In China, democratization may provide an opportunity for Tibet either to separate from China or to establish genuine autonomy, and for Taiwan to establish an independent state, recognized by the international community, or to unify with mainland China. Chinese democratization could produce a diverse range of outcomes.

The Chinese leadership seems to be reluctant to initiate large-scale democratization at the national level. For example, the attempt to lift restrictions on opposition parties was abandoned in 1998, and the experiments of direct election of township heads were frozen in 2001. Indeed, Chinese state nationalists remain opposed to

---

[2] Hung-mao Tien, "Toward Peaceful Resolution of Mainland–Taiwan Conflicts: The Promise of Democratization," in Edward Friedman (ed.), *The Politics of Democratization: Generalizing East Asian Experiences* (Boulder: Westview Press, 1994), p. 189.

[3] Theorists of referenda suggest that the referenda principle should be widely adopted to settle the boundary dispute. See David Butler and Austin Ranney, *Referendums around the World— The Growing Use of Direct Democracy* (Washington: AEI Press, 1994); Jurgen Habermas, "National Unification and Popular Sovereignty," *New Left Review*, No. 219 (September–

democratization, which they believe threatens China's national unity and territorial integrity. In particular, the breakup of the former USSR and the separation of East Timor from Indonesia have made Beijing more fearful of democracy, whereas China has become more convinced, as a result of its successful reunion with Hong Kong and Macau, that it is only power, and not democracy, that can unify the country.

In this context, this chapter tries to analyze the two challenges mentioned above for the fourth generation leadership and explore why China has difficulty adopting the democratic approach to the national identity question. It also examines the conditions under which democracy cannot or can be introduced in China to solve its national identity question. It will demonstrate the logic of the conflict between the democratic approach and China's unity in the context of the national identity issue. It should be noted that this chapter aims at providing an explanation or an understanding of the Party/state's resistance to the democratic approach, not a justification of it.

October 1996), pp. 3–13; Harry Beran, "A Democratic Theory of Political Self-determination for a New World Order," in Percy B. Lehning (ed.), *Theories of Secession* (London: Routledge, 1998), pp. 32–59. Theorists of democratization look for potential solutions to the boundary question in the democratization process and democratic strategies of management. See Alfred Stepan, "Toward a New Comparative Analysis of Democracy and Federalism: Demos Constraining and Demos Enabling Federations," paper given at IPSA XVII World Congress, Seoul, August 17–22, 1997. Theorists of secession advocate the constitutional right to secession as a democratic procedure to resolve the national identity/boundary problem. See Allen Buchanan, *Secession: The Morality of Political Divorce from Fort Sumter to Lithuania and Quebec* (Boulder: Westview Press, 1991). Theorists of transnational democracy can be extended to consider the national identity/boundary problem from the perspective of cosmopolitan democracy. See David Held, *Democracy and Global Order: From the Modern State to Cosmopolitan Governance* (Polity Press, 1995); and Daniele Archibugi, "From the United Nations to Cosmopolitan Democracy," in D. Archibugi and David Held (eds), *Cosmopolitan Democracy: An Agenda for a New World Order* (Oxford: Polity Press, 1995), pp. 135–155. Theorists of civil society challenge the state's monopoly of identity/boundary issues and stress the role of civil society in defining the identity/ boundary of a political community. See Craig Calhoun, "Nationalism and Civil Society: Democracy, Diversity and Self-determination," in C. Calhoun (ed.), *Social Theory and the Politics of Identity* (Cambridge: Blackwell Publishers, 1994); Michael Freeman, "Democrat and Dynamite: the Peoples' Right to Self-determination," *Political Studies*, XLIV (1996),

The national identity problem can be regarded as two sides of a coin, the coin of China's unity. One side of the coin is that sections of the national population, such as Tibetans, do not identify with the Chinese nation-state in which they live, and they try to create their own political identity through the reconstruction of a Tibetan cultural and ethnic identity. The other side of it is the question of reunification with Taiwan. In the writings of Linz and Stepan, the national identity question is seen as a "stateness problem;"[4] in Chinese writings, it is often referred to as a "nationality question." I will use the term "national identity question" in general but "nationality question" as used by Chinese leaders when I quote from them. Of course, the nationality question contains connotations and meanings different from the national identity question, but both share one critical issue concerning China's unity, namely, territorial integrity. The chapter will focus on the territorial dimension of the national identity or the nationality question and leave out its cultural, ethnic, and economic dimensions, except where they are related to territoriality and China's unity. Also, while Taiwan and Tibet are different cases and require different treatment,[5] Beijing's response to

pp. 746–761. Theorists of minority rights challenge majority-rule-democracy, and defend the institutionalization of the internal boundaries between communities within a nation-state. See Will Kymlicka, *Liberalism, Community and Culture* (Oxford: Clarendon Press, 1989); *Multicultural Citizenship: A Liberal Theory of Minority Rights* (Oxford: Clarendon Press, 1995). Finally, "democratic peace" theorists argue that democratic states rarely use military force against one another and that democracies are less likely to escalate conflict to war in general. For example, see Bruce M. Russett, *Grasping the Democratic Peace: Principles for a Post-Cold War World* (Princeton: Princeton University Press, 1993); and David L. Rousseau, Christopher Gelpi, Dan Reiter and Paul K. Huth, "Assessing the Dyadic Nature of the Democratic Peace, 1918–1988," *American Political Science Review*, Vol. 90, No. 3 (1996), pp. 512–533.

[4] See Juan J. Linz and Alfred Stepan, *Problems of Democratic Transition and Consolidation: Southern Europe, South America, and Post-Communist Europe* (Baltimore and London: The John Hopkins University Press, 1996), pp. 16–19.

[5] While Tibet has its unique cultural identity, Taiwan's cultural identity, despite reconstruction in recent years, has been associated with Chinese cultures. Tibet is a "state" in exile without territory; while Taiwan has had its own state with a clearly defined territorial boundary for more than 50 years.

the two questions is the same, that is, it refuses to adopt a democratic approach. We need to ask why this is so.

China's national identity problem has to be understood in historical terms, because explanations for today's politics of national identity can be found in Qing history.[6] The chapter, therefore, adopts a historical approach, starting with a brief critical review of modern Chinese history.[7] The historical approach is useful to reveal historical trends and patterns, from which we can find clues as to how the four generation leadership is likely to deal with China's national identity question. However, the chapter does not provide a detailed description of the formation of national identity issues so as to avoid controversial historical claims and counter-claims. It must be also admitted that the historical approach is incapable of providing a definite answer to the question whether or not democracy can manage China's national identity question. This is because a historical, law-like generalization does not determine the future, because it cannot rule out the innovation of agents. This is also because the historical approach cannot replace a logical analysis or deny the moral demand for self-determination by minority nationalities.

---

[6] See Evelyn S. Rawski, "Presidential Address: Reenvisioning the Qing: The Significance of the Qing Period in Chinese History," *The Journal of Asian Studies*, Vol. 55, No. 4 (1996), pp. 829–850.

[7] I have discussed the national identity question and the democratic approach to it from different perspectives and in different contexts. See *Nationalism, National Identity and Democratization in China* (with Yingjie Guo) (Aldershot: Ashgate Publishers, 2000); "Democracy, Transnational Problems and the Boundary Question: Challenge for China: An Interview with David Held," *Social Alternative*, Vol. 16, No. 4 (1997), pp. 33–37; "National Integrity, Elites and Democracy: Russia and China Compared" (with J. Pakulski). *Journal of Communist Studies and Transition Politics*, Vol. 15, No. 2 (June 1999), pp. 69–87 (A translation version is also published in Russian, *Far East Studies*, Moscow, No. 1 (1998)); "The Roles of Civil Society in Defining the Boundary of a Political Community: the Case of South Korea and Taiwan," *Asian Studies Review*, Vol. 23, No. 1 (March 1999), pp. 27–48; "The National Identity Problem and Democratization: Rustow's Theory of Sequence," *Government and Opposition: An International Journal of Comparative Politics*, Vol. 36, No. 1 (Winter 2001), pp. 97–119;

THE "EMPIRE THESIS"

Let us start with the Qing empire and the empire thesis, which is essential to my argument. The core idea of the empire thesis is that the empire is most likely to break up if democracy is to be established. Or, in a different formula, colonial power is most likely to give up its colonies when the colonial state or its colonial "subjects" embark upon democratization. This is because democratization undermines the domination of one people over another, of a stronger over a weaker community, and challenges the territorial basis of the empire that conquered territories and subjects in the past by use of force. Let us examine this thesis first in other contexts and then in the context of China.

After a period of expansion during the 15th and 16th centuries, Ottoman domination was extended over much of central Europe, the Balkans, the Middle East, and North Africa. The empire underwent a lengthy period of contraction and fragmentation. In July 1908, constitutional monarchy was instituted and democratization started. The election of November–December 1908 led to the success of the Unionists, who tried to transform and rescue the empire. However, the Ottoman Empire collapsed, and its territorial question was resolved as a result of the internal struggle between military and civil forces and between fundamental and secular forces; the demand for independence from non-Muslim and the non-Turkish

"The Question of Sovereignty in the Taiwan Strait: Reexamining Peking's Policy of Opposition to Taiwan's Bid for UN Membership," China Perspectives, No. 34 (March 2001), pp. 7–18 (this is also reprinted in French, "Chine-Taiwan: l'imperieuse question de la souverainete," Perspevtives chinoises, Numero 63 (janvier–fevier 2001), pp. 7–20); "Why Does Beijing Reject the Dalai Lama Autonomy Proposal?" Review of Asian and Pacific Studies, No. 22 (July 2001); "Cosmopolitan Democracy and the National Identity Question in Europe and East Asia," International Relations of Asia Pacific (Oxford University Press, Vol. 2, No. 1. 2002, pp. 47–68; "Civil Society and Democracy," a chapter in April Carter and G. Stokes (eds), Democratic Theory Today (Cambridge: Polity Press, 2002, pp. 203–227); "Democratization and the National Identity Question in East Asia," a chapter in Yeung Yue-man (ed.), Towards Twenty-First Century Asia Pacific (Chinese University of Hong Kong Press, 2002, pp. 245–273).

communities; and a disastrous alliance with Germany during World War I.[8] During Mustafa Kemal's rule, a process of Turkeynization occurred, so that the old Ottoman identity was replaced by a new Turk identity. Elections were held in 1946, and the People's Party was replaced by the Democratic Party in 1950.[9]

In Portugal, opposition parties were legalized in 1969, the new constitution came into effect on April 25, 1976, and an election to the Assembly of the Republic was held the same day. In 1974, the military government of Vasco dos Santos Goncalves recognized the right of the Overseas Territories to "self-determination" with all its consequences, including independence. Guinea-Bissau gained its independence in 1974; Mozambique in 1975; and Angola in 1976. Portugal's initial refusal to grant independence provoked fighting and guerrilla warfare.[10]

The Sovietization of the Russian center retained and expanded the territories of the Russian empire in the wake of World War II. However, the Soviet empire underwent imperial decay in the 1980s and 1990s, finally breaking up when democratization began.[11] The emergence of ethnic nationalisms played a decisive role in generating centrifugal forces to tear the Soviet Union apart.[12] According to S.N. Eisenstadt, given the center–periphery relations in the former USSR, the collapse of the Soviet empire was inevitable. Historically, a highly active Russian center exercised centralized control over a politically passive periphery. However, during the Soviet period, the

---

[8] See Feroz Ahmad, *The Making of Modern Turkey* (London: Routledge, 1993), ch. 3, "From Empire to Nation 1908–1923."

[9] D.A. Rustow, "Transitions to Democracy: Towards a Dynamic Model," *Comparative Politics*, Vol. 2 (1970), p. 362.

[10] Arthur S. Banks, Alan J. Day and Thomas C. Muller, *Political Handbook of the World 1997* (NY: CSA Publications, 1997), p. 682.

[11] Mette Skak, *From Empire to Anarchy: Postcommunist Foreign Policy and International Relations* (London: Hurst, 1996), ch. 3, "Shadows of the Past: The Soviet Empire."

[12] Wang Weimin and Yi Xiaohong, "Minzu yishi: lijie qiansulian minzu wenti de guanjian" [National Consciousness: Understanding the Crux of the National Problem of the Former Soviet Union], *Shanxi shida xuebao, Sheke ban* (Linfen), No. 4 (1996), pp. 17–21.

political center mobilized the periphery and activated it socially and politically to such a degree that it changed the balance between the center and the periphery. The totalitarian regime maintained effectively tight controls, forbidding the formation of autonomous subsystems, but legitimating national cultures within a universalistic framework. Once the totalitarian controls weakened, ethnic tensions were enhanced by the rise of ethnonationalism, leading to the breakdown of the empire system.[13] As another example, East Timor gained its independence through referendum and international intervention in 1999 following the democratization of Indonesia.

The territory of today's China is a product of the Qing empire, from the long historical interactions of Inner and East Asia. China was incorporated into a Qing empire that spanned Inner Asia and East Asia. The Qing was the most successful of China's dynasties in terms of territorial expansion. Under the Qing empire, ethnic minorities were colonized. Xinjiang became a province in 1884. But neither Mongolia, Qinghai, nor Tibet was ever converted into provinces during the Qing. When the Qing was overthrown in the 1911 Revolution, the Provisional Law of the Republic (1912) specifically identified Mongolia, Tibet, and Qinghai as integral parts of the nation. However, loyalty to the Qing dynasty did not automatically translate into loyalty to the Republic of China. The Mongols, for example, never considered themselves part of Zhongguo [China], and indeed, Outer Mongolia managed to break away from China.[14] Even today, the Dalai Lama claims that the Qing dynasty is not Chinese, and Tibet and China do not have the same sort of relationship as did Tibet and the Manchu dynasty.[15]

In the republican period, China struggled to retain all the Qing territories in the new nation-state. Like its predecessors, the People's Republic of China (PRC) worked hard to retain the inherited Qing territories through the consistent repression of independence

---

[13] Teresa-Rakowska Harmstone, "Soviet Nationalities and Perestroika," *Canadian Review of Studies in Nationalism*, Vol. XXIV, No. 1–2 (1997), p. 92.

[14] Rawski, "Presidential Address," p. 840.

[15] Xu Mingxu, *Intrigues and Devoutness: The Origin and Development of the Tibet Riots* (Canada: Mirror Books Ltd., 1999), pp. 122–123.

movements in Tibet, Xinjiang, and Inner Mongolia.[16] And Communist leaders declared: the vast ethnic regions of the former Empire were transformed into inalienable parts of the motherland.[17] China's "family" union was achieved under the Qing empire and has been retained by the PRC through force, the communist ideology, and pan-Chinese nationalism.

China has successfully frustrated attempts by Tibetans, Manchus, and Uygurs to establish independent statehood, but it failed to stop the Republic of Mongolia. It also successfully reclaimed its sovereignty over Hong Kong in 1997 and Macau in 1999. Nevertheless, it still confronts secessionist movements in Tibet and Xinjiang, and the reunification question with Taiwan, which has coexisted with the PRC since 1949.

Nevertheless, China is still seen as the "last empire," or "a residual empire." It is "residual" not only because the imperial way of exercising central power still prevails, but also because China is haunted today by the shadows of the Qing empire and burned by the Qing legacy, including the Tibet problem. Moreover, China's own empire history and its residual question were overshadowed by the struggle against Western imperialism. However, when Western imperialist forces were driven out in China after 1949, the residual question soon became an urgent problem and led to the conflict between the Dalai Lama and the CCP in the 1950s.

It is believed that China is likely to break into several natural organisms or natural political units, like all other empires. The rise and persistence of ethnic nationalism and independence movements in the PRC are seen as part of the logic of the breakdown of the world's "last empire." The driving forces come from the tension between China's empire history and the demands for modern nation-states by minority nationalities. It is the transformation from "empires" to nation-states that challenges China's territorial integrity. This

---

[16] Rawski, "Presidential Address," p. 841.

[17] Harald Bockman, "The Future of the Chinese Empire-State in a Historical Perspective," in Kjeld Erik Brodsgaard and David Strand (eds), *Reconstructing Twentieth-Century China: State Control, Civil Society, and National Identity* (Oxford: Clarendon Press, 1998), p. 317.

process often gives rise to ethnonationalism and inevitably to the proliferation of smaller and more ethnically homogeneous states.

There are different versions of the empire thesis. Victor Louis, a member of the KGB, presented his version of the empire thesis as a rationale to justify a Soviet "war of liberation" against the PRC in 1979. Louis outlined three key ideas of this thesis. First, the Chinese leadership, continuing the traditional imperial expansionist line, was laying claim to vast areas of the Soviet Far East, Siberia, and Central Asia. Second, for several decades, the people of the outlying regions of China, all along the Sino–Soviet border, had been waging an unrelenting struggle for their national self-determination and independence.[18] Third, the solution, according to Louis, was to grant independence to the people of Manchuria, Mongolia, Eastern Turkestan, and Tibet. For him, this was a just solution of the national identity problem (in his terms, the "nationalities question") and would largely remove the threat of Chinese expansion towards the adjacent territories.[19] Louis predicted that future developments would show how soon the national aspirations of the Manchu, Mongols, Uighurs, and Tibetans could become a reality.[20]

Zhuang Wanshou, a Taiwanese scholar, presents another version of the empire thesis. He argues that Taiwan's independence movement is historically determined by the inevitable breakdown of the Chinese empire.[21] In a more sophisticated version, Lee Teng-hui, who has been silent on the empire issue, suggests that China should get rid of pan-Chinese nationalism and allow Taiwan, Tibet, Xinjiang, Mongolia, and other three regions to enjoy complete self-determination and compete with one another.[22]

[18] Victor Louis, *The Coming Decline of the Chinese Empire* (New York: Times Books, 1979), p. 186.

[19] *Ibid.*, p. 186.

[20] *Ibid.*, p. 187.

[21] See Cheng-Feng Shih (ed.), *Taiwan Nationalism* (Taipei: Qianfeng, 1994), pp. 276–277.

[22] Lee Teng-hui, *Taiwan's View* (Taipei: Yuanliu Publishers, 1999), p. 216.

Similarly, it is often said that Tibetan independence should be seen as a just and ineluctable outcome of this same historical trajectory. It is often said that China annexed and colonized Tibet: both the International Committee of Lawyers for Tibet and the International Commission of Jurists confirmed Tibet's statehood under international law from 1913 to 1950.[23] Although China modernized Tibet with a flow of central financial and technological supports, the colonization or decolonization experience show that rapid modernization always empowers indigenous people, who will demand autonomy and independence. On the other hand, if modernization fails, indigenous people tend to blame the failure on the colonizers' policy. Modernization thus works in both ways against the colonizers. Viewing Tibet in such a way, it would appear that whatever Tibet has achieved is insignificant; a "golden cage" is still a cage. The best option for China is to pull out.

Needless to say, the above three versions of the empire thesis with special reference to China do not represent China's view. Beijing certainly dislikes the empire thesis and tries to avoid the term "empire." For Beijing, the empire system already ended in 1911, which was China's contribution to the global trend of ending the era of empire.[24] One may add that as the Qing empire was already broken up in 1919, the empire thesis does not apply to today's China. In the eyes of Beijing, Tibet is not a Chinese colony, and China did not colonize Tibet, because Tibet has been a part of China for several centuries. Beijing will also question the applicability of the empire thesis and even the term "empire." It is indeed questionable if China can be seen as an empire. The Chinese government will never see today's China as a residual empire. China can make a strong and creditable argument that it is currently a modern

---

[23] See http://www.tibet.com/Status/icj-es.html; and http://www.tibeticlt.org/reports/occupied.html.

[24] In 1917–1918, the imperial principle lost its major European stronghold; and Germany, Austria–Hungary, Russia-in-Europe, and the Ottoman empire, all gave way to a sorting out of the nations. See R. Emerson, *From Empire to Nation: The Rise to Self-Determination of Asian and African Peoples* (Cambridge: Harvard University Press, 1960), p. 3.

multinationality state, not an empire at all. Transformation from empire to nation-states does not have to result in a multiplicity of ethnic states. For Harald Bockman, a Western scholar, however, China is still an empire-state, and a new Chinese nation based on citizenship has not yet formed. Bockman even concludes that "The country is not a nation-state in the regular sense of the term, and it probably never will be."[25]

In rebutting the empire thesis, one may point out the dual legacies of Chinese modern history: China being semi-colonized and a colonizer at the same time. China inherited Qing's territories, but importantly, as Chinese history texts stress, all Chinese people have suffered from the Western imperial invasion and expansion during modern Chinese history. All the people unified to struggle against Western imperialism. Mao Zedong claimed that the self-determination of China's nationalities was decided, once and for all, by their common revolutionary struggle and voluntary incorporation into the PRC.[26]

Nevertheless, some Western leaders and commentators, and more importantly those who struggle for independence inside or outside China, believe in the empire thesis. China's national identity faces a stiff challenge if secessionist minorities regard China as an empire and demand independence.

SUN YET-SEN AND THE KMT

In the struggle against the Qing rule, Sun Yet-sen and the Kuomintang played up ethnic politics, urging the Han to overthrow the Manchus. As soon as the Qing was overthrown, Sun faced the new task of building the republic, which compelled him to stress coexistence, equality, and harmony among five major nationalities.[27] In order to retain the territories of the former Qing "empire" and

---

[25] Bockman, "The Future of the Chinese Empire-State," 1998, p. 332.

[26] Warren W. Smith, "China's Tibetan Dilemma," *The Fletcher Forum of World Affairs*, Vol. 14, No. 1 (Winter 1990), p. 78.

[27] Sun Yet-sen (Sun Zhongshan), *Selected Works of Sun Yet-sen (Sun Zhongshan)* (Beijing: People Press, 1981), p. 586, 588.

build a modern nation-state, Liang Qichao has further proposed a pan-Chinese notion and identity. Super or pan-nationalism employed visions of a broad political community binding together different nationalities and preventing the disintegration of the nation. As Rawski points out, "Only a definition of the nation that transcends Han identity can thus legitimately lay claim to the peripheral regions inhabited by non-Han peoples, since these claims rest on the empires created by the Mongols and the Manchus."[28] To strengthen Chinese national identity, local identities have been reconstructed in terms of vertical hierarchy so as to discover and defend the national significance of the local identities.[29] In contemporary China, the Party/state has done its best to redefine and homogenize Han Chinese images of national minorities and to gain more control over the Han majority.[30]

Not only was the idea of pan-Chinese national identity invented and constructed; a democratic solution to the national identity question was also advocated. In 1924, Sun Yet-sen addressed the nationality issue, writing in the manifesto of the 1st Chinese Nationalist Congress:

> "The Kuomintang solemnly declares that the right of self-determination is recognized for all the nationalities inhabiting China; following the victory of the revolution over the imperialists and militarists there will be established a free and united (formed on the basis of a voluntary union of all nationalities) Chinese republic."[31]

Later this policy of self-determination was completely abandoned, both in theory and practice, by the Kuomintang. Sun Yet-sen also

---

[28] Rawski, "Presidential Address," p. 841.

[29] Antonia Finane, "A Place in the Nation: Yangzhou and the Idle Talk Controversy of 1934," *The Journal of Asian Studies*, Vol. 53, No. 4 (1994), pp. 1150–1174.

[30] Dru C. Gladney, "Representing Nationality in China: Refiguring Majority/Minority Identities," *The Journal of Asian Studies*, Vol. 53, No. 1 (1994), pp. 92–123.

[31] Sun Yet-sen (Sun Zhongshan), *Selected Works of Sun Yet-sen (Sun Zhongshan)*, p. 592; also cited in Victor Louis, *The Coming Decline of The Chinese Empire* (New York: Times Books, 1979), p. 114.

advocated a federal system that would curb the power of the central government and grant autonomy to the provinces and minority regions. This was abandoned by Sun himself when he witnessed the rise of regional militarists [geju]. Chen Duxiu, a radical Marxist, also discredited the idea of federalism. Chen, who had originally favored self-government and federalism, realized that the circumstances of feudalistic politics meant the self-governing movement was doomed to become a pawn in the game of the militarists. If federalism was built upon the aspirations of regional militarists, it could, he concluded, never achieve national unity and strength.[32]

From 1934 to 1935, the national identity and unity issues again rose to prominence. This time there was heated debate among the Chinese intellectuals over the "democracy versus dictatorship" question. In rejecting "military unification," Hu Shi favored "political unification"—which involved the establishment of a national congress where people from different provinces would be invited to take part in national politics. This, he believed, would cultivate the centripetal force that would help to build a strong national identity.[33] Hu Shi outlined four proposals:

1. From now on, the first priority is to create an exemplary model of central politics;
2. Developing communication is the material basis for national unification;
3. Power should be shared between the center and provinces to form a republic unity;
4. A representative institution should be established to create a central authority above the regional militarists and to lay down a political basis for national unification.[34]

---

[32] Prasenjit Duara, "Nationalism as the Politics of Culture: Centralism and Federalism in Early Republican China," The Woodrow Wilson Center, Asia Program Occasional Paper, No. 37, June 11, 1990, p. 12.

[33] Cheng Yishen, Dulipinglun de minzhu sixiang [The Democratic Ideas of the Journal of Independent Forum] (Taiwan: Lianjing chuban Gongsi, 1989), pp. 88–91.

[34] Hu Shi, "The Road towards Unification," Independent Forum, No. 28 (November 1932), p. 6.

By contrast, Jiang Tingfu and Chen Zhimai expressed a preference for an authoritarian leadership that could unify China by force. They asserted that the political reality of China was such that the parliament could be closed down by a few soldiers. For them, even though a few representatives were sent to central governmental organizations, those who did not favor unification were considered untrustworthy because it was felt they might use parliament for political purposes.[35] Here, the problem of fostering national identity was intertwined with the problem of choosing a political system. For liberal intellectuals, democracy was seen as the best means to overcome local division and develop a national identity, while antiliberal intellectuals saw dictatorship as the best option. In the end, rather than adopting the idea of democratic national identity and unification, Chiang Kai-shek (Jiang Jieshi) opted for an authoritarian one-party government to maintain his monopoly of power and to combat the warlords and communists. The Chiang regime had an outward parliamentary form that made no attempt at revolutionary translation of power to the masses. Moreover, when the Japanese army invaded and occupied northern China, most Chinese liberal intellectuals and democrats gave up the democratic enterprise and became nationalists in defense of national unity.

MAO ZEDONG AND CCP

The Chinese Communist Party agreed and supported Sun Yet-sen's policy on the right of self-determination by national minorities, passed by the first Chinese Nationalist Congress.[36] Article 14 of the Constitution of the Chinese Soviet Republic declared in November 1931:

> "The Soviet government in China recognizes the right of self-determination of the national minorities in China, the Mongols, Moslems, Tibetans, Miao, Li, Koreans, and others inhabiting the territory of China enjoy the complete right to self-determination,

---

[35] Cheng Yishen, *Dulipinglun de minzhu sixiang*, ch. 3.
[36] Mao Zedong, *Selected Works of Mao Zedong*, Vol. 3 (Beijing: People Press, 1966), p. 1033.

that is, they may either join, or secede from, the Federation of Chinese Soviets, or form their own state as they may prefer."[37]

In 1945, Mao Zedong wrote, in "On a Coalition Government," that the future People's China would "grant nations the right to be their own masters and to voluntarily enter into an alliance with the Han people." "All national minorities in China must create, along voluntary and democratic lines, a federation of democratic republics of China." In the later edition of Mao's *Selected Works*, that passage had vanished, and the original words "granting of the right to national self-determination to all national minorities" were replaced by the phrase "the granting of the right to national autonomy to all national minorities."[38]

Mao developed his theory of autonomy to deal with the nationality question. He went through an ideological transformation from his early idea of federalism and self-determination to regional autonomy as a solution to China's nationality question. He initially supported the right of self-determination (in the 1920s and 1930s) but quickly abandoned it on the following grounds:

1. Lenin's theory of self-determination was used by Japan to support the independence of Mongolia.
2. The right to self-determination should be denied except in the case of oppressed nations casting off the rule of imperialism and colonialism to fight for independence.
3. The right to self-determination is not feasible in China where different nationalities overlap and are interdependent.[39]

---

[37] *Selected Documents of Central Committee of the CCP*, Vol. 7 (1931), reprinted by the Central Data Library (Beijing: The Central Party School Press, 1991), pp. 775–776. In Louis' translation, he stresses "their (national minorities) right to complete separation from China, and to the formation of an independent state for each national minority." See Louis, *The Coming Decline*, pp. 114–115.

[38] *Ibid.*, p. 115.

[39] Yang Jingchu and Wang Geliu, "Woguo de minzu quyu zizhi: Mao Zedong dui Marxism's minzu lilun de gongxian" [National Regional Autonomy in China: Mao Zedong's Contribution to Marxist Theory of Nationality], *Minzu yanjiu* [Nationality Study], No. 1 (1994), pp. 1–8.

4. The self-determination of China's nationalities had been decided, once and for all, by their common revolutionary struggle and voluntary incorporation in the PRC.[40]

Federation was one way of exiting the Qing empire. After 1949, Mao once entertained the idea of Soviet-style federalism, but eventually rejected it on the grounds that (1) Marx, Engels, and Lenin all supported a unitary centralized system; and (2) China, as a unitary country, in which many nationalities have lived together for centuries, is different from Europe in general and Russia in particular, where federalism was adopted in the wake of the communist revolution.[41] The rejection of Soviet-style federalism was also on the grounds that it would enable various nationalities of China to form separate states and thus allow the national autonomous regions to secede.[42] In the 1990s, some Chinese scholars argued that the Chinese unitary system, comprising many autonomous nationality regions, is better than a federal system. This is demonstrated by the fact that the federal system of the former Soviet Union and Yugoslavia promoted localism and ethnonationalism and finally led to the collapse of the socialist system.[43]

Following Marxism, Mao Zedong maintained that the nationality question is by nature a question of class, and that nationality and ethnicity will wither away after the end of class conflict. Mao also held that class division is much more important than ethnic division,

---

[40] See Chen Yanbin, Liu Jianzhong and Qiao Li, "Mao Zedong sixiang minzu lilun yanjiu huigu." [Review of the Studies on Mao Zedong Thought about Nationalities], *Heilongjiang minzu congkan* [Heilongjiang Nationality Series] (Ha'erbin), No. 4 (1998), pp. 33–38; W. Smith, "China's Tibetan Dilemma," *The Fletcher Forum of World Affairs*, Vol. 14, No. 1 (1990), p. 78.

[41] Ma Xing and Zhong He, "Minzu quyu zizhi yanjiu huigu" [Review of the Studies on National Regional Autonomy], *Heilongjiang minzu congkan* [Heilongjiang Nationality Series] (Ha'erbin) (March 1998), pp. 29–38.

[42] Louis, *The Coming Decline*, p. 116.

[43] See Chen Qinghua and Wei Yingxue, "Deng Xiaoping minzu lilun yanjiu huigu" [Review of the Studies on Deng Xiaoping's Theory about Nationalities], *Heilongjiang minzu congkan* [Heilongjiang Nationality Series] (Ha'erbin), No. 4 (1998), p. 49.

that the majority of any nationality are peasants and workers, and that working classes across different nationalities could and should be unified against their common enemy, the exploiting class.

DENG XIAOPING'S ECONOMIC APPROACH TO THE NATIONAL IDENTITY QUESTION[44]

To a large extent, Deng continued to follow Mao's theory and practice on the nationality question. Like Mao, Deng asserted that the autonomous nationality system was suited to the Chinese situation and worked much better than federalism. He claimed that this system could not be given up, for it had many advantages.[45] In Deng's theory, a unitary system with autonomous regions for nationalities was the best system to defend the unity of the nation-state against secessionism, and it therefore worked best for China.

Deng emphasized the implementation of "genuine autonomy" in terms of the rule of law. He said clearly that genuine autonomy involved putting into effect all self-governing rights according to laws, that is, all the autonomous rights to be defined by the Constitution and the Autonomous Law.[46]

Mao's class analysis of the nationality question, and his idea of the "vanishing" of nationalities, had no place in Deng's pragmatism. In fact, Deng repudiated the importance of class background and turned his attention to the market and economic development as a

---

[44] Chen Qinghua and Wei Yingxue, "Deng Xiaoping minzu lilun yanjiu huigu," pp. 39–44; Sun Yi, "1996–1997 nian minzu wenti lilun yanjiu zongshu" [A Summary of the Theoretical Studies on Nationalities between 1996 and 1997], *Heilongjiang minzu congkan* [Heilongjiang Nationality Series] (Ha'erbin), No. 3 (1998), pp. 43–48.

[45] See Deng Xiaoping, *Deng Xiaoping Wenxuan: Volume 3* (Beijing: People's Press, 1993), p. 257.

[46] Guojia minwei zhengce yanjiushi, "Jiaqiang minzu quyu zizhi lilun yanjiu, jianchi he wanshan minzu quyu zizhi zhidu" [Enhance the Theoretical Study on Regional National Autonomy, Uphold and Improve the System of Regional National Autonomy], *Dangdai zhongguoshi yanjiu* [Contemporary Chinese History Studies], No. 5 (1997), p. 83.

way of dealing with the nationality question. For him, without economic development, autonomy was an empty word.[47] Deng stressed the economic prosperity of ethnic nationalities. For Deng, economic development was the way to prosperity, and prosperity was the *final solution* to the nationality question.

Deng's theory of modernization required economic development to override any consideration of ethnic identities. Deng therefore highlighted the centrality of the stability of the autonomous regions. For him, maintaining stability was a precondition for economic development and improvement of the autonomy system.[48] Deng's concern with stability might override the need to protect some rights of autonomy.

Deng said: "Tibet is so big but has a small population. Developing Tibet only by Tibetans is not enough. It is not bad for Han Chinese to help them to speed up economic development."[49] Accordingly, the influx of Han Chinese into Tibet's minority areas was a necessary step in economic development.[50] To encourage economic development in Tibet, Beijing had exempted Tibet from the general rule that one must be a permanent resident of a given area to start a business there. The result was that Tibetan cities, Lhasa in particular, were inundated with a so-called "floating population" of Han Chinese from other provinces. Typically possessed of better linguistic and technical skills than the locals, the Han Chinese tended to take business away from native Tibetans. There was also a widespread feeling that it was the Han Chinese, and not the local people, who profited from tourism.[51]

---

[47] Deng Xiaoping, *Deng Xiaoping Wenxuan*, 1993, p. 167.

[48] See Guojia minwei zhengce yanjiushi, 1997.

[49] Cited in Wang Dewen and Huang Xiaohong, "Minzu quyu zizhi zhengce zai xizang de weida shijian" [Great Practice of Regional Autonomy Policy in Tibet], *Xizang ribao* [Tibet Daily], August 11, 1995, p. 3.

[50] For example, Deng told the former President Carter that "it is not a bad thing if the number of Han population increases in minority areas; the key issue is whether the economy has developed there." Certainly, Carter cannot fully understand Deng's remark in terms of Confucian culture. See Deng Xiaoping, *Deng Xiaoping Wenxuan: Volume 1* (Beijing: People's Press, 1993), pp. 246–247.

[51] June Teufel Dreyer, "Unrest in Tibet," *Current History*, Vol. 88, No. 539 (September 1989), p. 282.

Some Tibetans hold a different view of economic development. As Lobsang Sangay, an exile Tibetan and now a PhD candidate in Harvard University, put it:

"Tibetans have felt increasingly marginalized in their own territory and see themselves as mere observers of an economic development benefiting others. This has made the ethnic "us versus them" sentiment all the more concrete, since it is usually the Han Chinese who reap the profits of change."[52]

JIANG ZEMIN'S APPROACH TO THE NATIONAL IDENTITY QUESTION

The nationality question was one of his priorities when Jiang came to power. One lesson he learned from the collapse of the Soviet Union was that the Soviet Union failed to deal with the nationality question properly, and he was anxious to avoid a similar disaster in China.[53] He took imperial-style inspection tours to Tibet, Xinjiang, and Mongolia in 1990, followed by a central committee conference on the nationality question in 1992, the first kind of high-level conference since 1949.

Generally speaking, Jiang followed Deng's idea. In his attempt to implement the nationality autonomy law, Jiang combined the unity principle and the flexibility principle in emphasizing that the Chinese style of autonomy must strengthen the unity of China and the central authority; at the same time, it should be flexible enough to accommodate the needs of minority nationalities and stimulate their initiatives.[54]

---

[52] Lobsang Sangay, "China in Tibet: Forty Years of Liberation or Occupation," *Harvard Asia Quarterly* (Summer 1999), p. 27.

[53] Jiang Zeming, "Pay Special Attention to the Nationality and Religion Work," The Data Institute of Central Committee of the CCP (ed.), *Selected Important Documents Since the Fourteen Party Congress* (Beijing: People Press, 1996), p. 512.

[54] Jiang Zemin, "Strengthening the Great Nationality Solidarity and Constructing Socialism with Chinese Characteristics," The Data Institute of Central Committee of the CCP (ed.), *Selected Important Documents Since the Thirteen Party Congress* (Beijing: People Press, 1993), p. 1834.

Jiang also put forward a number of innovative ideas about the nationality question. First, he stressed its importance, reiterating that "nationality and religion contain nothing trivial."[55] For him, the nationality question mattered because it was of central importance to national unity.

Second, Jiang extended Zhou Enlai's argument that the Han cannot do without minority nationalities, and minority nationalities cannot do without the Han; Jiang added that "one minority nationality cannot do without other minority nationalities."[56] Third, following Deng's economic development approach, Jiang implemented two concrete projects: helping poor minority regions to get rich, and developing Western China. He emphasized that these two projects were not only economic projects but also political tasks central to the stability and unity of China.

Jiang took advantage of the national identity question and appropriated it as a part of what might be called a "crisis management program." He propagated the idea that democracy threatened the unity of China and undermined the pan-Chinese national identity project. He warned that if parliamentary democracy and the three divisions of powers were adopted in China, 1.2 billion people would not have enough food to eat, and general disorder and chaos would occur.[57] He warned the people that China faced disintegration. He also tried to make the people believe that CCP = China; thus if the CCP collapsed, China would break up. His warning has not fallen on deaf ears; many people actually believe that only the CCP is able to maintain the unity of China. The Chinese Party/state clearly relies on such an argument as a basis of legitimacy in order to shore up its power.

So far as Jiang is concerned, there is a *negative* correlation between democracy and the nationality question, that is, the West's promotion of democracy is a conspiracy aimed at China's disintegration. The

---

[55] Jiang Zeming, "Pay Special Attention to the Nationality and Religion Work," p. 513.
[56] *Peoples Daily*, October 1, 1990.
[57] *Mingpao*, August 11, 2001, October 8, 2001.

US now uses human rights and democracy, not the CIA, to support Tibetan independence and to interfere in China's internal affairs. At the same time, separatists use democracy and human rights to split China.[58] Jiang obviously fails to see a *positive* correlation between democracy and the nationality question; he apparently does not believe democracy can provide an answer to the nationality question. However, Jiang has made a small compromise. In response to Taiwan's insistence on democracy as a precondition for unification, Jiang cited village elections as an example of China's democracy. It looks as though Jiang does not reject the idea of *democratic* unification.[59]

HU JINTAO[60] AND THE NATIONALITY QUESTION

Hu's political career has been related to nationality areas. He was the party secretary of Guizhou Province (1985–1988) and of the Tibet Autonomous Region (TAR) (1989–1992). He, along with other 414 cadres, was sent to Tibet to deal with the numerous independence activities and events taking place there between October 1987 and December 1988. Tibet was a specially "lucky" place for Hu's career. Because he was in Tibet, he did not have to deal with the student demonstration in 1989 and easily survived the subsequent political struggle.[61]

In early January 1989, as soon as he arrived in Tibet, Hu emphasized social stability and the solidarity of cadres in TAR and promised a stable central policy towards Tibet.[62] In the wake of the

---

[58] Jiang Zemin, "Strengthening the Great Nationality Solidarity," p. 1838, 1847.

[59] Bai Shazhou, *The Illusion and Reality: Jiang Zemin's Political Reform* (Canada: Mirror Books, 1998), pp. 211–213.

[60] Ting Wang, *Hu Jintao: The Leader of Beijing in the 21st Century* (HK: Celebrities Press, 1999), pp. 161–200; Ren Zhichu, *Hu Jintao: China's First Man in the 21st Century* (Canada: Mirror Books, 1998), the third print; pp. 179–203.

[61] For a detailed description, see Yang Zhongmei, *Hu Jintao: The Successor of the CCP in New Century* (Taipei: Shibao Cultural Publisher, 1999), pp. 132–156.

[62] *Tibet Daily*, January 18, 1989, p. 1.

independence demonstrations in March, he implemented forcefully martial law in Tibet. While taking resolute and effective measures to suppress the separatists, Hu promoted economic development. His policies in Tibet were summarized in his slogan-like formula: stabilizing situation is a precondition; economic construction is central; training cadres is the key; maintaining the Party's leadership is imperative; and strengthening solidarity is a guarantee.[63]

Hu emphasized the importance of selecting and training minority cadres. He noticed that there was a substantial shortage of higher level and technical minority cadres. For Hu, the key to holding China together is human resource. It is the minority cadres who constitute a significant part of unity forces against fragmentation and disintegration.[64] Hu's stress on personnel reveals his commitment to the tradition of the rule of man over the nationality question and raises the question of whether Hu is interested in an institutional approach to it. Obviously, like Jiang, Hu does not favor the democratic approach to the nationality question.

CONCLUSION

China has confronted the national identity or unity problem, and among the various options for dealing with it, nationalist and democratic approaches have been advocated. Ideas of self-determination and federalism, that is, elements of the democratic approach for managing the national identity problem, were advocated and adopted by both the nationalist and communist parties but were abandoned later on. The democratic approach towards the national identity question was advocated by liberal-minded intellectuals in the 1930s and by contemporary liberals such as Yan Jiaqi and

---

[63] *Tibet Daily*, May 18, 1989, p. 1.

[64] Hu Jintao, "Pay Special Attention to and Effectively Handle the Selecting and Training of Minority Cadres," The Data Institute of Central Committee of the CCP (ed.), *Selected Important Documents Since the Fourteen Party Congress* (1996), pp. 295–310.

Hu Ping, but it was not taken seriously and implemented. The winners were always the nationalists, authoritarians, or centralists. Sun Yet-sen, Chiang Kai-shek (Jiang Jieshi), Mao Zedong, Deng Xiaoping, Jiang Zeming, and Hu Jintao, and their ways of handling the national identity question, demonstrate the existence of a consistent pattern, that is, all have failed to adopt the democratic measure to deal with the nationality question. It is their shared belief that the right of self-determination and federalism would undermine the unity of China. Their fundamental statist considerations overrode all the differences between the nationalists and the Communists.

It can be concluded that the difficulty associated with adopting the democratic approach to the national identity question is historically embedded; that is, Chinese democratization challenges the territorial basis of the Qing Empire. In other words, the clash between China's unity and the democratic approach to the national identity question derives from China's unique position as a multinational country with an empire legacy. Any fighting over national territorial integrity is likely to alter the direction of democracy, because as a general rule whenever the unity of China is threatened, the course of democracy has changed. In the case of such a conflict, the drive for national unity is sure to subordinate the claims of the individual, and liberal democracy will give way to an authoritarianism in which the actual and diverse wills of the people are replaced by a leader who, in some mystical fashion, is able to express the national ethos. Pan-Chinese nationalists are driven to defend their nation even at the cost of democracy if it threatens to break up China.

The logical tension can be seen as a "historical accident." It is "accidental" insofar as the historical circumstance of each country, as a starting point, is highly contingent. Australia as a new nation-state was confirmed through referenda and parliamentary vote, because of the influence of the British democratic tradition and the nature of its immigrant society. China, like the former Soviet Union, has a historical burden as an "empire," and its state was formed through wars. It is difficult for China, therefore, to reconstruct a new nation in accordance with democratic procedure. In short, the special context and circumstances of China do not favor the democratic procedure to settle the national identity question by any Chinese nationalists.

However, we should be cautious enough to allow for other possibilities, and the historical argument should not exclude the role of agents. While it is most likely for the fourth generation leadership to continue to reject the democratic approach, they do have a choice of developing an approach that draws on Chinese theories of autonomy developed by Mao Zedong, Deng Xiaoping and Jiang Zemin, Chinese pragmatism, Confucianism, and *some* elements of democratic principle, procedure, and institutions. It is important to distinguish the different components of the democratic approach. It is unlikely for the fourth generation leadership to take such a democratic procedure as a referendum as a central decision mechanism to settle the national identity question. However, it is possible for the fourth generation leadership to develop specific democratic institutions to accommodate ethnic nationalism[65] and to embark on a top-down democratization program as a way of gaining regime legitimacy. Indeed, China's regional autonomy system contains minority rights and autonomy principles, which serve as a potential basis for the democratic approach to the nationality question. More importantly, China does not lack an intellectual tradition of democratic thinking. Liang Qichao, Hu Shi, and Yan Jiaqi, for instance, all advocated the democratic solution. The fact that their ideas have not been put into practice indicates that there might be a potential. If their ideas were adopted, China would have managed its national identity question in a different way with a different outcome.

In short, China's national identity question poses a serious challenge to the fourth generation leadership. The democratic

[65] See Arend Lijphart, *Democracy in Plural Societies: A Comparative Exploration* (New Haven: Yale University Press, 1977); and Atul Kohil, "Can Democracies Accommodate Ethnic Nationalism? Rise and Decline of Self-Determination Movements in India," *The Journal of Asian Studies*, Vol. 56, No. 2 (May 1997), pp. 325–344.

approach may help better manage, but cannot provide a perfect answer to it, and it may even add another layer of problem to it. Ironically, refusing the democratic approach also perpetuates the existing national identity question. Whatever Hu Jintao and his colleagues decide to do, the national identity question and the democratic approach to it remain a challenge for them.

In particular, some Taiwanese demanding for a referendum to solve Taiwan's status question was is and will continue to be a serious challenge to the fourth generation leadership.

Chapter 7

The Challenges of Managing a Huge Society under Rapid Transformation*

X.L. DING

INTRODUCTION

If you ask any person who has received some training in social sciences and who has closely observed China for years to provide a briefing on the social problems China is confronted with in the early 21st century, he can easily give you an impressive list of problems. Because, as everyone knows, China is big; its civilization is aged; its economic restructuring is complex; its legal system is absurd; and its administrative structure is outdated. If China is trouble-free, then which nation on earth is likely to have so many gigantic social problems?[1]

* The views expressed herein are the author's own, who sincerely welcomes comments and suggestions. The author also thanks Ms. He Dan for her research assistance. The research for this chapter was supported by a grant from The Research Grants Council of Hong Kong (HKUST 6167/00H).

[1] It is interesting to note that the Russians perhaps are the most easily identifiable people who share similar feelings about their own country, which is understandable given the two nations' immense sizes and their strong traditions of statism. For more on this mentality, see two excellent insider reexamination of Russia under state socialism and during the transition: Georgi Arbatov, *The System: An Insider's Life in Soviet Politics* (New York: Random House, 1993); and Nikolai Zen'kovich, *Secrets of the Twentieth Century* (Moscow: Olma-Press, 1998), especially Chapters 17 and 21.

Instead of going over a comprehensive list of social problems in today's China,[2] I will select four for discussion: unemployment, income gap, rising crimes, and official corruption. On the basis of several years of fieldwork in various parts of China and from reading many insiders' and outsiders' empirical works, I believe that these are among the most significant social problems China faces now and that they are more dangerous than the others, in the sense that they are prone to trigger largescale social unrest and political conflict. A discussion of these major problems will help us assess the kind of challenges the new generation of Chinese leadership—which is in the formative process—is encountering; to what extent the leaders are equipped to meet these challenges; and what may happen politically if they fail to reduce substantially the strains generated by these problems.

UNEMPLOYMENT

The possibility of losing one's job is definitely a matter of worry for the urban Chinese. Ask the state sector employees, social and economic researchers, government officials, journalists, and others about the two or three issues that they have tremendous difficulty in dealing with in their own lives or in their public and professional service, and you will be told that unemployment is one of them.[3]

---

[2] For those who want to have an overview of such problems, the annual publication of *China Review* (Hong Kong: The Chinese University of Hong Kong Press) is a good source. Over the years, the editorship and chapter contributors have been changing, but the format of the discussions is basically the same. In some years, the publication also has a Chinese language version. Besides, the Institute of Sociology at the Chinese Academy of Social Sciences in Beijing has an annual Chinese language publication known as the "sociological blue book," but its research quality varies as it is susceptible to the changing political climate in China. Severe social problems are often watered down.

[3] With China's entry into WTO, job prospects for the average Chinese are worsening, and I have learned that a few of the most recent surveys conducted by Chinese

But you will not get a clear picture of the magnitude of the problem by looking only at the formal government statistics handed out by senior bureaucrats.[4] During the National People's Congress of March 2001, the spokesman of the Ministry of Labor and Social Security told the official media that by the end of 2000, China's urban unemployment rate was 3.1%, which was based on the total number of six million registered job-hunters.[5]

But social policy researchers working in the government had for years questioned that simplistic methodology of arriving at unemployment rates.[6] They had argued as early as 1997 that while the publicly registered layoffs numbered between 5.5 and 6 million, the undisclosed number actually exceeded nine million. Put together, the actual unemployment rate in urban China in the late 1990s was 7.5%, and the total number was around 14 million. This estimate later on seemed to be confirmed by government statistics.[7]

In addition, in the early 21st century, every year about 10–11 million working-age urban youths enter the job market,[8] but new job openings are far from being sufficient. In the countryside, there are 150–175 million peasants who cannot be absorbed into agriculture and rural industries and who, therefore, have to move into cities to find something to do. With the recent relaxation of urban residency restrictions, the rural-to-urban migration is accelerating naturally.[9] When all these factors are taken into consideration, the

research bodies show that unemployment is becoming the chief cause of worry (based on interviews in December 2001).

[4] For a solid empirical study on this problem, see Dorothy J. Solinger, "Why We Cannot Count the 'Unemployed'," *The China Quarterly* (December 2001), pp. 671–688.

[5] Based on news conference reports by the Xinhua News Agency, March 10, 2001.

[6] See, for example, Hu Angang, "The Present High Unemployment Rate in China and Its Background," *Liaowang Weekly*, No. 31, 1997.

[7] "For this Year the Job-Market Pressure is Tremendous," *People's Daily*, February 16, 2001, p. 5.

[8] I thank Dorothy J. Solinger for this statistics.

[9] The State Council has declared that, from October 1, 2001 onward, there will be no quota limits on peasants settling down in towns and small cities. See the Ministry of Public Security's Notice in *Chinese Youth Daily*, May 29, 2001, p. 1.

unemployment picture appears very gloomy. Some senior Chinese economists suggest that, at the beginning of this new century, the unemployment rate in urban China may go beyond 20%, reaching 150 million or so. Such a huge army of the jobless is likely to become the chief destabilizing force in Chinese society.[10]

INCOME GAP

Chinese academic researchers and government statisticians have shown a certain degree of consensus and, more noticeably, differences on how to assess the income gaps within the huge population. On the one hand, they agree that, owing to the decades-long strict *hukou* segregation policy (i.e., the household registration system), China actually has two basic socioeconomic structures, the rural versus the urban, and therefore each one's internal wealth distribution should be assessed independently. Only then can a meaningful comparison between the two be made.

Internationally, professional and government bodies take Gini coefficient 0.4 as the alarming threshold for family income inequality, beyond which the disparity will be seen as sufficiently worrying. Chinese experts, within and outside the government, seem to have agreed to set Gini coefficient 0.4 as the alarm index for the rural and urban societies, respectively, and 0.45 as the general alarm index for the nation as a whole.[11]

On the other hand, Chinese academic researchers and government statisticians often disagree on the basis for making private income estimation and thus the seriousness of economic inequality in the broader society. Until the autumn of 2000, senior government statisticians and policy analysts had in public generally played down

---

[10] Feng Lanrui, "Structural Transformation of Chinese Society: Recent and Mid-Term Trends and Potential Crises," *Strategy and Management*, No. 5 (1998); and the above two footnotes.

[11] See the State Statistical Bureau, "Examining Rich–Poor Disparities by Gini Coefficients," *Zhongguo Guoqing Guoli*, No. 1 (2001).

the income disparity problem.[12] They observed that from 1978, the onset of the reform program, to 1999, Gini coefficients in the urban society moved from 0.150 up to 0.295, in the rural society from 0.212 up to 0.336, and in the whole nation from 0.180 up to 0.397. The urban–rural per capita income ratio at the end of 1999 was 3:1, considering only the category of disposable incomes. But that ratio became 5:1 or 6:1 if the numerous urban welfare benefits were taken into account.

Less than four months later, however, the National Taxation Bureau released a few new figures,[13] which immediately put the general Gini coefficient as high as 0.458, significantly larger than the previously published estimate, making China a society with a wider income gap than the largest capitalist system, the US (about 0.4), and comparable to those notoriously corrupt economies such as Russia (about 0.48) and the Philippines (about 0.43).

According to the Ministry of Finance's data, in 1998, 66% of the total private savings (above 6 trillion yuan in *renminbi* or US$ 723 billion) in China belonged to 10% of its population. In late 1999, a nationwide urban survey discovered that less than 5% of the richest were in possession of nearly a half of the total bank deposits.[14] A veteran Chinese sociologist, who followed the trend of income distribution since the mid-1980s, explained that on this particular issue, official statistics tend to systematically underestimate the seriousness of the problem, because official surveys and inspections can normally obtain residents' formal income only. Various types of informal income, not all of which are illegal, can contribute significantly to the size of household wealth. According to this sociologist's and his team's

---

[12] Yang Yubao, "Looking through Gini Coefficients to See How Wide are the Rich–Poor Gaps," *Zhongguo Xinxi Bao*, November 20, 2000.

[13] Based on the director of the National Taxation Bureau Jing Renqing's comments on questions from delegates of the National People's Congress, Xinhua News Agency, March 10, 2001.

[14] "To Regulate the Class of Upstarts in China," *Beijing Youth Daily*, August 18, 2000; and "Our Government is Concerned with the Rural–Urban Rich–Poor Gap," *Wenhui Bao*, July 23, 2000.

empirical research in several parts of China, Gini coefficients in 1996 had already reached 0.4323 within the rural population, 0.4003 within the urban population, and 0.4577 nationwide.[15]

RISING CRIMES

When this chapter was being drafted, a 10-month "strike-hard campaign" against crime in China was at its peak, the largest of such nationwide actions since the early 1980s. It was the central government's response to the outcry against rising violent crimes frequently aired at public opinion polls, the mass media, and the local and national People's Congress meetings.

Chinese police have not published comprehensive data on the recent anticrime operations. They may never become public; yet reports on individual areas and cases reveal a few significant dimensions of crime in general. These general traits can be summed up in four words, "syndication," "modernization," "internationalization," and "politicization." This classification makes good sense when we place it against this background: for several decades, China was known for rarely having serious crimes because it was the state that monopolized virtually all the means and ways, thereby making big criminal operations impossible. But the China at the turn of the century is no longer such a case.

The syndication of criminal agents is the most worrisome development for the law-enforcement system, though the country's criminal laws have not formally established the categories of "organized crime."[16] In recent years, in every province and in numerous cities,

---

[15] Based on Li Qiang's interview on March 7, 2001, and his two books: *Zhongguo Dalu de Pinfu Chabi* [The Rich–Poor Gap in the Chinese Mainland] (Beijing: Chinese Women's Publishing House, 1989); and *Shehui Fencheng yu Pinfu Chabi* [Social Stratification and the Rich–Poor Gap] (Xiamen: Lujiang Publishing House, 2000).

[16] On December 5, 2000, the People's Supreme Court for the first time issued an "explanatory note" on handling criminal cases that "share certain attributes of black societies (i.e., organized crime)." See the *Legal System Daily*, December 10, 2000, p. 1.

there have been complaints or court proceedings against criminal gangs. Between 1992 and 1999, the public security organs nationwide discovered and eventually levied punishments on more than one million criminal groups of various types. Some had a membership as big as several hundreds, but most of them were relatively small. By early April 2001, the ongoing "strike-hard campaign" had already crushed more than 800 criminal groups in Henan and more than 900 criminal groups with some 3740 members in Sichuan, the two most populous provinces.[17] In the capital city of Hainan, between April and late May 2001, 22 criminal gangs with 105 members were penalized.[18]

Chinese legal scholars and law-enforcement analysts have tried to make a working typology of organized crime observed over the years. They suggest that in criminal activity or "operational specialization," there exist at least six subtypes: those who seize wealth directly for themselves by using naked force; those who charge fees by contracting out their services such as blackmailing, kidnappings, and killings; those who exercise extralegal power over a community by simultaneously occupying high positions in the grassroots government and in the local rings of hooligans; those who make excessive business gains by monopolizing a line of trade in a particular locality through threats and retaliations; those who specialize in illegal trafficking of drugs or people; and, finally, those who run underground financial markets, for example, usury.[19]

By the "modernization" of crime, I refer to the phenomenal updating of hardware and software employed in criminal operations

---

[17] Based on "Black Societies Penetrate Chinese State Organs Quickly," *Renmin Gongan Bao*, April 10, 2001; "The Social Control Situation in China is Serious," *Xianfengwang*, April 11, 2001; "How Bad are China's Black Societies?" *Xianfengwang*, April 9, 2001.

[18] Based on Xinhua News Agency's report from Beijing, June 2, 2001.

[19] Lu Gensong, "Six Subtypes of Black Society-like Criminal Organizations in Contemporary China," *Renmin Gongan Bao*, April 17, 2001. It goes without saying that this typology has obvious conceptual and methodological deficiencies, but it has been widely used in China.

Weaponry for outlaws in China is no longer limited to self-made knives and spears, but includes the standard armyʼs handguns, automatic and semiautomatic rifles, bombs, and advanced explosive devices.[20] Criminal ringsʼ transportation and communications equipment often outperform those of the police, because the former is mostly imported and the latter is largely indigenous. Foreign gang motion pictures and television programs are used by sharp-minded Chinese criminals for self-training.[21] White-collar criminals become more and more sophisticated in manipulating computer programs to steal assets from state banks, alter police data, or coordinate actions across vast areas.

Internationalization of crime has been helped by several structurally powerful factors, suggesting that this is an inevitable trend and will most probably grow further. They include the steady increase in commercial and social interaction between the mainland, Hong Kong, Macao, and Taiwan; the booming international tourism that makes people of various nationalities enter and leave the country more easily;[22] and the growth of cross-border trade with neighboring countries. Criminals at home and abroad exploit these factors to

[20] By the end of May 2001, two monthsʼ operation of the "strike-hard campaign" had led to the confiscation of 330,000 illegal firearms and tens of thousands of grenades, among other things. See "The Public Security Organs have Achieved First-Stage Success in Controlling Firearms and Explosives," Legal System Daily, June 13, 2001. But this statistics, seemed to be an understatement—in a separate report by the official news agency Zhongguo Xinwenshe, police in one province, Guangxi, seized 240,000 illegal firearms during a four-month "seize guns and prevent explosion" campaign a year earlier. Cited from "Chinaʼs Gun Problem," Far Eastern Economic Review, June 29, 2000, p. 10.

[21] Zhang Jun, boss of the most notorious criminal gang in China during 2000–2001, admitted that he had methodically studied many imported crime movies and video tapes in order to perfect his counter-measures against the police. His gang killed 28 people and injured 20 between December 1996 and September 2000. The police officers who captured and executed him showed a fair amount of respect for his organizational and operational techniques. Based on interviews.

[22] By May 2001, the Chinese government had signed agreements with 14 countries to allow Chinese citizens to visit them on tourist visas. Based on the PRC National Tourist Bureauʼs public notice of May 31, 2001.

cooperate on particular deals or become organizationally integrated.[23] After the crime networks' big operations in the mainland are accomplished and the loot needs to be relocated or when their joint ventures run into trouble, arranging for the key agents' escape into foreign territories has become a commonplace affair nowadays.

Some of the more refined criminals are not content with staying in the outlaw domain; instead, they take great effort to penetrate and even take over the leadership of local governmental organs. This is what I mean by the "politicization" of crime, a development that disturbs ordinary citizens as well as the central government, though their worries stem from very different considerations.[24] The marriage between outlaws and local government leaderships takes a number of forms. The oldest form is that in which the criminal offers the official money, sex, and other benefits, and the official provides him protection in return. Then there is the system by which the official hires hooligans to back up his power abuses in his area of jurisdiction. Gradually, criminal groups in some localities become capable manipulating local politics, including village elections, and appoint persons of their choice to official posts.

OFFICIAL CORRUPTION

Although the central leadership and international observers disagree on many things about the country, they share at least one important perception: corruption has penetrated China's public sector, and there is nothing to show that the problem has been curbed despite the anticorruption campaigns.

Publications in English and in Chinese on corruption in contemporary China are numerous, and this section points only to a few structural

[23] It is disclosed that some of the big criminal organizations in Taiwan, Hong Kong, and Macao have tried to set up their branches in the mainland, and one even tried to shift its headquarters to Shanghai. Based on "Black Societies in China are in the Takeoff Stage," *Chinese News Weekly*, February 19, 2001; *Zhongxinwang*, news from Guangzhou city on the sentences of eight members of a Hong Kong-based criminal group, September 16, 2001.

[24] Based on interviews, and see also the long report: "Black Societies Penetrate Chinese State Organs Quickly," *Renmin Gongan Bao*, April 10, 2001.

developments in the area, which can perhaps tell us more about how severe the problem is than unverifiable official statistics on corruption—the only general quantitative data available on this sensitive issue.

Firstly, corruption in China seems to have become a sort of *hang gui* in certain industries and professions. The Chinese term originally means "guild regulations;" ironically, it has in recent years turned out to refer to informal and illicit rules obeyed among a good part of an industry or profession. The construction industry and the state financial sector have been known to be suffering from this. In both areas, side payments and kickbacks have been indispensable for contracts to be offered and loans to be given in most transactions. Unauthorized use of public funds for making private gains has been commonplace. These types of corruption have become industry-wide practices, largely because open and fair tender in the building business is far from being a firm institution, because the staff of the state financial sector rarely bear the brunt of financial loss caused by their mismanagement and misappropriation, and because the outdated formal regulatory frameworks can no longer cover the new economic environment.[25]

Secondly, corruption is confined not merely to individual or private conduct; it has become part of the official organizations. Corruption by individuals, syndicates, or private corporations is prevalent in many politico-social systems, and China is not an exception. What is remarkable about corruption in China is that it is practiced by official bodies as a whole—state-owed companies, Communist Party cells, government departments, police divisions, public hospitals, etc. Officials heading these bodies and the staff plan and carry out schemes like imposing illegal taxes or diverting government funds, in the same way they would plan and discharge their legitimate duties. This practice is termed *jiti weiji* [the collective as an offender] or *danwei fanfa* [a work unit's breach of law].[26] Under

---

[25] For detailed studies see X.L. Ding, "Systemic Irregularity and Spontaneous Property Transformation in the Chinese Financial System," *The China Quarterly*, No. 163 (September 2000), pp. 655–676; X.L. Ding, "The Quasi-Criminalization of a Business Sector in China," *Crime, Law and Social Change*, Vol. 35, No. 3 (April 2001), pp. 177–201.

[26] See recent legal discussions summarized in *Chinese Youth Daily*, July 27, 1999, p. 2.

these circumstances, it becomes extremely difficult or even dangerous for others to fight corruption, because these official bodies can and do use their organizational power and resources to prevent interference from insiders and outsiders, and also to retaliate against those who dare pursue the case.

Lastly—and as a logical development of the above—corruption in China has become the enterprise of a regional state. A regional state in this context does not refer to one or two official bodies, but to almost all the branches of the state machinery in a particular area, such as a county, city, or prefecture. A typical regional state has an overriding Communist Party branch, a civilian administration, a police division, a court, a bunch of state financial institutions, and a border control unit with a Customs office if there is a terminal for international transportation. In the smuggling cases in Xiamen, Zanjiang, etc., in the tax fraud schemes in Shantou, and in the joint corruption and criminal ventures by bureaucrats and gangsters in the industrial center of Shenyang city, nearly every part of the regional state was implicated.[27] That explains why such corrupt and criminal enterprises were carried out for many years and on such a colossal scale, involving tens of billions of yuan. Should the law be impartially applied to the perpetrators, the entire region would be left with no government.

IMBALANCE BETWEEN SOCIAL PROBLEMS AND PROBLEM-CONTROL RESOURCES

None of these problems can be resolved easily. Worse still, they are all interrelated and they constantly interact with each other. For instance, unemployment is the main cause of urban poverty and expanding disparity in household incomes. The sharp contrast

---

[27] Hai Yun, *Xiamen Yuanhua Da'an* [The Big Yuanhua Case in Xiamen] (Beijing: Chinese Customs Publishing House, 2001); Gu Wei, "The Criminal Mayor of Shenyang has Left a Big Question Mark," *Workers' Daily* (Beijing), July 19, 2001; James Kynge, "Chinese Officials Detained in 'Mafia' Inquiry," *The Financial Times*, June 21, 2001.

between the haves and the have-nots has prompted many to seek wealth or take revenge by violent means. Official corruption also contributes to the growing income gap, because many of the newly rich have amassed large assets not by lawful means but by misuse of public property or public office. And in many localities, criminal rings receive protection from, or are even organized and controlled by, police officers and public officials.

To cope with these problems, the government needs various resources, especially financial, human, and institutional ones. Consider just the unemployment issue. To provide each of the 22-million-odd unemployed urban dwellers with 300 yuan in *renminbi* (US$ 36) per month, which is just about enough for a family of two to keep itself from starvation,[28] the government has to prepare a welfare budget of between 60 and 80 billion yuan a year to issue pay checks! But, according to official reports, the total government expenditure for the unemployed was only about 4.73 billion yuan for the first half of 2000,[29] a small fraction of what is needed. It goes without saying that the law of equilibrium works here too: the huge gap is likely to be filled eventually with human suffering, crime, and so on.

The shortage of competent personnel is also a severe drawback. The greater part of the Chinese state apparatus was designed for the control of a society structured by Leninist politics and state-socialist economics. In the past years, particularly since Zhu Rongji became the Prime Minister, the Chinese government has taken visible steps to reorganize its higher level departments in order to meet the increased needs of managing a market-oriented society. Despite this, the Chinese state desperately lacks qualified staff to fill those units and roles that primarily deal with new problems generated by the creative and destructive forces of the market (e.g.,

---

[28] Cui Li, "The Lowest Standards of Living for the Urban Chinese," *Chinese Youth Daily*, April 4, 2000, p. 1; and "Reports on the Minimum Social Security System in Cities," *The Business Weekly of China*, August 13, 1998, pp. 1–2.

[29] Based on the National Institute for Economic Research under The Fund for Studies on Chinese Economic Reforms in Beijing, "Report on the Third Quarter of 2000," pp. 4–5.

property volatility, easier movements of people and equipment within the country), the impact of globalization on domestic corruption and crime, etc.

For example, to help retrenched workers find new jobs, cadres of official labor unions (the only workers' organizations permitted to function in China) themselves have to be sensitive to the ups and downs in the job market and be fairly skillful in fitting different types of job hunters in suitable posts. To curb white-collar (including high-tech) crimes in the financial sector, the Chinese police forces need to know very well sophisticated computer programs and the financial markets. To trace transnational operations in the theft of public property, Chinese law-enforcement agents have to be familiar with the laws and customs of the destination countries. In reality, however, these well-trained professionals are not highly valued by the Chinese governmental recruitment units, and many of them do not want to join the government, given the poor work conditions and rewards.

INFORMATION FIDELITY: KEY TO A SUCCESSFUL MANAGEMENT OF THE SOCIAL PROBLEMS

Of the just-mentioned institutional resources, I particularly want to point to the information mechanism in China, because it is of vital importance in administering such a rapidly changing country with tremendous differences in regions, local cultures, ethnic communities, and social strata. Given the scale and the heterogeneity of the Chinese society, the informational process, the very foundation upon which decisions are made, is very likely to suffer from distortion.

But far more harmful to the informational process in China than its scale and heterogeneity is what can be termed "the incentive structure for not telling the truth." To explain this structure, we need to review at least five contextual factors.

The first is the age–position linkage policy; that is, for each rank in the Communist Party-state's bureaucratic appointments, there is a rather strict age ceiling.[30] If an official is approaching a certain age limit but has just been passed over in a recent round of personnel arrangements, he has a very slim chance of moving up in his bureaucratic career. When the next round of overall personnel restructuring (every three to five years, depending on ranking) comes up, that official may have to accept a less powerful position (at the same rank), or be transferred to a less influential department, or even be required to take earlier retirement. This situation is described by the popular Chinese saying: "Once you pass by this hotel, you can never find another one on your journey."

The second contextual factor is the rule of positive publicity for upward mobility and negative publicity for downward mobility, an institution not unfamiliar to most appointees of today's governments. Other things being equal, a Chinese official has a better chance of obtaining a promotion if there are "visible" accomplishments within his domain (which may be his own work or his subordinates' contribution); and an official is more likely to experience stagnation or demotion in his bureaucratic career if there are "visible" mistakes and failures within his domain (which may be his own fault or his colleagues' and subordinates' responsibility). Here I place emphasis on the "visibility" of achievements or mistakes: how easily others, especially the bosses, can see these? This is far more important than how substantial these are in real life. Over critical issues or at critical times, this policy can take the rigid form of forced "personal responsibility contracting;" that is, the upper government level sets

---

[30] For example, in the most recent overall arrangements in the preparation for the transition to the fourth generation leadership, the personnel policy requires that for a county and *chu* administrative headquarters, at least two of the main officials should be as young as about 30 years, for a prefectural/municipal and *ting/jue* administrative headquarters, one or two main officials ought to be about 40 years, and for a provincial and ministerial administrative headquarters, at least one main official should be about 40 years. In order to give way to these younger people, current officials at the three administrative levels are pushed to take complete or partial retirement two years before the legally specified retiring ages set for each rank. Based on interviews and "The CCP's New Retirement Regulations and Its Policy of Promoting Younger Cadres," *Wenhui Bao* (HK), September 27, 2001.

up a specific objective, for example, preventing something from happening or producing a quantity of something. If that objective has not been met, the local official will be held personally responsible: he may lose his job or pay heavy fines. But the upper government level rarely stipulates the legal framework for the use of means to achieve the ends.[31]

The third contextual factor is the established institution of a unified governing body over a geographic area. It was well known in the Mao Zedong era as *di-fang yi-yuan-hua-de ling-dao*. During the 20-year reform process, the political institution has been affected by the decentralization of economic activity and the growth of social networks outside the state sector. But several main features of the institution remain in place: all the state law-enforcement bodies and the Communist Party discipline-maintenance units in an area (county, city, or prefecture) are under the single unified Party-government leading group's ultimate control; so are the media and communication organizations; and so are the local People's Congress and the local political consultation conference. By "ultimate control," it is meant that the unified leadership may not keep a close eye on every operational detail of the organizations within its jurisdiction on a daily base, but on the most important issues or at critical moments, it will do everything possible to prevent undesirable operations.

The fourth contextual factor is also a time-honored Chinese bureaucratic practice, which is "stratified distribution of information." The question of who gets to know what, when, and how depends on where that person is placed in the political and administrative hierarchy.

---

[31] For a detailed portrayal of how this "personal responsibility contracting" has been used in a particular region in the campaign against the *Falun Gong* movement, see Ian Johnson, "Death Trap: How One Chinese City Resorted to Atrocities to Control *Falun Dafa*," *The Wall Street Journal*, December 26, 2000, p. 1. But there is a crucial aspect of the "contracting" method that the report does not mention—its military background. It can be traced back to earlier dynastic periods; when there was a war, a *junling zhuang*, a military pledge, could be made between an army officer and his superior. The officer would be severely punished if he failed to accomplish the particularly difficult mission.

This manner of sorting and channeling data has the advantage of not allowing the lower strata to know too much, but it also has, among other things, an inherent negative consequence. Because the data is distributed along distinctly separate "pipelines," and because different recipients have little chance to cross-check and verify and expose themselves to contention, the quality of information is inevitably distorted.

The last, and perhaps the most influential, contextual factor is Beijing's firm stand of "stability above everything" [wen-ding ya-dao yi-qi], that is, "maintaining political and social stability is the uppermost task for all Party and government bodies." The Communist Party central leadership has been routinely reissuing this policy instruction since mid-1989, immediately after the massive protest movement. Its message is unambiguous: although other tasks, such as economic growth, use of new technology, international scientific and scholarly exchanges, educational and social development programs, and cultural activity may be important, whenever the political and social order is believed to be threatened by some ingredients of these programs, they must be sacrificed instantly.

Almost all the policies described above contain certain reasonable elements, and some even contain legitimate considerations, for example, the first and the second policies. But, when placed together and implemented under the general constraints of the Chinese political environment, these policies, often contrary to their objectives, have helped to form an incentive structure on the part of Party–state officialdom that systematically distorts the flow of administrative information. Here is a sketch of how that happens:

- Because an official's term in a particular geographic area or government department is limited to a few years, the wise thing for him to do is to prevent big problems from surfacing during his tenure.
- But we know that the real world can hardly be so ideal, and that under China's profound economic and social transformation, serious problems are likely to occur frequently.
- The official's reactions to problems occurring within his jurisdiction could be (a) that he takes an active approach to

tackle them; or (b) that he maintains a passive attitude and does not touch them at all; or (c) that he adopts a middle-of-the-way approach.

- The active approach requires resources, which are often scarce, and personal guts, because tackling problems is always risky. Therefore, it is irrational to expect the majority of officials to take this approach.
- The greater part of officialdom is more likely to take the (b) and (c) approaches. In both cases, deliberate distortion of information by the official is necessary because problems within his domain are either intact or are only partially resolved; he needs to cover up the problems, or overreport on his problem-handling efforts, or do both.

This is one scenario—how information distortion serves an official's personal career interest when he encounters problems that are not created by himself. Now we need to briefly look at two other scenarios: when the problems an official faces are created entirely or mainly by himself, and when he takes the initiative to produce positive results (i.e., achievement oriented).

In circumstances where the official is the direct cause of the problems, his incentive for a complete or near complete coverup is particularly strong. (Typical of this pattern is that an official, his relative, or his crony is found to be involved in corruption or crime.) In circumstances where an official wants to show his extraordinary dedication and ability, his distorting of administrative information can take the form of exaggerating the achievements and/or underreporting the cost for a given level of achievement.[32]

---

[32] Mr. Hu Jianxue, the party secretary of the city government of Tai'an, Shandong province, provided a classic example. As the youngest municipal leader of that province in the first half of the 1990s, he was eager to present fresh evidence of great accomplishments to his superiors. When the provincial government urged peasants to raise more cows and they did not respond enthusiastically out of economic reasons, Hu instructed his assistants in charge of agriculture to buy a large herd of well-fed cows from another region but claimed that these were home-grown. Every time higher levels of government cadres came to his jurisdiction to inspect agricultural production, Hu

If the media makes efforts to investigate the matter and report the facts, or if some brave local residents who know the truth try to bring the issue to the attention of the higher government levels and the general public, the targeted official(s) can exercise the institutional power of "unified leadership" to discipline the media organizations (if locally based),[33] or mobilize the local police to kick nonlocal media investigators out, or retaliate against the local residents in various ways.[34]

---

arranged the herd of cows to be transported to the villages where the inspectors were scheduled to visit, who, of course, were very impressed by what they saw. The villagers remarked: "Those cows recognize Hu Jianxue as an old friend. They have seen him so many times accompanying high-level visitors." In 1996, Mr. Hu was sentenced to death with two-year suspension for extraction of huge money and company stocks. During investigation, it was found that many of his "outstanding accomplishments" that had helped him in his promotion were not real. Based on case-books Yang Shuwen and Chen Zhengyun (eds.), Zuian Shilu [Factual Records of Criminal Cases] (Beijing: Law Publishing House, 1997), pp. 253–260; Zhong Jian (ed.), Dalaulide 74 min Shizhang [Seventy-four Mayors in Prison] (Beijing: Economic Daily Publishing House, 1998), pp. 501–507; and interviews.

[33] On January 2, 2001, a local newspaper Chengdu Shangbao in Sichuan province published a front-page news on a hit-and-run accident. On the 2001 New Year's eve, the official vehicle of Mr. Zhao Congrong, a deputy party secretary of the Peng'an county government in that province, hit three villagers on the road. One was killed instantly and the other two were in critical condition. Angry villagers stopped the vehicle, but Zhao was rescued by another official sedan, leaving behind the victims on the spot. The two injured died a few hours later. On January 11, nine days after this shocking exposure, the newspaper was ordered by the provincial authorities to publish a self-criticism for "inaccurate details in parts of the report," and Mr. Chen Qing, the reporter, was fired. Based on interviews and the dated material in the newspaper.

[34] In March and May 2000, several Chinese newspapers, including the most outspoken one, The Southern Weekend, based on the city of Guangzhou, published investigative reports on the case of Li Lusong, a young peasant of Lanxian county, Shanxi province. In 1999, Li first made formal complaints to the county government against local cadres' misuse of education funds. Without much effect, he then posted his criticism of official corruption in public places. The county–town police unit immediately detained him and tortured him for 12 days, and cut off half his tongue. After his release, Li was unable to talk and work, and his family had to sell all valuable items to pay for his medical bills. Based on the front-page reports in The Southern Weekend, May 12, 2000 and March 1, 2001.

Students of Chinese bureaucracy know well the historical pattern that within state officialdom "those airing good news receive bonus and those airing bad news receive penalties."[35] This bureaucratic "custom," so to speak, is a double-edged sword, helping the government as well as hindering its function. The national leadership in the capital city cannot rely entirely on rosy reports to govern the immense country, and it has to use other long-established channels to learn about the real situation. Those include the "elite information pipelines" run by the central news organizations, such as the Xinhua News Agency and the *People's Daily*, and important government departments, such as those responsible for civil affairs, financial regulation, public health, and law enforcement in particular.

From what we have read from overseas Chinese language publications that often expose "internal reports and notes," information flowing through the "elite pipelines" focuses more on how to deal with disturbing issues than on how to promulgate flattering material, and its quality is unmistakably higher than that of the official mass media coverage. Despite that, we can assert, on the basis of our experience as well as social science theory, that such elite information process still has great potential to mislead the audiences. First of all, every state apparatus, government department, state-run news agency, or state-owned financial body has its distinct self-interest and bias (the two always reinforce each other). There is no incentive for them to "regularly" reveal their own operational errors and misconduct to their superiors, even if these negative things would not be disclosed to the general public. When one segment of the state machinery (e.g., a news agency's regional bureau) makes

---

[35] The best eyewitness work on this pattern in the PRC era is Li Rui, *Lushan Huiyi Shilu, 2nd Edition* [A Factual Record of the 1959 Lushan Conference, Revised Edition] (Zhengzhou: Henan People's Publishing House, 1994). For historical reviews of that bureaucratic tradition, see Wang Yanan, *Zhongguo Guanliaozhengzhi Yanjiu* [A Study of Chinese Bureaucratic Politics] (Beijing: Chinese Social Science Publishing House, 1981) (originally published in 1948); Ray Huang, *1587, A Year of No Significance* (New Haven, CT: Yale University Press, 1981); and Etienne Balazs, *Chinese Civilization and Bureaucracy* (New Haven, CT: Yale University Press, 1964).

confidential critical reports about another (e.g., the regional police division), the central leadership will normally let the higher police authorities follow up on the case. The result is rather predictable. Moreover, as the "elite information pipelines" are separately operated and kept secret from the public, grossly biased observations, imbalanced judgments, half-truths, and even trumped-up charges against the innocent can reach the top level without being promptly verified, challenged, and counterbalanced.[36] This leaves the upper echelons of the decision-making bodies in a state of systemic misinformation.

To sum up, the administrative information mechanism in contemporary China is composed of two basic processes, separable analytically yet complementary operationally. The first process is a formal one, in the sense that it runs bottom up through all segments of the state system and is more or less open to the public. Information distortion through this process is mainly in the manner of screening out bad news and inflating or even manufacturing good news.

The second process can be labeled as a "segregated" one, for it goes through selected parts of the state system and is not open to the public. Despite the higher quality of some of its portions, such

---

[36] On March 6, 2001, an explosion in a rural elementary school in Jiangxi province killed many people, mostly school children. The official version of this tragedy, which was based on the local government-provided material, issued by the Xinhua News Agency, and read out to the international media by the nation's senior leaders including the Prime Minister Zhu Rongji, was: A total of 42 people were killed, of which 38 were children, and it was caused by a deranged adult who killed himself at the spot too. (So, no one alive should be blamed for that bloody incident.) But the survivors, the victims' families, and local news reporters voiced via web sites that at least 54 people were killed, and the explosion resulted from illegal child labor. At the village school, the 8–11 years' old children had been forced to make fireworks in drafty classrooms to support the school, and the local officials had allowed this highly dangerous practice to go on for a long time. Immediately after the blast, the police surrounded the village to prevent Chinese and foreign journalists from interviewing the farmers. All the counter-official-version reports and protests on the web were quietly removed. For more details see Joanne Lee-Young and Sharon Walsh: "Beijing Backs Down on School Explosion Story," *Reuters*, March 16, 2001; Joanne Lee-Young, "Beijing Cracks Down on Firecracker Scandal," *Reuters*, March 15, 2001; and Chinese web site material of March 6–14, 2001.

problem-oriented elite information also suffers from distortion, which is mainly in the form of shifting one's responsibility to others and stepping up vigilance against the so-called "political enemies."

To put it differently, if the first type of information distortion can be characterized as "turning off the alarm," the second type can be characterized as "turning on the alarm at a wrong location."

A DANGEROUS PROBABILITY: TRANSLATING THE SOCIAL INTO THE POLITICAL?

One of the best-known theories of classical political sociology is that the most dangerous moment for a once dreadfully tough regime is when it implements reforms in some spheres of its governance.[37] Subsequent studies point out the cognitive and emotional reasons for why those who are ruled regard their situation as particularly unfair and feel their lives utterly unbearable as the society experiences dramatic changes.[38]

The Chinese society at the start of the 21st century is placed exactly in such circumstances—it is under a structural transformation that is equally profound and drastic, and as a result, many groups and strata feel misplaced. Since the Chinese government wants to be a successful reformist state capable of keeping a balance between change and continuity, it is vital that it confines issues like unemployment, poverty, and crime to the domain of social problems and keep them from becoming explosive political problems.

The top Chinese leadership, with its fresh memory of the Spring 1989 political crisis, is definitely committed to the goal of "depoliticizing" those problems, and that intention has been manifested in the central government's constant calls to maintain order and stability in society.

---

[37] Alexis de Tocqueville, *The Ancient Regime and the French Revolution*, introduction by Hugh Brogan and translated by Stuart Gilbert (London: Collins/Fontana, 1966).

[38] John Urry, *Reference Groups and the Theory of Revolution* (London: Routledge & Kegan Paul, 1973); and Peter Calvert, *Revolution and Counter-Revolution* (Minneapolis, MN: University of Minnesota Press, 1990).

Ironically, however, a number of the policies that the Chinese central state has designed for the depoliticization objective appear to be producing the opposite effects. The incentive structure unintentionally brought out by those policies, as elaborated before, plays a key role in the counterproductive process, because it leads public officials at most administrative levels and in most areas to provide false information to the decision makers above. One cannot make the right decisions on the basis of low-quality information, let alone false information—this is one of the experiences of bureaucratic administration and thus a key instruction of contemporary economic and social sciences.[39]

Concrete social problems, small and big, routinely get covered up or distorted in nature and in scope, and therefore the best time to deal with them is often missed, and the proper means are discarded. While some of the problems can be dispelled, many are simply translated into other forms of troubles. Once the ways to cover up or suppress them are exhausted, the magnitude and acuteness of the accumulated and fermented social problems pose real political challenges to the government. They are turned into political problems, because the people blame the political system rather than individual officials for the failure to tackle the problems, and because angry citizens sometimes turn to collective protests to demand justice and compensation.[40]

---

[39] See Jean-Jacques Laffont and Jean Tirole, A *Theory of Incentives in Procurement and Regulation* (Cambridge, MA: The MIT Press, 1993), pp. 1–19, 515–536.

[40] Two recent incidents provide us with a good opportunity to observe this trend of politicization. The first is about corruption in public works projects. Farmers in Yunyang county in the Three Gorges dam area accused local officials of embezzling resettlement funds. Four elderly men representing the farmers for lodging complaints in Beijing were taken by Yunyang police in March and put in detention. They faced sentences of up to five years, and one of their fellow villagers stated: "We will not give up our struggle and plan to organize more protests." See Jasper Becker, "Lengthy Sentences Feared for Outspoken Farmers," *South China Morning Post*, April 2, 2001, p. 9. Another regards peasants' tax grievances. The whole village in Yujiang county, Jiangxi province refused to pay what they called illegal high local taxes and fees, and local officials labeled the villagers a "criminal gang," using the current "strike-hard campaign" to break their

Although solid and comprehensive data on protests and other types of collective action in China are not available, scattered information does suggest that their scope and intensity are alarming. According to a State Council's document issued on April 23, 1997,[41] during the first three-and-a-half months of that year, about 2.35 million urban residents took part in demonstrations, gatherings, and petition giving, triggered by loss of jobs, economic hardship, and bureaucratic ill-treatment. Nearly 280,000 citizens came to Beijing to urge the central government to step in on issues for which they could not get proper help from the local governments. And, worse still, the Communist Party and state organs received about 2500 threat letters, telephone calls, and fax messages. In 1998, the Guangdong provincial courts alone handled 1500 collective petitions and demonstrations.[42] The Hong Kong-based Human Rights Information Center reported that the PRC police statistics it obtained show that in 1998, large-scale protests nationwide amounted to 60,000; and in 1999, the number rose to 100,000, including some very violent incidents such as blocking the railways and attacking local government/police buildings.[43]

A few in high places are aware of this political danger of a popular ferment. At the annual meeting of National People's Congress in March 2001, Wei Jianxing, a member of the Politburo Standing Committee,

---

resistance. In mid-April 2001, more than 600 police stormed the village and opened fire on unarmed farmers, killing at least two and wounding 18. Based on *The New York Times* report: "Unarmed Tax Protesters Killed as Police Storm Village," *South China Morning Post*, April 21, 2001; and Frank Langfitt, "Chinese Peasants Slain amid Tax Dispute," *Baltimore Sun*, April 18, 2001. This incident was confirmed a few days later by the Chinese government. In the same province there was another collective tax protest in August 2000, which involved about 10,000 farmers.

[41] This document is entitled "Guanyu yao renzhenqiuoshidi jiejue zhigong xiagang, daiye, shiyedi wenti," cited on a web newsletter *Shuidao* [*Tunnel*], No. 24, pp. 5–6, September 17, 1997.

[42] Quoted from the "Work Report" by the head of the Guangdong Provincial High Court, Lu Botao, *Nanfang Ribao*, January 31, 1999.

[43] Quoted from *Chengbao* (HK), A04, December 18, 1999; and *Xinbao* (HK), A14, June 29, 2000.

who oversees the legal system and the official labor unions, issued a rather unusual statement. He admitted that in the reform era, many ordinary people have strong grievances, not because they are politically ill-intentioned, but because their legitimate rights are infringed upon by others, and their basic material interests are denied by changing economic and social conditions. Many of their demands for compensation could have been met quickly and positively if state agencies had handled them according to established laws and polices. However, some government bodies and leading officials are so bureaucratic and irresponsible and others so corrupt that they eventually provoke strong popular reactions and collective protests.[44]

To reduce the frequency of such happenings that senior leaders like Wei Jianxing do not want to see, the Chinese state system— not just its top level or a particular division but its numerous levels and sections—must implement several "administrative rationalization" measures. Indispensable among them are:

1. the development of an information system that is basically transparent, allowing multidimensional reports on and data about social and economic problems to flow into the responsible state agencies and officials, without being distorted, delayed, or just omitted; and
2. the creation of legally regulated channels through which the ordinary citizens can routinely express their nonpolitical demands for social and economic justice.

These rationalization measures are not terribly radical and should not be read as a call to alter the fundamentals of the Chinese political structure. Rather, their implementation will prevent small

---

[44] "Wei Jianxing Joined the Liaolin Provincial Delegation's Discussion," *People's Daily*, March 14, 2001, p. 4. The much talked-about report, "China Investigation Report 2000–2001: Studies of Contradictions within the People under New Conditions" compiled by a research group of the Communist Party's department of organization made very similar assessments. See Erik Eckholm, "Chinese Warn of Civil Unrest across Country," *New York Times*, June 2, 2001.

issues from becoming big and nonpolitical problems from ironically becoming political. Because the four types of issues this chapter has discussed are quite common to market economies across the world, one cannot just want to have an increasingly market-oriented and internationally connected economy keep the society in the Maoist mode. The challenges of managing a huge society under rapid transformation are enormous, particularly when the top leadership is at a politically difficult time of succession. However, I am convinced that unless such rationalization measures are gradually but firmly introduced into the governing process, the fourth generation Chinese leadership will most probably be confronting a society which will have a deceitful appearance of things being "under control" but which have a "time bomb" lurking underneath its calm surface.

Chapter 8

Three Dimensions of Rural Issues and Policy Options

WANG TONGSAN & ZHANG TAO

INTRODUCTION

Thanks to the economic reform of 1978, the Chinese rural economy has made remarkable progress. The total grain production was maintained at 50 million tonnes and the supply of other agricultural products was sufficient; township and village enterprises (TVEs) developed rapidly and became an important force in economic growth; the living standards of the rural peasants improved dramatically along with a significant decline in rural poverty.

However, at the turn of the century, new trends have emerged. For example, growth in farmers' income is slow, economic performance of the TVEs is deteriorating, and more importantly, the income disparity between the urban and the rural areas is getting wider—all potential threats to the stability of the society. The rural economy will be affected with China's entry into the World Trade Organization (WTO). Therefore, achieving rural industrialization and rural urbanization and increasing the farmers' income are three urgent tasks facing policymakers.

This chapter consists of six sections. The first reviews the changes that have taken place in the rural areas since China's implementation of economic reforms and the open-door policy. The second section outlines the three dimensions of rural issues and the third shows their causes, such as uneven distribution of national income, the deteriorating performance of the TVEs, and the heavy burden on the farmers. The fourth section analyzes the impact on the rural economy of China's entry into the WTO. The fifth section puts forward some policy recommendations to deal with the three-dimensional issues, such as increasing investment in agricultural infrastructure, accelerating the tax reform, promoting the pace of urbanization, and developing labor-intensive industries to absorb surplus labor. The final section is the conclusion.

DEVELOPMENT OF AGRICULTURE AND THE RURAL ECONOMY

Before 1978, an immense rural population, low productivity, and serious shortage of agricultural products all severely restricted the development of the economy, leading to a decline in the standards of living of the Chinese people. However, since the economic reform, the situation has changed dramatically owing to the rapid growth of the rural economy.

From 1978 to 2000, the gross output value of agriculture increased at a rate of 6.6% per annum, which is peculiar by international standards (Table 1). The supply–demand ratio of primary agricultural products has changed considerably, from shortage to balance in total volume. In addition, the production structure of agriculture has changed from the traditional unitary or single farming (mainly in grain production) to mixed farming.

Table 1. Gross Output Value of Agriculture (billion yuan)

Year	Gross output value	Agriculture	Forestry	Herd	Fishery
1978	139.7	111.76	4.81	20.9	2.21
2000	2495.18	1387.36	93.65	739.31	27.13

Source: *China Statistical Abstract: 2001*, China Statistics Press.

Since the economic reform of 1978, the nonagricultural sectors, especially the TVEs, have developed rapidly and played an important role in the growth of China's economy. Till now, 60.8% of the total value added to rural areas, 31.8% of farmers' income, 46.3% of the total value added to industry, and 34.8% of export profits emanated from the TVEs. Meanwhile, the TVEs have absorbed nearly 100 million laborers during the last two decades, and this has contributed greatly to the stability of the country. There is no doubt that the success of the TVEs is the most prominent aspect of China's reform.

During the past two decades, there has been a significant increase in the farmers' income and living standards. The average farmers' income increased from 133.6 yuan in 1978 to 2253.4 yuan in 2000, with an average growth rate of 7.89% per annum. Along with this, the average farmers' consumption level rose gradually from 138 yuan in 1978 to 4998 yuan in 2000, with an average growth rate of 6.86% per annum. The Engel's coefficient declined, at the beginning of the reform era, from 67.7 to 50.13% in 2000. At the same time, by implementing the Removal Policy, the poverty level of the total rural population stood at 5.2% in 1998, down from 31.6% in 1978. As a result, the issue of clothing and feeding almost 900 million farmers has largely been resolved.

Development of the economy, however, needs institutional guarantee. From the prevailing system of contracted responsibilities of the household with remuneration linked to output, to the construction of the rural market system, and to the reform of the grain distribution system, institutional innovation is pertinent in the development of China's agriculture. In fact, "institutional innovation has positive effect on the growth of rural economy."[1]

China's reform was initiated from the rural areas. After more than 20 years of economic reform, there has been rapid and steady progress in agriculture and rural economy. This brought the agricultural structure and agricultural industrialization to a new stage. Meanwhile, the construction of rural infrastructure was reinforced, and the rural

---

[1] Wang Xiaolu and Fan Guang, *Zhongguo jingji zengzhang de ke chixuxing* [The Sustainability of China's Economic Growth] (Beijing: Jingji kexue chubanshe, 2000).

tax-fee system reform made great progress. However, at the turn of the century, worrying trends emerged. There is stagnant growth in farmers' income and widening income disparity between the urban and the rural folks. China's entry into the WTO will further aggravate the problems of agriculture, rural areas, and the peasants.

ISSUES CONCERNING AGRICULTURE, RURAL AREAS, AND FARMERS

The "three dimensions of rural issues" refers to the increase in farmers' income, structural adjustment of agriculture, and finally, industrialization and urbanization of the rural areas. It has become one of the most important problems in the development of the Chinese economy. How to increase the peasants' income is the pivotal issue.

Declining Growth Rate of Farmers' Income

Time Series Data Analysis

From the time series data, it is observed that the growth rate of farmers' income has been declining in the recent years. Per capita income increased from 2090.13 yuan in 1997 to 2253.4 yuan in 2000, but the average annual growth rate declined from 8.5% in 1997 to 2.8% in 2000 (Table 2). The growth rate of farmers' income has declined consecutively since 1997, something that has never happened before. As a result, the rural consumption demand is

Table 2. Growth Rate of Farmers' Per Capita Income

Time period	Nominal growth rate (%)	Real growth rate (%)
1978–1985	16.8	15.2
1986–1991	20.1	2.8
1992–1996	20.1	5.1
1997–2000	2.8	3.7

Source: *China Statistical Yearbook*, various issues.

insufficient, and the rural market has stopped expanding. In recent years, the government implemented the "startup domestic demand" policy to stimulate economic growth, but the result is not significant. One important reason is poor rural consumption.

Cross-Section Data Analysis

Meanwhile, the disparity in wealth is widening. This is due to many reasons. First, the income disparity between urban and rural residents has widened. The ratio of per capita income of urban and rural residents was up to 2.78 in 2000, much higher than 1.6—the world's average level. Second, the income disparity among different regions has also widened. In 2000, the income gap between the most wealthy and the poorest regions (Shanghai and Tibet) increased to 4.2:1. Third, the disparity in inner rural areas has widened gradually. The Gini coefficient of the farmers' income has reached 0.43, exceeding the line acknowledged by a worldwide society (Table 3). From 1995 to 2000, the extent of the income disparity among the rural people widened by almost 10%.

Structure Data Analysis

Owing to the decline in prices of agricultural products, the growth rate of the family operating income has decreased in absolute terms (see Table 4). In 2000, the average family operating income was 6380.91 yuan, 295.39 yuan less than that in 1995.

Table 3. Gini Coefficient of Farmers' Income in China

Year	National	East	Central	West
2000	0.4296	0.4229	0.3564	0.4094
1995	0.3932	0.3875	0.3283	0.3798

Source: The National Rural Fixed-Investigation-Point Office, "Analysis of Farmers' Income in China during the Period of Ninth Five-Year Plan," *Issues in Agricultural Economy*, Vol. 22, No. 259 (2001).

Table 4. Average Net Income of Each Rural Household, 1990–2000

	1990	1995	1996	1997	1998	1999	2000
Net income (yuan)	3920.16	9555.40	10392.65	10572.96	10229.43	10260.63	10642.91
Family operating income (yuan)	2900.68	6676.30	6911.29	6955.99	6713.16	6394.28	6380.91
Nonproductive income (yuan)	1019.48	2879.1	3481.36	3616.97	3516.27	3866.35	4262
Income structure (%)							
Family operating income (%)	73.99	69.87	66.50	65.79	65.63	62.32	59.95
Nonproductive income (%)	26.01	30.13	33.5	34.21	34.37	37.63	40.05

During the "Eighth Five-Year Plan," the growth rate of the family operating income reached 18.4%, more than 19.3% higher than that (–0.9%) during the "Ninth Five-Year Plan." Although the share of family operating income in the net income of farmers is decreasing every year, it accounts for nearly 60% at present. Therefore, we can conclude that the continuous decline of the family operating income is a major factor that reduces the growth rate of the farmers' income.

Underdevelopment of Agricultural Product Markets

China is a unique agrarian country with a large rural population and sparse arable land. This makes it different from the resource-rich countries like America and Canada, including resource-scarce nations like Japan and Holland (see Table 5). Furthermore, owing to the decentralization of the farm production belt and the inefficiency of service organizations, the farmers often have to face the big market directly, paying much money in dealing with information, and therefore incurring much higher transactional costs. As a result, the supply–demand ratio fluctuates frequently.

Currently, the basic structure of agricultural products consists mainly of primary and low-end products, being short of high quality,

Table 5. Comparison of Agricultural Input and Output between
China and Other Countries

	Time period	America	Canada	Japan	Holland	China
Cultivated area Per capita hectare	1994–1996	0.71	1.54	0.03	0.06	0.08
Added value by farmers Per capita dollar	1994–1996	–	30202	16712	41245	193
	1996–1998	39523	–	30272	–	307

Source: The World Bank, 1998, 2000, *World Development Indicators,* Development Data Center of the World Bank.

slapup and deep-processing ones. It cannot satisfy the diversified, specialized, and high demands of residents in the rural and urban areas. As a result, the products cannot compete in the international market, a key reason why their prices keep declining.

Withering Township Enterprise

With the transformation from a shortage to a surplus economy and from a buyer's market to a seller's market in recent years, some external factors that restrict the development of TVEs emerged, such as a small and dispersed distribution network, poor management, and outdated techniques. These severely affected the growth of farmers' income and also decelerated the process of urbanization of rural areas.

Since the "Ninth Five-Year Plan," TVEs had experienced much faster growth in absolute terms, but the extent of growth is much slower than that during the "Eighth Five-Year Plan." At the same time, with increasing mechanization, the capacity of TVEs to absorb surplus labor force is declining. For example, in 1997 and 1998, the growth rate of farmers participating in TVEs was only –3.4 and –4.0% respectively. There is no evidence that the declining trend will halt in 2001. Moreover, the losses incurred by TVEs is another serious issue. Although the extent of the losses has been reduced, the average loss incurred by every enterprise increased rapidly; as a result, the total/aggregate losses are increasing (Table 6).

Table 6. Economic Indicators of Township Enterprise*

Year	Value-added of industry (%)	Practitioners (%)	Range of loss (%)	Total loss of every enterprises (yuan)
1995	33.56	7.02	4.95	48,800
1996	21.00	5.02	8.43	22,600
1997	17.40	−3.40	6.80	243,100
1998	17.30	−4.00	6.70	260,600

*All indicators except column 4 refer to growth rate.

Source: The Institute of Rural Development, the Chinese Academy of Social Science, Zhongguo nongcun jingji xingshi fenxi yu yuce [The Analysis and Forecast of Rural Economy in China] (Beijing: Fazhan Chubanshe, various years).

Causes of the Three-Dimensional Issues

Factors Affecting the Increase in Farmers' Income

Declining Prices of Agricultural Products

In the rural areas, the farmers' income comes mainly from the operating income, which accounts for over 70% of the total income. From 1997 to 1999, the operating income decreased 0.3% per year, which was 18.6% lower than that in the six years from 1990 to 1996. In 2000, the average income from planting was 784 yuan, 11.2% lower than that of last year.[2] The reason was that the prices of agricultural products kept decreasing since 1997. The decline in key agricultural products, including grains, cash crops, eggs, fruits, and aquatic products, was as high as 20%. Meanwhile, the prices of agricultural products sold in the retail market also came down. As a result, the income of farmers who sold agricultural products declined.

Heavy Burden on Farmers

Although the Chinese government issued orders repeatedly to relieve the burden on farmers, the local governments always tried to levy

[2] The National Statistical Bureau, 2000.

various fees on them. From 1994 to 1999, the per capita net income of the farmers increased by 12.6% per year, as against all kinds of rural taxes, integrated fee, and the social burden, which increased by 12.7, 10.3 and 29.3%, respectively. In many regions, the tax fee accounted for more than 10% of the per capita net income, largely surpassing the regulation level (5%) of the central government.[3] In 2000, the ratio of urban residents' personal disposable income to total income accounted for as much as 1.4 times that of rural residents. The heavy burden on farmers, the unreasonable tax-fee structure, and the income disparity between rural and urban residents severely affected the growth of their income and discouraged production.

Growth Rate of Farmers' Reward From TVEs Declining

At present, both the institutional and market situation that the TVEs faced have changed fundamentally. In comparison with state-owned enterprises, the TVEs have distinct advantages in operating mechanism at the beginning. However, with the reform of state-owned enterprises, resistance to market forces is accumulating, because many advantages previously enjoyed by TVEs have now virtually disappeared. In terms of quality or competition, TVEs lag behind those in the cities. Moreover, lack of funds is yet another important factor that prevented TVEs from establishing new businesses. With the overhaul of the financial system, TVEs now encounter more difficulties in getting finance from banks. In 1998, the total loans provided by banks amounted to 865.4 billion yuan, an increase of 15.5% over 1997, but the loan balance of TVEs decreased by 11.3% than that in last year. The share of TVEs' loans in nationwide loans declined from 7.1% in 1997 to 5.4% in 1998, which is far below the ratio of output value of TVEs in GDP.

[3] Xu Lianzhong, "Analysis of the Rural Residents Income Change and Influential Factors," *Issues of Agricultural Economy*, Vol. 22, No. 257 (2001).

Some Basic Reasons for the Three-Dimensional Rural Issues

Distorted National Income Distribution Structure

Primarily, the main objective in agricultural development is that the central government needs to increase the input for agricultural development. But for a long time, under the policies of "inclining towards city and the stated-owned industries," the fiscal expenditures in agriculture out of the total expenditure has been far below the agricultural output–GDP ratio. In 2000, the output value of agriculture accounted for 15.9% of GDP; this was in contrast to the fiscal expenditure in agriculture which accounted for 5.5% of the total, which is not consistent with the position and function of agriculture in the national economy. In addition, the ratio has been declining since 1990. In 1998, the central government issued 100 billion yuan of national debt, but only 2 billion yuan was used directly for agriculture. In the 60 billion yuan of national debt issued in 1999, none was used for agriculture. With the decline of the fiscal expenditure on agriculture, the tax revenue from agriculture increased to a large extent. During the first three years after implementing the reform of "tax-sharing system" policy, the expenditure on financial support to agriculture increased by only 68%, but the revenue from agriculture increased nearly two times than before. Various agricultural taxes had been increased from 12.574 billion yuan in 1993 to 39.88 billion yuan in 1998. The average net value of the increase reached as high as 5.46 billion yuan per year. This kind of distorted national income distribution structure weakened the rural economy and thus restricted the growth of farmers' income.

"Dualistic Structure" Between Urban and Rural Areas

The segregation between urban and rural population still continues. To prevent the urban population from overexpanding, the government divided the population into urban and rural residents and separated them through a strict census registration system. Rural residents who wish to enter the city face many obstacles, such as their census register, employment, children's admission to school, and so on. Although industrialization has reached as high a level as 0.7, the urbanization level is as low as 0.4 or so. The abnormal relationship between urban and rural areas and the stagnancy of urbanization has widened the income disparity.

ENTRY INTO WTO AND CHINA'S AGRICULTURE AND RURAL ECONOMY

During the WTO negotiations, China undertook a number of commitments on agriculture. The first was the reduction in tariff. China promised to continue to reduce average tariff on agricultural products from 19 to 17% (2005), among which tariff on important products would be reduced to 14.5%. Excluding the bulk of farm products, the import restriction on most agricultural products would be eliminated in quantity, that is to say, single tariff would be implemented. The second was the market access to agricultural products. The third was eliminating the state-management monopoly. As promised, during the transition period, the government could maintain the state-management foreign trade system on grain, cotton, edible vegetable oil, edible sugar, tobacco leaf, etc. It would later open the import–export trade system of agricultural products according to WTO requirements. The fourth was eliminating the export subsidy. China promised not to give any export subsidy, especially on corn, rice, cotton, etc., to its farmers.

From the above, we can conclude that the key aspects of China's entry into the WTO are reduction of tariff on agricultural products, opening up of agricultural markets, elimination of nontariff barriers, and abolition of state-management monopoly. All these will present both opportunities and challenges to China's agriculture sector and industry.

Advantages

It is beneficial to adjust the domestic agricultural structure and the import–export structure. Previously, China's insistence on grain self-sufficiency (to feed its entire population) had resulted in environmental degradation. After entering the WTO, China has to import resources, especially certain land-intensive products, that other nations have comparative advantages in producing. As a result, entering WTO will favor agricultural structure adjustment. Furthermore, it is beneficial to introduce technology from outside for improving the quality of agricultural products. When China becomes a member of the WTO, it will be easier for foreign capital to enter the country directly, which may bring in advanced technologies that will improve the quality of agricultural products. Finally, with the improvement in resource allocation and structure of agricultural production, rural labor will enter nonagricultural sectors. As a result, free trade will help to increase farmers' income in the long run.

Disadvantages

Trade liberalization will no doubt bring some opportunities for China's agriculture. But it will also produce some negative effects on the rural economy.

Firstly, it will affect agricultural production. During the past decade, the cost of grain production increased at the rate of over 10% per year, with the price of grain going up rapidly. The domestic prices of important products, such as wheat, corn, soybean, cotton, oil bearing crops, and edible sugar, exceeded by 20–50% those of international levels. Clearly there is a lack of competitive advantage. According to forecasts, by 2005, the output of domestic corn will decrease by as much as 8.3% and that of wheat by 3.8%. This increases the pressure on importing some important agricultural products. On the one hand, increasing imports will create pressure on the northern regions. On the other hand, when China enters the WTO, the pattern of corn distribution will change; some southern regions that need fodder grain can purchase directly from international markets instead of from the northern regions. These two aspects can result in the rapid decline in farmers' income, especially for those who depend only on cultivation. Furthermore, it does affect the macroeconomic adjustment of the central government. It becomes more difficult for the government to adjust and control the demand and supply of grain. According to US requirements, the import quota of agricultural products must be distributed to non-state-owned enterprises yearly to prevent state-owned trade enterprises from failing to play their import quota role. Under this condition, once international price is lower than the domestic price, non-state-owned trade enterprises will transfer the quota into import. So the government cannot control import through its monopoly in foreign trade, and then the uncertain factors in grain adjustment will increase. Also, it becomes more difficulty to solve the economic and social conflicts in rural areas. At present, there is increased tension in the rural areas. For example, farmers have much more difficulty in selling their products, and their income remains almost stagnant, and it is very hard for rural labor to relocate to cities. All these problems will perhaps become more pronounced with China's entry into the WTO.

COUNTERMEASURES AND POLICY RECOMMENDATIONS

Short-Term Policy Recommendations

Accelerating Reform of Rural Tax-Fee System to Relieve the Farmers' Burden

In the early 1980s, China began to implement the farmland family contract system. The increase in farmers' income came mainly from agricultural production. After 1984, farmers encountered difficulties in selling their products. The increase in income depended mainly on adjusting the rural industry structure, developing diversified management systems, and boosting the development of rural enterprises. After 1992, farmers' income increased when the prices of agricultural products were raised and the inputs were added to agriculture. But in recent years, owing to the improvement in agricultural productivity and the variation of relative demand to agricultural products, the prices of most products have reached or exceeded the international average level, and the constraint on consumer demand has already restrained price increase. For these reasons, it is imperative to relieve the farmers' burden soon. One solution is to accelerate the reform of the rural tax and fee system.

Readjusting Planting Structure to Stabilize Rural Operating Income

Rural family operating income is the most important part of the farmers' net income. Because it is impossible to further raise the prices of the agricultural products, adjusting the planting structure becomes an essential way to increase the farmers' income. Under the leadership of the central government, the local government should guide people to develop various operating ways to process the primary agricultural products in accordance with the local conditions, while solving the oversupply problem and the high production costs.

Long-Term Policy Recommendations

Readjusting National Income Distribution Structure to Increase Financial Support for Agriculture

Owing to the peculiar nature of agriculture, the government should invest more in it. Presently, optimizing the structure of financial support and increasing the supply of agricultural goods is an important means of eliminating the constraints on agricultural development, promoting the demand structure of investment in agriculture, and improving the equilibrium of supply structure. Government support for agriculture should adapt itself to new situations and create new conditions for input, policy, and service. Government should lay emphasis on infrastructure, such as irrigation and water conservancy, market construction, conservation of agricultural products, and transport. At the same time, it should also take into account technology and information service. Thus, combined with the farmers' efforts, the limited financial support from the government can play a more active role. Furthermore, considering the low income of farmers, the government should encourage research, especially for popularizing advanced technology, and put the results into practice.

Agricultural Industrialization and Agricultural Structure Adjustment

When China becomes a member of the WTO, its agriculture will face intense competition from both international and domestic markets. With the development of agriculture and the changes in international and domestic markets, the agricultural structure must be optimized to solve deep-rooted problems. As a new kind of operating system, agricultural industrialization plays an important role not only in realizing the integration of production, processing, and selling, but also in taking agricultural structure adjustment to a new level. Domestic and international markets place a higher demand on agricultural structure adjustment. Agricultural structure adjustment is not just a problem of deciding what to plant and how much to plant, but rather one of considering the quantity, quality, production, process, and sale.

Development of Nonagricultural Sectors and Urbanization of Rural Areas

Accelerating the development of nonagricultural sectors is an effective way of moving rural surplus labor out of agriculture, which is also crucial in increase the farmers' income. Therefore, the secondary and tertiary industries should develop vigorously so as to widen the employment channels and reduce the dependence of farmers on farmland. A large and comparatively cheap labor force in rural areas is an advantage. Therefore, it is appropriate to develop labor-intensive industries to absorb the rural surplus labor force.

In a sense, rural urbanization can improve resource allocation. It can also alter the existing unreasonable "dualistic structure," save resources, and reduce the cost of rural industrialization. From another angle, it can make rural industries and people more cohesive to create the necessary conditions for optimizing the agricultural structure and developing nonagricultural industries.

CONCLUSION

Presently, the problems concerning agriculture, rural areas, and farmers have become pressing issues in China, and these have a great impact on the sustainable growth of the economy. These issues are not merely agricultural or rural; they are connected closely with the macroeconomy as a whole. To resolve these issues, the whole economic structure must be adjusted to allocate the resources optimally throughout the country. The peasants' income should be increased with urbanization and reform of the TVEs. Comprehensive measures are needed to solve all these issues. Only then can farmers' income be improved and the stability of the society maintained while bringing about modernization of the economy.

Chapter 9

Direct Election of Township Heads: Perspectives of Chinese Peasants*

LI LIANJIANG

One of the most daunting challenges that China's fourth generation leadership will face is how to maintain political stability in the countryside. Since the late 1980s, a major destabilizing factor has been popular protests against township governments. Numerous conflicts, many of which turned violent, have taken place of late between peasants and township officials. In 1997 alone, for instance, angry peasants in Jiangxi province blew up dozens of township government buildings. Policy analysts in Beijing have frequently warned that township governments have become "the weakest link" in the government structure. Even official media, such as the *People's Daily*, which are generally reticent when it comes to unpleasant information, have occasionally criticized township officials for jeopardizing stability by mistreating peasants.[1] Finally, central Party leaders themselves have begun to express concern over the prospect

* For generous financial support, I thank the Asia Foundation, the Henry Luce Foundation, the Research Grants Council of Hong Kong, and Hong Kong Baptist University. I would also like to acknowledge a grant for Research and Writing from the John D. and Catherine T. MacArthur Foundation. For helpful comments on earlier drafts, I thank Kevin O'Brien, Baogang He, and Yongnian Zheng.

[1] For conflicts between peasants and township officials, see Thomas P. Bernstein, and Xiaobo Lu, "Taxation without Representation: Peasants, the Central and the Local States in Reform China," *The China Quarterly*, No. 163 (September 2000), pp. 742–763; Xiaobo

of rural unrest. In 1999, President Jiang Zemin, for instance, told his entourage during an inspection tour in Guangdong province that township governments must be strengthened, because "without a solid foundation, the earth quakes and the mountains shiver."[2]

The top leadership has sought time and again to address the tension between peasants and township governments. In the late 1980s, under the auspices of the Ministry of Civil Affairs, an administrative innovation was introduced in a few counties of Hebei and Shandong. Known as "streamlining government and decentralizing power" [jianzheng fangquan], this reform was designed to make the county government devolve some of its power and revenues to township governments so that the latter could offer more services. This effort was foiled quickly, however, by power-thirsty county leaders.[3] Since the early 1990s, the central government has also tried to reduce the tensions between township governments and peasants by capping the total fees that townships could collect. In December 1991, the State Council issued "Regulations Concerning Peasants' Fees and Labor" [Nongmin chengdan feiyong he laowu guanli tiaoli], which stipulated that the total fees levied on peasants must not exceed 5% of their previous year's net income (Art. 6). Two years later, Agriculture Law (1993) explicitly stated that peasants "have the right to reject" unauthorized fees, fines, and other impositions (Arts. 18–19). Official media, such as the People's Daily, have frequently encouraged peasants to defend their "lawful rights and

Lu, "The Politics of Peasant Burden in Reform China," The Journal of Peasant Studies, Vol. 25, No. 1 (October 1997), pp. 113–138; and Kevin J. O'Brien and Lianjiang Li, "The Politics of Lodging Complaints in Chinese Villages," The China Quarterly, Vol. 143 (September 1995), pp. 756–783. Also author's interviews in Jiangxi, December 1999.

[2] Interviews, Guangzhou, October 2001.

[3] See Li Xueju, Wang Zhenyao and Tang Jinsu (eds), Zhongguo xiangzhen zhengquan de xianzhuang yu gaige [The Current Situation of Township Government and its Reforms] (Beijing: Zhongguo shehui chubanshe, 1994); and Zhang Houan, Bai Yihua and Wu Zhilong (eds), Zhongguo xiangzhen zhengquan jianshe [The Construction of Political Power at the Township Level] (Chengdu: Sichuan renmin chubanshe, 1992).

interests." In a few cases, local courts have gone so far as to accept class action lawsuits against township governments for imposing illegal fees and have ruled in favor of the plaintiffs.[4] But overall these measures have been largely ineffective, primarily because local officials are institutionally predisposed to overextracting resources, and local courts are often ordered not to accept lawsuits related to peasant burdens.[5] Most recently, a reform known as "tax-for-fee" [*fei gai shui*] was experimented with, first in a few counties of Hebei and Shandong and then throughout Anhui province. Once again, the reform was designed to prevent township officials from collecting unauthorized fees. But the initial plan to extend this reform throughout the country was aborted in 2001 after Beijing realized that the central government would have to offer huge subsidies to keep township governments functioning.[6]

Another experimental palliative that has not been officially adopted by the central government concerns direct election of township heads. Advocates of this reform have argued that such elections will reduce the tension between peasants and township officials by making township leaders more accountable to peasants. According to them, direct elections will help check peasant burdens by making it possible to remove from the state payroll those who lose elections. Supporters of this measure have also argued that there is a strong popular demand for direct township elections, and that the best way to maintain rural stability is to open up institutional channels to accommodate popular participation. They have warned

---

[4] See Zhao Changfan, "Jian qing nongmin fudan yao kao falu" [The Reduction of Peasant Burdens Depends on Laws], *Minzhu yu fazhi* [Democracy and Legality], No. 2 (February 1993), pp. 28–29.

[5] For a discussion of the incentive system faced by township leaders, see Kevin J. O'Brien and Lianjiang Li, "Selective Policy Implementation in Rural China," *Comparative Politics*, Vol. 31, No. 2 (January 1999), pp. 167–186.

[6] Interview with a senior researcher from Beijing, Hong Kong, December 2001. On the financial crisis of township governments and the tax-for-fee reform, see "China's Rural Governments are Bust," *The Economist*, December 15, 2001, p. 26; Josephine Ma, "Rural Cash Crunch Taxes Reformers," *South China Morning Post*, January 7, 2002, p. 3

that, without introducing such reforms popular grievances will continue to grow and may eventually explode as massive unrest. These analysts have also argued that the overwhelming majority of peasants are perfectly capable of participating in direct elections at the township level.[7]

Some other analysts, however, disagree. They generally do not contest the need for democratic reforms, but instead argue that most peasants are not overly interested in direct township elections. They often cite a remark, allegedly attributed to villagers: "We care a lot about who serves as our village head. As to who serves as township head or county magistrate, we do not care." It has also been suggested that most peasants are not educated enough to participate in direct township elections, and so if such elections are introduced, they may vote irresponsibly, irrationally, or even sell their votes. As a result, direct elections may produce worse township leaders, thus further jeopardizing rural stability.[8]

Do Chinese peasants think that township heads should be directly elected? If they do, do they think that such elections can be introduced right away? Who tends to hold what view on direct

---

[7] See Li Fan, "Buyun xiang shi Zhongguo zhengzhi tizhi gaige de 'Xiaogang cun' ma?" [Is Buyun Township the 'Xiaogang Village' for China's Political Reforms], Zhongguo shehui daokan [Journal of Chinese Society], No. 2 (February 1999), pp. 14–17; Wu Shiyi, "Du Runsheng shuo: nongmin ying biancheng ge 'ziyouren'" [Du Runsheng Says: Peasants Should Become Free Men], Beijing guancha [Beijing Observations], No. 1 (January 1999), p. 12; Wang Dexian, "Li Changping: shangshu shi wo xiang nongmin chanhui" [Li Changping: by Submitting a Petition to the Center I was Repenting to Peasants], Workers' Daily, September 14, 2001, p. 1; and Li Changping, Wo xiang zongli shuo shihua [I Told the Premier the Truth] (Beijing: Guangming ribao chubanshe, 2002). Also interviews, Beijing, September 2001.

[8] For a summary of arguments against introducing direct township elections, see Li Fan, "Buyun xiang shi Zhongguo zhengzhi tizhi gaige de 'Xiaogang cun' ma?" [Is Buyun Township the 'Xiaogang Village' for China's Political Reforms], Zhongguo shehui daokan [Journal of Chinese Society], No. 2 (February 1999), pp. 14–17. Also see Zha Qingjiu, "Minzhu bu neng chaoyue falu" [Democracy Must Not Overstep the Law], Fazhi ribao [Legal Daily], January 19, 1999, p. 1; and Lang Youxing, "Zhixuan ke xing hu—Buyun xiang zhijie xuanju ji qita" [Is Direct Election Practical?—Direct Election in Buyun Township and Others], Dongfang [Orient], Nos. 4–5 (April–May 1999), p. 83.

township elections? Using survey data and interviews, this research tries to address these questions. First, I identify four representative views held by peasants about direct township elections:

1. the "liberal" view that township heads should be directly elected and such elections can be conducted right away;
2. the "moderate" view that township heads should be directly elected but conditions for holding such elections are not yet ripe;
3. the "conservative" view that township heads should not be directly elected by peasants, now or anytime in the future; and
4. the "no opinion" view.

I then present the results of a multivariate regression analysis, which showed that

1. villagers who were dissatisfied with the performance of township officials were more likely to hold the "liberal" view rather than the "conservative" position;
2. politically more assertive villagers were most likely to be "liberal";
3. economically better-off villagers were most likely to hold the "liberal" position; and
4. better-educated villagers were less likely to hold the "no opinion" position, but they were also more likely to be "moderate" than "liberal."

These findings suggest that further deterioration of the relationship between township officials and peasants, the growth of peasant political assertiveness, and economic development may heighten popular demands for direct election of township heads.

DATA

The data on which the following analysis is based comes primarily from a survey conducted from December 1997 to February 1998 in 478 villages in Anhui, Beijing suburbs, Fujian, Hebei, Jiangsu,

Jiangxi, and Shandong. The questionnaire had 99 questions, took about 60 min to complete, and permitted respondents to include open-ended responses. The interviews were carried out primarily by trained college and high school students. Better-educated respondents were allowed to fill in the questionnaires by themselves, if they so chose. Altogether, 10,041 questionnaires were completed and collected,[9] 2217 of which included comments written by the respondents or recorded by the interviewers.[10] Those comments, together with research notes submitted by some interviewers, provided supplementary evidence that was useful for understanding the villagers' attitudes towards direct township elections.

Owing to the restrictions on politically sensitive surveys in rural China, the survey was conducted in an opportunistic manner.[11] In

---

[9] In earlier research that uses the same survey data, the total number of valid questionnaires was reported as 8302, see Kevin J. O'Brien and Lianjiang Li, "Accommodating 'Democracy' in a One-Party State: Introducing Village Elections in China," *The China Quarterly*, No. 162 (June 2000), p. 485. I later realized that the standards of data-cleaning I applied at that time were too stringent. A closer check on reports of the interviewers and respondents' comments showed that most of the apparently suspicious questionnaires were in fact genuine. So in a later article, I reinstituted most of the formerly excluded cases, see Lianjiang Li, "Support for Anti-Corruption Campaigns in Rural China," *The Journal of Contemporary China*, Vol. 10, No. 29 (November), p. 575. Since then I have done one more round of data-cleaning and recovered some more cases. The survey was designed to explore the dynamics of political contentions in rural China. Of particular interest was who tended to engage in and organize collective protests against local governments. Since such political activists constitute only a very small fraction of the rural population, I decided to have my collaborators interview as many villagers as possible.

[10] Written comments totaled 7954 lines, of which 741 were from Anhui, 963 from Beijing, 643 from Fujian, 1428 from Hebei, 639 from Jiangsu, 3129 from Jiangxi, and 1152 from Shandong.

[11] For a discussion of such restrictions, see Tianjian Shi, "Survey Research in China," in Michael X. Delli Carpini, Leonie Huddy, and Robert Y. Shapiro (eds.), *Research in Micropolitics: Rethinking Rationality*, Vol. 5 (Greenwich, CT: JAI Press, 1996), pp. 216–220. Also see Lianjiang Li, "Surveying Chinese Peasants: Costs and Benefits of Not Seeking Approval," Paper presented at Conference on Surveying China, The Sigur Center

most places, the requirements of probability sampling were compromised to avoid attracting unwanted attention. In Fujian and Jiangsu, one county was selected by convenience, then three townships representing high, middle, and low levels of economic development were selected from each county, and three or four administrative villages were chosen, again according to levels of economic development. Finally, in each selected village all available adult members of a randomly chosen small group [*cunmin xiaozu*] (former production team) were interviewed. In the other five provinces, accidental sampling was employed. Interviewers, most of whom were college students, were dispatched to their home villages during winter vacation to interview up to 30 villagers.

Since no strict probability sampling procedure was enforced, the data set obtained from these surveys, though very large, may not be representative of the rural population in the six provinces. For this reason, all findings presented in this paper are only descriptive, not inferential. In other words, they describe only the respondents included in the analysis. We cannot infer with certainty whether the observed patterns hold true for the entire rural population of these six provinces, let alone all of China. Though the extensive geographical reach of the survey and the heterogeneity of the sample enhance our confidence in the generalizability of the findings to some extent, this research is only exploratory. My main goal was to collect reliable data on sensitive political issues, such as lodging collective complaints, and to use this data to generate hypotheses to be tested in future research. Definite conclusions about the issues discussed below cannot be drawn until national probability samples of China's rural population are available.[12]

for Asian Studies, George Washington University, Washington, DC, USA, June 9–10, 2000.
[12] On the use of local probability samples, see Melanie F. Manion, "Survey Research in the Study of Contemporary China: Learning from Local Samples," *The China Quarterly*, Vol. 139 (September 1994), pp. 741–765.

ATTITUDE TOWARDS DIRECT ELECTIONS OF TOWNSHIP HEADS

Rebuilt after the dissolution of the commune system in 1982, township [*xiang*] and town [*zhen*] government is the lowest level in the Chinese governmental hierarchy.[13] In 1999, there were 44,741 townships and towns in China, 19,184 of which were towns.[14] (Towns are generally more urbanized and industrialized than townships. For simplicity, I use "township" to refer to both townships and towns in this paper.) On an average, each township has around 20,000 residents and 20 villages.[15] Townships are governed by the township Party committee, the township people's government, and the township people's congress. Leaders of the three institutions are chosen in three different ways. The township Party secretary, for instance, is appointed by the county Party committee. But according to the Constitution (Art. 101) and the *Organic Law of Local People's Congresses and Local People's Governments* (1979, revised in 1982, 1986, and 1995), the head and deputy heads of the township government should be elected by the township people's congress deputies, who in turn are to be directly elected by the residents of the township.[16] In reality, however, most township heads are selected by the county leadership, and the election at the township people's congress is little more than a formality.

---

[13] On the reconstruction of township government, see Vivienne Shue, "The Fate of the Communes," *Modern China*, Vol. 10, No. 3 (July 1984), pp. 259–283.

[14] National Statistics Bureau, *Zhongguo tongji nianjian* [China Statistical Yearbook] (Beijing: Zhongguo tongji chubanshe, 2000), p. 369.

[15] Here I mean "administrative villages" [*xingzheng cun*], which are usually equivalent to the brigades of the commune era. Most administrative villages are natural villages, though a large, natural village is sometimes divided into two or more administrative villages, and several small natural villages can be combined into one administrative village. Each administrative village has its own villagers' committee.

[16] For an account of revisions to the *Organic Law*, see Shi Weimin, *Gongxuan yu zhixuan* [Open Selection and Direct Elections] (Beijing: Zhongguo shehui kexue chubanshe, 2000), pp. 283–297.

Appendix 1. Demographic Profiles of Respondents

	Anhui	Beijing	Fujian	Hebei	Jiangsu	Jiangxi	Shandong nation
Gender							
Male	80.5	56.6	49.8	61.3	50.3	65.3	61.3
Female	19.5	43.4	50.2	38.7	49.7	34.7	38.7
Age							
18–25	12.3	19.7	7.3	26.8	10.5	12.5	23.2
26–35	33.9	32.6	37.7	25.5	28.2	31.9	30.3
36–45	29.4	23.4	35.4	25.8	26.9	29.3	23.9
46–55	12.7	15.8	12.6	15.6	25.5	18.5	15.5
56–65	5.5	6.8	4.1	4.8	8.2	6.6	5.5
66–above	0.6	1.1	0.1	0.3	0.1	0.4	1.2
Missing	5.7	0.6	2.9	1.2	0.6	0.8	0.4
Education							
No schooling	6.8	3.3	3.8	6.3	10.2	8.8	2.3
Primary school	30.1	18.5	22.2	21.1	33.9	36.7	22.2
Junior middle	49.6	51.0	49.8	46.9	42.4	39.8	48.5
Senior middle	12.7	26.8	23.8	25.5	13.2	14.7	26.8
Missing	0.8	0.4	0.3	0.2	0.3	0.0	0.2
Party membership							
Party member	13.1	12.4	6.4	9.3	6.6	10.9	11.0
Non-member	82.2	83.3	91.0	89.0	92.5	88.3	87.8
Missing	4.7	4.2	2.6	1.7	1.0	0.7	0.2

Note: Anhui, $N = 528$; Beijing, $N = 990$; Fujian, $N = 1529$; Hebei, $N = 1304$; Jiangsu, $N = 1445$; Jiangxi, $N = 2101$; Shandong, $N = 2144$; numbers in cells are percentages; columns may not sum to 100 due to rounding effects.

It is therefore no surprise that most township heads are responsive mainly to their superiors in the county and pay comparatively little attention to the needs and demands of peasants.[17]

[17] For a recent discussion of elections of township people's congresses and elections of township heads, see Melanie Manion, "Chinese Democratization in Perspective: Electorates and Selectorates at the Township Level," *The China Quarterly*, No. 163 (September 2000), pp. 764–782.

By late 1997 and early 1998, when the survey was conducted, no direct elections of township heads had been held anywhere in China.[18] Still, the survey indicated that popular support for introducing such elections was fairly strong. When asked "Do you think that township heads should be directly elected by peasants?"[19] 42% of the 10,041 respondents (whose demographic profiles are summarized in Appendix 1) thought that township heads should be directly elected, and that such elections could be held immediately. I call this the "liberal" view. Another 24.1% thought that township heads should be elected directly but maintained that conditions for such elections were not ripe. I call this position "moderate." Only 9.1% of the respondents thought that township heads should not be directly elected. I call this view "conservative." Yet another 23.2% claimed to have "no opinion," and the remaining 1.7% declined to answer the question.

THE EFFECT OF DEMOGRAPHIC PREDICTORS

Who tends to hold which of the four identified views? A multivariate multinomial logistic regression analysis was conducted to answer this question. Of the four positions of the dependent variable (response), "liberal" was used as base category in order to highlight what might contribute to a respondent's choice between "liberal" and "conservative," between "liberal" and "moderate," and between "liberal" and "no opinion." Independent variables (predictors) included five demographic variables— gender, age, level of education, annual household per capita income, and Party membership. The other four predictors were respondents'

---

[18] The first direct election of a township head was conducted in Sichuan in late 1998, see Baogang He and Youxing Lang, "China's First Direct Election of the Township Head: A Case Study of Buyun," *Japanese Journal of Political Science*, Vol. 2, No. 1 (May 2001), pp. 1–22; and Joseph Y.S. Cheng, "Direct Elections of Town and Township Heads in China: The Dapeng and Buyun Experiments," *China Information*, Vol. XV, No. 1 (2001), pp. 104–137.

[19] *"Nin ren wei xiang zhen zhang shifo yinggai rang nongmin zhijie xuanju?"*

assessment of the performance of township officials, their awareness of "local policies that peasants dislike," their assertiveness vis-à-vis local governments, as well as their experience of village elections.

The regression analysis suggested that, of the five demographic variables, gender was not significant in predicting respondents' attitude towards direct township elections, when the effects of the other eight predictors were held constant. Age was significant only in predicting whether a respondent would take the "liberal" position or claim to have "no opinion." The positive coefficient of Age in the column "No opinion" in Table 1 indicated that, as the age of the respondent increased, the likelihood of choosing "no opinion" rather than holding the "liberal" position also increased.[20] More precisely, for every unit of increase in age (one year), the odds of having "no opinion" rather than adopting the "liberal" position increased by 1.008 times (odds ratio = 1.008).[21] But when it came to predicting a respondent's choice between "liberal" and "moderate," or between "liberal" and "conservative," age was statistically insignificant ($p > 0.05$).

---

[20] Logistic regression coefficients reflect the change in the log odds of the dependent variable that a one-unit change in the independent variable would cause. A positive coefficient increases the probability of an event occurring, while a negative value decreases the predicated probability of an event occurring. When interpreting the meaning of a given coefficient in multinomial logistic regression, we need to take into account which category of the dependent variable is used as base category. In addition, we need to take into account which category of a predictor is used as base category if it is a nominal variable, and the meaning of an increase of numerical value of a predictor if it is a continuous variable. In this case, since the "liberal" position is used as base category (defined as "0"), Table 1 is the summary of three binary logistic regressions.

[21] The odds of an event occurring are defined as the ratio of the probability that it will occur to the probability that it will not occur. In other words, when p is the probability of an outcome, the odds of the same outcome are $p/(1-p)$. The odds ratio is the ratio of the odds of an outcome when one particular predictor is, say, 1, compared with the odds of an outcome when that predictor is, say, 0. The odds ratio, always predicated on a particular independent variable, is the increase (or decrease) in the odds of an outcome when that independent variable increases by 1. For a detailed discussion of odds and the odds ratio, see Tamas Rudas, *Odds Ratios in the Analysis of Contingency Tables*, Sage University Papers Series on Quantitative Applications in the Social Sciences, Series No. 07-119 (Thousand Oaks, CA: Sage Publications, Inc., 1998).

Table 1. Multinomial Logistic Regression Predicting Attitude Toward Direct Elections of Township Heads

	Conservative		Moderate		No opinion	
	Logit	Odds ratio	Logit	Odds ratio	Logit	Odds ratio
Intercept	-0.539 (0.384)		-0.819** (0.268)		-0.875** (0.328)	
Age[a]	0.003 (0.005)	1.003	-0.001 (0.003)	0.999	0.008* (0.004)	1.008
Gender[b]						
Men	0.089 (0.102)	1.093	-0.054 (0.069)	0.947	-0.058 (0.83)	0.944
Women	0		0		0	
Education[c]	0.042 (0.065)	1.043	0.284*** (0.045)	1.329	-0.152** (0.054)	0.859
Income[d]	-0.078** (0.029)	0.925	-0.049** (0.069)	0.952	-0.056* (0.024)	0.945
Party member[e]						
Yes	0.413** (0.142)	1.512	0.441*** (0.101)	1.555	-0.373* (0.156)	0.689
No	0		0		0	
Assessment[f]	-0.097*** (0.029)	0.907	-0.013 (0.019)	0.987	0.004 (0.024)	1.004
Local policies[g]						
Do not know	-0.620*** (0.162)	0.538	-0.218 (0.114)	0.804	0.804*** (0.128)	2.235
Many	-0.862*** (0.167)	0.422	-0.555*** (0.114)	0.574	-0.286* (0.146)	0.751
Some	-0.299* (0.120)	0.742	0.037 (0.090)	1.038	0.025 (0.119)	1.025
None	0		0		0	
Assertiveness[h]	-0.126*** (0.016)	0.882	-0.064*** (0.011)	0.938	-0.072*** (0.014)	0.930

Village election[i]					
Do not know	0.034 (0.139)	1.034	-0.206 (0.095)	0.814	0.414*** (0.110)	1.513
Primary	-0.120 (0.138)	0.887	0.012 (0.091)	1.012	0.047 (0.118)	1.048
No primary	0.137 (0.141)	1.146	-0.040 (0.097)	0.961	-0.121 (0.128)	0.886
No election	0		0		0	

Note: $N = 5801$–2 log likelihood $= 13,760$, Nagelkerke $R^2 = 0.10$. $*p \leq 0.05$, $**p \leq 0.01$, $***p \leq 0.001$. The dependent variable is a multinomial variable; "liberal" is used as base category; standard errors appear in parentheses.

a Ranging from "18" to "70".

b Female is coded as "2," male as "1."

c Measured by the level of school finished, where (1) "no schooling," (2) "primary school level," (3) "junior middle school," and (4) "senior middle school."

d Household per capita annual income, measured by an 8-level index, where "1" stands for "below 200 yuan," "2" for "200–500 yuan," "3" for "501–1000 yuan," "4" for "1001–2000 yuan," "5" for "2001–4000 yuan," "6" for "4001–6000 yuan," "7" for "6001–10,000 yuan", and "8" for "10,001 yuan and above."

e Coded "1" if a Party member, "2" if not a Party member.

f Assessment of performance of township officials measured a constructed scale that ranges from 2 to 10, where "2" stands for "very positive" and "10" for "very negative."

g Existence of local policies disliked by peasants, "1" stands for "do not know," "2" for "many," "3" for "some," and "4" for "none."

h Measured by a constructed scale that ranges from "–6" to "6," where "–6" stands for least assertive," "6" for "most assertive."

i Village elections, "1" stands for "do not know if there were any village elections," "2" for "election with primary," "3" for "election without primary," and "4" for "no election."

Unlike gender and age, Party membership was significant in predicting a respondent's choice between the "liberal" position and the three alternatives. Perhaps because of their affiliation to the ruling Party, whose Leninist principle of democratic centralism runs against the idea of popular election of political leaders, Party members surveyed in this research were in general more conservative than nonmembers in regard to direct election of township heads. As we see in Table 1, compared to respondents who had not joined the Party, Party members were over one-and-a-half times more likely to hold the "conservative" view rather than the "liberal" (odds ratio = 1.512). This finding was corroborated by remarks made by many respondents. A Party member from Jiangxi, for instance, wrote: "Township heads should be elected by Party members only, not by all villagers. Otherwise there will be chaos" (JX0358).[22] Even when Party members agreed that township heads should in principle be directly elected, they were more likely than nonmembers to adopt the "moderate" position rather than the "liberal" view (odds ratio = 1.555). Interestingly, perhaps because of their stronger sense of political efficacy, Party members were less likely than nonmembers to take the "no opinion" position rather than the "liberal" view (odds ratio = 0.689). This indicates that Party members in the countryside tend to be either for or against the introduction of direct township elections, while nonmembers tend to be more likely than Party members to be uninterested in this issue.

Corroborating the argument that economic development may generate stronger popular demand for political participation,[23] this research showed that respondents with higher income tended to

---

[22] In this paper, respondents' written comments are referred to by the serial number of the questionnaire, for example, HB0085. Here HB stands for Hebei. The abbreviations for the other provinces are: AH for Anhui, BJ for Beijing, FJ for Fujian, JS for Jiangsu, and JX for Jiangxi. Since the survey in Shandong was administered by two independent teams, the serial numbers of the questionnaires start respectively with SDA and SDB.

[23] For classical statements of this argument, see Daniel Lerner, *The Passing of Traditional Society* (Glencoe: Free Press, 1964); Karl Deutsch, "Social Mobilization and Political Development," *American Political Science Review*, Vol. 55 (September 1961), pp. 493–514; and Samuel Huntington, *Political Order in Changing Societies* (New Haven: Yale University Press, 1968).

be more supportive of direct township elections. In this research, annual household per capita income was measured by an eight-level index, ranging from "1" (below 200 yuan) to "8" (over 10,001 yuan).[24] This predictor remained significant when the effects of other eight predictors were held constant. The regression coefficients of income in all three columns—"conservative," "moderate," and "no opinion"—were negative, indicating that respondents who reported higher household per capita incomes were less likely to choose these three positions over the "liberal" one. In other words, the higher a respondent's income, the more likely was he or she to hold the "liberal" view. For instance, holding other predictors in the model constant, a respondent whose annual household per capita income was "201–500 yuan" was less likely than those whose income was "below 200 yuan" to be "conservative" instead of "liberal" (odds ratio = 0.925). Conversely, one level of increase in income increased the odds of holding "liberal" rather than "conservative" views by nearly 1.1 times (odds ratio = 1.081). If this pattern holds true in the entire rural population, we may expect to see that popular demands for direct township elections are stronger in the more economically developed regions than in the less developed ones.

Perhaps the most interesting demographic predictor was education. It is not surprising that the better-educated respondents were less likely than the less educated to have "no opinion" on township elections. Contrary to a widely accepted argument that the better educated are more likely to hold democratic values, higher level of education does not make a respondent choose the "liberal" over the "conservative"

---

[24] The question was worded: "Approximately what was the net per capita income of your family last year?" [*Nin quanjia qunian renjun chun shouru dayue shi duoshao yuan?*]. Of the 10,041 respondents, 7% said it was below 200 yuan, 18.0% between 200 and 500 yuan, 19.9% between 501 and 1000 yuan, 16.1% between 1001 and 2000 yuan, 13.2% between 2001 and 4000 yuan, 7.5% between 4001 and 6000 yuan, 4.2% between 6001 and 10,000 yuan, 2.4% over 10,000 yuan, 10.4% said they did not know, and 1.3% declined to answer. There is no way to independently assess the reliability of the respondents' estimates.

position.[25] Also surprising is that the better-educated respondents turned out to be more likely than the less educated to be "moderate" rather than "liberal." That is to say, they were more likely to think that conditions for holding direct township elections were not ripe. Respondents' written remarks suggested that some better-educated villagers seemed to regard themselves as culturally superior to the less educated. A senior middle school graduate from Shandong, for instance, wrote: "Township heads should be elected directly by peasants, but at present such elections cannot be held because the cultural level of the masses is too low" (SDA0143). Another senior middle school graduate from Jiangsu sounded even more condescending: "Many peasants are either timid or greedy. If direct township elections are held now, the rich and bad guys can easily collect enough votes to win the election by offering bribes to the greedy and by hiring thugs to menace the timid" (JS0762). It will be interesting to see how this kind of elitism may affect collective action in the countryside, because most so-called "peasant leaders" [nongmin lingxiu] are better educated than their followers.[26]

ASSESSMENT OF TOWNSHIP OFFICIALS

Since the introduction of direct election of township heads will almost certainly bring about major changes in township governance, we may expect that villagers who are dissatisfied with the current township leadership are more likely to wish for changes and therefore support direct township elections. This hypothesis was largely confirmed.

---

[25] For a discussion of high level of education as a necessary condition of democracy, see Seymour Martin Lipset, "Some Social Prerequisites of Democracy: Economic Development and Political Legitimacy," American Political Science Review, Vol. 53 (1959), pp. 78–81.
[26] For reports on "peasant leaders," see Duan Xianju, Tan Jian, and Chen Bin, "'Yingxiong' hai shi 'diaomin'?" ('Heroes' or 'diaomin'?), Banyuetan (neibuban) [The Semi-monthly] (Internal Edition), No. 2 (February 1999), pp. 8–12; and Li Junde, "'Jianfu yingxiong' za cheng le fanzui xianyiren" [How did Heroes of Reducing Burdens Become Criminal Suspects], Banyuetan (neibuban) [Semi-monthly] (Internal Edition), No. 2 (February 2000), p. 14.

Two questions were raised about the performance of township officials in this research. The first one was "How well do you think township officials are doing in governing by law?"[27] Corroborating field observations made by other researchers, the survey showed that the majority of the responses were not particularly positive. Out of 10,041 respondents, only 3.6% found the performance of township officials in this respect very good, 11.4% good, 39.8% so-so, 11.5% poor, and 9.7% very poor. In addition, 22.9% said they had "no opinion," and 1.1% declined to answer the question. Some respondents offered examples of how township officials blatantly violated laws and mistreated peasants. A villager from Jiangxi, for instance, wrote: "Peasant burdens are determined by township leaders. If peasants raise any objections, township officials will order hired thugs to rough them up and confiscate their valuables such as TV sets and livestock" (JX1000). Some respondents even called township officials "bandits" [*tufei*], who frequently broke laws and preyed upon peasants: "Today's township officials are not much different from bandits. If township officials enter your house, that means ill fortune has fallen upon you. When township officials enter the village, it is just like when the [Japanese] devils arrived. Everybody keeps a wide berth from them" (JX1230, similar remarks were made by HB0084 and HB0098).

The second question about the performance of township officials was "How do you think township officials are doing in practicing the mass line and respecting the will of the people?"[28] The results were even less positive: out of 10,041 respondents, only 3.0% found the performance of township officials very good, 9.7% good, 37.1% so-so, 14.7% poor, and 12.8% very poor. The nonresponse rate was similarly high, as 21.9% said they had "no opinion," and 0.8% declined to answer the question. The high nonresponse rates are worth noting, because quite a number of interviewers reported that many respondents were hesitant to answer questions about the performance of village cadres and township officials, apparently

---

[27] "*Nin renwei xiangzhen zhengfu ganbu zai yifa banshi fangmian zuode hao bu hao?*"

[28] "*Nin renwei xiangzhen zhengfu ganbu zai zou qunzhong luxian zunzhong minyi fangmian zuode zenmoyang?*"

fearing possible retaliation by local cadres if they were found to have spoken critically.

To simplify the analysis and, more importantly, to avoid the problem of multicollinearity that would result if two or more highly correlated variables were included as separate predictors in the regression model, the two questions about the performance of township officials were treated as indicators of a respondent's overall evaluation. "No opinion" was treated as a missing value. A simple summation index of respondents' assessment of township officials was then constructed (Cronbach's alpha = 0.85).[29] The index ranges from "2" (most positive) to "10" (most negative).

The regression analysis showed that assessment of township officials had a significant impact on a respondent's attitudes towards direct township elections. The negative coefficient of the variable "assessment" in the column of "conservative" indicated that the more positive a respondent's evaluation was, the less likely was he or she to hold the "conservative" view vis-à-vis the "liberal" one. Put the other way round, the more positive a respondent's assessment of township officials was, the more likely was he to think that township heads should not be directly elected. To be more precise, holding the other eight independent variables constant, a one-level increase in the evaluation of township officials increased the odds of taking the "conservative" position versus the "liberal" position by 1.1 times. It is interesting, though, that a respondent's evaluation of township officials had no significant impact on one's choice between the "liberal"

---

[29] The most popular way of measuring the reliability of a construct scale is to calculate Cronbach's alpha coefficient, which is between 0 and 1. There is, however, no universally accepted threshold for this coefficient. Some methodologists suggest that it should be 0.65 or larger; for a discussion, see Robert F. DeVellis, *Scale Development: Theory and Applications* (Newbury Park, CA: Sage Publications, Inc., 1991), p. 85. Others consider 0.70 as acceptable; see, for instance, W. Paul Vogt, *Dictionary of Statistics and Methodology: A Nontechnical Guide for the Social Sciences*, 2nd edn. (Thousand Oaks, CA: Sage Publications, Inc., 1999), p. 64 and p. 245. It should be noted that the alpha tends to be higher when the number of items used in constructing the index is large, so when a large number of items is used, the threshold for the alpha should accordingly be higher.

and "moderate" positions. This may indicate that villagers who were more dissatisfied with township officials' performance did not necessarily think that direct elections could be held right away.

AWARENESS OF UNPOPULAR LOCAL POLICIES

The last two decades have witnessed numerous peasant protests against harmful "local policies" [*tu zhengce*]. Though it is not always justifiable, peasants often blame township governments for making such policies. As one villager from Hebei said: "Nowadays central policies have changed their taste when they reach the county and township levels. Particularly bad are township officials, who deceive their superiors and repress their subordinates" (HB0642). Since the township government is often thought to be the main source of local policies that peasants dislike, we may expect that villagers who wish to see few such policies are supportive of direct township elections, because they may believe that popularly elected township heads will be less willing and less capable of making such policies.

The survey showed that the majority of respondents were keenly aware of the existence of unpopular local policies. When asked "Are there any local policies that peasants dislike in your locale?"[30] 16.8% of the 10,041 respondents said there were many [*henduo*] such policies, 41.0% said there were some [*you yixie*], only 15.9% said there was none, 24.7% said they did not know, and 1.6% declined to answer. Examples of such local policies identified by respondents included:

1. fining peasants for selling their grains on the free market;
2. issuing IOUs for grain procurement;
3. tearing down the houses of villagers who could not pay fees or fines; and
4. hiring local bullies to beat up villagers who rejected the unlawful demands of township officials.

[30] "*Nin zheli you mei you nong min bu xihuan de tuzhengce?*"

In the words of an indignant villager from Jiangxi: "There are quite a lot of such local policies here. We peasants have suffered so much that it is hard to explain in a few words" (JX0609).

The regression analysis showed that awareness of unpopular local policies was positively correlated with support for direct election of township heads. Compared to those who said there were no unpopular local policies in their locality, respondents who believed there were "many" of them were less likely to hold the "conservative" position rather than the "liberal" view (odds ratio = 0.422). Conversely, respondents who perceived many local policies were over two times as likely than those who found none to be "liberal" than "conservative" (odds ratio = 2.368). To a lesser extent, respondents who find "some" unpopular local policies are also more likely to hold the "liberal" view rather than the "conservative" (odds ratio = 1.757). Even those who claimed to not know if there were any local policies were more likely to be "liberal" rather than "conservative" (odds ratio = 1.273). Moreover, awareness of local policies seemed to heighten one's sense of urgency in introducing direct township elections. Compared to respondents who saw no local policies, those who found "many" were less likely to hold the "moderate" position vis-à-vis the "liberal" one (odds ratio = 0.574). A further indicator of the significance of the problem of local policies is that, compared to those who said there was no such policies, respondents who said they did not know if such policies existed were more likely to take the "liberal" position rather than the "conservative."

POLITICAL ASSERTIVENESS

In the post-Mao era, Chinese peasants have demonstrated remarkably different levels of assertiveness in dealing with local governments. Some villagers are usually passive and compliant, others unyielding and defiant, and still others have tried to use laws and central policies to defend their interests and rights.[31] This research showed that respondents who believed it lawful and rightful to contend against rogue officials were more likely than those who thought otherwise to be "liberal" in regard to direct township elections.

Three questions tapped the political assertiveness of the respondents. The first question was: "Do you think it is lawful to lodge collective complaints?"[32] Since the mid-1980s visiting local governments en masse to lodge a complaint against a local cadre or an unpopular local policy has been a common way of staging public protests in the countryside. As local officials always try to discourage villagers from engaging in such disruptive collective action, the lawfulness of lodging collective complaints has become a matter of contention. Local officials have often informed villagers that it is unlawful to lodge collective complaints, particularly after the State Council issued *The Regulations Concerning Works of Letters and Visits* in December 1995. They like to argue that the *Regulations* outlawed lodging collective complaints by stipulating that complainants should send no more than five representatives to the government (Art. 12). Resourceful peasants, however, often insist that the *Regulations* do not outlaw collective complaints. They instead argue that if the *Regulations* indeed outlawed such action, then it would have had listed it as legally punishable in the same way it did with actions such as besieging government buildings and disrupting government work (Art. 22). So, in spite of warnings from local officials, assertive peasants have continued to lodge collective complaints. They seem to understand that without the safety of numbers leaders of collective protests will be highly vulnerable. They also seem to understand that without boisterous demonstrations their demands will almost certainly go unmet.

The survey showed that the majority of respondents regarded lodging collective complaints as a lawful action. Of the 10,041 respondents,

[31] See Lianjiang Li and Kevin J. O'Brien, "Villagers and Popular Resistance in Contemporary China," *Modern China*, Vol. 22, No. 1 (January 1996), pp. 28–61; and O'Brien and Li, "The Politics of Lodging Complaints."

[32] *"Nin renwei jiti shangfang hefa ma?"*

50.7% said that it was entirely lawful [wanquan hefa], 11.7% not very lawful [bu da hefa], only 3.7% said it was unlawful [bu hefa], 32.2% said they had no opinion, and 1.7% declined to answer. Comments made by respondents indicated how strongly some peasants felt about the necessity and lawfulness of lodging collective complaints. A villager from Hebei, for instance, wrote that "it is suicidal for us commoners to fight with officials individually; we must act together" (HB0361). A villager from Shandong argued that the lawfulness of lodging collective complaints came from the lawfulness of complainants' demands: "If complainants' demands are in accord with central policies, then it is entirely lawful to lodge collective complaints" (SDB0068).

A similarly contentious issue is whether it is lawful to bypass levels when lodging complaints. Again, the State Council's *Regulations* is not entirely clear on this matter. It stipulates that complainants should lodge their complaints either with the level of government that has the authority to handle such complaints or with an immediately higher level (Art. 10), but it also says that if complainants bypass one or more levels, their complaints may still be accepted (Art. 19). One of the reasons why the *Regulations* do not outlaw bypassing levels may be that doing so would run against the Constitution, which stipulates that Chinese "citizens have the right to make to relevant state organs complaints or charges against, or exposures of, any state organ or functionary for violation of the law or dereliction of duty" (Art. 41). "Relevant state organs," of course, could be at any level. It is therefore no wonder that local officials and assertive peasants often clash over the lawfulness of bypassing levels. In spite of warnings from local officials, Chinese villagers have often resorted to this tactic in order to step up pressure on local governments; in fact, sometimes they travel directly to Beijing to seek an audience with possible patrons.

The survey showed that there was strong popular support for the practice of bypassing levels.[33] When asked "Do you think it is lawful to bypass levels of government when lodging complaints?" 33.1% of the 10,041 respondents found it entirely lawful, 16.8%

---

[33] *"Nin renwei yueji shangfang hefa ma?"*

said it was not very lawful, only 9.1% found it unlawful, 38.7% said they had no opinion, and 2.3% declined to answer. Again, some respondents judged the lawfulness of this tactic based on the lawfulness of the complainants' demands: "As long as we are right [*you li*], it is lawful for us to visit any level of government" (JX0027). Some respondents also pointed out that it was necessary for them to bypass levels: "Township officials did not pay attention to us, so we had to go to the county government" (JX0032), "Without bypassing levels nobody will pay any attention to complainants" (HB0925), and "It is useless to lodge complaints level by level. Without bypassing levels we can only wait for death" (HB0434).

An even more contentious issue is whether it is reasonable [*heli*] for complainants to hold off paying taxes until their grievances are redressed. The practice of using tax payments as a leverage to apply pressure on local governments has been adopted by peasants in many places.[34] Since this action is quite sensitive, the question was phrased indirectly: "Some complainants say that they will not deliver public grain [*gongliang*] until the problems they reflected have been resolved, do you think it is reasonable to say so?"[35] Remarkably, 18.3% of the 10,041 respondents found this statement entirely reasonable [*wanquan heli*], 27.6% not very reasonable [*bu da heli*], 30.1% unreasonable [*bu heli*], 22.4% said they had no opinion, and 1.7% declined to answer. Respondents who found it entirely reasonable to withhold tax payments suggested two arguments to defend their position. One argument came very close to the rallying cry of "no taxation without representation" discussed by Bernstein and Lu: "Taxpayers pay taxes to their own government so that the government can more effectively fulfill its legal obligation to taxpayers. If the government fails to perform its duties, then taxpayers do not have to pay taxes"

---

[34] See Li and O'Brien, "Villagers and Popular Resistance," pp. 47–48.

[35] "*You de shangfang qunzhong shuo, tamen yao dengdao shangfang de wenti jiejue yihou zai jiao gongliang, zhezhong shuofa heli ma?*"

(AH0001).[36] Villagers who held this view seemed to view the relationship between peasants and the state as one of a contractual nature, in which peasants pay taxes in exchange for services such as effective and impartial enforcement of laws. The other argument in favor of holding tax payment was more instrumental: "We must exact a tooth for a tooth, otherwise nobody pays attention to us" (JX1494), and "only by doing this can we pressure them [officials] into resolving our problems promptly" (JX1500). Even respondents who found it unreasonable to postpone tax payments admitted that they might do it anyway, either because they found it an effective means of applying pressure on local governments, or because they saw no alternative. In the words of a respondent from Anhui: "It is unreasonable to hold off giving public grains, but we have to do so if the government repeatedly refuses to resolve our problems" (AH0583). A Hebei villager agreed: "If we continue to pay taxes, our problem will never be resolved" (HB1256).

Again, to simplify the analysis and to avoid the problem of multicollinearity, I treated these three questions as indicators of the respondents' overall political assertiveness. For the first two questions, the response "entirely lawful" was assigned the value of "2," "not very lawful" the value of "1," and "unlawful" the value of "−2." For the third question, the response "entirely reasonable" was assigned the value of "2," "not very reasonable" the value of "1," and "unreasonable" the value of "−2." For all the three questions, the response "no opinion" was treated as "neutral" and assigned the value of "0." A simple summation index on assertiveness was then constructed (Cronbach's alpha = 0.74), ranging from "−6" (least assertive) to "6" (most assertive).

Regression analysis showed that political assertiveness remained a significant predictor of respondents' attitudes towards election of township heads when the effects of the other eight predictors were held constant. As we see in Table 1, more assertive respondents were more likely than less assertive ones to be "liberal" rather than "moderate,"

---

[36] "Na rui ren xiang ziji de zhengfu narui, shi wei le zhengfu neng geng youxiao di shishi falu zeren, fan zhi, ze wu."

"conservative," or having "no opinion." More precisely, for every level of increase in political assertiveness, the chance of adopting the "liberal" position vis-à-vis the "conservative" position increased by over 1.1 times (odds ratio = 1.134), the chance of holding the "liberal" view rather than adopting the "moderate" position increased by nearly 1.1 times (odds ratio = 1.066), and the chance of being "liberal" instead of having "no opinion" also increased by nearly 1.1 times (odds ratio = 1.075).

THE IMPACT OF VILLAGE ELECTIONS

One of the arguments in favor of introducing direct election of villagers' committees (VCs) was that it would provide democratic tutelage for Chinese peasants. Peng Zhen, former chairman of the National People's Congress, argued that villagers' self-government would help overcome China's long feudal tradition by serving as the "democratic training class of hundreds of millions of Chinese peasants."[37] Wang Zhenyao, a longtime advocate of village democracy, has further argued that after peasants have realized that they can defend their rights and interests by using their ballots to topple corrupt and coercive village cadres, they will wish to do the same at the township level and so demand that township heads be directly elected.[38] By the time this survey was conducted, village elections had been introduced on a trial basis in some places. It is therefore interesting to see if the elections of VCs had any impact on peasants' attitudes towards township elections.

[37] For a discussion of Peng Zhen's role in introducing VC elections, see Lianjiang Li and Kevin J. O'Brien, "The Struggle over Village Elections," in Merle Goldman and Roderick MacFarquhar (eds), *The Paradox of China's Post-Mao Reforms* (Cambridge: Harvard University Press, 1999), p. 131.

[38] See Wang Zhenyao, "Village Committees: The Basis for China's Democratization," in Eduard B. Vermeer, Frank N. Pieke and Woei Lien Chong (eds), *Cooperative and Collective in China's Rural Development Between State and Private Interests* (Armonk: M.E. Sharpe, 1998), pp. 239–256. For a similar argument, see Tianjian Shi, "Village Committee Elections in China: Institutionalist Tactics for Democracy," *World Politics*, Vol. 51, No. 3 (April 1999), pp. 394–395.

In this research, I first asked the respondents whether VCs in their villages were elected. Of the 10,041 respondents, 47.9% answered yes, 21.0% answered no, 29.7% said they did not know,[39] and 1.3% declined to answer. Since the quality of VCs elections is known to vary considerably from place to place, I tried to assess it by looking at how official candidates were chosen, because "in many ways, the process of nominations is as critical, if not more so, than the elections themselves."[40] It turned out that 27.2% of the 10,041 respondents said that official candidates for VCs were selected either by villagers or villagers' representatives in primary elections, 20.7% said that official candidates were selected either by the township government, or by the village Party branch, or by the incumbent villagers' committee.

Interestingly, the regression analysis suggested that neither the existence/absence of VC elections nor the selection of official candidates had a significant impact on respondents' attitudes towards direct election of township heads. As we see in Table 1, the only significant correlation between the predictor "village elections" and the response was that respondents who said they did not know if there were any VC elections were more likely to adopt the "no opinion" position rather than the "liberal" position.

The lack of significant correlation between VC elections and peasant attitudes towards township elections may be due to a number of factors. First, when the survey was conducted, the *Organic Law of Villagers' Committees* (1987, revised in 1998) was still being

---

[39] This is a remarkably high number, suggesting that these elections were still not all that salient.

[40] Allen C. Choate, "Local Governance in China: An Assessment of Villagers Committees," Working Paper, No. 1 (San Francisco: The Asia Foundation, 1997), p. 10. On nomination procedures and their importance, see Jorgen Elklit, "The Chinese Village Committee Electoral System," *China Information*, Vol. 11, No. 4 (1997), pp. 7–9. Anne Thurston has also concluded that "the selection of nominees is a vital, but often overlooked, part of the democratic process," see *Muddling Toward Democracy: Political Change in Grassroots China* (Washington, DC: United State Institute of Peace, 1999), p. 26.

implemented on a trial basis. The Law said nothing about key electoral procedures such as nomination of candidates, candidate winnowing, and balloting. In addition, local officials in many places simply ignored it.[41] Second, I did not collect data systematically on other important indicators of electoral quality, for example, whether elections were competitive [*cha'e*], whether voting was done by a show of hands or by anonymous balloting, and whether candidates were allowed to do any public campaigning. As a result, the measurement of electoral quality used in this research may be too crude to isolate the impact of the procedural quality of VC elections on peasants' attitudes towards township elections. Lastly, it may take a number of free and fair elections before peasants are convinced that Beijing is serious about grassroots democracy; only then they may start thinking about how to take advantage of this political opening to improve their position vis-à-vis the township government. Indeed, in-depth interviews and the comments by respondents suggested that VC elections might well in the long run exert some influence on peasants' attitudes towards township elections. One respondent from Jiangxi, for instance, said that "it is completely impossible to have direct election of township heads. As of now even the elections of village cadres are not truly democratic" (JX0921). Villagers like this man may think differently about township elections if one day VC elections become truly democratic.

CONCLUSIONS

Three tentative conclusions seem warranted. First, if the respondents are representative of the rural population, popular support for introducing direct election of township heads is fairly strong. The

---

[41] For more discussions of the *Organic Law* and its implementation, see Kevin J. O'Brien, "Implementing Political Reform in China's Villages," *Australian Journal of Chinese Affairs*, No. 32 (July 1994), pp. 33–59; O'Brien and Li, "Accommodating Democracy;" and Robert A. Pastor and Qingshan Tan, "The Meaning of China's Village Elections," *The China Quarterly*, No. 162 (June), pp. 490–512.

fact that nearly two-thirds of over 10,000 respondents from seven provinces thought that township heads should in principle be directly elected is particularly remarkable, because at the time of the survey no such elections had been conducted. In fact, direct election of township heads was not even a popular topic for discussion until after the Buyun election in December 1998. This finding implies that direct election of township heads will be welcomed by most peasants, should Beijing decide to introduce it. It also suggests, albeit indirectly, that current township heads who are appointed by the county leadership may not enjoy a particularly high level of legitimacy.

Second, peasant support for direct township elections seems to be mainly instrumental. This research showed that respondents who were more dissatisfied with the performance of township officials in governing by law and respecting the will of the people were more likely to support the introduction of direct township elections right away. Moreover, it showed that villagers who saw many or some unpopular local policies in their locality were more likely than those who felt there were none to be "liberal" rather than "conservative" or "moderate." These findings suggest that the villagers expect direct election of township heads to bring forth a number of positive changes. They seem to hope that elected township heads will enforce laws and central policies rather than violate them, respect the will of the people rather than trample it, and refrain from making harmful local policies. The respondents' remarks also suggest that they expect other changes, for example, elected township heads will be less corrupt and more capable, more understanding of peasants' living conditions and less callous, more willing to meet the demands of villagers and help those in need, more respectful of peasants, and less ready to use coercion against them.

Last, and perhaps most important, this research shows that a significant number of peasants are quite assertive in dealing with local governments, and that political assertiveness is positively correlated with support for direct election of township heads. This finding indicates that consciousness of rights may be stronger among

Chinese peasants than scholars have typically assumed. Some villagers are very skillful in using "rights talk."[42] Quite a few respondents, for instance, argued that it was their "democratic right" [*minzhu quanli*] or "citizen's right" [*gongmin quanli*] to elect township heads, just as it was their lawful right to lodge complaints, bypass levels, and even withhold tax payments. Some respondents even argued that direct election was the only appropriate way to choose government leaders. As a villager from Hebei put it: "All cadres, including the president, should be elected directly by the masses, not appointed by higher levels" (HB0038). Some respondents also argued that direct township elections would protect their other rights: "Only with direct township elections would peasants really have the right to speak. At present the words of township leaders are like emperor's edicts. Whatever officials say must be right, whatever we say must be wrong, even though we are in fact right" (JX1347). Although most villagers seem to consider their "rights" to be claims against rogue local governments rather than against the regime, their efforts, especially collective ones, to assert such rights may nonetheless have revolutionary implications. For one, what appears to be misbehavior by local officials may in fact be rooted in the political system, and so resisting malfeasant local officials amounts to indirectly challenging the authoritarian regime itself. For another, once the peasants act based on growing rights consciousness, they may learn more about the regime's policy intention and capacity and adjust their political behavior accordingly. If they successfully assert their rights against the township government, for instance, they may gain confidence in their power to defend their rights and interests, see the need for asserting rights against the county and even higher level governments, and seek to win such rights. If their efforts to assert their rights against the township government are frustrated, as they often are, they may

---

[42] For discussions of rights consciousness and citizenship rights in China, see Kevin J. O'Brien, "Rightful Resistance," *World Politics*, Vol. 49, No. 1 (October 1996), pp. 31–55; and Kevin J. O'Brien, "Villagers, Elections, and Citizenship in Contemporary China," *Modern China*, Vol. 27, No. 4 (October 2001), pp. 407–435.

conclude that more systemic changes are necessary and therefore raise more radical demands. In short, China's leadership will perhaps soon face the challenge of peasant struggles for rights. Whether the Party leadership can handle well this challenge will determine to a considerable extent whether political reforms will unfold gradually and without incident or be supplanted by more dramatic forms of political action.

Chapter 10

The Private Economy: Will the Ugly Duckling Become a Swan?

Tian Xiaowen

After the establishment of the People's Republic of China in 1949, the Communist Party launched one campaign after another to replace private ownership with public ownership. Private enterprises were by and large looked down upon as an "ugly duckling" during the whole socialist planning period, particularly during the Cultural Revolution, when any private businesses and economic activities were regarded as "capitalist seedlings" that had to be eradicated. Under this hostile policy, the private economy shrank dramatically, with its share in the value of industrial output declining from 55.2% in 1952 to 0.2% in 1978. With market-oriented reforms after 1978, the government relaxed its policy, and the private economy began to revive spontaneously.

China's official attitude towards the private economy was, however, ambiguous—a love–hate relationship. Discrimination against the private economy prevailed in many areas, such as legislation, finance, taxation, business entry, and market entry. This was understandable given that the prosperity of the private economy was, on the one hand, crucial to the efficient operation of the economy, and on the other was dangerous to a communist regime committed to the abolition of private property. To overcome this dilemma, the Party advocated partial privatization, promoting the development of an informal private sector, where private property rights existed within the framework or under the disguise of public ownership.

Is partial privatization a solution or a transition? Will the private economy remain a half-grown swan or become a full-grown swan in China? In a sense, the answer to this question depends neither on the will of the Party nor on ideological considerations, but on the economic performance of the private economy in the transition to a market system. In competitive markets, the private economy is certain to outperform the public sector in productivity. To maintain the growth momentum, the Chinese government will have to adopt more radical reform measures to eradicate discrimination against the private economy. Therefore the private economy is expected to become a full-grown swan in the near future.

This chapter is organized as follows: The first section discusses how the Chinese government gradually changed its policy towards the private economy from 1978 onwards, and also the economic compulsions for the change. The second section describes how the private economy fared in China after 1978 and the specific composition of the private sector. The third section analyzes the limitations of the policy change and the discrimination against the private economy. The fourth section shows the rise of an informal private sector under such policy constraints and discrimination. The fifth section explains, from both theoretical and empirical perspectives, why the private economy will become a full-grown swan in the process of China's transition to a market-based economic system and gives the concluding remarks.

PRESSURE FOR POLICY CHANGE

The Chinese government relaxed its policy towards the private economy not because it wanted to but because real economic pressures operated. After nearly 30 years of socialist development, China suddenly found itself still a relatively developing country in 1978, with per capita GDP much lower than most of its Asian neighbors that had adopted a capitalist system after independence. The fundamental cause of China's economic underdevelopment was found in the public ownership that stifled incentives for hard work and competition. State enterprises ran inefficiently, incurring massive losses. The People's Communes suffered from low productivity and could not even provide the basic necessities for their members. To demonstrate the superiority of the socialist system over capitalism, the government had to reform the economic system to achieve rapid economic growth and improve the living standards of its people. The reforms of the commune system were quite successful, but little progress was made in the reform of state-owned enterprises (SOEs). The number of loss-making SOEs was increasing, and the government had to spend more to subsidize them. In the meantime, the private economy emerged spontaneously and played a key role in revitalizing the economy both in the countryside and in the cities. If the government had prohibited the development of the private economy, China would not have achieved rapid economic growth and attained decent living standards. Economic pressure pushed the government to advance one step after another to change its policy towards the private economy.

China divided what is considered as the private economy in the West into individual-owned enterprises [*getihu*] and private-owned enterprises [*siyingqiye*] according to the number of workers employed in them. Individual-owned enterprises have less than eight employees and private-owned enterprises more than eight. China started encouraging individual-owned enterprises immediately after the launch of economic reforms. According to the government, individual-owned enterprises were private in nature only in the sense that they had their own means of production. They were, however, based on self-employment, not exploitation. That is, owners of individual-owned enterprises were laborers at the same time. Although they were allowed to have one or two assistants and, if they had special skills, 3–5 apprentices, they were considered laborers, not exploiters. They were less incompatible with socialism than private-owned enterprises that were "exploitative" in nature according to orthodox Marxist literature. Therefore, China's attitude towards individual-owned enterprises was quite stable during the reform period, that is, it protected, encouraged, and helped them. This policy was written into the Constitution as early as 1982.[1]

By contrast, the government was very cautious about private-owned enterprises and relaxed its policy only gradually and reluctantly as market-oriented reforms progressed. In a sense, the whole policy debate over the private economy focused on the private-owned enterprises, rather than on the individual-owned enterprises. At first, China hesitated to recognize the private-owned enterprises that grew spontaneously in the early 1980s. There was, for instance, a policy debate in the Party over the issue of the "fool melon seed," a private enterprise in Anhui province, which had developed into a large firm with more than 100 employees and with assets of several million yuan by the year 1984. In response to conservative criticism, Deng Xiaoping proposed that "we leave it alone for two years and then see what happens."[2] The wait-and-watch policy towards private-owned enterprises was written down in a number of official documents over that period and maintained until 1987.[3]

The driving force behind the policy change in 1987 had to be found, among others, in the advantage that private-owned enterprises had over individual-owned enterprises. The small scale of individual-owned enterprises limited their capacity to compete in markets. To survive in competitive markets, individual-owned enterprises had to expand both capital and employment. From 1982 to 1988, according to official data, the average number of workers in an individual-owned enterprise increased from 1.22 to 1.59, while the assets of an individual-

---

[1] *People's Daily*, December 6, 1992.

[2] Deng Xiaoping, *Selected Works of Deng Xiaoping*, Vol. III (Beijing: People's Press, 1994), p. 91.

[3] See Zhang Houyi, "A New Force Suddenly Coming to the Fore: The Revival and Development of the Private Economy Since the Reform and Opening-Up" [Youyizhi Yijun Zai Tuqi: Gaigekaifang Yilai Siyingjingji De Zaisheng Yu Fazhang], in Zhang Houyi and Ming Lizhi (eds.), *A Report of the Development of Private Enterprises in China* [Zhongguo Siyingqiyie Fazhan Baogao] (Beijing: Social Sciences Literature Press [Shehui Kexue Wenxian Chubanshe], 1999), p. 36.

owned enterprise, on an average, increased from 273 to 2147 yuan, respectively. In fact, individual-owned enterprises expanded far beyond what was shown by the official statistics, and many of them became de facto private-owned enterprises with a large number of employees and assets. Without official endorsement or legal protection, however, these de facto private-owned enterprises existed under such titles as "specialized large production household" [zhuangye dahu], "large individual household" [geti dahu], "employee enterprises" [gugong qiye], "new economic joint units" [xinjingji lianheti], or under the disguise of collective ownership.[4] According to a survey conducted by the State Administration Bureau of Industry and Commerce in 1987, there were 225,000 private-owned enterprises with a total of 3.6 million employees. That is, on an average, there were 14 employees in a private-owned enterprise. Fifty-one percent of these private-owned enterprises were registered as individual-owned enterprise, 22% as township and village enterprises (TVEs), and 27% as cooperative enterprises.[5]

It became increasingly clear that large-scale private-owned enterprises can better meet market competition. To deepen market reform, the government had to give up the wait-and-watch policy. In preparation for a new round of economic reforms and an opening-up featured as the "economic development strategy of coastal regions," the 13th Party Congress, held in 1987, announced that the Party would encourage the development of both individual-owned enterprises and private-owned enterprises. This position was later clearly stated in Article 11 of the Amendment to the Constitution passed in 1988:

> The state allows the private economy to exist and develop within the limits set by the law and regulations. The private economy is a complement to socialist system of public ownership. The state protects the legal rights and interests of the private economy, and provides guidance, surveillance, and administration for it.[6]

---

[4] *Ibid.*, p. 26.
[5] *Ibid.*, p. 50.
[6] *People's Daily*, March 24, 1988. Here the private economy referred to is private-owned enterprises.

Private-owned enterprises, therefore, obtained legitimacy a decade after the reforms started. In the same year, the State Council promulgated the Provisional Regulations on Private-Owned Enterprises of the Peoples' Republic of China, which contained detailed regulations on private-owned enterprises in business startup, surveillance and administration, labor management and protection, taxation, distribution of profits, etc.

Following the Tiananmen Square incident in 1989, however, hostility against the private economy gained momentum. There appeared criticisms in leading Chinese newspapers that "the private economy was the social basis of capitalist liberalism," that "the development of the private economy was equal to privatization," and that "private entrepreneurs were the middle class who stirred up the disturbance."[7] Under increased pressure, top Party leaders revised the policy on private economy so as to "place restrictions to the negative impact of the private economy on socialist economy."[8] Hostility towards and discrimination against private enterprises became widespread, and some private entrepreneurs were treated as the "targets of revolution" or even arrested without legal ground. The conservative crosscurrent gained force until 1992 when Deng Xiaoping made his historic tour of southern China.[9] With his tour, China's market-oriented reforms were accelerated, and the policy towards the private economy became more relaxed.

The 14th Party Congress, held immediately after Deng Xiaoping's tour, asserted, for the first time, that the goal of economic reforms was to establish a socialist market economic system, and that the state would create conditions for economies under various forms of ownership to compete in the market on an equal footing, and treat

---

[7] *Ibid.*, p. 42.

[8] Jiang Zemin's speech at the 40th anniversary of the establishment of the Chinese Communist Party. Cited from Zhang Houyi, *ibid.*, p. 39.

[9] During the tour, Deng Xiaoping called for ending the meaningless debate over socialism and capitalism and for speeding up market reforms. He particularly mentioned the issue of "fool melon seed," to affirm the friendly policy towards the private economy.

all enterprises equally without discrimination. In 1997, the 15th Party Congress further raised the status of the private economy from a "complement to the socialist system of public ownership" to "an important component of the socialist market economy." This new position was written into the Amendment to the Constitution passed in 1999.[10]

THE DEVELOPMENT OF THE PRIVATE ECONOMY

In accordance with the changes in the government policy, the development of the private economy passed through three distinct stages. The first stage covered the period 1978–1988 and was characterized by the rise of individual-owned enterprises and the hidden development of private-owned enterprises. According to Chinese official classification, individual-owned enterprises included only those in industry and commerce, not individual farming under the household contract responsibility system that was still formally under collective ownership. Individual-owned enterprises increased in the late 1970s and grew rapidly in the 1980s. From 1981 to 1988, as shown in Figures 1–3, the number of individual-owned enterprises increased by nine times, the number of employees in them by 10 times, and their registered assets by 62 times. From 1983 to 1988, as shown in Figure 4, the value of retail sale of consumer goods of individual-owned enterprises increased by five times. By contrast, there was no official data of private-owned enterprises that were developing quietly and covertly. Private-owned enterprises were not formally registered until 1988.

The second stage of the private economy development covered the period from 1989 to 1992. Following the Tiananmen Square incident, the private economy experienced a crisis. Under the influence of the conservative crosscurrent, businessmen in both individual-owned and private-owned enterprises feared

---

[10] *People's Daily*, March 17, 1999.

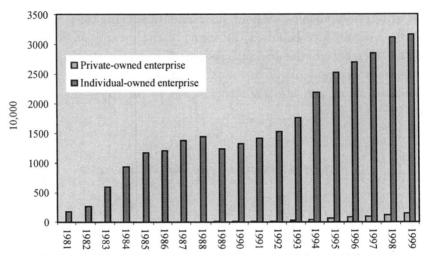

Source: Yearbook of China's Administration and Management of Industry and Commerce (Beijing: Industry and Commerce Press, 1994–2000).

Figure 1. Number of Private Enterprises in China (1981–1999)

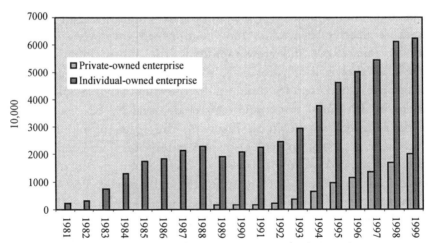

Source: Yearbook of China's Administration and Management of Industry and Commerce (Beijing: Industry and Commerce Press, 1994–2000).

Figure 2. Employment of Private Enterprises in China (1981–1999)

political persecution and infringement of property rights. The number of individual-owned enterprises dropped from 1453 in 1988 to 1247 in 1989—a negative growth rate of 14.2. It was

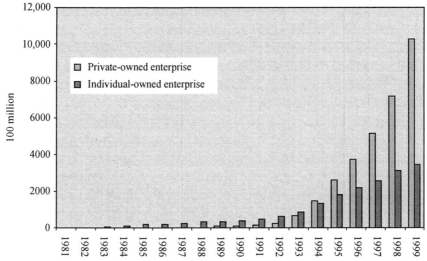

Source: *Yearbook of China's Administration and Management of Industry and Commerce* (Beijing: Industry and Commerce Press, 1994–2000).

Figure 3. Assets of Private Enterprises in China (1981–1999)

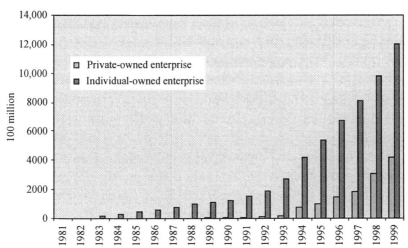

Source: *Yearbook of China's Administration and Management of Industry and Commerce* (Beijing: Industry and Commerce Press, 1994–2000).

Figure 4. Value of Retail Sale of Consumer Goods of Private Enterprises
in China (1981–1999)

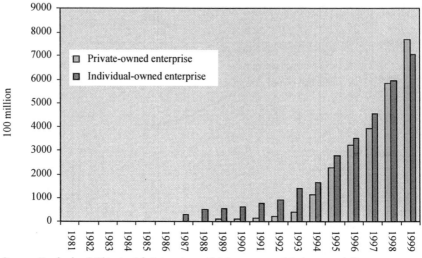

Source: Yearbook of China's Administration and Management of Industry and Commerce (Beijing: Industry and Commerce Press, 1994–2000).

Figure 5. Output Value of Private Enterprises in China (1981–1999)

not until 1992 that the number of individual-owned enterprises reached the precrisis level. The negative impact on private-owned enterprises was even greater. The registered private-owned enterprises numbered 90,500 in 1989, which was only 40% of the number estimated by the State Administration Bureau of Industry and Commerce in 1987! This figure implied that most private-owned enterprises either quit or preferred to exist as individual-owned enterprises or under the guise of collective ownership.

The third stage began after 1992 when Deng Xiaoping reconfirmed the friendly policy towards the private economy during his tour. This period was marked by a boom in the private economy, particularly the private-owned enterprises. From 1993 to 1999, as shown in Figures 1–5, the number of private-owned enterprises increased by 6.2 times, the number of employees in them by 5.4 times, their assets by 15 times, the value of retail sale of consumer goods by 22 times, and the output value by 18.2 times. Individual-owned enterprises also grew, though at a slower

Table 1. The Development of the Private Economy in China

Year	Individual-owned enterprise					Private-owned enterprise				
	Unit (10,000)	Employment (10,000)	Registered assets (100 million yuan)	Value of output (100 million yuan)	Retail sale (100 million yuan)	Unit (10,000)	Employment (10,000)	Registered assets (100 million yuan)	Value of output (100 million yuan)	Retail sale (100 million yuan)
1981	183	227	5							
1982	261	320	8							
1983	590	746	31		160					
1984	933	1304	100		288					
1985	1171	1766	169		479					
1986	1211	1846	180		585					
1987	1373	2158	236	306	744					
1988	1453	2305	312	516	1024					
1989	1247	1941	347	559	1147	9	164	84	97	34
1990	1328	2093	397	642	1270	10	170	95	122	43
1991	1417	2258	488	782	1526	11	184	123	147	57
1992	1534	2468	601	926	1861	14	232	221	205	91
1993	1767	2939	855	1387	2710	24	373	681	422	190
1994	2187	3776	1319	1638	4211	43	648	1448	1140	759
1995	2528	4614	1813	2791	5355	66	956	2622	2295	1006
1996	2704	5017	2165	3539	6706	82	1171	3752	3227	1459
1997	2851	5442	2573	4553	8074	96	1349	5140	3923	1855
1998	3120	6114	3120	5960	9780	120	1709	7198	5853	3059
1999	3160	6241	3439	7063	12015	151	2022	10287	7686	4191

Source: Yearbook of China's Administration and Management of Industry and Commerce (Beijing: Industry and Commerce Press, 1994–2000).

rate. From 1993 to 1999, the number of individual-owned enterprises increased by 1.8 times, the number of workers in them by 2.1 times, their assets by four times, the value of retail sale of consumer goods by 4.4 times, and the output value by 5.1 times. In the meantime, the average scale of private enterprises increased remarkably. As shown in Table 1, from 1993 to 1999, the average assets of private-owned enterprises increased from 280,000 to 680,000 yuan, whereas the average assets of individual-owned enterprises increased from 4800 to 10,900 yuan. By 1999, private-owned enterprises had accounted for 74% of the total assets and 53% of the total industrial output generated by the private economy.

As far as the industrial distribution of the private economy is concerned, as shown in Figure 6, the majority of individual-owned enterprises (83%) were concentrated in the tertiary industry, while the rest were located in the primary industry (5%) and the secondary

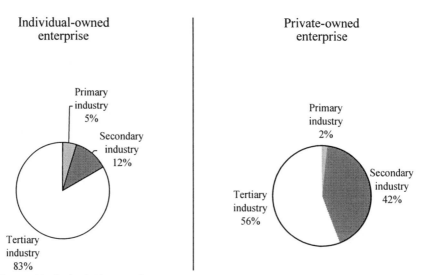

Source: Yearbook of China's Administration and Management of Industry and Commerce (Beijing: Industry and Commerce Press, 1994–2000).

Figure 6. Industrial Distribution of the Private Economy in China (1998)

industry (12%). Sixty-four percent of individual-owned enterprises were located in rural areas while the rest were in towns and cities. This suggests that individual-owned enterprises were mainly engaged in services such as food, hotel, and transportation in rural China. By contrast, private-owned enterprises were mainly engaged not only in tertiary industry (56%) but also in secondary industry (42%), and the majority of them (63%) were located in towns and cities.

As far as regional distribution of the private economy was concerned, as shown in Figure 7, 45% of individual-owned enterprises were in the eastern region, 38% in the central region, and 17% in the western region. The concentration of the private economy in the eastern region is even more prominent in the case of private-owned enterprises. Sixty-five percent of private-owned enterprises were located in the eastern region, 22% in the central region, and 13% in the western region.

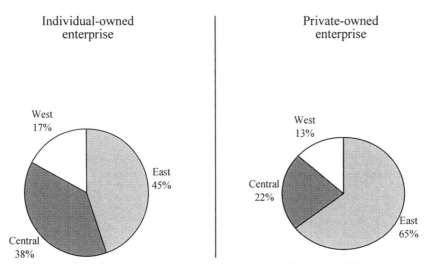

Individual-owned enterprise

West 17%

East 45%

Central 38%

Private-owned enterprise

West 13%

Central 22%

East 65%

Source: Yearbook of China's Administration and Management of Industry and Commerce (Beijing: Industry and Commerce Press, 1994–2000).

Figure 7. Regional Distribution of the Private Economy in China (1998)

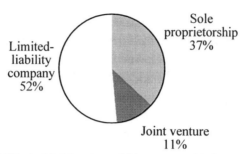

Source: Yearbook of China's Administration and Management of Industry and Commerce (Beijing: Industry and Commerce Press, 1994–2000).

Figure 8. Organizational Forms of Private-Owned Enterprises in China (1998)

Unlike individual-owned enterprises, private-owned enterprises took various organizational forms. According to official classification, private-owned enterprises were divided into three categories: sole proprietorship [duzi qiye], ventures in partnership [hehuo qiye], and limited-liability company [youxianzeren gongsi] The third category experienced the fastest growth in the 1990s. From 1989 to 1998, for instance, the growth rates of the number of the three categories of private-owned enterprises were 27.92, 15.18, and 76%, respectively. By 1999, as shown in Figure 8, 52% of private-owned enterprises were limited-liability companies, 37% ventures exclusively with one's own investment, and 11% ventures in partnership.

We should realize that the development of private economy was still very limited in China. By 1999, the private economy accounted for only about 10% of industrial output value and 11.6% of employment.[11] This was mainly due to policy constraints and discrimination against private enterprise.

---

[11] Individual-owned enterprises accounted for 4.7% of industrial output value and 8.8% of employment, while private-owned enterprises accounted for 5.34% of industrial output value and 2.86% of employment. These figures are from Yearbook of China's Administration of Industrial and Commerce 2000.

POLICY CONSTRAINTS AND DISCRIMINATION

Unlike in some of the eastern European transition economies where communist parties have lost power, policy changes and development of the private economy have been very limited in China, where the Communist Party remains in power. Bound by communist ideology, China has never called for privatization and has repeatedly claimed that public ownership should be dominant in the whole economy in the sense that "public assets dominate the total assets in society; the state-owned sector controls the lifeblood of the national economy and plays a leading role in economic development."[12] In other words, it is no problem for the private economy to exist and develop as long as it does not achieve dominance in the total assets of the society, does not execise control over the lifeblood of the national economy, and does not play a leading role in economic development. Beyond that limit, the government has to do something about it. That is to say, the Chinese government has actually adopted a policy of limited development of the private economy. In other words, the development of the private economy has to be limited in a way that will not threaten the dominance of public ownership. This policy had led to serious discrimination against the private economy.

Legislation

The first, and the most significant, discrimination is at the legislative level. China's Constitution states clearly that "socialist public property is sacred and inviolable. The State protects public property and prohibits any organization or any individual to encroach upon or do damage to state and collective property with any means."[13] By contrast, the Constitution refers to the protection of private property

---

[12] See Jiang Zemin's speech at the 50th anniversary of the establishment of the People's Republic of China, *People's Daily*, October 1, 1999.

[13] See Amendment to the Constitution in 1993, *People's Daily*, March 30, 1993, and Amendment to the Constitution in 1999, *People's Daily*, March 17, 199.

with a very general and weak wording. It states that "the state protects the legal rights of the citizen to legal income, savings, house, and other legal properties. The state protects the citizen's rights to private property and inheritance according to legal regulations."[14] China has never declared that "private property is sacred and inviolable," as it did for public property. It seems that China is unwilling to do so because it will fundamentally undermine the communist principle of "abolition of private property." The discrimination implies that legal protection provided for the private economy is limited, leaving room for possible policy change later.

Finance and Taxation

Owned and controlled by the government, large banks and financial institutions in China maintained a lending policy in favor of public enterprises, particularly the SOEs. In principle, they did not give loans to private enterprises for investment in fixed assets; only limited loans for short-term working capital were given under strict conditions. Therefore, private enterprises could get little loan from formal state-owned financial institutions. It was estimated that private enterprises accounted for only 2.3% of the total loans from state banks in China in 1994. In Shanghai, of the total loans of 377.7 billion in 1997, 53.33% went to SOEs, 22.36% to collective enterprises, 6.75% to foreign-funded enterprises, and only 0.15% to private enterprises.[15] In addition, private enterprises were denied access to the two stockmarkets in Shenzhen and Shanghai. As a result, businessmen under private ownership had to turn to so-called "non-governmental financing" at an interest rate much higher than the official rate. It was estimated that in the 1990s, the interest rate

---

[14] Ibidem.

[15] Zhu Fangming, Yao Shurong, Zou Yi and Hu Shifa, The Private Economy in China: Reality, Puzzle and Trend of the Change of the Private Economy [Siyingjingji Zai Zhongguo: Siyingjingji Shanbian De Xianshi, Kunhuo Yu Qushi] (Beijing: China City Press [Zhongguo Chengshi Chubanshe], 1998), p. 454.

for non-governmental lending was two or three times as high as the official interest rate.[16]

In the meantime, as compared with SOEs that enjoyed financial subsidies from the government and foreign-funded enterprises that enjoyed taxation deduction and exemption, private enterprises did not enjoy any preferential policy treatment in this regard. On the contrary, they suffered from so-called "arbitrary fines, arbitrary charges, and arbitrary financial levies" set by government departments at various levels. It was estimated that they were normally under the administration of more than 20 government departments, to which they had to pay about 50–80 types of taxes and fees. Fifty percent of the taxes and fees were arbitrarily collected by the government departments themselves. The arbitrary taxes and fees were two or three times higher than the official tax rate.[17]

Business Entry and Market Access

Private enterprises were denied entry to key industry sectors under the state monopoly, such as banking, telecommunication and post, railway, airline, electricity, and ammunition. The policy is understandable because some of these key industry sectors are in state hands even in market economies. Private enterprises are, however, denied entry to certain industry sectors that are not normally under state monopoly in market economies. They are, for instance, not allowed to engage in production of a wide range of goods, such as tobacco products, steel products, petrol products, gold and silver products, coffin and related products, army uniform and police uniform, printed trademarks, film-recording and picture-recording products, tea products of minorities, toy guns, dangerous chemicals, hunting rifles, medicines under special regulations, explosive goods for civil use, and round spring scales.

---

[16] G. Qi, *20 Years of Ownership Reform in China* [Zhongguo Suoyouzhi Gaige 20 Nian] (Zhengzhou: Zhongzhou Guji Press, 1998), p. 69.

[17] Zhang Xuwu, Xie Minggan and Li Ding (eds.), *Yearbook of the Private Economy in China: 1978–1993* [Zhongguo Siyingjingji Nianjian] (Hong Kong Economic Herald Press, 1994), p. 71, pp. 102–104.

Private business and enterprise are also banned from selling wholesale certain goods, such as goods under state monopoly and under state planning, necessities closely related to people's living, books and periodicals, Western medicine, and goods for labor protection. They are denied the retail sale of a wide range of goods, such as imported books and periodicals, cotton, nonferrous metal including discarded nonferrous metal, discarded productive metal, color TVs including discarded color TVs, silks, fertilizers, farm chemicals, cultural relics, pearls, and crystals.[18] In addition, private enterprises also suffer from restrictions on entry into international markets, and only a very few large private enterprises are qualified for the right of direct import and export.[19]

Private enterprises are also discriminated against in other areas. They are virtually not allowed to make requisition for land. They have to pay much higher fees for certain public goods and services than SOEs. It was estimated that in 1997, the fee for electricity was two or three times higher for private enterprises than for SOEs. Private enterprises have to pay a much higher fee for renting railway carriages than state enterprises have to.[20] There were restrictions on business startups for private enterprises, and the approval procedure took a very long time. In addition, businessmen in private enterprises were discriminated against in joining the Party and working in the government.[21]

---

[18] Wei Guanglang, (ed.), *China Policy: 1998.1–1999.1* [Zhongguo Zhengce] (Beijing: China Legislation Press, 1999), pp. 411–413.

[19] According to recent regulations, for instance, only private enterprises with assets more than 8.5 million yuan, business income more than 50 million yuan, and export goods more than US$ 1 million can apply for the rights to imports and exports.

[20] G. Qi, *20 Years of Ownership Reform in China*, p. 69.

[21] The Chinese government has recently taken measures to remove these restrictions and simplify the procedures. The Party has also recently announced that private entrepreneurs can join the Party.

THE PREVALENCE OF PARTIAL PRIVATIZATION

Owing to the policy constraints and discrimination, partial privatization became popular in China. Partial privatization meant that there was an informal private sector along with the formal private sector described above. Expressed in various terms, such as "partial private," "mixed forms of ownership," "intermediate forms of ownership," "hybrid property forms," the informal private sector referred to economic units in which private property rights developed within a formal framework of, or in association with, or under the guise of public ownership. The most important factor was the rights to land in agriculture. Along with the adoption of the "household contract responsibility system" in the late 1970s and early 1980s, farmers obtained the rights to use a piece of land for a period of time. From the mid-1980s onwards, the length of the land contracts were extended, first to a minimum of 15 years, and then to a minimum of 30 years. In the meantime, the land could be subcontracted, and the rights to use land traded. As a result, a second market for the rights to use land emerged. Although collective ownership to the land was formally maintained, "the land was reprivatized de facto" under the household contract responsibility system,[22] because "such a long duration brought lease contracts close to full ownership."[23]

Another example of informal privatization could be found in public enterprises that were transformed into shareholding companies or joint ventures. Some SOEs turned into shareholding companies with property rights reassigned to individual shareholders to varying degrees. It was estimated that by 1997, 9200 SOEs had been

---

[22] J. Kornai, "The Affinity between Ownership Forms and Coordination Mechanisms: The Common Experience of Reform in Socialist Countries," *Journal of Economic Perspectives*, Vol. 4, No. 3 (1990), p. 451.

[23] B. Krug, "Privatization in China: Something to Learn From?" in H. Giersch, (ed.), *Privatization at the End of the Century* (Berlin: Springer, 1997), p. 279.

transformed into shareholding companies, accounting for one-fourth of the total shareholding companies. Although they were officially called "mixed ownership" by the Chinese authorities, they acted in much the same way as private shareholding companies. Furthermore, some public enterprises were combined with, or even de facto merged in, private enterprises in the form of joint ownership or joint operation. Some of them were "effectively controlled if not formally owned by an individual", and were therefore "much closer to private enterprises."[24]

A third example of informal privatization could be found in the so-called "fake collectives," that is, enterprises which were private in nature but which used collective labels for political protection and economic benefits. A large number of TVEs were, for instance, found to be "fake collectives." Many case studies suggested that the kind of TVEs that served as a form of "disguising of private enterprises" were commonly observed in coastal regions, but were rare in interior region in the 1980s. Into the 1990s, however, the interior began to "feel this trend."[25] Official estimates of "fake collectives" varied from one survey to another, but a nationwide survey, conducted by the State Administration of Industry and Commerce in 1995, suggested that 20.8% of collectives were in fact fake collectives in the sense that private-owned assets accounted for more than 51% of the total assets.[26] If one included collectives that, despite having less than 51% of private-owned assets, were de facto under private control, the share of fake collectives would be even larger. According to an official survey, about 83% of TVEs were fake collectives to varying degrees.[27] As a result, many found that "the labels 'collective' and

[24] World Bank, *World Development Report 1996*. (New York: Oxford University Press), p. 51.

[25] J.C. Oi and A.G. Walder (eds.), *Property Rights and Economic Reform in China* (Stanford: Stanford University Press), 1999.

[26] Zhang Houyi, "A New Force Suddenly Coming to the Fore," p. 51.

[27] Zhang Xuwu, Xie Minggan and Li Ding (eds.), *Yearbook of the Private Economy in China*, p. 71.

'private' would tell us little about the actual property rights relationships."[28]

Other examples of informal privatization were found in shareholding cooperatives, leased public enterprises, and public enterprises with foreign direct investment in the form of equity joint ventures and cooperative joint ventures, etc.[29] The informal private economy played an extremely important role in China's economic reform and development, and it was described by many China observers as "partial privatization," "hidden privatization," and "covert privatization."[30] Therefore, although Chinese leaders have resisted calling for "widespread formal privatization of majority stakes in the larger state firms," large-scale informal private economy has been growing in China quietly, and "much of the Chinese economy has moved away from state ownership, some into private hands but most into intermediate forms of ownership."[31] As a result, the Chinese economy is now much more diversified in ownership structure than ever before. Owing to the nature of the informal private sector, it is very difficult, if not impossible, to estimate exactly from official statistics to what extent the Chinese economy has been partially privatized.

The Party appeared to be more comfortable with the informal private sector than with the formal private sector, because it could easily arrange various forms of mixed ownership in a way that public ownership still looked as if it was dominating the whole economy, and yet made use of private property rights that were developing in the framework of public ownership to

---

[28] Oi and Walder (eds.), *Property Rights and Economic Reform in China*, p. 12.

[29] Up to 1997, there were four million shareholding cooperatives, and about one-third were located in rural China.

[30] B. Krug, "Privatization in China: Something to Learn From?" in H. Giersch (ed.), *Privatization at the End of the Century* (Berlin: Springer, 1997); C.B., Francis, "Bargained Property Rights: The Case of China's High-Technology Sector," in Oi and Walder (eds.), *Property Rights and Economic Reform in China*, pp. 227–247.

[31] World Bank, *World Development Report 1996*. (New York: Oxford University Press), p. 49.

improve economic efficiency. In 1984, the Party pronounced clearly that it would "develop a wide range of flexible and diversified forms of cooperation and economic combinations between the state and the collective and individual economies on the basis of voluntariness and mutual benefit."[32] In 1987, the Party officially endorsed the shareholding system and encouraged "enterprises to combine, merge, or organize themselves into conglomerates."[33] In 1992, the Party acknowledged that "along with the flow and rearrangement of property rights, economic units under mixed ownership of property would increase and form a new ownership structure of properties."[34] In 1997, the Party clearly stated that the "public economy includes not only the state economy and collective economy, but also the state components and collective components in economic units under mixed ownership," and promised to encourage the development of shareholding cooperatives.[35] On the one hand, private businessmen felt politically safe and economically comfortable under the umbrella of public ownership, because it enabled them to get rid of various forms of discrimination against the private economy. Many private enterprises willingly merged with state or collective enterprises or reorganized themselves as shareholding cooperatives.[36] It seems that the Party had found in partial privatization a solution to the dilemma in its policy towards the private economy.

[32] G. Qi, 20 Years of Ownership Reform in China, p. 12.

[33] Ibid., p. 13.

[34] Ibid., p. 15.

[35] Ibid., p. 17.

[36] Economic Daily, June 7, 1998; also see S.H. Whiting, "The Regional Evolution of Ownership Forms: Shareholding Cooperatives and Rural Industry in Shanghai and Wenzhou," in Oi and Walder (eds.), Property Rights and Economic Reform in China, pp. 2171–2202; E.B. Vermeer, "Shareholding Cooperatives: A Property Rights Analysis," in Oi and Walder (eds.), pp. 123–144.

BECOMING A FULL-GROWN SWAN

After two decades of economic reform as shown above, the private economy is no longer an ugly duckling, but it has not yet become a full-grown swan either. It is a half-grown swan in the sense that the formal private sector, particularly the private-owned enterprise, is still very small and weak and is still seriously discriminated against. It is a half-grown swan also in the sense that private property rights have to develop within the framework, or under the guise, of public ownership in the informal private sector. Will the private economy become a full-grown swan? In other words, will the day come when the private economy is not discriminated against and when it does not have to merge with public ownership, as has been done in market economies? Recent developments in China give a positive answer to this question.

First, the Party has shown its commitment by moving towards a market-based economic system. According to the property rights theory, well-defined private property rights are the basis for the proper functioning of markets and for economic gains in productivity and efficiency. The more clearly the private property rights are defined, the greater are the efficiency gains, and the better is the economic performance.[37] On the basis of this theory, if China is to establish a properly functioning market system and achieve efficiency gains, it has to move towards more and more clearly defined private property rights. Therefore, the formal private sector has to be developed, because mixed ownership is only a transition towards full private ownership.

Secondly, the Chinese government has shown its determination to respect facts rather than doctrines. The Party has repeatedly stated that practice is the sole criterion against which truth is tested, and that everything has to be judged by whether it promotes the

---

[37] See, for example, Eirik G. Furubotn and Svetozar Pejovich, "Property Rights and Economic Theory: A Survey of Recent Literature," *Journal of Economic Literature*, Vol. 10 (1972), p. 1137.

development of productive force. There is increasing evidence that private enterprises indeed performed better than both the partially privatized sector and the public sector in productivity gains; that as more property rights are assigned to private hands, the better is the economic performance; and that partial privatization of SOEs through shareholding did not achieve the desired effect.[38] To achieve efficiency and maintain growth momentum, the Party has to, albeit its orthodox doctrine, move further to develop the private economy.

We therefore expect that China will take radical reform measures to abolish all kinds of discrimination against the private economy in the coming years. On January 4, 2000, Zeng Peiyan, the Chairman of the State Commission for Economic Planning and Development, announced that China would "eliminate all restrictive and discriminatory regulations that are not friendly towards private investment and private economic development in taxes, land use, business startup, and import and export."[39] China's entry into the WTO will further push the country in this direction, because domestic private enterprises will ask for treatment equal to that accorded to foreign investors. The reform process is painful and lengthy because it touches the cornerstone of the orthodox communist doctrine, but it is inevitable in the transition to a market-based economic system.

---

[38] See, for example, R. Garnaut and L. G. Song, (eds.), *Private Enterprises in China* (London: Routledge, forthcoming); Sun Qian, "Partial Privatization via Overseas Listing in China: Does it Work," *mimeo*, School of Banking and Finance, Nanyang Technological University.

[39] *People's Daily*, January 4, 1999.

Chapter 11

Adapting to the WTO Dispute Settlement Mechanism

KONG QINGJIANG

DISPUTES EXPECTED BETWEEN CHINA AND OTHER TRADE PARTNERS AFTER CHINA'S ENTRY

In laborious negotiations with the World Trade Organization (WTO) members, particularly with the US and the European Union, China agreed to make vast market-opening changes in its hybrid economy.[1] However, there is a growing feeling that trade between China and the rest of the world (in particular the US) may become contentious as China gains marketing and manufacturing prowess, particularly after it enters the WTO.

Firstly, the conflict of interests between China and other WTO members is the source of trade disputes between them. As China's cheap products pour into the developed countries after its WTO entry, the industries in the developed countries will most probably be affected. Similarly, relatively cheap Chinese products will intensify the competition between China and those developing countries with similar economic and export structures. All these will bring political pressure on the governments to restrict Chinese

---

[1] For a description of China's commitments, see, for example, Qingjiang Kong, "China's WTO Accession: Commitments and Implications," 3 *Journal of International Economic Law*, Vol. 4 (2000) pp. 655–690.

exports. Take China–US trade as an example. The trade imbalance,[2] antidumping,[3] intellectual property rights protection,[4] the US export control,[5] trade in textile[6] and prison product export[7] are the main areas where trade disputes are likely to occur between the two countries.

Secondly, China is woefully unprepared to do so much work in so little time. Given the magnitude of preparatory work necessary to implement the WTO agreements fully, it will not be surprising to see the details of many implementing measures not worked out beforehand.[8] In this context, trade friction is expected to arise from China's inability to meet all of the many concessions it has made to gain entry into the WTO.

---

[2] Despite the difference between the Chinese Customs' statistics and those of the US, it is a fact that China has gained substantial annual trade surplus over the US.

[3] Antidumping has remained a major problem in the trade relations between China and the US. From 1980 to the end of 1999, the US had launched 73 antidumping investigations against imports from China, thus creating a major barrier for Chinese exports. According to the bilateral agreement between China and the US on China's WTO accession, the US will be able to apply the current US antidumping acts that treat China as a nonmarket economy.

[4] Inadequate protection of foreign intellectual property rights has been a major concern for US traders and investors in China. Although Chinese intellectual property law is up-to-date and basically compatible with the TRIPs Agreement, enforcement of intellectual property law is still a problem.

[5] The US has maintained control over high-tech exports to China, and China has been complaining about the practice. The bilateral agreement between China and the US does not cover US export control, and therefore the US practice will probably continue.

[6] Textile is one of the major products that China exports to the US. According to the bilateral agreement between China and the US, the US will maintain its current quota arrangement for China before January 1, 2009, although the WTO agreement on Trade in Textiles and Clothing requires an earlier relaxation.

[7] Although the bilateral agreement does not cover Chinese exports of prison products, the bill that the US Congress passed concerning China's permanent normal trade status required the US administration to monitor China's export of prison products.

[8] For example, China has to redraw its rules and regulations to come into compliance with its new responsibilities. Government officials, bureaucrats, and judges have to be trained to ensure enforcement. All these constitute a formidable task for China.

Thirdly, although China has a generally satisfactory history of adhering to international treaties,[9] there are bound to be lingering struggles between China and its trade partners about the exact nature of some of its commitments.[10] As a result, it may be reluctant to yield to the claims of its trade partners; still, it is a good fighter for its presumed legitimate interests[11] and will predictably begin using the WTO rules to protect its perceived interests.[12]

In all, trade disputes are sure to occur between China and other WTO members after China joins the WTO.

UNDERSTANDING THE CHINESE PRACTICE OF DEALING WITH TRADE DISPUTE WITH ITS TRADE PARTNERS

Statutory Provisions Concerning Dealing with Trade Disputes

Until the promulgation of the Foreign Trade Law,[13] there had been no legal grounds for China engaging in trade disputes with other countries. The Foreign Trade Law lays down a provision for dealing

---

[9] See Margaret M. Pearson, "China's Track Record in the Global Economy," *China Business Review* (January–February 2000), available at http://www.chinabusinessreview.com/0001/pearson.html.

[10] For example, soon after China and the EU reached agreement on China's WTO accession in May 2000, the two parties disputed on the number of licenses that should be awarded to allow European insurance companies to operate in China. The EU said China had failed to implement previous agreements on market access for the insurance companies.

[11] One may wonder why China, in the following China–Japan case, has taken a tough approach to Japan on the eve of China's entry into the WTO. One explanation is that it is never shy to defend its perceived interests. This speculation being true, China's behavior after the WTO accession could be expected.

[12] The promulgation of the Antidumping and Antisubsidy Regulations of the People's Republic of China is already a good example.

[13] Adopted at the Seventh Session of the Standing Committee of the Eighth National People's Congress on May 12, 1994.

with trade disputes with other countries. Article 7 of the Law provides that "[I]n the event that any country or region applies discriminatory prohibition, restriction or other similar measures against the People's Republic of China (PRC) in respect of trade, the PRC may, as the case may be, take countermeasures against the country or region in question."

The Antidumping and Antisubsidy Regulations,[14] which were adopted in accordance with this provision of the Foreign Trade Law, further provide that "[b]ased upon actual circumstances, the PRC may adopt corresponding measures against any country or region adopting discriminatory antidumping or antisubsidy measures against its exports" (Art. 40).

The statutory provisions give China leeway to restrict foreign imports for indefinite periods while engaging in trade disputes.

Case Studies

As its trade expanded,[15] China had scuffles with its major trading partners. The US, European Union, South Korea, and Japan have all had disputes with China.

A look at how China managed these disputes would not only shed light on the Chinese practice in trade dispute settlement, but also help predict how it will behave regarding the WTO dispute settlement mechanism after its WTO accession.

China–US Dispute on Textile Transshipment

In this case the dispute was settled with China making concessions. China is the second largest supplier of imported textile and apparel products to the US.[16] Textile exports account for 10% of the overall

---

[14] Promulgated by the State Council, March 25, 1997.

[15] According to the WTO, China was the seventh largest exporter and the eighth largest importer in the world in 2000.

[16] See Bernard A. Gelb, "Textile and Apparel Trade Issues," *Congressional Research Service*, Report for Congress, RS20436, March 20, 2001.

Chinese exports to the US. Because of the importance of the textile industry to the Chinese economy and of the trade in textiles to Sino–US trade relations, textile exports to the US has been a major source of dispute in China's trade relations with the US. Alleged transshipment, which involves Chinese companies labeling textiles made in China as having originated elsewhere (usually Hong Kong or Macau) to avoid quota limits, is a conspicuous example.[17]

In February 1997, China and the United States concluded a new agreement on textile trade.[18] Under this four-year agreement, the US promised to extend quota arrangement for Chinese textile imports under the previous agreement (1994 agreement)[19] in exchange for Chinese promises to reduce tariff and nontariff barriers to US textile imports[20] and to crack down on transshipments. The new agreement maintains strong enforcement measures including the ability to "triple charge" quotas for repeated violations of the agreement, that is, cutbacks in those areas where investigations have discovered illegally shipped products. Also, the agreement incorporates arrangements to implement an "electronic visa" information system to more effectively track

---

[17] According to a US Customs Service study, in 1999, as much as $ 10 billion in Chinese textile exports were not officially accounted for; much of this was believed to have entered the US market. Quoted from Greg Mastel, *Testimony before The Trade Deficit Review Commission (US)*, February 24, 2000.

[18] Before this pact, there were four agreements on textile trade between the US and China, the first being concluded in 1980 and the recent one in 1994. Under the 1994 agreements, the USTR imposed sanctions against China's apparel quotas on three occasions, including imposing triple charges for illegally transshipped merchandise in September 1996.

[19] The 1994 agreement generally provides that there is an annual increase in quota for Chinese textile export to the US. Ironically, the new agreement reduces quota levels in 14 apparel and fabric product categories where there were repeated violations of the 1994 agreement through transshipment or overshipment.

[20] These barriers related to a number of products including high volume, high quality cotton and man-made fiber yarns and fabrics, knit fabrics, printed fabrics; high volume knit apparel like t-shirts, sweatshirts and underwear; and advanced specialty textiles used in construction of buildings and highways and filtration products.

textile and apparel shipments. In addition, a number of procedural measures are provided to improve the bilateral consultation process, which states that consultation shall be held within 30 days after either party has requested for it and concluded within 120 days. However, the agreement authorizes the US to impose the aforesaid "triple charge" measures on proved transshipments if the parties cannot reach a settlement.

On May 5, 1998, the US announced that it would impose punitive charges of US$ 5 million for exporting textiles to the US via third countries to circumvent quotas. China initially responded by accusing the US of "wantonly" violating the bilateral agreement with the unilateral deduction of the quotas. China was not happy because it had not been consulted. Interestingly, despite the vehement rhetoric, the Chinese did not resort to retaliation. Instead, given the widespread transshipment, it tightened the enforcement of the rule against transshipments.

China–EU Dispute on Interpretation of Trade Agreement

This is a case where the dispute ended in an agreed resolution based on China's concession. The Agreement on Trade and Economic Cooperation between the European Economic Community and the PRC (1985) is the guiding agreement on trade relationship between China and the EU. However, the Agreement does not contain a provision for the resolution of disputes, and therefore no reference can be made to this Agreement to solve the trade disputes between the two parties.

As a result of the conclusion of Memorandum of Understanding on the Protection of Intellectual Property between the US and China in January 1992, China adopted the Regulations on the Administrative Protection of Agrochemical Products on December 26, 1992 and the Regulations on the Administrative Protection of Pharmaceuticals on December 19, 1992. The Regulations grant administrative protection to pharmaceuticals and agrochemical products patented in other countries.[21] In 1994, China and the

EU reached the agreement on administrative production for phamaceuticals and agrochemical product inventions. At the conclusion of the agreement, the EU consisted of 12 member-states. This changed when three other states, namely Austria, Finland, and Sweden, later acceded to the EU. As a result, the Chinese authorities, who had always previously adopted restrictive interpretation and application of the Agreement, denied administrative protection to applicants from these new EU member-states. This caused the European industry an estimated loss of €25 million. Following the incident, the EU raised the issue of equal treatment to these member-states on several occasions. In June 2000, EU Commissioner Pascal Lamy requested urgent action for equal treatment for all EU member-states from China's Trade Minister Shi Guangsheng. At the subsequent EU–China Joint Committee in October 2000, Minister Shi agreed in principle to an extension. The European Commission Delegation in Beijing and the Chinese Ministry of Foreign Trade and Economic Cooperation in February 2001 finally reached a new agreement. The new agreement confirms that administrative protection for phamaceuticals and agrochemical products in China will extend to applicants from Austria, Finland, and Sweden.[22]

China–EU Dispute on Telecommunications Investment

China prohibited foreign participation in telecommunications network ownership, operations, and management. However, China Unicom, the second largest telecommunications operator, and its incorporators devised a model—the *Zhong-Zhong-wai* [Chinese–Chinese–foreign] mode—to circumvent this regulation. In a *Zhong-Zhong-wai* arrangement, a foreign investor (foreign) forms a joint venture with Chinese partners (Chinese) which is either the incorporator of China

---

[21] Administrative protection is a system that grants market exclusivity in China to foreign patented pharmaceutical and agrochemical products.

[22] "EU and China Settle Long-running Dispute over Pharmaceuticals, European Commission Delegation in China," *Press Release*, Beijing, February 6, 2001.

Unicom or the companies designated by China Unicom (these Chinese partners are not in the field of telecommunications sector).

The joint venture will build the network and sign revenue sharing and other network services agreements with China Unicom (Chinese). The foreign investor typically contributes the majority of the funding needed for network buildup, and in return, shares the revenue allocated to the joint venture from China Unicom. In this way, the foreign investor seemingly could reap "equity-like" returns without breaking Chinese rules. According to one study, during the four years from 1995 to late 1998, nearly 50 *Zhong-Zhong-wai* projects were established, involving US$ 1.4 billion of foreign investment from companies from the US, Canada, Germany, France, Italy, Japan, South Korea, and Singapore. In September 1998, the Chinese government issued a decree banning the *Zhong-Zhong-wai* investment model.[23]

The move was apparently a major setback for the ambitious EU telecommunications operators, who were using this model to circumvent the Chinese government ban on foreign participation in the telecommunications services industry. The European Commission intervened on behalf of the European telecommunications investors in China Unicom. In the process of bilateral negotiation between China and the EU concerning China's WTO entry, the EU secured from its agreement with China a satisfactory settlement concerning the mobile investments of EU telecommunication companies.

China–Korea Dispute on Garlic Export

This is another case where China and a disputant agreed on a settlement, with the latter making concessions. China is the third largest trading partner of Korea, and Korea is the fourth largest

---

[23] See He Xia, "Strategic Selections for Financing China's Telecommunications Industry," in Zhang Xinzhu et al. (ed.), *Regulation and Competition in China: Theories and Practice* [Zhongguo guizhi yu jingzheng: lilun he zhengce], (Beijing: Shehui kexue wenxian chubanshe, 2000), pp. 310–312.

trading partner of China. The total volume of the trade between the two countries exceeded US$ 300 billion in 2000. Korea enjoyed a trade surplus of US$ 11.9 billion in 2000.

The year 1999 saw a 30% drop in garlic prices in Korea. The Korean farmers suffering from such a drastic price decline blamed the cheap foreign imports for their loss. The Korean Finance and Economy Ministry issued its No. 141 order on May 31, 2000 which declared that from June 1, 2000, Korea would adopt restrictive measures on garlic imports, and that a tariff rate as high as 315% would be levied on imported garlic.

China was the major garlic exporter to Korea. It thought that Korea's restriction on garlic import was actually targeted at China. It dismissed the assertion that "the increase of garlic imports has caused a reduction in garlic prices and damaged the garlic industry in Korea" as unjustified. It argued that "[a]ny damage to Korea's garlic industry is caused entirely by the sharp increase of its garlic production at home, instead of the minor increase of its garlic imports."[24] It further asserted that the unilateral measures endorsed without consulting China, not only seriously obstructed China's garlic exports and affected the normal development of bilateral trade—from which China had sustained huge deficits for a long time—but also did not comply with the WTO regulations.

Following that, China suspended the import of Korean mobile telephones (including vehicular mobile sets) and polyethylene on June 7, 2000. However, on August 1, 2000, it lifted its two-month ban after the two countries reached an agreement on garlic trade.

Under the agreement, Korea would import 32,000 tonnes of Chinese garlic at low tariffs in 2000, and the amount would grow by 5.25% annually within three years.[25] For implementing the

---

[24] Citing the Korean Customs statistics, the MOFTEC pointed out the domestic output of garlic in Korea increased by 90,000 tonnes in 1999, while its import increased only by 1200 tonnes. It concluded that the price drop in Korea's garlic market was mainly due to overproduction in Korea.

[25] It was reported that the South Korean government had asked local mobile phone and polyethylene exporters instead to share the cost of importing the remaining 10,000 tonnes of garlic, worth some 10 billion won (US$ 7.5 million). See *People's Daily*, April 17, 2001.

agreement on the Chinese side, the MOFTEC promulgated the Provisional Rules on Management of Export of Garlic to South Korea to regulate garlic exports to Korea.

China–Japan Dispute on Agricultural Products

This was a case where the ongoing dispute was likely to be settled with the other disputant making concessions. Japan is now China's largest trading partner while China is Japan's second largest trading partner, with almost no imbalance, importing US\$ 41.7 billion worth of goods from China and exporting US\$ 41.5 billion in 2000.

On December 22, 2000, Japan decided to investigate the import of three farm products—leeks, shiitake mushrooms, and straw—more than 90% of which came from China.[26] On April 11, 2001, the Japanese Embassy in Beijing informed the Chinese government that Japan had decided to impose "provisional safeguard measures" on the imports of Chinese leeks, shiitake mushrooms, and straw for 200 days starting from April 23, 2001. China protested that Japan was adapting double standards. From the Chinese perspective, Japan's decision was politically motivated.

The MOFTEC argued that the Japanese decision ran counter to WTO rules in several respects: selection of products to investigate, basic conditions to impose the safeguard measures, and the objectiveness of the decision.[27]

---

[26] According to the MOFTEC, although the import of other three farm products, that is, tomato, green pepper, and onion, sharply increased from 1996 to 2000 and the prices of the same products from Japan have been evidently affected by the imports, the Japanese side, which had planned to investigate, finally decided not to make any investigation into the import of the three products: See *China Daily*, June 28, 2001.

[27] According to the Agreement on Safeguard (Art. 2.2), safeguard measures shall be applied to a product being imported "respective of its source." The MOFTEC elaborated that the Japanese side selected the three farm products, rather than those surging imports of farm products from some WTO members, for investigation. Such an investigation constituted nondiscrimination principle of the WTO. The MOFTEC complained that the Japanese side provided only Chinese statistics on the increase of

While strongly urging Japan to retract the decision, China threatened that a possible retaliation would be imminent if Japan did not suspend the restrictions. Japan disregarded China's opposition, arguing that it had imposed provisional safeguard measures under the WTO rules, which precluded retaliation. On June 19, 2001, an angry China announced that it would soon impose "prohibitively high tariffs" of 100% on imports of Japanese cars, mobile phones and air conditioners, valued at about US$ 500 million. Seemingly, this would be the most severe retaliatory measure taken by the Chinese authorities against Japan's "wrong decision and discriminatory actions."

The trade dispute has the following features:

1. On the Japanese side, the disputed items from China constituted only a very small portion of Japan's total imports in terms of value.[28] From the Chinese perspective, therefore, the restrictions are politically motivated.[29]
2. On the Chinese side, it had reason to fear that the Japanese import curbs could spread to other Chinese agricultural

---

imports and the decline of relevant industries without an objective, just and convincing conclusion of investigation, nor an explanation of the relations between the import increase and the decline of the industries, which according to the MOFTEC, are "a must to impose import curb in accordance with relevant rules of the WTO." It further complained that the Japanese side repeatedly claimed that although China is not a WTO member, it was willing to handle bilateral trade and economic affairs within the framework of WTO.

[28] According to Japanese statistics of 2000, Japan imported four billion yen worth of leeks, 10 billion yen worth of mushrooms, and 10 billion yen worth of rush from China. Totaling 24 billion yen, the three imported items accounts for only 0.05% of Japan's total imports of 40.938 trillion yen. See *Asahi*, August 31, 2001, from http://www.asahi.com/english/op-ed/K2001083100556.html.

[29] First, the ruling Liberal Democratic Party (LDP) had to secure the votes of farmers, which are traditionally the LDP's supporters. Secondly, the government was seemingly trying to divert public attention from domestic problems such as structural reform and bad debts.

products and eventually to light and heavy industry products.[30]

3. While Japanese safeguards are limited to Chinese agricultural products, China's retaliatory measures target leading Japanese industrial products. However, the additional tariffs are not expected to have much influence on Japanese manufacturers, because the affected Japanese exports account only for a small portion of Japan's total exports in value.[31] Furthermore, the majority of these brands, except for some cars, are manufactured in China.[32] The Chinese move was believed to be more symbolic than anything else,[33] necessary only to dissuade Japan from extending its protective and discriminatory measures to other Chinese exports and also to dissuade other countries from adopting similar measures against China.

One has reason to believe that both parties' ensuing behavior brought about a lull in, rather than an escalation of, the dispute. A clear indication is that, although Japan accused China of violating the 1974 Trade Agreement between China and Japan and the WTO rules,

---

[30] In fact, Japan decided on June 7, 2001 to temporarily stop the import of Chinese poultry on alleged "bird flu" fears, while China denied any local outbreak of the virus. It is reported that Japanese necktie makers who have been persuading the Japanese government to take similar protective measures are delaying their own quest for tariff help. See *South China Morning Post*, Editorial: "Trading troubles", June 21, 2001.

[31] Japan exported 45.2 billion yen worth of automobiles, 11.1 billion yen worth of mobile phones, and 5.6 billion yen worth of air conditioners to China for a total of 61.9 billion yen, accounting for 0.12% of Japan's total exports of 51.654 trillion yen. Incidentally, Japan's automobile exports to China make up only 0.65% of Japan's total automobile exports, worth 6.93 trillion yen. See *Asahi*, August 31, 2001, from http://www.asahi.com/english/op-ed/K2001083100556.html.

[32] Japanese statistics show that no mobile phones and air conditioners are imported from Japan.

[33] Xu Changwen, a senior researcher with the Chinese Academy of International Trade and Economic Co-operation under the MOFTEC, holds the view. See "Counter-tariffs Set to Warn Japan," *China Daily*, June 20, 2001.

in the aftermath of China's announcement of retaliation, both China and Japan soon sent each other conciliatory signals. While playing down the adverse impact of the dispute, China said that it would resort to the WTO dispute settlement mechanism for resolution of disputes after its accession to the WTO.[34] Japan also said that it would approach the dispute in a flexible manner and in accordance with the WTO rules.[35] In fact, the two parties have held talks.[36] All these leave room for speculation that the trade dispute may be resolved without resorting to a war of retaliation. Very likely, the dispute will be solved as the "duration of provisional safeguard measures" lapses on November 8, 2001.[37]

---

[34] When Japanese Prime Minister Junichiro Koizumi visited China on October 8, 2001, Chinese Premier Zhu Rongji reportedly said the dispute was not insurmountable. Zhu's views were reportedly echoed by Long Yongtu, Vice-Minister of the MOFTEC. *Lianhe Zaobao*, August 23, 2001.

[35] Japanese Economic, Trade and Industry Minister, Takeo Hiranuma, was quoted to have said that. *South China Morning Post*, October 26, 2001.

[36] The first talk was held from July 3 to 4, 2001 in Beijing. According to the Chinese side, in this talk, Japan only proposed to turn the provisional safeguard measures into formal safeguard measures and did not intend to negotiate a compensation plan for the losses incurred, with the Chinese side, owing to the safeguard measures of Japan, which is also stipulated in WTO rules. Although it ended failing to reach a settlement, both parties stressed the importance of China–Japan trade relations. Japanese Prime Minister Junichiro Koizumi's talks with Chinese Premier Zhu Rongji during his China visit on October 8, 2001 and with President Jiang Zemin during his attendance of the APEC Summit on October 22 further precipitated a second talk, which started on November 1, 2001 and renewed on November 7, 2001. In the former talk, the leaders cited the importance of an early solution through mutual discussion and expressed their wish to resolve the trade dispute from a broad perspective through friendly consultation; in the latter talk, the leaders reportedly agreed to the dispute being resolved through negotiation. See, respectively, Ministry of Foreign Affairs of Japan, Visit to the People's Republic of China by Prime Minister Junichiro Koizumi (Overview and Evaluation), October 8, 2001 (from http://www.mofa.go.jp/region/asia-paci/china/pmv0110/overview.html) and *Lianhe Zaobao*, October 22, 2001.

[37] According to the WTO Agreement on Safeguard, the "provisional safeguard measures" shall not exceed 200 days (Art. 6). Moreover, according to the Japanese law, the aforesaid investigation shall conclude within one year (the duration for investigation will lapse on December 21, 2001) and then the Japanese government shall decide whether to impose formal safeguard measures up to a four-year period (including the duration of the "provisional safeguard measures") (Art. 6 and 7).

However, if the Japanese government continues to bow to domestic pressure, restricting import of such goods as towels, then the Chinese response will probably not be so restrained.

A study of the above cases shows that China employs different strategies to resolve trade disputes with its trade partners. It clearly depends on the existing agreement and the generally recognized trade and legal norms as part of its bargaining posture. In the China–EU case concerning trade agreement interpretation, China was justified from the perspective of international law when it stuck to a narrow interpretation of the relevant agreement and when it yielded to the interpretation of the EU. Its eventual concession was, to some extent, a reward to the EU for maintaining good bilateral relations. In the China–US case, China accused the US of breaching its obligations under the textile trade agreement between the two countries. In the China–Japan case, it accused Japan of violating trade liberalism and the principle of fairness. In the China–Korea case, it regarded the Korean measures as a violation of the WTO rules. In the China–EU case concerning telecommunications investment, as it knew that it had gone back on its promise by annulling the previous approval, it took a conciliatory stance in the negotiation.

China is also good at using its trade status to strengthen its bargaining posture. In the China–Korea case, the realistic Chinese government succeeded in using the trade deficit issue to force concessions from Korea. However, its trade partners can also use the trade status against China. In the China–US case, Chinese textile export's reliance on the US market and China's huge trade surplus became a hindrance.

Political relations with the disputant country at the time of the dispute are also taken into consideration in formulating an approach to the dispute in question. In the China–US case, when the US unilaterally reduced the quotas, alleging that China had violated the agreement on textiles, what China opposed was merely such unilateral measures, hinting that it would be willing to accept a bilateral deduction of the quotas. This softened tone was obviously the result of fear over the deteriorating China–US relations.[38] In the China–Japan case, China seemed to have had an understanding of the Japanese government's decision resulting from domestic political pressure, and therefore imposed seemingly punitive but de facto minor measures to warn Japan. This was understandable against the backdrop of the bilateral relations between China and Japan.[39]

Nevertheless, there are common elements in the different approaches to various disputes. Firstly, it is noteworthy that China attached great importance to consultation as a means of trade dispute settlement. A close look at the practice would reveal a link between advance consultation and the tone of China's position. There is no empirical evidence indicating that an imminent trade dispute would be avoided if China were consulted in advance over a trade issue that, if improperly dealt with, would lead to a dispute. However, it is obvious that China opposes any of its trade partners' unilateral trade measures without advance consultation. Unilateral trade measures by its trade partners often give rise to trade disputes. Moreover, China would normally react strongly to such unilateral measures. Apparently, Korea learned this from the process of resolving the garlic export dispute.[40]

---

[38] China has just succeeded in forging closer relations with the US as a result of the US' engagement policy. Chinese President Jiang Zemin paid the first state visit to the US since the Tiananmen incident and China–US relations recovered from the shocking Taiwan Strait missile launch during Taiwan's first presidential election.

[39] Relations between China and Japan have been suffering from a series of events, such as the history textbook, pro-independence former Taiwan leader Lee Teng-hui's visit to Japan, and Junichiro Koizumi's visit to the Shrine. China was reluctant to see a further deterioration of bilateral relations.

[40] The agreement ending the garlic export dispute between China and Korea states: "The two countries also agreed to operate regular negotiation channels between the Korean Ministry of Foreign Affairs and Trade and the Chinese Ministry of Foreign Trade and Economic Cooperation in order to prevent trade disputes that may occur as the economic and trade cooperation between the two countries increase. And in case of disputes, the two countries agreed to resolve them as early as possible through close cooperation and mutual negotiations between relevant ministries."

Secondly, China has shown an inclination to resort to retaliation where its trade partners impose restriction on its exports in ways it sees as unfair. In both the China–Korea and China–Japan cases, China did not hesitate to use retaliation to force or try to force concessions from the other disputants.

DISPUTE SETTLEMENT MECHANISM WITHIN THE WTO FRAMEWORK

The WTO Agreement set up a new institutional framework for the governance of international trade with a vigorous dispute settlement system.[41] The system is presided over by the Understanding on Rules and Procedures Governing the Settlement of Disputes (DSU), which is an integral part of the single undertaking package of the organization. The WTO dispute settlement mechanism is the central element in providing security and predictability to the multilateral trading system.[42] It is essential to the enforcement of WTO agreements.[43]

The WTO established a DSB charged with creating panels, adopting panel and appellate body reports, and monitoring compliance with decisions and recommendations. Only members can initiate WTO dispute settlement against other members. Refusal of a WTO member involved in a dispute dealt with by a WTO panel to take recommended compliance measures would lead to unilateral retaliation. The WTO agreements require its member-states to take measures to ensure observance of the WTO agreements by its regional or local governments and authorities.[44] Given this, the WTO Dispute

---

[41] See, generally, Ernst-Ulrich Petersmann, *The GATT/WTO Dispute Settlement System: International Law, International Organizations and Dispute Settlement* (London: Kluwer Law International, 1997); David Palmeter and Petros Mavroidis, *Dispute Settlement in the World Trade Organization* (The Hague: Kluwer Law International, 1999).

[42] Article 3 (2) of the DSU.

[43] Confidence in the system is borne out by the number of cases brought to the WTO—167 cases by March 1999 compared to some 300 disputes dealt with during the entire life of GATT (1947–1994).

[44] For example, Article XXIV (12) of GATT also provides that WTO member-states "shall take such reasonable measures as may be available to it to ensure observance of

Settlement Mechanism could result in sanctions even where it is a provincial or municipal government rather than the central government that is responsible for the breach.

PROSPECT OF CHINA'S BEHAVIOR RELATING TO THE DISPUTE SETTLEMENT MECHANISM

In this regard, it should be first pointed out that the WTO dispute settlement mechanism can play a role only in areas covered by WTO agreements. Part of the reality is that many dimensions of China's politico-economic system are not accounted for by the current WTO agreements.[45] Where such a practice culminates in a dispute between a WTO member and China, the DSB might be frustrated in dealing with it.

---

the provisions of this Agreement by the regional and local governments and authorities within its territories."

[45] For example, the draftsman of the GATT, who designed an article (i.e., Art. XVII) to discipline activity by state enterprises, could never have anticipated that this article and the GATT as a whole would not sufficiently address problems created by the accession of a country as big as China and with such a big role for state enterprises.

Even according to the most generous estimates of the extent to which China's market has liberalized, at least 35% of Chinese GDP is still attributed to state-owned enterprises (SOEs). Therefore, questions relating to SOEs are sure to be encountered in China. The risk is that action by SOEs has the potential to undermine the fundamental rules of the GATT. For the most part, the GATT assumes that economic decision making is done by producers and consumers based on price, but SOEs do not always make decisions based on price. It is not difficult to see that SOEs that consume computer chips purchase all of their computer chips from state-owned chip manufacturers. This would not only contravene the primary requirement of Article XVII, that is, state enterprises shall make purchases or sales "solely in accordance with commercial considerations," but also effectively undermine the GATT's Article III national treatment provision. Similar arguments can be made about how SOEs may engage in behavior that would undermine the GATT Article I commitment to the most favored nation (MFN) treatment, the Article II commitment to a schedule of concessions, and the Article XI commitment against maintaining quantitative restrictions. Given that the reason for purchases or sales by state enterprises is not transparent, none of these disciplines could be effective.

As Professor Jackson pointed out, "[a] very important consideration affecting a nation's willingness to accept the WTO dispute procedures is that nation's view of the role that the treaty and its institutions should play in its international economic diplomacy."[46] China has consistently opposed any unilateral measures by its trade partners. However, the multilateralism of the WTO dispute settlement mechanism will not necessarily provide an impetus for China's preference for the multilateral approach. Three factors may account for this.

Firstly, China is more used to the bilateral approach. To some extent, it is one of the Chinese legacies. China has demonstrated its sophisticated skills in dealing with different negotiating partners at the bilateral level. Owing to lack of experience, however, China is still clumsy at multilateral fora. It has remained out of the international arena for too long; even becoming a UN member took place just 30 years ago. Western specialists on international affairs have no difficulty noticing that though China is a permanent member, it has been "cooperative" on almost every issue referred to the UN Security Council. It reflects how little creative thinking there is in China when it comes to managing world affairs. Indeed, there is arguably no huge gap between bilateral and multilateral approaches. It will take time for China to feel comfortable with multilateral fora.

Secondly, because of its culture, China is never shy to express its preference for amicable means of dispute settlement in diplomacy.[47] Furthermore, it has been reluctant to accept any international tribunal. There has never been a dispute involving China that was adjudicated by an international tribunal. The only exception is that China acceded to the Convention on Settlement of Investment Disputes between Nations and Nationals of other Nations, which obliges China to accept the jurisdiction of the International Centre

---

[46] John H. Jackson, *The World Trade Organization: Constitution and Jurisprudence* (London: The Royal Institute of International Affairs, 1998), pp. 76–78.

[47] Probably, the traditional preference for consultation and other amicable means for dispute settlement may find support in the new context. A major power, with attractive market potential, presumably owns more bargaining power in diplomacy-negotiation-oriented processes of dispute settlement.

for Settlement of Investment Disputes (ICSID) on the condition that China and the disputant foreign national have reached an agreement on the jurisdiction matter.

Thirdly, even if China is willing to use the dispute settlement mechanism, or if other WTO members "grill" China on the dispute settlement mechanism, the limited capacity of the WTO dispute settlement mechanism to handle disputes[48] may frustrate China and its partners to use the mechanism to resolve disputes involving China. The amalgam of these factors boils down to this: China may be cautious to use, or even accept, the adjudicating method used by WTO panels for dispute settlement, which is arguably the strength of the WTO mechanism.[49]

Nevertheless, since its accession to the WTO, China is bound by the WTO agreements including the DSU. Even its inclination to resort to retaliation should be restrained. Unlike other international organs for dispute settlement, the jurisdiction of the DSB is compulsory. Whenever China's partner feels Chinese trade measures are violating the WTO agreements, it can bring China to the DSB without getting China's consent. China cannot challenge the jurisdiction of the DSB that receives the application of that member. Needless to say, in cases where a complainant can show that China has violated WTO rules, the WTO dispute settlement system mechanism will be able to recommend that China should change its behavior and comply with WTO regulations. Moreover, if compliance is not forthcoming, the DSU will ensure an automatic right to retaliation by the injured WTO member.

In addition, the adjudication and consultation processes are not mutually exclusive. In fact, they are compatible within the procedures

---

[48] Given its tremendous responsibilities, the WTO has few professional staff in its secretariat and it has a tight budget. The dispute settlement mechanism can handle only about 45 cases annually.

[49] The DSU indeed leaves room for members concerned to engage in consultation to settle their disputes. It, however, only requires parties to mutually "give sympathetic consideration to and afford adequate opportunity for consultation." See Article 4 (2) of the DSU.

of the WTO dispute settlement mechanism. This provision leaves more room for China to participate. Furthermore, the WTO mechanism, since the inauguration of the WTO, has had a history of successfully and efficiently settling trade disputes between member-states.

Finally, subjecting itself to the dispute settlement mechanism—no matter how unwilling China is—would result in desirable side effects per se; China may develop an interest in defending its rights through a generally viable and fair quasijudicial body.

CONCLUDING REMARKS

While Chinese law provides China with the teeth to engage in trade disputes with its trading partners, its peculiar approaches to trade disputes, as exemplified by its practice of dealing with such disputes, give a murky sign that it will probably accustom itself to the adjudicating procedures of the WTO dispute settlement mechanism while pursuing its own interests within the framework. However, as it wishes to become a key player in the WTO, it therefore has a fundamental interest in both the promotion and the proper regulation of trade at the global level. Based on this, one has no reason to believe that China will become a rogue elephant of the trade rules embodied in WTO.

Chapter 12

WTO Accession and Growth Strategy Adjustment

LU DING

INTRODUCTION

Market opening sets the tune of China's commitments in its deals with the World Trade Organization (WTO) members to clear the way for the nation's entry into the organization. These commitments are about trade and investment. With regard to trade, China will make sweeping cuts in tariff rates, reducing the current average level from about 15 to about 10% in a few years. For certain industrial products (such as cars and IT products) and agricultural goods, the tariff cuts will be more substantial. On top of that, China will remove many of its complicated nontariff barriers, such as quotas, trading right restrictions, local content requirement, technology transfer requirement, and government procurement rules that favour domestic producers. For instance, all quotas on civil aircraft, medical equipment, and IT products should be eliminated upon accession. Quotas on auto will grow 15% annually until completely eliminated.

As for investment, China will relax and gradually phase out various restrictions imposed on foreign businesses in sectors such as telecommunications, car manufacturing, banking, insurance, security trading, energy supply, distribution service, and retails. For instance, foreign banks will be allowed to conduct domestic currency business with Chinese firms two years after the WTO entry and with Chinese individuals five years after the entry. Foreign telecom carriers were allowed to hold a 25% share in Chinese telecom firms upon entry, and the permitted share will be increased to 49% in three years.

These changes in trade and investment openness will have profound microeconomic as well as macroeconomic impact on the Chinese economy. A number of researchers have pointed out the efficiency gains China will reap from its WTO accession. By reviewing the implications of China's WTO commitments on domestic institutions, Xiao and Zhou emphasize the huge potential of transaction cost savings arising from the better economic institutions that will come with the procedures, disciplines, and rules of the WTO.[1] Similar views are shared by Yang, who perceives that a real constitutional negotiation initiated by the WTO entry will be instrumental to the start of a new round of institutional reforms.[2] Woo observes that WTO-enforced rules will help Chinese reformers to overcome the resistance to further market-oriented reforms from the entrenched interest within the country's ruling structure.[3] On the basis of a study of the state-owned enterprises (SOEs) that operate in markets with varying degrees of protectionism and different restrictions on foreign direct investment (FDI), Liu and Woo expect the greater foreign competition after WTO entry to force domestic SOEs to form alliances with foreign companies.[4] Production efficiency will thus be enhanced in the more diversified ownership structure in the post-WTO economy.

Apart from institutional reforms, China's WTO entry is likely to improve significantly interindustry resource allocation and trade structure. A study by Chen and Feng shows that China's pre-WTO tariff policy reflected a balance of an industrial policy that

[1] Geng Xiao and Zhou, "WTO and China's Economic Transformation: Institutional Perspectives and Policy Options," *China Review* (2000).

[2] Xiaokai Yang, "China's Entry to the WTO," *China Economic Review* (US), Vol. 11, No. 4 (2000), pp. 437–442.

[3] Wing Thye Woo, "Recent Claims of China's Economic Exceptionalism: Reflections Inspired by WTO Accession," *China Economic Review* (US), Vol. 12, No. 2/3 (2001), pp. 107–136.

[4] Guy S. Liu and Wing T. Woo, "How will Ownership in China's Industrial Sector Evolve with WTO Accession?," *China Economic Review* (US), Vol. 12, No. 2/3 (2001), pp. 137–161.

favors high-tech industries and a social policy that aims at political stability characterized by a gradual phase-out of the protection for those declining industries.[5] With the WTO entry, both tariff and nontariff barriers in resource-intensive products (agriculture, wood, paper, etc.) and capital/technology-intensive products (chemicals, autos, and IT products) will be significantly reduced. Imports of these products from developed countries are expected to increase.[6] Consequently, domestic production in these sectors has to be adjusted. China's economic structure will also be affected by less restrictive FDI after accession to the WTO. Its industrial policy must be revamped, because many of the elements that form the foundation of the regime will have to be dismantled or phased out in a few years.[7] Resources will be reallocated to those sectors where China has comparative advantages or potential comparative advantages and to the newly developed service sectors. With such resource reallocation, exports from the sectors with comparative advantages will increase. While some of the previously protected industries may have problems after the WTO entry, the economy will benefit and gain in overall comparative advantages, as indicated by a number of computable general equilibrium analyses.[8,9,10] These

[5] Baizhu Chen and Yi Feng, "Openness and Trade Policy in China: An Industrial Analysis," *China Economic Review* (US), Vol. 11, No. 4 (2000), pp. 323–341.

[6] Wen Hai, "China's WTO Membership: Significance and Implications," CCER *Working Paper*, E2000007, 2000.

[7] Ding Lu, "Industrial Policy and Resource Allocation: Implications on China's Participation in Globalization," *China Economic Review* (US), Vol. 11, No. 4 (2000), pp. 342–360.

[8] Shantong Li and Fan Zhai, "Impact of WTO Accession on China's Economy—A Dynamic General Equilibrium Analysis," in Yongding Yu, Zheng Bingwen and Song Hong (eds.), *The Research Report on China's Entry into WTO* (Beijing: Social Science Documentation Publishing House, 2000).

[9] Xuesong Li and Arjan Lejour, "The Sectoral Impact of China's Access to the WTO: A Dynamic CGE Analysis", Paper presented at Workshop on China's Accession to the WTO: An Overview of Recent Analyses, Beijing, October 19–20, 2000.

[10] Arjan Lejour, "China and the WTO: The Impact on China and the World Economy," Paper presented at Annual Conference of the Development Economic Study Group, Nottingham, UK, March 27–29, 2000.

studies project that the WTO-initiated trade liberalization will enhance China's long-run growth and economic welfare.

When China fulfills its WTO commitments, its economy will be integrated into the global economy on an unprecedented scale. This will drastically change the conditions and environment of China's macroeconomic management and long-term development strategy. The post-WTO-accession environment will pose serious challenges to the Chinese policymakers, compelling them to redefine the nation's macroeconomic management framework and the long-term growth strategy. The purpose of this chapter is to look into the implications of the WTO membership on these issues. The rest of the chapter is arranged as follows: Section 2 discusses how the WTO accession will change the internal balance and external balance of the Chinese economy. Section 3 will examine the growth model that has so far guided China's economic development and its prospect after the WTO accession. The concluding section suggests that a shift towards an America-type, trade deficit-based growth model may be necessary to sustain long-term growth for the Chinese economy.

CHANGES IN MACROECONOMIC CONDITIONS

China has experienced two decades of rapid economic growth with an average annual growth rate of over 9%. Between 1980 and 2000, in real terms, China's GDP sextupled, and per capita income quintupled by rising six times as fast as the world average. The World Bank summarizes four major factors that explain the success.[11] First, the favorable initial conditions ranging from the "advantage of being backward" and "a dry prairie parched by years of planning, awaiting the first sprinklings of market reform." Second, the pragmatic economic reforms that have effectively promoted economic efficiency while maintaining social stability. Third, the structural changes that transit the

[11] World Bank, *China 2020* (Washington, DC: World Bank, 1997).

labor force rapidly out of the agricultural sector. Fourth, the unusually high saving rate that supports and generates high investment rate and growth.

As shown in Figure 1, China's gross saving rate has been above 35% of GDP in most years since the mid-1980s, and it jumped to above 40% during the major part of the 1990s. According to the World Bank, such a high saving rate is quite unusual by international standards. World Bank economists attribute the phenomenon to three factors, namely, the rising aspirations of the Chinese households, the changing demographics that compel people to save more for the longer retirement years, and institutional factors such as the state banks' systematic efforts to attract deposits. In the more recent years, market-oriented reforms ended lifelong employment in state sectors, privatized home ownership, and restructured the social security system. As more and more individuals and households found themselves left on their own to swim or sink in a market-based

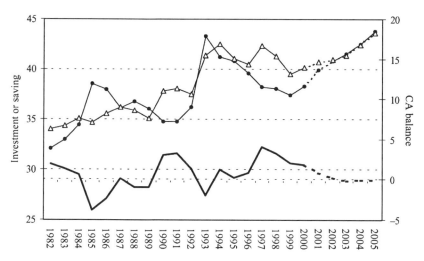

—•— Investment as % of GDP   —△— Aggregate saving as % of GDP   ——— CA balance as % of GDP

Source: EIU database, October 2001, figures for 2001–2005 are EIU estimates.

Figure 1. Investment, Aggregate Savings, and Current Account Balance
as Percentage of GDP

economy, people had to save more to prepare for the greater uncertainties in life.

Rapid economic growth supported by a high saving rate has contributed to China's successful export-oriented growth strategy and the open-door policy to attract FDI. In the past two decades, China's exports have increased at a hefty annual rate of 17%, from US$ 13.7 billion in 1979 to US$ 250 billion in 2000 (Figure 2). China has now become the world's seventh largest exporting economy. The composition of trade shifted drastically from primary products to manufactures, which today account for about 90% of Chinese exports and 80% of imports. The country's efforts to attract FDI have been even more successful. From 1988 to 2000, actual or utilized FDI in China increased at an annual rate of 23% to reach a cumulative total of US$ 339 billion. No other country, except the

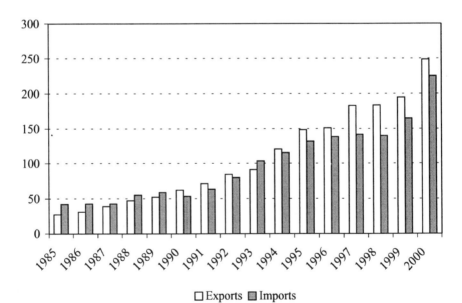

□ Exports ■ Imports

Source: China Statistical Yearbook, various issues.

Figure 2. Growth of China's Foreign Trade (US$ billion)

US, has received such massive amounts of FDI in such a short period. (Figure 3).

With merchandise trade balance turning towards surplus and FDI inflow drastically surging in the 1990s, China started accumulating huge foreign reserves (Figure 4). By mid-2001, the nation's foreign reserves approached close to US$ 190 billion, second only to Japan's. The rapid accumulation of foreign reserves in the recent decade is not a surprise, given China's persistent current account surplus and net FDI inflow. According to a textbook equation in macroeconomics, balance-of-payment surplus (B) is trade surplus $(X - M)$ minus the net private capital outflow (F) and net transfers to foreigners (R):

$$B = (X - M) - F - R \tag{1}$$

The surge of FDI inflow on the prospect of greater openness for foreign businesses after the WTO accession is likely to continue for

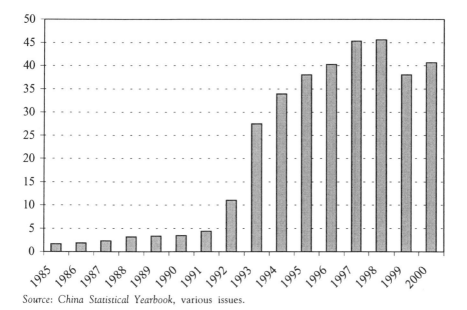

Source: *China Statistical Yearbook*, various issues.

Figure 3. Foreign Direct Investment to China (Utilized, US$ billion)

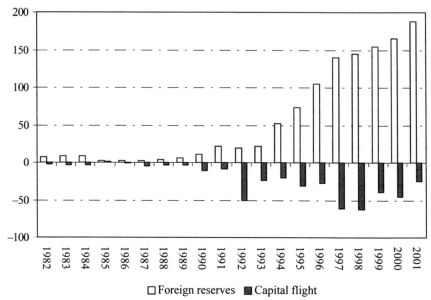

☐ Foreign reserves ■ Capital flight

Note: The 2001 figure is of July.
Source: China Statistical Yearbook, various issues; EIU database, October 2001.

Figure 4. China's Foreign Exchange Reserves and Capital Flight (in US$ billions)

a while. It is, however, unlikely for China to maintain the same scale of trade and current account surplus it has had during the major part of the last decade.

As shown by Hai, most OECD members' export potential to China have been suppressed in the past. The reduction of trade barriers will lead to increase of imports that were once kept out by those barriers. The impact is equivalent to an increase in marginal propensity to import, which will reduce net export or trade balance, according to Dornbusch.[12] Define national income or output as

$$Y = D(Y, p, b) + G + M^*(Y^*, p) \qquad (2)$$

where domestic demand (*D*) is dependent on income (*Y*), relative price of domestic products (*p*) and business confidence (*b*),

---

[12] Rudiger Dornbusch, *Open Economy Macroeconomics* (New York: Basic Books, 1980).

government purchase (G) is exogenously determined by fiscal policy, and foreign imports (M*) of home country's exports depends on foreign income Y* and relative price. Meanwhile, aggregate spending by domestic residents is defined as

$$E = C + I + G = D(Y, p, b) + G + M(Y, p) \tag{3}$$

which is composed of consumption (C), investment (I) and government purchase (G), or the sum of spending on domestic goods (D + G) and home country's imports (M). Subtracting (3) from (2) we have

$$Y - E(Y, p, b, G) = TB(Y, Y^*, p) \tag{4}$$

where TB = M* − M is trade balance. Equation (4) can be depicted in Figure 6, where the upward schedule shows output-less absorption with slope equal to marginal propensity to save (s), and the downward schedule shows trade balance with slope equal to the negative of marginal propensity to import (−m).[13]

After October 1997, the Chinese economy entered a period of deflation and rising unemployment (Figure 5). The government has used expansionary fiscal and monetary policies to pump prime the aggregate demand. An increase of government purchase G can be seen in Figure 6 as an outward shift of output-less-absorption schedule, leading to an increase of equilibrium output Y and a reduction of trade balance T, other things being equal.

The trade barrier reduction caused by WTO entry will, nevertheless, make import more elastic to income, or in other words make the value of marginal propensity to import (m) larger. This will be represented by a steeper slope of trade balance schedule, as

---

[13] Dornbusch also discusses the case when the home economy is not "small" compared to the foreign economy in the sense that repercussion effects associated with income and import changes in the latter interact with the home economy's variables. He shows that taking the repercussion effects into account will make the trade balance schedule flatter.

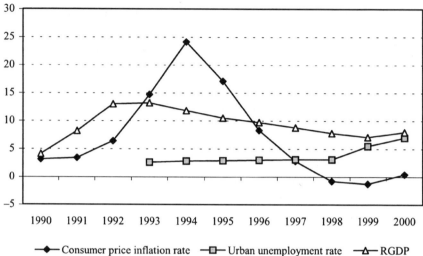

Source: *China Statistical Yearbook*, various issues.

Figure 5. Inflation, Unemployment, and Real GDP Growth (1990–2000)

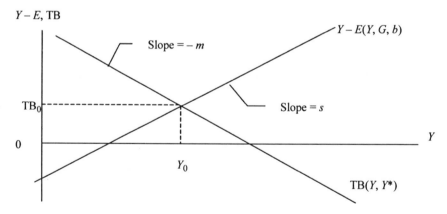

Figure 6. Equilibrium Output and Trade Balance

shown in Figure 7, which reduces the output increasing effect of fiscal pump priming while aggravating its trade balance reducing effect.

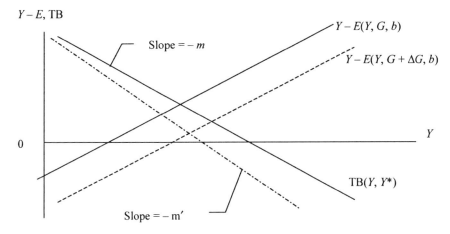

Figure 7. Impact of Trade Barrier Reduction on the
Effectiveness of Fiscal Pump Priming

Several factors will add to the trade balance reducing effect. First is the rising business confidence that supports the surge of (domestic and foreign) investment in China before and after the WTO entry, which will shift the output-less-absorption schedule in Figure 6 further outwards. The second factor is the current world economic downturn that reduces overseas demand for Chinese exports, which will cause the trade balance schedule in Figure 7 to shift inwards. The third factor is the Chinese currency's appreciation in trade-weighted terms.

In April 1994, China's foreign exchange regime entered the era of current account convertibility with strict controls over cross-border capital flows. The regime guarantees foreign exchange purchasing/ payment needs for all current account transactions to be met by state-designated foreign exchange banks. Two mechanisms prevent funds from being diverted from current account uses to capital account uses.[14] One is the principle of immediate settlement, which requires all current account incomes be either sold to or deposited in designated foreign exchange banks within a deadline after they are received. The second mechanism is the principle of transaction

---

[14] Ding Lu, "China's Currency Control: Features, Mechanisms, and Effects," *Issues and Studies* (Taiwan), Vol. 35, No. 3 (1999), pp. 134–149.

on needs, which requires all purchases/payments of foreign exchanges for trading and nontrading expense to be supported by transaction documents verifiable by banks.

China's central bank, the People's Bank of China (PBOC), sets foreign exchange reserve ratios for the designated foreign exchange banks according to their asset value. Banks maintain their foreign exchange reserve ratios by buying and selling foreign exchange at the interbank foreign exchange market. The PBOC supervises the banks' foreign exchange reserves and, through open-market operation, intervenes in the interbank foreign exchange market to maintain the exchange rate fluctuation within its desired range. In fact, the PBOC has restricted fluctuation of the currency within a narrow range of RMB 8.2–8.4 per US dollar for most of the time since 1994, maintaining a de facto peg to the US dollar. This has caused a considerable appreciation of Chinese RMB in trade-weighted terms (Figure 8).

All these factors will push China's trade balance further towards the deficit range. This trend may dampen the economy's aggregate demand to some extent but will not necessarily undermine the pump priming efforts that have started taking effect. On the whole, the move towards trade deficit could be a positive development for China's macroeconomic management.

The persistent current account surplus and FDI inflows in the 1990s have exerted pressure on China's banking system in the context of the above-mentioned foreign exchange control system. The immediate settlement principle requires all foreign currency income to be kept in the banks, forcing the PBOC to passively issue notes or credits to buy up the foreign currencies, resulting in reserve accumulation. Although the expansionary mechanism is consistent with the Central Bank's contemporary monetary policy, it nevertheless diminishes the monetary authorities' control over money supply. As shown in Figure 9, foreign exchange purchase has risen to a remarkable ratio to the total bank loans in the last few years. Meanwhile, accumulation of reserves also carries a social cost measured by the cost of servicing the foreign fund inflow minus the income earned on the reserves. A World Bank study estimates the

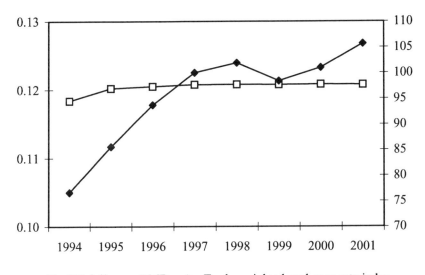

—□— US dollar per RMB —◆— Trade-weighted exchange rate index

Source: EIU database, October 2001.

Figure 8. RMB's Nominal Exchange Rate to US Dollar and
Trade-weighted Exchange Rate (1994–2001)

cost to be 0.10–0.16% of GDP a year for some developing countries.[15] An alternative to reserve accumulation is monetary sterilization, a process by which the authorities sell domestic bonds or increase reserve requirements to offset the inflationary impact of fund inflow. This measure proved to be costly and risky by the experience of other developing countries, because interest payment on domestic bonds may well exceed the interest earned on foreign reserves, causing rising fiscal costs for the government. Sterilization also could cause higher domestic interest rates, attracting more capital inflows.

In this context, a move towards trade deficit will release some pressures. The PBOC may also consider widening the range of

[15] World Bank, *Global Economic Prospects and the Developing Countries* (Washington, DC: World Bank, 1999), p. 131.

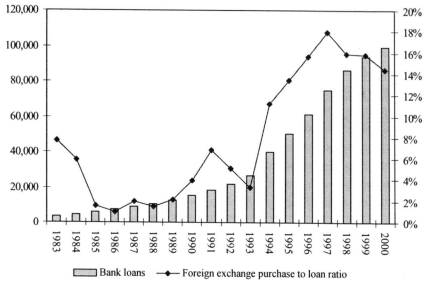

Source: *China Statistical Yearbook*, various issues.

Figure 9. Bank Loans (RMB 100 million) and Foreign Exchange Purchase as Percentage of Total Loans

exchange rate fluctuation to accelerate RMB's appreciation on a trade-weighted basket of currencies by allowing RMB to appreciate against US dollar in nominal terms. This will in turn push trade balance further towards deficit. Will that be harmful to China's long-term development?

ADJUSTING THE GROWTH MODEL

Around the late 1960s and early 1970s, the success of a small number of East Asian manufacture exporters started changing people's views on the relative merits of export-oriented growth strategy and import substitution strategy. "The 1980s debt crisis, combined with slow economic growth in many countries that were following the import substitution strategy, further reinforced support for export-led growth. By the early 1990s, there was widespread consensus (although not complete agreement) on the advantages of this strategy for developing countries."[16] One of the most influential documents that represent this consensus is the World Bank's 1993 World Development Report, which relates export performance to growth success in high-performing Asian economies.[17]

When China launched its ambitious modernization program around 1980, the Chinese leadership headed by Deng Xiaoping was quick to adopt an export-oriented growth model. The Chinese government started by applying policies and measures adopted by other export-oriented pioneers, such as setting up export-processing zones, improving infrastructure to attract FDI projects, duty exemption programs for imported parts and materials in export industries, and fiscal subsidies to exports in forms of priority loans and tax exemptions. China also developed many innovative incentives and restrictive measures to ensure that trade balance would be improved by export-oriented growth. For instance, there have been requirements imposed on foreign-funded enterprises for maintaining a ratio of local contents of their products, the foreign exchange balance in fund usage, and an export ratio of output. Export-oriented manufacturers can enjoy a wide range of administrative supports, tax benefits and subsidies, such as subsidized credits, value-added tax (VAT) rebates, import duty exemptions and rebates for materials and equipment, corporate tax reductions, and tax refund for reinvested profits.[18]

As presented in the previous section, China has been very successful so far in pursuing this strategy to achieve rapid growth and structural changes. The Chinese economy has, no doubt, benefited from pursuing an export-oriented growth, such as specialization and economies of scale in export production, job

---

[16] Dwight H. Perkins, Steven Radelet, Donald R. Snodgrass, Malcolm Gillis and Michael Roemer, *Economic Development* (W.W. Norton & Company, 2001), p. 706.

[17] World Bank, *The East Asian Miracle: Economic Growth and Public Policy* (Washington, DC: World Bank, 1993).

[18] Ding Lu and Zhimin Tang, *State Intervention and Business in China: The Role of Preferential Policies* (London: Edward Elgar, 1997).

creation by labor-intensive export manufacturing, foreign exchange earnings to pay for imported materials and capital goods, and new technologies and new ideas through export-oriented openness. However, the question remains whether this strategy is feasible for the next stage of China's economic growth.

For the successful export-oriented growth experience, there have been heated debate among scholars about the magnitude of export-growth correlation and the channels through which trade policies operate.[19] As many of the successful Asian exporters fell victim to the 1997–1998 Asian financial crisis, new skepticism about the advisability of the export-oriented growth strategy was rekindled. As summarized by Perkins et al., there are three central issues of concern. The first is the extent to which the export-oriented strategy can continue to succeed as more and more countries shift to manufactured exports. The second is the extent to which the countries pursuing the strategy could replicate the magnitude and speed of the gains by the early practitioners, especially when surging exports from developing world pushes the industrialized countries towards more protectionist policies. The third is whether it is really worthwhile for a developing economy to gain export competitiveness with "sweatshop" level of wages and working conditions.

As for the Chinese economy, a recent article by Feldman and Xie suggests signs that China is moving away from an export-oriented growth model towards a trade deficit-based, internal demand-driven growth model.[21] This is evident if we perceive Hong Kong and Chinese trade data as one integrated unit (Figure 10). The rationale to do so lies in the fact that "a large portion of Hong Kong's imports flow to adjoining Guangdong province, without being recorded by the Customs service in China. The correct trade balance for China

[19] Francisco Rodriguez and Dani Rodrik, "Trade Policy and Economic Growth: A Skeptic's Guide to Cross-national Evidence," Working Paper, No. 7081, National Bureau of Economic Research, 1999; Ann Harrison and Gordon Hanson, "Who Gains from Trade Reform? Some Remaining Puzzles," *Journal of Development Economics*, Vol. 59 (1999), pp. 125–154.

[21] Robert Feldman and Andy Xie, "The New East Asian Economic Model," http://www.chinaonline.com/commentary analysis, August 15, 2001.

is thus the total of the two." From the perspectives of national saving and investment, the essence of the export-oriented strategy is to build capital stock and wealth "by serving markets abroad first and then serving domestic markets after income had risen far enough to become self-sustaining". Recent trends in the Chinese economy, however, suggest that China has come to rely on foreign capital (Japanese, Taiwanese, American, and European) for a greater portion of incremental savings and on domestic sources for incremental demand. The duo perceive these trends as signs for the emergence of a new Chinese development model, similar to that of the US in the 19th century.

Let us take a close look at this issue with rigorous analysis on macroeconomic balances. Equation (2) can be written alternatively as

$$Y = C + I + G + (X - M) \tag{2\textprime}$$

where national output or income Y is the sum of consumption (C), investment (I), government purchase (G), and net export [the difference between export (X) and import (M)]. The export-oriented

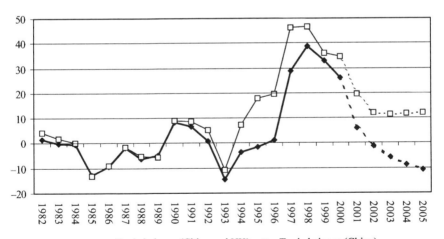

—◆— Trade balance (China and HK) —□— Trade balance (China)

Note: Figures of 2001–2005 are EIU estimates.
Source: EIU database, October 2001.

Figure 10. Trade Balance of China and China with Hong Kong (US$ billion)

strategy that increases net export has thus a positive impact on income growth. The standard Keynsian income-determination analysis reveals that net export increment leads to multiplying impact on equilibrium income increment.

On the other hand, according to the fundamental equation of macroeconomic balances, current account or trade surplus $(X - M)$ should equate domestic net saving, which is the sum of saving (S) in excess of investment (I) and government revenue (tax, T) in excess of government purchase (G):

$$X - M = (S - I) + (T - G) \tag{5}$$

When current account or trade is in surplus, domestic net saving must be positive, a scenario of net lending to foreigners. No wonder that a successful practitioner of export-oriented growth strategy is also typically a high saving economy.

The snag, however, is the impact of persistent net lending (or equivalently trade surplus) on capital formation, which is the most important source of economic growth. For a developing economy at a fast-growing curve, interest returns to lending to foreign land are likely to be lower than returns to investment at home. Export-promoting policies often twist the use of domestic savings by channeling them to foreign hands through trade surplus. They may therefore reduce the savings available for domestic capital formation and eventually slow the long-term growth.[22]

Define $\underline{C}$ = autonomous consumption, s = marginal propensity to save, t = income tax rate, $\underline{T}$ = fixed tax, m = marginal propensity to import, $\underline{M}$ = autonomous import, and G and I as above. Equation $(2)'$ can be rewritten as

---

[22] According to Yongding Yu, "Guanyu Waihui Chubei he Guoji Shouzhi Jiegou de Jige Wenti" [Some Issues of Foreign Reserves and Balance of Payment Balance], *China and the World*, No. 25 (1998), http://160.79.248.165/98/zs9811a.htm#2, LTC + STC − [ΔFR + (M − X)] = 0, where LTC = net long-term capital inflow, STC = net short-term capital inflow, and ΔFR = changes in foreign reserves. China's "twin surpluses" of trade and capital flow in recent years must lead to accumulation of foreign reserves, a de facto lending to foreign monetary authorities.

$$Y = \underline{C} + (1-s)(Y - tY - \underline{T}) + I + G + (X - \underline{M} - mY) \tag{5}'$$

Rearrange (5)' and define $TB_a = (X - \underline{M})$ as "autonomous trade balance," we have

$$[t + m + (1-t)s]Y - \underline{C} - I - G - TB_a + (1-s)\underline{T} = 0 \tag{6}$$

With a given level of labor force, Y is a function of capital stock:

$$Y = f(K) \quad \text{and} \quad f'(K) > 0, f''(K) \le 0 \tag{7}$$

And capital stock is a function of investment stream at period t:

$$K_t = K(I_t) \tag{8}$$

Substituting (7) and (8) into (6) and totally differentiating the equation, we can derive comparative statics of investment stream to autonomous trade balance as

$$\frac{dI}{d(TB_a)} = \frac{1}{[t + m + (1-t)s]f'(K)K'(I) - 1} \tag{9}$$

To get a glimpse at how the comparative statics change over time, we run a simulation exercise by making some reasonable specifications of the production function and investment function: $f(K) = AK^\alpha$ and $K_t = (1 + r)K_{t-1}$, where A is a constant, α and r are both between 0 and 1. Substituting these into (9) we have

$$\frac{dI_t}{d(TB_a)} = \frac{1}{[t + m + (1-t)s]A\alpha\left((r+1)I_t/r\right)^{\alpha-1}(r+1)/1} \tag{10}$$

Figure 11 displays results with the assumptions that $\alpha = 0.25$, $s = 0.30$, $t = 0.15$, $m = 0.10$, $K_0 = 1$, and $A = 1$. Several interesting observations can be made. First, in the early stages of capital accumulation, the autonomous trade balance has positive impact on value of investment stream. Second, the magnitude of this impact increases over time at a surging rate until it suddenly reverses itself into the negative range. Afterwards, the impact gradually diminishes. Finally, the higher the investment rate, the earlier the reversion.

The policy implication of this simple model is illuminating. Autonomous trade balance is determined by external market conditions and government policies. Export-oriented strategy usually contains government interventions that augment this balance. The model simulation indicates that such interventions may be very effective in raising investment streams and consequently growth rates at early stages of capital accumulation. However, when capital accumulation reaches a certain level, the effect may become highly uncertain and unstable. Eventually, the economy would be mature enough so that further augmentation of autonomous trade could only have negative impact on investment and growth.

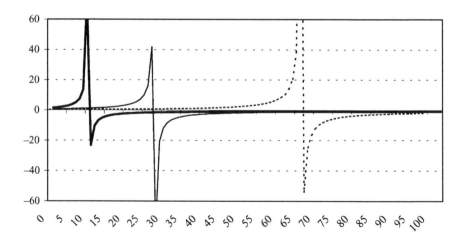

Figure 11. Impact of Autonomous Trade Balance on Investment Stream at Different Investment Rates

CONCLUDING REMARKS

This chapter discusses mainly the impact of China's imminent WTO accession on the economy's external balance and its implications for macroeconomic management and long-term growth strategy. Our theoretical analysis of macroeconomic data suggests a tendency for the Chinese economy to move towards a deficit trade balance in the coming years. Macroeconomic management should move along this tendency to take advantage of the changes. In the longrun, China must adjust its export-oriented strategy towards an internal-demand-driven growth strategy. This will become increasingly necessary as the industrialization process deepens. No doubt, further studies are needed to assess China's economic structure in order to determine the optimal timing for the economy to shift to an internal-demand-driven growth strategy. It is, nevertheless, time to start phasing out various interventionist policies that seek to augment trade surplus. China's accession to the WTO provides an impetus to move in the right direction.

Chapter 13

Cross-Strait Relations in the 21st Century: More Integration, More Alienation?

CHIEN-MIN CHAO

Three forces are currently working towards integrating the two sides of the Taiwan Strait. The first can be referred to as the cultural integration theorem, which argues that the people of Taiwan and China are of the same ancestry, sharing the same culture, language, customs, and traditions. Their common culture is considered important in the new world order in which the old forces of ideology and power alignment have given way to the cultural factor as the most vital determinant of the new order.[1] The cultural thesis is reinforced by the collapse of the socialist system that culminated in the fall of the former Soviet Union and its cohorts in Eastern Europe, resulting in what Francis Fukuyama termed the "end of history." The end of the socialist system as a viable model for economic as well as political development has revived the old conviction that there is indeed the possibility of a systemic and institutional convergence between the two diametrically divergent systems across the Taiwan Strait, engaged till now in a fierce competition of ideologies and development strategies.

The second force of integration is that of economics. Extracted from the European Union experience, this hypothesis argues that economic integration can ramify and generate spillover effects, and

---

[1] Samuel P. Huntington, *The Clash of Civilizations: Remaking of World Order* (NY: Touchtone Book, 1996), p. 125.

exchanges can over time move to higher levels, and a more integrated community will emerge. Although whether a political community without borders will ultimately surface remains debatable, the European Union has come a long way in bringing uniformity to previously divergent nations in areas such as finance, law, and defense.

The third force of integration is political. It is believed that as China grows in power, nations and subnational regions in the continental vicinity will be sucked into its orbit and become satellites. As of now, China is fast becoming a dominant regional power, and it is not inconceivable that China may one day surpass Japan as the largest economy in the world next only to the US. In fact, reports already conducted by major international financial institutions using new statistical methods have come up with the conclusion that China's economy is by now larger than Japan's.

Evidence seems to substantiate the view of integrationists. While there was barely contact of any kind between the two sides during the early 1980s, by the end of the last century business and other exchanges have multiplied: two-way trade amounted to a whopping US$ 30 billion in 2000, while Taiwan businessmen have poured roughly US$ 60 billion of money into the Chinese market. Between January and July 2001, Taiwanese people took more than two million trips to the mainland. Over 22 million such trips have been made across the Strait since 1988 (see Table 1). It is reported that over

Table 1. Cross-Strait Exchanges in the Past Decade

Year	Trade (US$ million)	Taiwan investment on the mainland (US$ million)*	Two-way telephone calls	Taiwanese visits to the mainland
1990	5160	844	8,830,093	948,000
1993	15,097	3139	47,958,683	1,526,969
1996	23,787	3475	96,497,184	1,733,897
1999	25,835	2599	178,328,419	2,584,648
2000	31,233	2296	206,652,715	3,108,650

* According to statistics released by mainland China customs.

Source: Cross-Strait Economic Statistics Monthly (Taipei), No. 108 (August 2001).

300,000 Taiwanese have settled in the Shanghai metropolitan area alone. The channel across the Taiwan Strait has become one of the busiest in the world as trade, personnel, and venture capital flow from one side to another.

Pummeled by the island's unprecedented economic woes, President Chen Shui-bian convened a cabinet-level Economic Development Advisory Conference in August 2001. The month-long conference ended with a move to replace the old restrictive "no haste, be patient" policy, formulated by former President Lee Teng-hui in 1996 to prevent Taiwan from being overly dependent on the mainland market,[2] with an "active opening and effective management" policy. Overall, 332 proposals were made, including suggestions on taxation and finance reforms. Among them, 36 items were aimed at developing closer economic ties with the mainland, with the most significant one being the lifting of the US$ 50 million cap on single investments in mainland China and the limit on total investments there by listed companies. The conference also urged the government to actively pursue direct trade, transport, and postal links (the so-called "three direct links") with the mainland.[3]

---

[2] Chen's motive was basically economic. Eighteen months after Chen's inauguration, Taiwan's economy is still whacked by the worst recession since the KMT government resettled its capital here after World War II. Stock prices have dropped almost 50% since the DPP became the ruling party, the New Taiwan Dollar has depreciated to the lowest rate in 17 years, unemployment has surged to an all-time high of 5.3%, and the real estate market has plunged precipitously. Domestic business tycoons such as Morris Chang, chairman of the world's largest chipmaker, Taiwan Semiconductor Manufacturing Company, announced that he now sees the mainland market as "irresistible." Well-known multinational corporations with interests in Taiwan such as Dell Computer have heightened the anxiety by suggesting that unless the problem of direct shipping is resolved, they are going to relocate their Taiwan headquarters to either Hong Kong or the mainland. Under these circumstances and in preparation for the crucial election to renew parliament and local administrators (which was held at the end of 2001), the Chen administration decided to convene the meeting. About Chen's policy towards China, see Chien-min Chao, "DPP's Factional Politics and Taiwan Independence," *Journal of Contemporary China*, forthcoming.

[3] *Zhongguo shibao*, August 28, 2001, p. 1.

A few months later, the Democratic Progressive Party (DPP) decided to elevate the "Resolution on the Future of Taiwan," passed in 1999 in which the Republic of China (ROC) was affirmed officially for the first time by the party as a sovereign entity, on par with the "Taiwan independence clause,"[4] passed and incorporated in the party platform in 1991. These developments have supported the integration argument that obstacles are indeed being swept aside as commercial concerns make their way into the arena heretofore dominated by political and security considerations. It is believed now that because the two entities have since joined the WTO, bilateral trade and commercial ties will be further strengthened.

Just as the integrationists are cerebrating their cause, the gap between the two sides seems to be widening. Even as Taiwan is ditching its conservative economic policy and making two-way exchanges and communications easier, and while at the same time the DPP is softening its rigid position on the issue of Taiwan independence, Beijing declined to allow former ROC Vice President Lee Yuan-tsu to participate in the Asia–Pacific Economic Cooperation (APEC) summit meeting held in Shanghai in October 2001, proving that a simple meeting of leaders between these two arch rivals is still difficult.[5] Indeed, it has been seven years since representatives of the two semiofficial organizations—Taiwan's Strait Exchange Foundation (SEF) and the People's Republic of China (PRC) counterpart, the Association of Relations across the Strait of Taiwan (ARATS), which were created by the two governments in 1990

---

[4] *Zhongguo shibao* (Taipei), October 22, 2001, p. 1.

[5] Taiwan had hoped that President Chen Shui-bian would be allowed to participate in the meeting, but the plan was abandoned as Beijing rejected the idea. Lee Yuan-tsu was named on Chen's behalf and a new title as advisor of economic development was added to better suit the nature of the APEC meetings; however, that was to no avail. See *Zhongguo shibao*, October 22, 2001, p. 1.

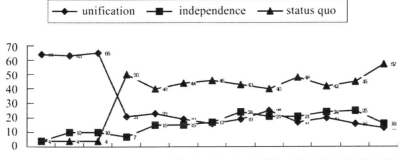

90.3 90.1 91.5 92.1 94.4 95.6 95.8 96.3 97.7 98.2 98.7 99.12 0.12

Note: Respondents questioned in surveys conducted before October 1992 were asked to express their opinions on the questions of Taiwan's independence or unification. After that date, however, a third option "status quo" was added to the questionnaire.

Source: Survey Center, *The United Daily News*.

Figure 1. Taiwan Residents' Attitude towards the Future

and 1991, respectively, to deal with problems arising from the increased wave of interaction—last met.[6]

In the past few years, an increasing number of Taiwanese have become disenchanted with the Beijing authority and have shown their displeasure by rejecting unification as a possible solution (see Figures 1 and 2). It seems that the two sides have differences not only in sovereignty and representation, but also in defining the meanings of democracy, liberty, and human rights. After over one century of separation, Taiwan and mainland China have grown accustomed to discordant political values and orientations. Immersed in the newly transplanted Western-style democratic values, Taiwan has seen the growth of its full-fledged civil society with individualism

---

[6] Representatives from the two organizations met in Singapore in April 1993 for the first time since the Chinese Civil War. Among the agreements reached at the meeting was one to institutionalize the meetings between the two institutions. They followed through with that agreement the next year. However, after former ROC President Lee Teng-hui made a trip to Cornell University in June 1995, all contacts have been cut off. Koo Chen-fu, head of Taiwan's SEF, did travel to Shanghai in 1998 to meet with Wang Daohang, head of the ARATS, but did so in an unofficial capacity.

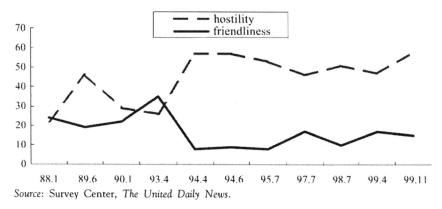

Source: Survey Center, *The United Daily News*.

Figure 2. Taiwan Residents' Perception of Cross-Strait Relations

at its core. Mainland China, on the other hand, is laden with a history of contemporary imperialist abuses and remnants of a collective mindset left by years of practicing socialism.

This article intends to explain the seemingly paradoxical developments in the two sides' association. I will first illustrate the discordant trends and then proceed to account for this unusual bilateral relationship. My research will argue that the discordance is rooted primarily in the growing divergent political cultures that have been developing across the Strait. Not only is a political cultural gap widening following a regime transition for both societies that began in the 1980s, causing them to see things with political implications differently, but a similar gap also exists within their own society, deriving from the same transition and thus making it hard for one side to make concessions to the other. These cultural gaps offset the positive effects generated by physical integration and are thus pulling the bilateral relationship towards the other end of the spectrum.

INTEGRATION, RAMIFICATION, AND SPILLOVER

Ever since Taiwan opened the door to allow its citizens to visit their families on the mainland in 1987, Cross-Strait contacts have shot up enormously. Two-way annual trade (conducted largely illegally) amounted to a mere US$ 460 million in 1981, but expanded to US$ 30 billion in 2000, an increase of nearly 70 times. Taiwanese businessmen knew nothing about investment on the mainland in the early 1980s, but by the end of last century they had dumped US$ 17 billion into PRC ventures, according to statistics released by the ROC Ministry of Economics. That figure could in fact be three times as much if mainland China sources are to be trusted, while even some private sources put that figure at a whopping US$ 100 billion. Whatever the number, the huge leap in trade can be seen in the 22 million excursions to the PRC that have been taken by Taiwanese over the last decade, with a good proportion of them conducting business there.

There does seem to be a certain degree of reciprocity when Taipei and Beijing interact with each other in this new era. Beijing reversed its Cold War hostility and unveiled in 1979 for the first time a policy—A Temporary Provision to Promote Trade with Taiwan—to engage Taiwan by nonviolent means. A while later, a similar regulation was pronounced, granting goods made in Taiwan the status of "domestic products," and waiving their duties. As a result, Taiwan eased its restrictions over the goods made in China and transported via Hong Kong and Macao. In a move to court Taiwan investors, the PRC's State Council passed a "Regulation Concerning Investment from Taiwan Compatriots" in July 1988. Barely a month later, Taiwan began formulating a policy to engage her arch rival and granted residents of both places the right to travel to the other side of the Strait. Statute governing relations between peoples of the Taiwan area and the mainland area was passed in November 1990.

As the integration theory suggests, economic and trade exchanges between the two sides of the Taiwan Strait have indeed ramified and spilled over to other areas. In order to expatriate immigrants crossing the Taiwan Strait and entering Taiwan illegally, representatives of the two Red Cross Associations, authorized by their respective governments, met in September 1990 for the first time to find a solution.[7] A month later, President Lee Teng-hui invited representatives from all political parties to form the National Unification Council and enacted the National Unification Guidelines.

In 1991, Taipei created the SEF to be its intermediary and liaison in its new engagement policy with China. After a few months of hesitation, Beijing followed suit by forming it own organization, the ARATS. Thus, a new era was ushered in, and in the next few years, the two former arch enemies engaged in over two dozen rounds of negotiation,[8] culminating in the historical summit meeting between Koo Chen-fu and Wang Daohan, heads of SEF and ARATS, respectively, in Singapore in April 1993. Two accords were reached at the meeting, marking the first documents conceded by the two governments since the Civil War in the 1940s. Working meetings of various levels between the two front organizations were also discussed and institutionalized.[9] What was more important was that SEF and ARATS agreed to "orally express the 'one-China principle' respectively" before the Singapore meeting.[10] Before the century

---

[7] In May 1986, a China Airlines cargo plane was hijacked to mainland China, and representatives of the airline met with a delegation from mainland China's China Air at Hong Kong to work out a solution. That meeting was indeed the first for the two sides since 1949. However, the September 1990 negotiation was the first initiated and monitored by the two governments. See Wu An-chia, *Taihai liangan kuanxi de huigu yu qianzhan* [Retrospection and Future Prospects of the Cross-Strait Relations] (Taipei: Yongye Publishing Co., 1996), pp. 81–93.

[8] Chien-min Chao, "Liangan shiwuxing tanpan jinyan pingxi: jianlun zhonggon dueitai juece tixi" [An Analysis of Cross-Strait Negotiations and Beijing's Decision-making Mechanism on Taiwan Affairs], *Wenti yu yanjiu* [Issues and Studies] (Taipei) (November 1995), pp. 11–23.

[9] Strait Exchange Foundation (ed.), *Koo-Wang huitan jiyao* [A Documentary of Koo-Wang Meeting] (Taipei: 1993); Chao, "Liangan shiwuxing tanpan jinyan pingxi: jianlun zhonggon dueitai juece tixi," pp. 11–23.

[10] Chien-min Chao, *Lianan huton yu waijiao jinzhu* [Cross-Strait Interaction and Diplomatic Competition] (Taipei: Yongye Publishing Co., 1992), p. 28. Beijing recanted by suggesting that no such agreement was reached, possibly after President Lee made a trip to Cornell University in June 1995. However, after the DPP won the presidency in 2000, Beijing reinvigorated its call for reverting to the agreement.

ended, the two sides even tested the waters of the possibility of holding their first political negotiation since their split in 1949.[11]

These facts attest to the following realities: First, ever since former President Chiang Ching-kuo relaxed restrictions in 1987 and allowed ROC citizens to travel to the mainland on humanitarian grounds, bilateral relations between Taiwan and mainland China have changed both in quantity and quality. Economic and trade exchanges have ramified and spilled over into areas of culture, news media, tourism, and even politics. As contacts increased, pressure began to mount, and officials became closely involved in the so-called "private" meetings between the two semiofficial organizations, SEF and ARATS. If the trend is to continue, it is not unlikely that official channels of communication may get activated. It is even argued that if every Taiwanese visitor meets three mainlanders, and those three share their experiences with their relatives and friends, 200 million mainlanders will be exposed to the Taiwan experience.[12] If popular culture in the form of pop music, movies, and novels is to be included, then the impact generated by the opening of contacts will be even more astounding.

The second reality is that because the ideologies and strategies of development adopted by the two governments have varied in the past, and the level of economic development is not the same, the two economies are in fact highly complementary to each other. The adoption of the Stalinist command economy model, implemented in the first half of the 1950s, led the mainland to pursue heavy and defense industries at the expense of light industries. On the other hand, as a small island whose development has been highly dependent on international markets, Taiwan has made light industries its priority. Furthermore, after three decades of self-imposed isolation,

---

[11] Chien-min Chao, "Weilai liangan zhengzhi huitan: beijing, xuqiu, wenti" [Cross-Strait Negotiations on Political Issues: Background, Demands, and Problems], *Zhengzhi kexue luncong* [Edited Works on Political Science] (Taipei) (December 1999), pp. 247–259.

[12] Gary Klintworth, *New Taiwan, New China: Taiwan's Changing Role in the Asia–Pacific Region* (NY: St. Martin's Press, 1995), p. 179.

China desperately needs managers and professionals to take care of its fledgling market economy. Bonded by a common history, culture, and language and equipped with the know-how of a modern market economy, Taiwan is poised to be the beachhead that many multinational corporations in the West desire when initiating commercial connections with mainland China.

The third point is that the end of the Cold War and the advent of democracy in Taiwan have greatly enhanced the prospect of a possible convergence of institutions and belief systems between Taiwan and the mainland. The displacement of the KMT's authoritarian regime has brought Taiwan into line with the third wave of democracy witnessed in the international community since the 1980s. Although Beijing remains hostile to the mechanism of western-style checks and balances, a more diversified civil society does seem to be in the making.[13] It is quite possible that people on both sides of the Taiwan Strait may find themselves in agreement one day with the way their respective political institutions and basic value systems are structured.

It is also no secret that helping mainland China to become more accustomed and receptive to the values of an open society has been a vital consideration for Taiwan's policymakers when deliberating policies concerning the mainland.[14] This expectation has no doubt been helped with Taiwan adopting more open mainland policies. Some even argue that rather than Taiwan and Hong Kong being drawn into the new economic orbit tacked by the mainland, it is China's southern regions that are actually being assimilated by forces emanating from Hong Kong and Taiwan.[15]

---

[13] See, for example, Larry Diamond and Ramon H. Myers, "Introduction: Elections and Democracy in Greater China," The China Quarterly (July 2000), pp. 365–386; Shu-Yun Ma, "The Chinese Discourse on Civil Society," The China Quarterly, No. 137 (March 1994), pp. 180–193; Mary G. Mazur, "Public Space for Memory in Contemporary Civil Society: Freedom to Learn from the Mirror of the Past?" The China Quarterly, No. 160 (December 1999), pp. 1019–1035.

[14] Klintworth, New Taiwan, New China, pp. 174–175.

[15] Ibid., p. 187.

The increased economic integration and cooperation across the Taiwan Strait area have been facilitated by the congeniality of a common culture and geographic proximity. Samuel P. Huntington argues that the new global politics is being reconfigured along cultural lines, where cultural identity is the central factor shaping a country's associations and antagonisms. Citizens and countries with different cultures are coming apart, and alignments defined by ideology and power politics are giving way to alignments defined by culture and civilizations. Cultural commonality facilitates cooperation and cohesion among people whereas cultural differences promote cleavages and conflicts. As a result, people rally to those with similar ancestry, religion, language, values, and institutions, and distance themselves from those with different ones. Consequently, the relation of culture to regionalism is apparent in economic integration. In the end, Huntington contends that cultural identity is the reason behind the increasing orientation towards being involved in and dependent on mainland China by the three lesser Chinas (Taiwan, Hong Kong, and Singapore) and the overseas Chinese communities in Southeast Asia.[16]

Huntington has a very solid point. The rise of the PRC's economy, along with the achievements realized by Hong Kong and Taiwan (two of the four Asian dragons), have prompted some to envision an enlarged Chinese economic community to rival the North American Free Trade Zone and the European Union. The economic compatibility of the three Chinese communities has induced some to address this possible alliance as the "golden economic triangle."[17] Among the names proposed are: the Chinese Economic Grouping, the Chinese Common Market, Asian–Chinese Common Market, China Economic Circle, Southern China Economic Community, the Greater China Economic Circle, the Chinese Economic Circle, the Greater China Co-prosperity Sphere, Greater

[16] Huntington, *The Clash of Civilizations: Remaking of World Order*, pp. 125–135.

[17] Jian Zheyuan, *Jueqizhong de jinji jinshanjiao* [A Rising Golden Economic Triangle: Mainland China, Hong Kong, and Taiwan] (Taipei: Yongye Publishing Co., 1994).

Cultural and Economic Community, the Chinese Economic Unity, Southern China Economic Region, and the Chinese Economic Coordinated System.[18]

LIMITATIONS OF THE INTEGRATION THEORY

It is evident that the integrationists have been quite successful in accounting for the recent expansion of exchanges in the Taiwan Strait area. Nevertheless, there are constraints in their application. Figures 1–3 vividly illustrate the centrifugal forces that have been working against the trend of integration. While integration has increased steadily, alienation too has been growing correspondingly. It would not be surprising to see that a similar trend is shaping the perceptions among the people on the other side of the Strait. The gradual integration of the two economies and the shared cultural lineage have not been able to bring closer the minds of the people separated by the narrow channel of water, nor have they been able to generate enough ramification and spillover effects to elevate contacts beyond the economic and humanistic spheres. As commercial ties are getting stronger, political ties are stagnant and in some cases even retrenching.

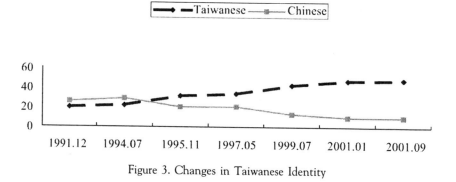

Figure 3. Changes in Taiwanese Identity

[18] Wu, *Taihai liangan kuansi de huigu yu qianzhan*, pp. 166–167.

Bucking economic and commercial trends, the mood for unification on Taiwan's side of the Strait has dropped by a gigantic 50% in the past decade (Figure 1). The number of Taiwanese with a negative perception of bilateral relations has tripled (Figure 2), and the number of those who would identify themselves as "Taiwanese" has gone up from less than 20 to nearly 50%, while those acknowledging themselves as "Chinese" have dwindled to a single digit, from a height of nearly 30% (Figure 3). The integration theory faces challenge when applied to Taiwan/mainland China relations.

One first notices that the common identity that the two sides share is crumbling. The democratization of Taiwan and the reform of the Stalinist socialist system in the PRC have not only transformed the two varying despotic political structures, but have also forged new identities and consciousness [*zhizhu yishi*] amid destruction of the old belief systems on which some shared consensus was based.[19] From Taipei's perspective, the contrast of the two entities is culturally reinforced as a more participant political culture on the island is emerging, as opposed to the subject political culture that is still dominant in China.[20] This newly surfaced divergence is exacerbated by the confrontation over sovereignty that the two have been unable to shake off over the past decades.

The concepts of China and Chinese culture are being increasingly regarded as irrelevant or even "alien" by the people of Taiwan.[21] People on the two sides are becoming more and more detached

---

[19] Chien-min Chao, "Taiwan zhuti yishi he zhongkuo dalu minzhu zhuyi de duikang" [A Confrontation between Taiwan's Sense of Selfness versus Mainland China's Nationalism], *Zhongguo dalu yanjiu* [Mainland China Studies] (Taipei), Vol. 41, No. 1 (January 1998), pp. 54–71.

[20] By subject political culture, Almond and Verba meant to suggest that there is a high frequency of orientation towards a differentiated political system and towards the output aspects of the systems, but orientations toward specifically input objects, and towards the self as an active participant, approach zero. See Gabriel A. Almond and Sidney Verba, *The Civic Culture* (Princeton: Princeton University Press, 1963), p. 19.

[21] In campaigning for the Taiwan Solidarity Union (TSU) candidates running for the Legislative Yuan and local administrators at the end of 2001, former President Lee Teng-hui constantly used the term "alien regime" in referring to the KMT.

from each other. For example, when in 1991 the PRC was whacked by the Yangtze river in one of the worst floods it had seen, the people of Taiwan responded by helping the flood victims.[22] However, when Taiwan suffered one of its worst natural disasters in history after a 7.0+ earthquake struck on September 21, 1999 (in which over 2000 people died), Beijing responded by engaging in a war of words with Taipei, warning international humanitarian agencies that all relief materials for the island must pass through mainland China.[23] Complaints about lack of compassion by the PRC were also voiced when Taiwan was hit by a typhoon that crawled slowly over the island for over three days in the summer of 2001, causing the worst flood of the last century. Similarly, the people of Taiwan showed very little enthusiasm when Beijing was awarded the 2008 Olympic Games, an event that brought hundreds of thousands of mainlanders to the streets to celebrate.

It was quite evident that the relative good relations at the turn of the 1990s were headed for a tailspin by mid-1990s. The PRC's firing of missiles over the waters near Taiwan on the eve of Taiwan's first direct presidential election in March 1996 and the subsequent *wengong wuhe* (which literally means to attack by pen and intimidate by force) by Beijing to suppress what it saw as an inclination to Taiwan independence—promoted first by former President Lee Teng-hui and then his successor, President Chen Shui-bian—were only tips of the iceberg. A lack of concern and affection may also be the reason for the lack of progress in cross-Strait negotiations. After two accords, one to authenticate official documents and the other to

---

[22] Taiwan donated US$ 30 million in cash and relief goods for the flood victims. See *Zhongguo shibao*, October 30, 1991, p. 2.

[23] Beijing donated, through the Red Cross, US$ 500,000 and prepared to send a team of experts for assistance. However, Taipei took the money and refused entry of the rescue team. Moreover, Taipei accused Beijing of rejecting the Russians to use its airspace for the rescue effort and forced a Jordanian rescue plane to wait for a day. At the same time, mainland China's foreign minister thanking the world for providing help on Taiwan's behalf also angered Taipei. See *Zhongyang ribao* (Taipei), October 22, 1999, p. 14; *Zhiyou shibao* (Taipei), October 16, 1999, p. 4.

verify registered mail, were signed at the 1993 Koo-Wang meeting between SEF and ARAFTS, negotiations failed to produce any tangible results. Not even talks over fishing disputes and the expatriation of criminals, deemed by both as crucial, yielded any results.[24] It has been increasingly apparent to the mainland that an increase in exchanges may not necessarily lead to an ultimate political union.

The second thing one notices is that the principles and code of conduct developed under the framework of the integration theory are based primarily on experiences extracted from interactions among sovereign states, which are not necessarily suitable in the handling of problems deriving from the division of sovereignty. Taipei and Beijing have been engaged in a diplomatic tussle over the issue of "one China" for the past half a century. As Taipei is drawing less reverberation for its cause,[25] it is less willing to play along in the losing battle, because its diplomatic maneuverability is being strangled day by day. Fewer people on this side of the Strait see the utility of fighting to keep the "one China."

A third observation is that although the integration theory (derived from the cooperative experiences of the Common Market in western Europe) does not preclude an ultimate political amalgamation, it is not an aim in itself. This is utterly different from the kind of interaction that is conducted between two parts of a divided state in which the principle of indivisibility of sovereignty is

---

[24] Chao, "Taiwan zhuti yishi he zhongguo dalu minzhu zhuyi de duikang," pp. 54–71.

[25] The ROC is recognized by only 27 countries now (mostly poor and small), as opposed to over 70 countries that supported the island regime before the ROC was forced out of the United Nations in 1972. See Chien-min Chao, "Balance Sheet: Lee Teng-hui's Performance in Diplomacy," in Chien-min Chao and Bruce Dickson (eds), *Lee Teng-hui's Legacy: Democratic Consolidation and Foreign Affairs* (NY: M.E. Sharpe, forthcoming). At the same time, in a move further restraining Taipei's foreign space, former US President Bill Clinton declared a new "three nos policy" while making a trip to China in 1998: that his country would not support Taiwan independence; one China, one Taiwan; and the US will not support Taiwan's quest for membership in international organizations with statehood as a requirement.

often proclaimed as the most sacrosanct credo in a non-zero-sum game. The difference in the nature of the conflict has led to different solutions. While the resolution of conflicts under the integration theory relies on compromises and reconciliation, the resolution of the same conflicts for a divided state is often composed of boycotts, intimidation, and even the use of brute force.

The reason for the detachment is due in large part to the emergence of a new genre of political culture after a long period of separation. People living on both sides tend to interpret political phenomena differently. One can take the negotiations as a prime example. As a highly commercialized society accustomed to a Western style of bargaining philosophy, Taiwan has had difficulties with the kind of bargaining honed by a culture of despotic collectivism.

The two sides also differ in almost everything, ranging from the nature, process, and agenda of any mediation. Taipei wants to begin with issues more negotiable and leave tough political disagreements to a later date when solutions are easier to come by. Therefore, issues like fishing disputes, expatriation of criminals and illegal immigrants, and investment agreements have shown priority. However, for Beijing, agreeing to enter into these kinds of negotiations with Taipei must be premised on the condition that they will lead to political negotiations over the issue of unification.

When Koo Chen-fu went to Shanghai in October 1998 to meet with Wang Daohang in an effort to revive suspended negotiations, the move was seen as a turnaround in Taipei's attitude, and Beijing billed it as "the first time that the two sides had sat down to discuss political issues."[26] To carry on the spirit of negotiation, the two top negotiators agreed that Wang would return a visit to Taipei in due time. The agenda that they arranged for a possible future visit by Wang were: political and economic dialogue, ways to facilitate contacts between the two semiofficial institutions, assisting in the protection and safety of Taiwanese businessmen on the mainland

---

[26] Tang Shubei, former Vice Chairman of the ARATS, made this point in an interview. See *Zhongguo shibao*, December 26, 1998, p. 14.

for individual cases, and a Wang Daohang visit to Taiwan in due time. According to Taipei's understanding, there was no ranking order among the four subjects, but Beijing insisted that the political and economic dialogues should precede Wang's visit and that "due time" meant only after the dialogues had proceeded well with tangible results.[27] For Taipei, all the discussions were predicated on the visit of Wang.

To show its sincerity about the visit, Taipei briefly flirted with the idea of a "peace accord" as a response to Beijing's call for "an end to hostility in the Taiwan Strait" area. Beneath a superficial resemblance lies a huge difference between these two political agendas. In Taipei's view, a peace accord was called for, so that Beijing would renounce the use of force in resolving differences with Taiwan; while for Beijing, "an end to hostility" meant Taiwan should end its independence drive and accept the "one-China" principle.

THE NEW TAIWANESE DOCTRINE AND CONSENSUS BUILDING

The different developmental ideologies and strategies that the two sides have adopted since their separation in 1949 have helped to create two very divergent political cultural identities across the Taiwan Strait. The capitalist development strategy that Taiwan undertook has laid the foundation for a belief system embedded in liberalism and individualism, while the socialist development strategy on the mainland has churned out a mentality with collectivism and nationalism at its core. However, the regime transitions that started in both places at the turn of the 1980s have not only fundamentally altered the nature of the previous regimes, but also resulted in the creation of two dual societies afflicted by a torn cultural identity. For Taiwan, the problem with the split identity is ethnically driven in which the three largest ethnic groups—the Fukienese, Hakka (the two are jointly labeled Taiwanese), and the mainlanders—have shown

---

[27] *Ibid.*

significant differences over major political issues. For China, the bifurcation is basically a continuation of the century-old debate over where the country is heading and the role traditional Chinese culture should play. While the former needs to continue to build up a consensus among the major ethnic subgroups, the latter must effectively search through the heap of Chinese history and socialist tradition in search of a new cultural identity.

As a former colony of imperialist Japan and ruled for a long time by a group of KMT elites who emigrated from the mainland, Taiwan has had problems with harmonizing its own cultural multiplicity. The discordance was earlier heightened by the February 28, 1947 incident in which thousands of Taiwanese were slaughtered by the first government installed by the KMT after the Japanese withdrew in 1945. The incident was primarily rooted in a conflict of cultures—an elite culture fomented by the mainlanders who fled to Taiwan after the Civil War and who took control of all major political resources versus a mass culture which had been molded by many immigrants who had come to Taiwan much earlier.

Most of the one million mainlanders who followed Chiang Kai-shek to Taiwan were teachers, factory owners, engineers, technicians, merchants, bankers, scholars, and professionals. They filled the gap in managerial skills for industrialization purposes, because Japan had purposely left the island under an "agricultural Taiwan" policy. The wave of immigration from China also provided the "seed money" as well as entrepreneurs for Taiwan's initial import-substitution manufacturing industry. For the ordinary Taiwanese, after having suffered many years of Japanese colonialism during which they were treated as second-class citizens, and then having experienced the February 28 incident, politics by that time had become prohibitively distant. Memories of the Japanese colonial past, such as the infamous Japanese military police, still loomed large. The land reform proposed by the KMT government and the island's subsequent industrialization kept people encapsulated in the commercial arena for decades to come.

The end of KMT authoritarian rule and the advent of democracy by the end of the 20th century were more than just a simple transition of power from old-guard mainlander politicians to a new breed of Taiwanese elites who had lived on the island longer than their predecessors. With the changeover of power, a new cultural identity was forged. Gradually, what had been suppressed previously is now coming out into the open. The myth of "one China", imposed by the mainlander ruling elites, has been sidelined during this cultural renaissance, as evidenced by the remolding of a new cultural identity that has been a vital part of the democratization process initiated by former President Lee Teng-hui. This explains why "indigenization" has been an indispensable segment of the political process in the past decade. Some call this new sense of selfness a "civic doctrine,"[28] or the "new Taiwanese doctrine," as coined by former President Lee.[29]

Affected by a Western liberalist tradition against a backdrop in which small- and medium-sized enterprises (SMEs) constitute the backbone of the island's economic structure, and aggravated by transitional pains in which a full scale of rule of law has yet to be realized, individual rights and selfness have been unusually exaggerated in Taiwan.[30] Family is still important, but social networking between individuals and families has been unremittingly reshaped.

The democratization process that started in the late 1980s has been essentially a redistribution of political resources (see Table 2). In addition to advocating local values, the indigenization process (as it is aptly termed) did manage to heal some of the old wounds inflicted by the ethnic division. The admission of wrongdoing by the KMT government and the recantation of the February 28 incident are but two examples. However, the reconfiguration of the

---

[28] Siew Chuan-chen, *Taiwan xinsiwei: guomin zhuyi* [Taiwan's New Thinking: Civic Doctrine] (Taipei: Shiying Publishing Co., 1995), pp. XV–XVII.

[29] President Lee coined the term in 1998 during the Taipei mayoral election. It was believed that the invention helped KMT candidate Ma Ying-jeou, a second generation mainlander, in winning the election over DPP opponent Chen Shui-bian, a native Taiwanese.

[30] This is evidenced by a recent episode in which a tabloid, the Scoop Weekly, distributed a VCD disk, showing a sexually explicit film of a popular young female politician having an affair with a married man. The owner of the tabloid defended his move by citing press freedom. See all major newspapers on September 18, 2001.

Table 2. Redistribution of Political Resources

Year	President	Vice President	Premier	Vice Premier	Cabinet members	Total (%)
1993						
Taiwanese	1	0	0.5*	0	17	18.5 (54.5%)
Mainlander	0	1	0.5	1	13	15.5 (45.5%)
2001						
Taiwanese	1	1	1	1	35	39 (95%)
Mainlander	0	0	0	0	2	2 (5%)

* Lien Chan, the Premier at that time, was a product of two ethnic groupings.
Sources: The Executive Yuan website, (http://www.ey.gov.tw/web/index-m4.htm); Singtao Ribao (Hong Kong), February 27, 1993, p. 9.

political map has also opened new fissures unwittingly, with one such by-product being the alienation of the previous ruling class, the mainlanders. The estrangement has worsened with major political parties, particularly the ruling DPP, trying to take advantage of the newly installed democratic procedures in order to reap political benefits by opening ethnic differences. Consequently, major ethnic groups have shown grave differences over political issues, particularly those concerning cross-Strait relations.

While a proportionally significant percentage of mainlanders living in Taiwan are more concerned about a possible attack from mainland China and henceforth more inclined to opt for conciliation when contemplating policies towards Beijing, the island's population of Fukienese and to some extent the Hakka have been less sensitive to that threat and are thus less intimidated by the PRC menace. In a recent survey conducted by the National Chengchi University Election Studies Center, while 37.5% of those with a mainland background expressed support for eventual unification with the mainland, only 16.5% of those with Fukienese (Taiwanese) blood felt the same; by the same token, 17.5% of Taiwanese opted for independence, while a mere 4.1% of mainland Chinese supported the demand. In the same survey, nearly 47% of Fukienese Taiwanese consider themselves "Taiwanese, not Chinese," while only 15.6% of the mainland Chinese concurred. Furthermore, 26.6% of mainland

Chinese identified themselves as "Chinese," with the number for Fukienese Taiwanese feeling the same way dwindling to 6.5%.[31] The third major ethnic group, the Hakka, has found itself somewhere in the middle of the two groups on issues of ethnic and national identity.

The ethnic divide does seem to be fluctuating in a reverse V-shaped curve. Spurred by the first transition of power from mainlanders to Taiwanese, the confrontation began to emerge when President Lee was sworn into office in 1988, and it culminated at the first elections for mayor of the two major cities, Taipei and Kaohsiung, and the governor of Taiwan in 1994. Rhetoric that was tuned to appeal to ethnic subgroupings was a common campaign strategy, with candidates identified under different ideological stripes risking their political careers when entering an "enemy camp." An infamous case in point was the violence that erupted when New Party (with its power base in the northern half of the island) candidates went to Kaohsiung (a southern port city and stronghold of the DPP) to campaign for votes. Politicians belonging to different ideological belief system had difficulty in even sitting down for a cup of coffee. However, after the initial surge, emotions seemed to have tapered off.

A new cultural identity actually seems to be shaping up, featuring a rising consensus on subjects concerning mainland China—traditionally the most divisive issue in Taiwan's ethnic confrontation.[32] A new sense of a political community seems to be in the making. A more secular culture with less ideological emphasis is in fact discernible.

The first wave of consensus building began when the DPP decided to tone down its Taiwan independence rhetoric—the most controversial issue affecting ethnic harmony.[33] Sensing the reality that the party would not be able to pull off a good outcome in the first direct presidential election (in March 1996) without recasting

---

[31] The survey was conducted in October 2001 with 1658 samples collected.

[32] Chao, "Taiwan zhuti yishi he zhongguo dalu minzhu zhuyi de duikang," pp. 54–71.

[33] Concerning DPP's transition, see Chao, "DPP's Factional Politics and Taiwan Independence."

its independence stance first, the party started to transform itself in the mid-1990s. In the ensuing years, the party underwent an amazing metamorphosis, resulting in what has been called a new type of Taiwan independence movement. The old independence movement based on Taiwanese nationalism was displaced, as the ROC had been transformed into a new democratic polity which many within the party had no problem embracing. This in turn foreordained the passage of the "Resolution of Taiwan's Future" in 1999, in which the principle that the ROC was a sovereign entity was affirmed officially for the first time in the party's short history.

During the second major convergence of a value system, consensus was reshaped across the party divide. At the Conference on National Development convened at the end of 1996, all major political parties agreed for the first time to a number of issues concerning the basic fabric of political establishment. They all agreed to the principles of ROC sovereignty and Taiwan's security being the first priority when contemplating the future of the country. The criterion that any policy agenda should be based on nothing but the principle of "Taiwan first" was upheld without question.

The third and last wave of consensus building came to fruition when President Chen Shui-bian called the previously mentioned Advisory Meeting on Economic Development in August 2000. At the conference, the core of Lee Teng-hui's mainland policy—the "no haste, be patient" policy—was unanimously cast aside, which was a major turnabout for the ruling DPP. It took a huge economic setback on the island to bring forth a more constructive and forward-looking policy towards mainland China. With the termination of the old policy, the biggest debate in ROC history on constructing a new policy towards the mainland (in the midst of a new era after ending the Cold War-style confrontation) was finally put to an end. From now on, it seems that a more constructive engagement policy will dominate the island's strategic thinking about its relationship with the PRC. Security has ceased to be the sole concern as was the case in the past.

Despite all these efforts, internal ethnic rivalry still lingers. At the year-end parliamentary election in 2001, instead of campaigning on their own causes, the three major political parties (the KMT, the

DPP, and the PFP) were divided into two forces, the Pan-Green and the Pan-Blue camps, with "indigenization" as the dividing criterion.[34] A new party, the Taiwan Solidarity Union (TSU), with former President Lee Teng-hui as its "spiritual leader" and "indigenization" as the core stumping issue, saw itself a victor after winning 13 seats in the 225-seat Legislative Yuan (the parliament).

The founding of the TSU and its prospect of luring some disaffected KMT legislators to join its forces in the future has rekindled tensions. The rise of ethnic confrontation and the threat of bifurcation have reduced the likelihood that the Chen Shui-bian administration will be able to make breakthroughs in the near future in its relations with Beijing. In a move that partly reflects this division, the Government Information Office introduced on December 31, 2001, a new logo for itself (a propaganda agency) with the conspicuous absence of a map of mainland China, and instead showing the national flag of the ROC. In another move, The Ministry of Foreign Affairs in mid-January 2002 began issuing new ROC passports with the English phrase "Issued In Taiwan" at the bottom of the front cover.[35] Logically speaking, "Issued In Taiwan" means that Taiwan is just a place in one country (potentially the PRC or ROC) from which the passport can be issued, and it does not mean that Taiwan is in fact its own country. But this no doubt reinforces Beijing's conviction that Taiwan under the stewardship of Chen Shui-bian is pursuing a policy to "culturally split China."

CULTURAL CRISIS AND IDENTITY-SEARCHING ON THE MAINLAND

After 20 years of economic reforms, the PRC has quadrupled its GDP. Before this decade ends, it is highly likely that the mainland

---

[34] Pan-Green camp refers to those sympathetic to the cause of the ruling DPP since the party has associated itself with the color green. Pan-Blue represents those close to the cause of the KMT since the party's emblem is blue. The former accused the latter of being deficient in "indigenization."

[35] "Pursuit of a separate identity may raise political tensions," *The China Post* (Taipei), January 2, 2002, p. 4.

economy will double again in output. The rapid rise of its economic power has made Beijing more assertive in the international arena. At the same time, as more reforms come about and as the market economy takes hold, elements of orthodox socialism are shrinking accordingly. Amid Jiang Zemin's dramatic proposal to grant communist Party membership to capitalists, in a speech to commemorate the Party's 80th birthday on July 1, 2001, the country's Maoist development strategy has formally become history. As the old socialist value system has disintegrated and a new one based on the capitalist rule of law is in the process of being transplanted wholly, it is evident that there is an ideological and, indeed, cultural void. China is once again searching for an identity—a task unfulfilled since the late Ching dynasty.

As a revolutionary force that has based its legitimacy on the opposition to traditional Chinese culture, it is unlikely that the "feudalistic Four Olds" are to be rehabilitated and installed as the core of the new moral code soon. Although the utility of traditional Chinese culture was widely debated in the 1980s, and relevant publications and discussions have also been on the rise, the focus in the PRC seems to be on critiquing and reevaluating. This also explains why Zhou Zuoren, a writer who was highly critical of traditional Chinese culture three quarter of a century ago, can still command so much attention.[36]

Economically, China is doing rather well, attracting an unprecedented amount of foreign direct investment. Nonetheless, culturally, it seems to be at the crossroads. After decades of experimentation, socialism seems to be dead in its tracks. For various reasons, capitalist political values continue to be negated, and the attitude towards traditional Chinese culture is ambivalent at best. There certainly is a crisis of cultural identity.

The predicament faced on the mainland originated when traditional Confucianism came under heavy attack with the

---

[36] Liu Dong, "Zhu zuoren: shiqu rujia zhiheng de 'gerenzhuyi'" [Zhu Zuoren: A Believer of Individualism Unconstrained by the Confucianism], *Ershiyi shiji* [The Twenty-First Century] (Hong Kong), No. 39 (February 1997), pp. 92–106.

introduction of Western influences in the mid-1800s. The frailty of the imperial Ching dynasty in the face of colonial penetration prompted many Chinese to reexamine the value of traditional culture, paving the way for the May Fourth Movement, also known as a "renaissance" in modern China. However, in the decades that followed, none of the three ideological paradigms—liberalism, Marxism, and neoconservatism—that had been introduced as possible ways to salvage the morbid traditional Chinese culture has been cataclysmic enough to reconstruct the citizen's moral and value underpinning. The failure laid the ground for a kind of material nihilism in which the pursuit of physical satisfaction has emerged as the only sensible goal in the midst of rebuilding a market economy after decades of practicing socialist public ownership system.[37] The rise of economic power, the craving for a reincarnation of its ancient hegemonic empire, and anti-Westernism have all converged to give rise to a new "nationalistic cultural nihilism."

Traditional Chinese culture has long been denounced as feudalism, but owing to a lack of liberal tradition and the meagerness of a middle class, it is difficult to hope for any reception of Western liberalism as a viable substitute anytime soon. The only alternative is to hark back to Chinese and socialist traditions for answers. Unfortunately, the shrinking authority of the central government is worrisome to many and has even prompted some contemporary Chinese writers to welcome back a strong center.[38] Others have tried to delve into nonmainstream academic writings in the West to prove that the liberal tradition in the West is losing steam and so a need for institutional innovation in China is justifiable.[39] These people have tried to dig deep into Chinese history and socialist practices during Mao's era to prove that the neosocialist institutional

---

[37] Xu Jilin, "erzhong weiji yu sanzhong sichao" [Two Crises and Three Thoughts: History of Thought in the 20th Century China], *zhanlue yu guanli* (Beijing), No. 38 (January 2000), pp. 66–71.

[38] Hu Angang, Wang Shaoguang, and Cui Zhiyuan are leading scholars in this school.

[39] Cui Zhiyuan, *Erci sixiang jiefang yu zhidu chuangxin* [Second Thought Liberation and Institutional Innovation] (Hong Kong: Oxford Press, 1997).

arrangements are a valid "third way." As an example, Cui Zhiyuan revisited the works of Fei Xiaotong in his study of Chinese rural areas in the 1940s and came up with the findings that the manufacturing doctrines of division of work and economy of scale developed by Ford Motors are false and that "post-Fordism" was already in existence in China long ago. Cui has a particular taste for "neocollectivism," and the juxtaposition of collective and private ownerships is being hailed as a "Chinese institutional innovation."

In the wake of searching for a new cultural identity, collectivism and nationalism have emerged as two key components, arguing that the past practice of public and collective ownerships has already been substituted by "neocollectivism" in which both the collective ownership based on old socialist idealism and a newly transplanted private ownership have been put on par. This is in accordance with the "Chinese reality," and therefore there is no need to duplicate the Western experiences.[40] At the same time, events such as the sympathetic attitude that the West extended to the "antirevolutionary" dissidents of the Tiananmen incident in June 1989 and the subsequent sanctions imposed on China, the reversion of Hong Kong to PRC sovereignty, the bombing of the Chinese embassy in Belgrade by US warplanes during the Kosovo war, and the rise of its economic power have all combined to give rise to a new kind of nationalistic sentiment in mainland China. In the face of what it perceives to be America's hegemonic presence, some have resorted to using "rational nationalism" to fight against the advocacy of "containment of China."[41] An inner thinking based, to a large extent, on neocollectivism and nationalism not only contradicts the pluralistic culture exuberated by the civil society that has emerged in Taiwan,

---

[40] Wang Yin, "Xinjitizhuyi yu zhongkuoteshe de shichang jinji" [Neo-collectivism and Market Economy with Chinese Characteristics], *Ershiyi shiji*, No. 25 (October 1994), pp. 11–14.

[41] Wu Guoguang, "Yi lixing minzhuzhuyi kangheng weidu zhongkuo" [Fight Against Containment of China with Rational Nationalism] *Ershiyi shiji* (April 1996), pp. 25–33; "Zailun lixing minzhuzhuyi" [On Rational Nationalism Again—An Answer to Chen Yan], *Ershiyi shiji* (February 1997), pp. 125–131.

but also makes Beijing less susceptible to making policies deemed conciliatory to Taiwan.

The new US strategy under the younger Bush administration has assigned China a status of "competitor" (at least before the September 11 terrorist attacks on the World Trade Center and the Pentagon[42]). Subsequent friendly overtures to Taiwan by this administration culminated in the sale of the biggest arms package since 1992, including eight diesel-powered submarines and four Kidd-class destroyers. Such actions have reinforced the misgivings that Beijing has held for a long time that Taiwan is not only politically, but also culturally, a part of the US sphere of influence.

CONCLUDING REMARKS

After over a century of separation, the two sides of the Taiwan Strait have grown into very divergent identities. These two political entities have managed to move forward from the Chinese Civil War and intense hostility towards a state of economic interdependence. Although still highly antagonistic in the political arena, exchanges in the fields of economy, commerce, culture, and tourism have remained unhindered. It is also further generally expected that with the simultaneous accession of both the PRC and Taiwan into the WTO on January 1, 2002, the pace of exchanges should only quicken.

The different development ideologies and strategies chosen by the separate regimes in the past have given rise to two very different cultural subsystems. For Taiwan, this new cultural identity (resulting from interplays of multiethnicity and a mixture of Chinese, Japanese, traditional Taiwanese, and Western influences) emphasizes

---

[42] Washington–Beijing relations were further damaged when a PRC jet struck an American surveillance airplane in midair over the sky of South China Sea on April 1, 2001. However, after the September 11 terrorist attack, Bush announced while attending an APEC summit meeting in Shanghai in October that the PRC is not an enemy and the two should strive to develop a "constructive cooperation."

individualism, an embrace of local values (as opposed to those imported from mainland China), and a growing identification of Taiwan as a political community. This mindset differs tremendously with the collective-minded Chinese way of thinking prevalent on the mainland in which socialism and nationalism, including reclaiming Taiwan back into its fold, have taken the center seat. The chronic political disputes that have hamstrung the two sides in the past half a century and mainland China's heavy-handedness towards the island have contributed to the rise of a sense of alienation that the people of Taiwan feel towards the mainland. The detestation and alienation towards the Beijing regime justify for many here in Taiwan the wish for more autonomy vis-à-vis Beijing, which angers the latter even more.

The identity crisis that the two have suffered, caused by their respective transformation of the ruling regimes in the 1980s, has made their policies less amenable towards each other. While "indigenization," a source of contention within Taiwan, continues to be an element of alienation for the people of Taiwan towards the Beijing regime, the identity crisis on the mainland has also reduced the probability of formatting a more conciliatory policy towards its compatriots across the Strait.

For now, cross-Strait relations are in a state of stalemate. The two cannot come to any agreement, not only on issues with political implications such as the issue of "one-China" policy, but also on nonpolitical issues. There is no reason why the two cannot work together to promote direct transportation and allow tourist and journalistic exchanges. On top of that, Taipei and Beijing have even succeeded in backpedaling from the rare consensus that was reached in 1992. Negotiations between SEF and ARATS have been shut down since 1995, and there seems to be no sign of their resumption. It is increasingly clear that the two need to tackle obstacles from a cultural perspective and overcome the split in their respective cultural identities from within, and then work to form a more congruous belief system between them. Maybe by doing so, a more stable bilateral relationship will show up on the horizon.

Chapter 14

The Rise of China: Challenges for the ASEAN Economies

JOHN WONG*

THE ECONOMIC RISE OF CHINA

The Chinese economy has experienced spectacular growth ever since it adopted economic reforms and an open-door policy some 20 years ago. Real growth during 1979–2000 was at an annual rate of 9.6%. The 1997 Asian financial crisis brought down many Asian economies. China's economy, however, was hardly affected—it continued to grow at the rate of 8.8% in 1997 and 7.8% in 1998. More recently, while economic growth in most of Asia has been falling to low or negative growth, and the world economy at large is creeping towards recession, China's economy alone is still steaming ahead with strong growth. In the first quarter of 2001, it grew at the rate of 7.6%.[1]

China is much less affected by the global economic downturn, mainly because about 70% of its economic growth is generated by domestic demand. However, its exports have also been growing at an average rate of 17% for the past two decades. In 2000, it exported US$ 250 billion worth of goods to become the world's seventh largest exporting nation. While many Asian economies currently find their

---

* The author would like to thank Research Officer Miss Sarah Chan for assistance in updating the statistical tables and making the charts.
[1] China's National Statistical Bureau source, *Mingpao Daily*, Hong Kong, October 17, 2001.

exports plunging, China's export machine is still going fairly strong, up by 7% for the first eight months of 2001.

For foreign direct investment (FDI), China has become the world's most favored destination of all developing countries since 1993. From 1988 to 2000, China's realized FDI grew at an average rate of 23% per annum to reach a cumulative total of US$ 339 billion. In fact, China in recent years has captured about 70% of all FDI in Asia. Currently, still more FDI is flowing into China in anticipation of its WTO membership. In the first nine months of 2001, the FDI inflow to China went up by 21% to US$ 32 billion.[2]

In all, China's total nominal GDP by 2000 reached US$ 1 trillion or about twice that of the original five ASEAN countries of Indonesia, Malaysia, the Philippines, Singapore, and Thailand, ranking it the world's seventh largest.[3] In terms of purchasing power parity (PPP), the Chinese economy in 1999 became the world's second largest after the US—one needs, of course, to be aware of the problem of overstating China's real GDP by the PPP measure.[4] As Singapore Prime Minister Goh Chok-tong recently put it, China's economy can be potentially 10 times the size of Japan's by the middle of this century.

Not surprisingly, the economic rise of China has suddenly become a "hot" issue in international and regional media. It has also become a real concern to many Asian governments. Many commentators saw the emergence of China as a disruptive force in the Asian economy. Others even point a finger at China for their current economic crises. The famous economist Kenichi Ohmae recently used a sensational title "Asia's Next Crisis: Made in China" to write about the rise of China.

In fact, Japan has recently grown apprehensive about the meteoric rise of China as a manufacturing powerhouse. According to Japanese

[2] *Mingpao Daily*, October 17, 2001.
[3] World Bank, *World Development Report 2000/2001*. Also, *Mingpao*, Hong Kong, September 20, 2000.
[4] World Bank, *World Development Report 2000/2001*. Also, *Mingpao*, Hong Kong, September 20, 2000.

Figure 1. China's Shares of World's Production of
Some Key Commodities (2001) (%)

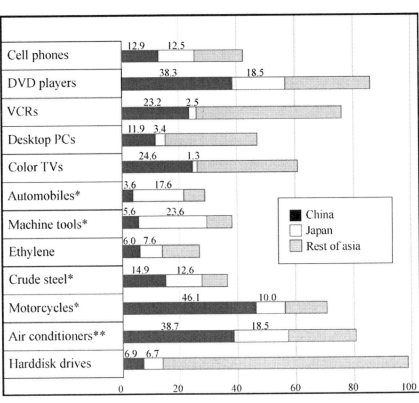

*2000; **1999.

Source: The Nikkei Weekly, August 6, 2001.

estimates, by the end of 2001, about one in two of the world's motorcycles, one in three of the world's air conditioners and one in four of the world's color TVs will be manufactured in China. China is indeed already producing more cell phones, more desktop computers, and more DVD players than Japan[5] (Figure 1).

In short, as China is undergoing its fourth major leadership transition, the "Chinese economic threat" seems to be looming large in many Asian countries. It may just be a perception. However,

[5] See "China Takes Production Lead as Foreign Firms Set Up Shop", The Nikkei Weekly, August 6, 2001.

China's younger leaders need to address this problem if they want to maintain a strong and stable political relationship with China's neighbors.

CHINA'S DYNAMIC GROWTH IN REGIONAL PERSPECTIVE

China's economic performance in the past two decades has indeed been breathtaking. Viewed in the overall East Asian (EA) context, however, China's hyper-growth is actually not so exceptional. Nor is it unprecedented, because many East Asian economies (EAEs) have also at one time or the other experienced high growth.

The EA region is commonly defined as comprising Japan, China, the four newly industrialized economies (NIEs) of South Korea, Taiwan, Hong Kong, and Singapore, and the four Association of Southeast Asian Nations (ASEAN) of Indonesia, Malaysia, the Philippines, and Thailand—the original ASEAN members. Situated on the western rim of the Pacific, many of these EAEs have displayed dynamic growth for a sustained period until 1997 when they were hit, in varying degrees, by the regional financial crisis. The World Bank in its well-known study referred to the high growth phenomenon of East Asia as the "EA Miracle."[6]

Japan was the first non-Western country to become industrialized. Its high growth dated back to the 1950s after it achieved its post-War recovery, and the momentum was carried over to the 1960s. Japan's economic growth was initially based on the export of labor-intensive manufactured products, but it was soon forced by rising wages and increasing costs to shed its comparative advantage of labor-intensive manufacturing in favor of the four NIEs, which started their industrial takeoff in the 1960s. These four NIEs, once dubbed "Asia's Four Little Dragons," constituted the most dynamic component of the EA region, and their near double digit rate growth has been sustained for three decades, from the 1960s to the 1980s.

---

[6] *The East Asian Miracle* (New York: Oxford University Press, 1994).

By the late 1970s and early 1980s, high costs and high wages had also caught up with these NIEs, which had to restructure their economies towards more capital-intensive and higher value-added activities and to pass their comparative advantage in labor-intensive products to the latecomers, China and the four ASEAN economies. Thus, China and some ASEAN economies experienced high economic growth in the 1980s and the 1990s. Some Japanese scholars like to depict this pattern of development as the "flying geese" model[7] (Table 1).

An important feature of these EAEs is their growing economic interdependence. The EAEs, despite their inherent political, social, and economic divergences, can actually integrate economically quite well as a regional grouping. This is essentially the underlying meaning of the "flying geese" principle. Thus, Japan is obviously the natural economic leader of the group and has in fact been the prime source of capital and technology for other EAEs. The resource-based ASEAN-four complement well with the manufacturing-based NIEs, while both are also complementary with the more developed Japanese economy. Then the huge potential of China, with its vast resource base and diverse needs, offers additional opportunities for all.

Not surprisingly, the EA region has already developed a significant degree of economic interdependence as manifested in its fairly high level of intraregional trade. As shown in Table 2, the EA region in 1999, although still recovering from the Asian financial crisis, absorbed 47% of China's total exports; 47% of the average of the NIEs', 48% of the average of the ASEAN-four's, though only 36% of Japan's—still unusually high for Japan as a global economic power.

Apart from intraregional trade, intraregional FDI flows have increasingly operated as a strong integrating force for the EA region, especially because a great deal of regional FDI is trade related. The EAEs are essentially open and outward looking in being heavily

---

[7] The "flying geese" concept of development was originally coined by a Japanese economist, Kaname Akamatzu ("A Historical Pattern of Economic Growth in Developing Countries," *Developing Economies*, Vol. 1 (March/August 1962)).

Table 1. Performance Indicators of East Asian Economies

	China	Japan	NIEs				ASEAN-4			
			South Korea	Taiwan	Hong Kong	Singapore	Indonesia	Malaysia	Philippines	Thailand
Population (Mn), 1999	1250	127	47	22	7	3	207	23	77	62
GNP per capita (US$), 1999	780	32,230	8490	13,248	23,520	29,610	580	3400	1020	1960
PPP estimates of GNP per capita (US$), 1999	3291	24,041	14,637	NA	22,939	27,024	2439	7963	3815	5599
Growth of GDP (%)										
1960–1970	5.2	10.9	8.6	9.2	10.0	8.8	3.9	6.5	5.1	8.4
1970–1980	5.8	5.0	9.5	9.7	9.3	8.5	7.6	7.8	6.3	7.2
1980–1990	10.2	4.0	9.4	7.1	6.9	6.4	6.1	5.3	1.0	7.6
1990–1998	11.1	1.3	6.2	NA	4.4	8.0	5.8	7.7	3.3	7.4
1996[b]	9.6*	3.3	6.7	5.6	4.7	7.5	8.1	8.0	5.9	8.5
1997	8.8	1.0	6.0	6.7	5.3	7.0	5.0	7.0	4.3	0.6
1998[a]	7.8	−2.5	−5.8	4.6	−5.1	0.3	−13.2	−7.5	−0.5	−10.4
1999[a]	7.1	0.8	10.0	5.6	2.1	5.6	0.1	5.4	3.2	5.0
2000[b]	8.0*	2.3	9.2	4.1	6.8	11	5.1	6.5	3.6	3.1
Annual export growth (%), 1990–1998	14.9	3.9	15.7	2.4	9.5	13.3	8.6	13.2	11.0	11.1

Manufacturing exports as % of total exports, 1997	85	95	87	96	93	84	42	76	85	71
Exports as % of GDP, 1999	22	11	42	42	132	135	54	124	56	57

Notes:

[a] Denotes data obtained from *Far Eastern Economic Review.*

[b] Denotes statistics from *Asiaweek.*

* Denotes figure extracted from State Statistical Bureau, China.

NA denotes not available.

Singapore exports/GDP ratio calculated from data in ADB, *Key Indicators of Developing Asian and Pacific Countries,* 2000.

Sources: World Bank, *World Development Report 2000/2001* (Washington, DC: Oxford University Press); Statistics Department, Taiwan Ministry of Economic Affairs, http://www.moea.gov.tw; "Bottomline," *Asiaweek,* May 4, 2001; and "Prices and Trends," *Far Eastern Economic Review,* April 13, 2000.

Table 2. Intra-Regional Trade in East Asia* (1999)

	Total exports (US$ million)	To industrialized countries (%)				China (%)	NIEs (%)	ASEAN-4 (%)	East Asia (%)	East Asia less Japan (%)
		Total	USA	Japan	EU					
China	194,931	57	21.5	16.6	16	–	27.3	3.2	47.1	30.5
Japan	419,207	53.7	31.1	–	18.7	5.6	21.6	8.6	35.8	35.8
NIEs										
South Korea	143,647	50.5	20.6	11	15.8	9.5	14.1	7.7	42.3	31.3
Taiwan	121,590	NA	25.4	9.8	15.7	2.1	26.7	7.3	45.9	36.1
Hong Kong	173,793	49.4	23.9	5.4	16.9	33.4	6.4	3.2	48.4	43
Singapore	114,730	45.6	19.2	7.4	15.5	3.4	15.7	23.4†	49.9	42.5
ASEAN-4										
Indonesia	57,282	55.7	16.1	20	15.3	4.8	23.4	5.7	53.9	33.9
Malaysia	84,550	53	21.9	11.6	16	2.7	28.5	6.3	49.1	37.5
Philippines	35,474	63.6	29.6	13.1	19.3	1.6	23.8	6.9	45.4	32.3
Thailand	61,797	57.5	21.5	14.5	17.8	3.6	19	7.3	44.4	29.9

Notes:
* East Asia region here comprises Japan, China, the four NIEs, and ASEAN-four.
† Figure for Indonesia is not available.
NA denotes not available.

Sources: IMF, Direction of Trade Statistics Yearbook 2000; Statistics Department, Taiwan Ministry of Economic Affairs, http://www.moea.gov.tw.

dependent on foreign trade and foreign investment for their economic growth. Both China and ASEAN have devised various incentive schemes to vie for FDI, which is generally treated not just as an additional source of capital supply but, more importantly, as a means of technology transfer and export market development. This is particularly so for China, which in recent years has become the most favored destination of all developing economies for FDI.

As can be seen from Table 3, the EA region, especially Hong Kong, Taiwan, Japan, Singapore, and South Korea, accounted for an overwhelming share of FDI inflow into China. In other words, Japan and the NIEs have been able to capture most of the benefits arising from China's open-door policy by investing in China. However, such regional predominance has been declining in recent years, as China tried to attract more FDI from North America and the EU. By 2000, the EA share of FDI in China declined to 55%, down from 88% in 1992.

Suffice it to say that China's economic growth fits in quite well with EA growth. In a broad macro sense, China's dynamic economic growth since 1978 has interacted with many high-growth EAEs positively to each other's advantage. On the one hand, China has been able to harness the region's trade and investment opportunities to facilitate its own economic growth. At the same time, China's growing economic integration with the region, at least in theory, also provides new opportunities to enhance the region's overall growth potential, including ASEAN.

Viewed from a different angle, however, the rise of China's economy can disrupt its neighboring economies, especially in the short run. This is particularly so for the ASEAN economies.

The ASEAN Economies

The ASEAN was formed in 1967 by the five Southeast Asian countries of Indonesia, Malaysia, the Philippines, Singapore, and Thailand to promote regional cooperation. Some 32 years later, ASEAN encompassed all the 10 Southeast Asian countries after

Table 3. Foreign Direct Investment in China (US$ million)

	1992		1993		1994		1996		1997		1998		1999		2000	
	Actual amount invested	%	Actual amount invested	%	Actual amount invested	%	Actual amount invested	%	Actual amount invested	%	Actual amount invested	%	Actual amount invested	%	Actual amount invested	%
Total	11,292	100	27,771	100	33,946	100	42,135	100	45,257	100	45,463	100	40,319	100	40,715	100
Asia Pacific	9900	87.7	23,333	84	28,267	83.2	32,714	77.6	30,389	67.1	26,626	58.6	23,210	57.4	22,202	54.5
Hong Kong	7706	68.2	17,445	62.8	19,823	58.4	20,852	49.5	20,632	45.6	18,508	40.7	16,363	40.6	15,500	38.1
Taiwan	1053	9.3	3139	11.3	3391	10	3482	8.3	3289	7.3	2915	6.4	2599	6.4	2296	5.6
Japan	748	6.6	1361	4.9	2086	6	3692	8.8	4326	9.6	3400	7.5	2973	7.3	2916	7.2
South Korea	120	1.1	382	1.4	726	2	1504	3.6	2142	4.7	1803	4.0	1275	3.1	1490	3.7
ASEAN	271.6	2.4	1005.9	3.6	2240.6	6.6	3184.3	7.6	3418	7.6	4197	9.2	3274	8.2	2837	7.0
Indonesia	20.2	0.18	65.8	0.2	115.7	0.3	93.6	0.2	80	0.2	69	0.2	129	0.3	147	0.4
Malaysia	24.7	0.22	91.4	0.3	509.4	1.5	460.0	1.1	382	0.8	340	0.7	238	0.6	203	0.5
Philippines	16.6	0.15	122.5	0.4	201.0	0.6	55.5	0.1	156	0.3	179	0.3	117	0.3	111	0.3
Singapore	125.9	1.1	491.8	1.8	1179.6	3.5	2247.0	5.0	2606	5.8	3404	7.5	2642	6.6	2172	5.3
Thailand	84.3	0.75	234.4	0.8	234.9	0.7	328.2	0.8	194	0.4	205	0.5	148	0.4	204	0.5
USA	519	4.6	2068	7.4	2491	7	3444	8.2	3239	7.2	3898	8.6	4216	10.5	4384	10.8
Others	873	7.7	2370	8.5	3188	9	5977	14.2	8192	18.1	10,729	23.6	9619	23.9	10,218	25.1

Sources: Statistical Yearbook of China (1992–2000); and China Monthly Statistics.

admitting Brunei in 1984, Vietnam in 1995, Laos and Myanmar in 1997, and finally Cambodia in 1999. It has also evolved into one of the world's politically influential regional groupings.

In this paper, discussion is focused on the five original founding members of ASEAN, namely, Indonesia, Malaysia, the Philippines, Singapore, and Thailand, the so-called "ASEAN-five" or the "ASEAN-four" as Singapore, is commonly grouped under the "NIEs." To begin with, newer members such as Brunei, Cambodia, and Laos are economically very small, while Myanmar is barely open for economic interaction with other countries, and Vietnam is still under transition towards the market system. On the other hand, the original ASEAN-five are politically and economically by far more important than the newer members.

Indonesia is the largest country in the region while Singapore is the most developed economy. Indeed, Singapore's per capita income in 1999 at US$ 29,600 ranked the ninth highest in the world, just below the US.[8] Other ASEAN countries such as Malaysia, Thailand, and the Philippines have clearly become middle-income economies, with their economic growth mainly driven by manufactured exports, as can be seen from Table 1.

By comparison, the other newer ASEAN economies, with the exception of the very small and oil-rich Brunei, are low-income countries, economically underdeveloped and still heavily dependent on primary-product exports for their economic growth. They are structurally much like the ASEAN-five were some 20 years ago.[9] Such diversity has always been the main feature of ASEAN as a regional grouping, which is characterized by sharp differences among member-states in not just their stages of economic development but also history, culture, language, and religion. That is why this paper is focused only on the old ASEAN-five in order to achieve a coherent discussion of their development problems.

Suffice it to say that these ASEAN-five have experienced intensive economic development for three to four decades under

---

[8] World Bank, *World Development Report 2000/2001*.

[9] See John Wong, *ASEAN Economies in Perspective: A Comparative Study of Indonesia, Malaysia, the Philippines, Singapore and Thailand* (London: Macmillan Press, 1979).

largely stable political and social conditions (except for the post-Marcos Philippines). As a result, these five economies have all been successfully industrialized. In particular, the ASEAN-four (which were originally resource-based economies, depending heavily on the export of natural resources and primary commodities for growth) have all become industrialized in the sense that their overall economic growth is now primarily fueled by the growth of their manufacturing sector, particularly manufactured exports.[10] In the early 1980s, for instance, oil and gas still constituted about 80% of Indonesia's total exports. By the end of the 1990s, as shown in Table 1, manufactured exports increased to almost half of its total exports. For Malaysia, the Philippines, and Thailand, manufactured products now accounted for about three-quarters of their total exports.

Table 4 brings out the industrialization processes of the ASEAN-five over the past three decades. In 1975, all the resource-based ASEAN-four still had a sizeable agricultural sector, which was 37% of GDP for Indonesia, 28% for Malaysia, 27% for the Philippines, and 31% for Thailand. By 1999, their relative share of the agricultural had dropped to 19% for Indonesia, 11% for Malaysia, 18% for the Philippines, and only 10% for Thailand. Correspondingly, the relative share of manufacturing sector in Indonesia had increased from 11% in 1975 to 26% in 1999, 16 to 32% in Malaysia, and 18 to 32% in Thailand, though it declined from 24 to 22% in the Philippines.

For Singapore as a city-state with virtually no agriculture to speak of, its industrialization was initially marked by the building up of export-oriented manufacturing activities at the expense of traditional commerce and entrepot trade. In recent years, the relative share of manufacturing in Singapore has actually declined owing to the expansion of modern, tradable service activities, much akin to the deindustrialization process that has taken place in developed economies.

In 1997, the ASEAN-five were struck by the "Asian financial crisis", causing their economic growth to collapse. By the end of

---

[10] Oil and gas used to constitute 80% of Indonesia's exports; Malaysia's exports used to be dominated by rubber, tin, and palm oil; Thailand used to depend heavily on rice and sugar; and the Philippines used to depend heavily on coconut products. Ibidem.

Table 4. ASEAN: Sectoral Distribution of GDP (%)

	Agriculture				Industry								Services			
					All				Manufacturing							
	1975	1980	1990	1999	1975	1980	1990	1999	1975	1980	1990	1999	1975	1980	1990	1999
Indonesia	36.8	24.8	19.4	19.4	27.3	43.4	39.1	42.9	11.1	11.6	20.7	25.8	35.9	31.8	41.5	37.7
Malaysia	27.7	23.8	15.2	10.8	26.8	30.0	42.2	46.2	16.4	18.6	24.2	31.6	45.5	46.2	42.6	43.1
Philippines	26.6	25.1	21.9	17.6	33.0	38.8	34.5	30.4	24.1	25.7	24.6	21.5	40.4	36.1	43.6	52.0
Singapore	1.6	1.3	0.4	0.2	30.4	38.1	34.4	35.6	21.4	29.1	27.1	25.9	40.4	60.6	65.3	64.1
Thailand	30.5	23.2	12.5	10.4	25.0	28.7	37.2	40.1	18.1	21.5	27.2	32.4	44.5	48.1	50.3	49.6
China	–	30.1	27.0	17.3	–	48.5	41.6	49.7	–	44.2	37.0	43.1	–	21.4	31.3	32.9
South Korea	24.5	14.9	8.5	5.0	33.8	41.3	43.1	43.5	26.0	29.7	28.8	31.8	41.7	43.7	48.4	51.5

Note: For 1975, GDP data are at constant market prices; 1980–1999, at current market prices.

Sources: Asian Development Bank, *Key Indicators of Developing Member Countries of ADB* (1984); *Key Indicators of Developing Asian and Pacific Countries* (2000).

Figure 2. Crisis and Prolonged Economic Recovery for ASEAN

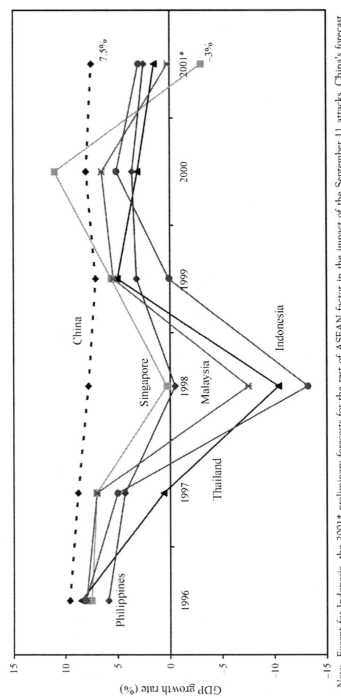

Note: Except for Indonesia, the 2001* preliminary forecasts for the rest of ASEAN factor in the impact of the September 11 attacks. China's forecast growth rate is estimated by IMF; Singapore's forecast is from official sources; estimates for Thailand (1.5%), Indonesia (around 3%), Malaysia (0.2%) and Philippines (2.5%) forecast by Ideaglobal.

1999, two years after the outbreak of the crisis, they bounced back to positive growth, in the form of a "V-shaped recovery," as a result of the recovery of their stockmarkets, rising exports, and greater stability of their exchange rates.[11] However, their recovery process was soon disrupted in 2001 by the onset of the global economic downturn, giving rise to a potential "W-shaped recovery" (Figure 2).

Nonetheless, the economic crisis had left behind many political and economic scars. Politically and socially, it altered a lot the institutional condition of ASEAN economic growth. It brought down the old regime in Indonesia and started the democratization experiment. There were also pressures on other ASEAN countries to open up their political systems. However, an economically backward young democracy may find it difficult to galvanize its contending political and social forces for the single-minded pursuit of economic growth. Economically, the crisis has laid bare the structural shortcomings of the ASEAN economies and pointed to their urgent need for reform and restructuring.

Even the external environment of ASEAN's economic growth has also changed. In recent years, economic growth momentum in the region has gravitated towards Northeast Asia as a result of the resurgence of the Chinese economy. In particular, the rise of China has presented ASEAN with formidable external challenges.

CHINA'S COMPETITIVE PRESSURES ON ASEAN

China's rapidly growing economy will inevitably carry important geo-economic implications. It will impact significantly on its neighboring economies in the Asia–Pacific region, which absorb about 50% of China's exports and supplies three-quarters of China's FDI. Broadly speaking, the spillovers of China's dynamic economic growth will produce both positive and negative effects for the region, as mentioned earlier. Japan and other EA NIEs may lose their comparative advantage for many of their manufactured exports. But

[11] See "Asia's Astonishing Bounce-back," *The Economist*, London, August 21–27, 1999.

they can also capture the benefits of the growing Chinese economy by exporting high-tech products and by investing in China. The EAEs will become more closely integrated with China.

However, China and ASEAN (minus Singapore) at their present stages of economic development tend to be more competitive than complementary towards each other. In many ways, China's dynamic economic growth has created strong competitive pressures for the ASEAN economies, which are vying for FDI with China as well as competing head-on with China's manufactured exports in the developed country markets.[12]

Initially, China's success in economic reform and development had produced very little impact on the ASEAN countries to its south. Sino–ASEAN trade was very small—in fact, only a small fraction of each other's total trade. Even by the early 1990s, when massive FDI began to flow into China, there was no evidence that China had "sucked" in a lot of capital from the ethnic Chinese in Southeast Asia.[13]

The picture has radically changed since the second half of the 1990s. While many ASEAN countries were plagued by persistent economic crises and domestic political instability, as we have mentioned earlier, China has been intent on its single-minded pursuit of economic modernization. This will soon enable China to close the development gaps and then take the lead over ASEAN. Right now, China's total foreign reserves, at US$ 190 billion, are second only to Japan's. China today has more mobile phones than the US. Its Internet population is getting close to that of Japan's. Thus, at least in total economic terms, its fast economic development seems to be leaving the ASEAN region behind.

Specifically, the change in China's export structure has produced the most serious implications for the ASEAN economies. When Deng

---

[12] For further discussion of this topic, see Prakash Loungani, "Comrades or Competitors? Trade Links Between China and Other East Asian Economies," *Finance and Development* (June 2000).

[13] See John Wong, *Southeast Asian Ethnic Chinese Investing in China*, EAI Working Paper No. 15, October 23, 1998.

opened up China in 1978, half of China's exports were made up of primary commodities like mineral and agricultural products. Today, manufactured products constitute about 90% of China's exports. Before 1995, traditional labor-intensive manufactures like textiles, clothing and footwear (TCF) used to dominate China's export structure. All developing economies have gone through the stage of exporting such traditional labor-intensive manufactured exports. Hence China's TCF exports were not much of a real "threat" to ASEAN's own exports, especially because many of ASEAN's TCF export items to developed economies are protected by the MFA quota system (Figure 3).

In recent years, the composition of China's manufactured exports has experienced even more significant changes, marked by the rise of nontraditional items like machinery, electronics, and other high-tech products.[14] China's rapid expansion of such nontraditional exports will clearly pose serious economic challenges for the ASEAN-four, which are directly competing with China in the third-country markets, particularly the US.

In future, Sino–ASEAN export competition in such nontraditional items as electrical and electronics products will grow even more intense, particularly after China's accession to the WTO. As illustrated in Figure 4, although the electrical and electronic exports of the ASEAN-four and the NIEs combined are higher than China's, China is rapidly taking on these Asian competitors, as evident in its increasing share of the US market for these products over the years.

In 1990, for instance, China's share of the US electronics market was only around 2%, but this share has now increased to 9.7% by 2000, comparable to 8.4% for Taiwan and 9.8% for South Korea, and higher than the ASEAN-four countries—9.2% for Malaysia, 1.02% for Indonesia, 3.0% for the Philippines, and 4.5% for Thailand. China is set to overtake both the NIEs (which are relocating their production bases to China) and the ASEAN-four whose export

---

[14] John Wong and Sarah Chan, "China's Rapidly Changing Export Structure," EAI Background Brief, No. 85, April 9, 2001.

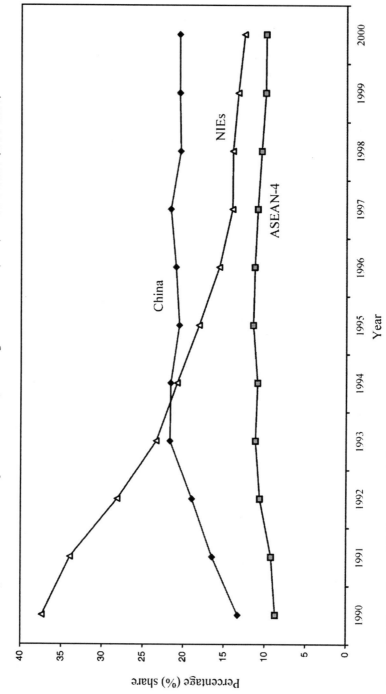

Figure 3. East Asian Exports of Textiles, Clothing and Footwear (TCF) to US Market (1990–2000)

Source: US Census Bureau, US Department of Commerce.

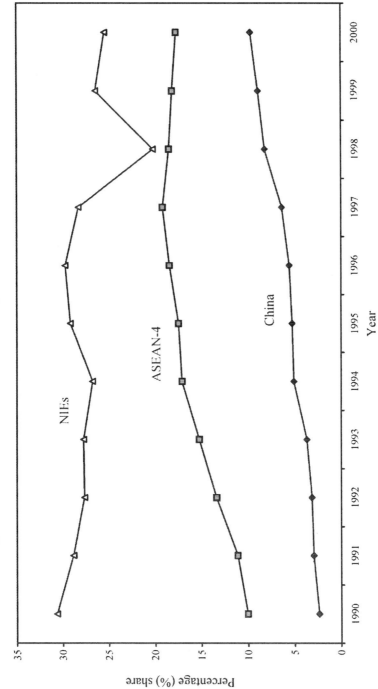

Figure 4. East Asian Electrical and Electronics Exports to US Market (1990–2000)

Source: US Census Bureau, US Department of Commerce.

competitiveness will be fast eroded by China's growing strength in these nontraditional items.[15]

What made China different from ASEAN is the fact that China has by far a much larger pool of skilled as well as nonskilled labor. China also has a large domestic market for all sorts of products, from high-tech to low-tech, to take advantage of the economies of scale effect. With lower average and marginal costs generated as a result of high-volume production, China is thus able to enjoy its natural cost advantage compared to ASEAN and other smaller developing countries. Furthermore, for both China and ASEAN, a high proportion of these nontraditional items are produced under OEM (original equipment manufacturing) arrangements whereby large multinationals are merely making use of China and ASEAN to process often the same products for exports. When a sharp cost gap arises, these multinationals may simply cut back their production facilities in ASEAN and move them to China.

It may be remembered that for Japan and other smaller NIEs, shifting comparative advantage had forced them to relocate their labor-intensive manufactures to their neighboring economies with lower costs. But China is a rare continental-sized economy with such great diversity that it can contain the evolution of comparative advantage within its own borders. As is already happening, the more developed coastal regions of China are transferring their losing comparative advantage in labor-intensive products to central and western China, which is currently the focus of China's future development efforts. This means that China can continue for years to flood the world market with low-cost manufactured items even after many parts of China have achieved middle-income status.

---

[15] China's top electric appliance maker, Haier, for instance, has penetrated the US market to compete against entrenched foreign firms on the basis of price and quality. It has established a plant in the US to manufacture consumer electronics like refrigerators and air conditioners. *Far East Economic Review*, March 29, 2001.

COPING WITH THE RISE OF CHINA

Without doubt, China's economy will continue to grow on its own momentum. No external forces barring a large-scale war can stifle China's dynamic growth. In fact, China for its own political and social reasons needs to continue with high economic growth, not just to satisfy the rising material expectations of the Chinese people, but also to maintain social stability and facilitate further economic reform. In particular, the fourth generation leaders need good economic performance to legitimize their rule.

It may be stressed that China today is not an economic threat to any country yet. However, every Asian country has to brace itself for the economic rise of China. To cope with the rising China, Asian governments have to develop a "positive attitude." Just crying wolf does not help. China is not the root cause of their present economic difficulty, and their governments should not use this as an excuse for not taking hard decisions to carry out their reform and restructuring.

For Japan, the rise of China seems to coincide with the decline of Japan. Many Japanese will naturally find it difficult to accept this, particularly because Japan is still technologically and economically much ahead of China. By comparison, South Korea and Taiwan seem more realistic in the sense that they have been quick to accept the rise of China.

Thus, Korean and Taiwanese businesses are actively repositioning themselves to find new niches or new opportunities in the expanding China market and to work out new areas of complementation with China. In this way, the rise of China is turned into a positive force for their mutual benefit.

For ASEAN, the rise of China poses a real challenge. Calling on the ASEAN countries to stand united and advance economic cooperation further in order to compete with China is merely political rhetoric. Some ASEAN countries have to put their house in order first by restoring social stability. Average labor costs per hour in Malaysia and Thailand are about US$ 2.0 compared to only

US$ 0.50 in China. These ASEAN countries need to address the real issue of economic restructuring and cost cutting.

The ASEAN countries, already under the shadow of China, have to accept the rise of China as a new political and economic reality. Smaller ASEAN economies, in particular, need to develop such open and pragmatic attitude to survive. In future, they may also have to accept the rise of India.

However, there is also a complementary angle to the Sino–ASEAN economic relationship. As the Chinese economy continues to grow, it will also increase the demand for exports from ASEAN, particularly for its primary commodities and natural resources. In fact, some ASEAN countries, particularly Malaysia and Thailand, tend to take the positive view that the rise of China in the long run could operate as a potentially new engine of economic growth for the region.

Chapter 15

Japan's "Challenges" to China in the Epoch of Terrorism

LAM PENG ER

In economics and geo-politics, Japan is the most important Asian country for China. This will not change when China's fourth generation leaders take over the helm. Whoever emerges at the top will have to deal with a Japan that is increasingly tied to the US global war strategy and also maintain mutually beneficial economic ties.

This chapter examines the international trends and Japanese domestic politics that may well pose a potential geo-political challenge to Beijing. In the aftermath of the September 11 terrorist attacks on the US, Tokyo has embarked on a larger military and diplomatic role ostensibly to support its alliance partner beyond "areas surrounding Japan." A higher military profile by Tokyo is likely to trigger concerns in Beijing that Japan is emerging as a "normal" nation that may use force in settling international conflict even before the Japanese have adequately addressed their "burden of history".

However, if the US and China (given its problems with separatists from Xinjiang) were to forge a United Front along with other nations (including Japan) against global terrorism, then American perceptions that China may emerge as the key strategic rival to the US are likely to weaken in the near future. In the Epoch of Terrorism, Washington will be increasingly preoccupied with real and immediate threats rather than speculating about potential threats emanating from China in two or three decades ahead. In this regard, Beijing should feel less threatened by the US–Japan Alliance even if Japan were to play a larger role within that framework. In addition, increasingly strong economic ties between China and Japan will provide incentives for both countries to maintain their overall relations on an even keel despite occasional friction over issues of history and trade. Simply put, Japan is most likely to present more of an opportunity than a serious challenge to the fourth generation leaders of the People's Republic of China.

The outline of the chapter is as follows: First, I argue that the events of September 11 and its aftermath will have a profound impact on the post-Cold War era, the central structure of international relations, and concomitantly, Sino–US relations. This, in turn, will frame Sino–Japan relations, especially when the latter is a close ally of the US. Indeed, a relaxation of tension between Washington and Beijing is likely to improve ties between Beijing and Tokyo. However, the US focus on wiping out global terrorist networks in the next few years does not mean that Washington will no longer regard China as the potential long-term challenger to US interests in East Asia. In this regard, any deterioration in relations between the US and China may well spill over to Sino–Japanese relations.

Second, I will identify the conceivable challenges posed by Japan to the new Chinese leadership. They include: a tighter alliance between Washington and Tokyo; Japan becoming a "normal" state that seeks a larger political and military role in the region and beyond; the potential rise of neorightist nationalism within and outside the ruling Liberal Democratic Party (LDP); addressing the history issue in a manner that will not embitter Sino–Japanese relations; allaying the fear among some Japanese that China is superseding their nation in East Asia; and managing the increasing trade friction between the two countries.

Third, I will identify areas of common interests between China and Japan that may mitigate differences over geo-strategic outlooks, historical understanding, and trade. They include: expanding economic ties, cooperating in environmental protection, and building nascent multilateral institutions such as ASEAN plus 3. The paper will conclude by arguing that among the many "challenges" posed by Japan to the fourth generation Chinese leadership, the greatest challenge is to ensure friendly relations with Tokyo. Indeed, a more stable and predictable regional environment and greater economic interdependence will benefit both countries. If this trend emerges, it will surely enhance China's economic development and social stability that is necessary to underpin the political legitimacy of the new Chinese leadership.

The Epoch of Terrorism

For a decade after the end of the Cold War, analysts have simply labeled it as the post-Cold War era. During the past decade of transition, while the world was marked by US unipolarity, intensifying globalization, and the persistence of primordial ethnic conflict in certain regions, there was lack of a single grand principle that simplifies, encapsulates, and defines the central feature of an era. Indeed, the central feature of the new epoch was not apparent. (During the Cold War, the central feature that polarized international relations was the ideological and geo-political competition between the US and the Soviet Union and their respective allies; whereas both superpowers avoided a direct war that would lead to mutual nuclear annihilation, competition and proxy wars took place in different regions of the world.) While the term "post-Cold War" states that the present epoch has moved away from the features of the preceding Cold War, it does not suggest what are the defining characteristics of the contemporary era.

A new global epoch began on September 11, 2001, when terrorists hijacked four passenger planes and, in *kamikaze* style, three planes struck against the symbols of American financial and military power, the World Trade Center (WTC) and the Pentagon. Civilian fatalities were in excess of 3000 when the WTC's twin towers collapsed. In the aftermath of September 11, the grand idea that shapes international relations is likely to be the US-led multilateral war against global terrorism. (During the Cold War, containing communism was Washington's guiding principle in the world.) For the US superpower, the war against terrorism will be the new compass in international relations: countries that oppose global terrorism will be deemed friends and those that do not, enemies.

New features of this war include: no fixed geographical scope, uncertain time frame, unconventional means to pursue political ends (terrorist-piloted *kamikaze* planes and possibly biological and chemical weapons) and shadowy enemies that are not necessarily nation-states but terrorist networks. The US and its allies also regard states that harbor such networks and training camps as foes, even if such states do not directly participate in terrorism. However, phantom-like terrorist networks that have tentacles beyond 30 countries and engage in a vicious cycle of violence cannot be easily and quickly eradicated even by a high-tech superpower; a successful *blitzkreig* attack by US-led multilateral forces like the 1991 Gulf War is highly unlikely. President George W. Bush has warned that the war against terrorism may take as long as two years. The mopping-up operation may last much longer. Although the future is unpredictable, the astonishing events unleashed by September 11 on an unsuspecting world are likely to transform international relations to the extent where the term "Epoch of Terrorism" may become apt.

Washington's new war against terrorism is perhaps fortuitous for China, because the Bush Administration's preoccupation with the immediate threat of terrorism means that it is likely to downplay its concern that China is a "strategic competitor" to the US.[1] Relations between Washington and Beijing have been prickly since the 1989 Tiananmen incident and the end of the Cold War, and the issues include tension in the Taiwan Strait, human rights in China, the bolstering of the US–Japan Alliance, the US bombing of the Chinese

---

[1] A Japanese commentator wryly noted: "A former Canadian ambassador to China I met in Shanghai said: 'Because the United States clearly defined its main enemy as terrorism, China escaped being the main US enemy. This is China's greatest gain.'" See Yoichi Funabashi, "Is China's Confidence Natural or Contrived?" *Asahi Shimbun*, *Asahi.com*, October 30, 2001. See also Ralph Cossa, "Chance for New U.S.–China Strategic Tie," *Japan Times Online*, October 20, 2001.

embassy in Belgrade, and the midair collision between a Chinese fighter plane and American espionage plane off the coast of mainland China.

Beijing has unequivocally condemned the terrorist attacks of September 11 and has not opposed US military retaliation against suspected terrorist training camps and facilities in neighboring Afghanistan.[2] Moreover, China has a problem with Muslim separatists in Xinjiang adopting violence to pursue their political goals.[3] In this regard, both China and the US can forge an alignment against terrorism.[4] If Sino–US tension were to be defused because of the new American preoccupation with eradicating terrorism, China is likely to enjoy a breathing space and concentrate on economic development, modernization, and reforms for at least the next decade. And if the country continues to chalk up around 7–8 GDP

---

[2] See, for example, "China and US Combat Terrorism," *Beijing Review*, September 27, 2001. The *Beijing Review* notes: "China will strengthen its cooperation with the United States and the international community to crack down on terrorist activities, President Jiang Zemin said in a September 12 phone call with US President George W. Bush. ... Jiang said China has been closely following rescue attempts and will provide as much aid as it can."

[3] A Japanese newspaper notes: "The United States is attacking the Taliban, which is also China's foe because it has been supporting separatists in the Xinjiang–Uygur Autonomous Region. ... China hopes that it would not be criticized for oppression of separatists as part of an international fight against terrorism and is counting on the United States to ease its criticism toward China concerning human rights violations." See Yoichi Funabashi, "Is China's Confidence Natural or Contrived?" *Asahi Shimbun, Asahi.com*, October 30, 2001.

[4] The *International Herald Tribune* notes that on the eve of President George W. Bush's first meeting with his Chinese counterpart in October, Secretary of State Colin Powell said that "Beijing's co-operation in tackling terrorism had further bolstered the relationship between the two countries after a rocky period during the first months of the Bush Administration. Secretary Powell said that Chinese support, which has included an offer to share intelligence, backing at the United Nations and cautious statements of support for US operations in response to the September 11 terrorist attacks, has built on progress in economic affairs." The Chinese foreign minister Tang Jiaxuan was quoted as saying: "Antiterrorism is the struggle of evil versus good, the civilized and the barbaric." See "Powell Credits China's Anti-Terrorism Effort for Improved U.S. Ties," *International Herald Tribune*, October 19, 2001.

growth every year for the next 10 years or so, it will become a much more developed and potentially powerful country that is likely to generate a great deal of ambivalence among many Japanese.

"CHALLENGES" FROM JAPAN

Addressing Japan's Relative Decline and Anxiety Syndrome

More than two millennia ago, Thucydides identified the fundamental cause of the Peloponnesian War: "What made war inevitable was the growth of Athenian power and the fear which this caused in Sparta."[5] In recent years, Robert Gilpin[6] and Paul Kennedy[7] have explored the same theme: that the uneven rate of growth in power capabilities among nations often leads to envy, fear, competition, and conflict. Both Gilpin and Kennedy affirm that international relations are often destabilized when a rising great power challenges a declining great power.

That Japan is the second largest economic power in the world is a source of pride for many Japanese. However, the country has suffered from economic stagnation since the bursting of its bubble economy in the early 1990s. Unemployment stands at a record 5.5% in December 2001 and is still climbing. Institutions and practices (a developmental state, a one-party-dominant system, an iron triangle among the ruling party, big business, and the bureaucracy, public works subsidies as a form of social and regional welfare, the *keiretsu* system, lifetime and seniority systems, and house unions) that worked

[5] Thucidides, *The Peloponnesian War* (Harmondsworth, Middlesex: Penguin, 1983), p. 23.

[6] Robert Gilpin, *War and Change in International Politics* (New York: Cambridge University Press, 1981).

[7] Paul Kennedy, *The Rise and Fall of the Great Powers* (New York: Random House, 1987).

well for post-War Japan have ironically become the obstacles to necessary reforms in Japan today.

Japan today is adrift and struggling to implement much-needed reforms. Owing to the strength of entrenched interest groups and weak political leadership, structural reforms may take many more years to be implemented.[8] Increasingly, the public mood in Japan is that the nation is suffering from malaise; despite the early promises of the Koizumi administration, there is still no light at the end of the tunnel. Indeed, Japan is further stagnating against the backdrop of a rising China.

While a military conflict between China and Japan is highly unlikely in the foreseeable future, the phenomenon of "China rising, Japan declining" may generate tension in bilateral relations.[9] Increasingly, many politicians, academics and the media in Japan have warned about a potential "China threat."[10] Moreover, they have been irritated by China's nuclear tests, and they perceive Chinese assertiveness in the South China Sea and over the disputed Senkaku (Tiaoyutai) islands, missile tests in the Taiwan Strait, Beijing's criticisms of a reinforced US–Japan Alliance, and the cynical use of the apology issue as political leverage on Japan. They also claim that Chinese vessels have sailed into Japanese territorial waters at a

---

[8] See Lam Peng Er, "Can Koizumi Carry Out Japan's Needed Reforms?" *EAI Background Brief*, No. 102, September 2001.

[9] Recent articles by both Japanese and Chinese scholars have alluded to the dynamics of "China rising, Japan falling." See, for example, Kokubun Ryosei, "Japan–China Relations After the Cold War: Switching from the '1972 Framework'," *Japan Echo*, Vol. 28, No. 2 (April 2001), Zhu Jianrong, "An Extended View of China's Prospects" in the same issue of *Japan Echo*, and Yang Bojiang, "Current Japanese Social trend of Thought and Neonationalism," *Contemporary International Relations*, Vol. 11, No. 5 (May 2001). See also the comment by Kato Chihiro: "As Japan's economy languishes in recession, people are increasingly envious of China's economic growth" in Kato Chihiro, "The New matrix of Japan–China Ties," *Japan Quarterly*, Vol. 48, No. 4 (October–December 2001), p. 71. To date, there is no detailed or systematic analysis of this phenomenon. It certainly deserves more study.

[10] For a very useful account which traces the rise of such sentiments, see Gilbert Rozman, "Japan's Images of China in the 1990s: Are They Ready for China's 'Smile Diplomacy' or Bush's 'Strong Diplomacy'?" *Japanese Journal of Political Science*, Vol. 2, No. 1 (2001).

rate of about 20 incursions a year; these ships are believed to be mapping the seafloor for Beijing's growing fleet of submarines.[11] However, many Japanese increasingly view the "China threat" as primarily an economic one as the Mainland becomes even more economically competitive against Japanese industries; factories are likely to be hollowed out in Japan (leading to increasing unemployment) and relocated to China to enjoy cheaper labor and land, and greater profits.

A consensus is also emerging in Japan that it should cut back on its ODA (Official Development Assistance) to China for at least three reasons: the mainland is already enjoying rapid economic growth, and modernizing its military and, therefore, has less need for Japanese foreign aid; Tokyo is suffering from a decade of economic doldrums and is thus less able to help Beijing;[12] it is illogical to continue ODA to the mainland if the Chinese appear ungrateful to or ignorant of Japanese assistance to their economic development.

An editorial in *Nikkei Weekly* noted:

"The domestic dissatisfaction with ODA for China centers around the fact that few Chinese are even aware of Japan's contributions. In the past 20 years, Japan has provided some 3 trillion yen ($ 24 billion) in ODA to China, more than half of all aid received by the country. In spite of this, bilateral relations are even worse now than they were before the aid started. If Japanese taxpayers' money is not appreciated by the Chinese and does not help improve ties with the country, the critics argue, there is no good reason that a country itself trapped in a fiscal quagmire should continue financial assistance for a neighbor which has become an economic threat as the 'factory of the world' and which has also grown into a major military power after years of aggressive military spending."[13]

[11] On China's alleged incursion into waters claimed by Japan, see *International Herald Tribune*, October 19, 2001.

[12] "Foreign Ministry Proposes Cutting Aid to China," *Japan Times On-line*, September 28, 2001.

[13] Editorial, "Tokyo Talks Tougher on ODA for Beijing," *The Nikkei Weekly*, October 29, 2001.

However, if Japan were to deeply and quickly slash its ODA to China, the act is likely to be viewed as unfriendly by Beijing. To the Chinese, Tokyo's ODA to Beijing is based not purely on altruism but also in lieu of war reparations which the mainland did not demand as a precondition to forge diplomatic relations. Moreover, the bulk of Japanese ODA is extended as a loan that has to be repaid with interest; ODA is also often tied to Japanese economic interests penetrating the China market.

Displacing the Leading Goose: Japanese Fear of China's Rise

The rapid rise of China is also likely to challenge Japan's preferred model of economic development for East Asia: the flying geese paradigm. According to many Japanese analysts, the economic regional order is (should be) led by a leading goose (read Japan) at the vanguard of technological development, followed by the next wave of newly industrializing economies (South Korea, Taiwan, Singapore, Hong Kong); another wave behind comprises Thailand, Malaysia, Indonesia, and the Philippines. The last wave probably includes even less developed economies such as Vietnam, Cambodia, and Burma. The flying geese model assumes that all birds will benefit from the economic logic of comparative advantage; as each echelon develops, it will shed less sophisticated economic production to the succeeding wave of geese.

The popularity of the flying geese paradigm among the Japanese elites is in a sense self-serving and flattering. It rationalizes and justifies the preeminence of Japan, even though much of its domestic market is closed to competition from other Asian countries. China's rapid rise as an economic power raises serious doubts whether the Japanese notion of a flying geese model is still valid.

In April 2001, Tokyo sought to restrict agricultural imports (*shitake* mushrooms, leeks, and straw for *tatami* mats) from China to protect its less competitive agrarian sectors. China retaliated by raising tariffs on Japanese auto exports and hand phones to its market. Though both countries resolved this particular dispute by December the same year, it is merely a precursor to more trade disputes ahead. In the near future, Chinese-manufactured products will increasingly penetrate the Japanese market. While both countries have become members of the rule-bound World Trade Organization (WTO), bilateral trade friction is likely to intensify when China exports cheaper and even high-end manufactured products to Japan. Those domestic sectors that suffer from Chinese competition are likely to seek political protection to limit such exports.

The fear that China will eventually displace Japan as the leading goose is likely to underpin greater anxiety and antagonism among many Japanese elites towards the mainland. Besides advocating a slash in ODA to China, they will react with greater hostility to any Chinese criticism about the lack of a sincere apology from Tokyo towards Japan's invasion of the mainland more than half a century ago; some will become even more sympathetic to an autonomous Taiwan; others will support a greater political and military role within the framework of an expanded US–Japan Alliance, and the revision of Article 9 of Japan's pacifist Constitution.[14]

Rise of Japanese Neonationalism?

The phenomenon of "China rising, Japan declining" may also stimulate the rise of neonationalism in Japan[15] especially if many voters become gravely disappointed with the failure of Prime Minister Koizumi to implement reforms and revitalize the nation. Politicians within and outside the ruling LDP who subscribe to neonationalism will promote Japanese tradition to underpin national revival and pride. Some will support the view that Japan was the liberator of Asia from Western colonialism during World War II; and there is really no further need to apologize and kow-tow to China.

---

[14] Article 9 of the Constitution obliges Japan not to adopt force to resolve international dispute.

[15] Unlike many fanatical Japanese nationalists during World War II, most neonationalists, while revering the Emperor institution, do not consider him to be a god or think that the Emperor should again play a larger political role; they also do not support the military displacing civilian rule.

The most prominent neonationalist today is probably Ishihara Shintaro, the present governor of Tokyo. The governor is well known for his fierce criticism of Beijing, a sympathizer for an independent Taiwan, and the view that Japan was not an aggressor nation during World War II. Apparently, Ishihara is waiting in the wings and is likely to seek a larger political role, especially if Koizumi and other mainstream politicians are utterly discredited by their failure to reform Japan and end its economic stagnation.

The rise of neonationalist sentiments in Japan is conceivably a potential challenge to Beijing's new leadership. If future Prime Ministers of Japan were to visit Yasukuni Shrine (where the spirits of Class A war criminals are reposed along with other Japanese war dead), and prominent politicians including cabinet ministers were to deny Japanese atrocities in the mainland, Chinese nationalism is likely to be stirred. Nationalism in China is potentially a double-edged sword to the new leadership. Robust responses by the new leadership to Japanese neonationalism will probably win considerable mass support in China over this issue and bolster regime legitimacy; an overreaction to it will further worsen Sino–Japanese relations, and perhaps inflame nationalism in China to the extent where it may not be easily managed by the new leadership. It remains to be seen whether the central leadership can easily manage well-educated Chinese youths and students (who have increasing access to the Internet) if they were to rally against Japanese neonationalism.

Managing Xenophobic Nationalism in China and Japan

Overly aggressive criticism of Japan over its reluctance to offer a sincere apology for its invasion of and atrocities in China will backfire and only add fuel to the rise of neonationalism in Japan.[16] In November

---

[16] Chinese critics of Japan's reluctance to apologize should also realize that China's political leadership often conveniently downplayed the apology issue when it was in its perceived interests to establish closer ties with Japan. A good case study is Beijing's numerous requests to invite the Japanese Emperor to visit China in 1992 and end its international isolation in the aftermath of the Tiananmen incident. The Chinese government pragmatically did not make any demands for a written apology from Japan

1998, during the first official visit ever by a Chinese head of state to Japan, President Jiang Zemin incessantly criticized Tokyo at every stop for not giving Beijing a sincere and adequate apology especially in a written form. To many Japanese, the behavior of Jiang was simply too crude and boorish for a guest, and his visit was a public relations disaster. The following year, Prime Minister Zhu Rongji visited Tokyo to repair bilateral relations, adopted a "smiling diplomacy," and avoided any vociferous criticism of Japan over the apology issue.

Increasingly, many Japanese (especially those born after the War) are suffering from "apology fatigue;" they do not feel a sense of guilt because they were not responsible for the War, and they also think that Japan has apologized enough.[17] If the fourth generation leaders were to continue Zhu's line of smiling diplomacy, Sino–Japanese relations are likely to improve.[18] Indeed, a challenge to the new leadership to keep Sino–Japanese relations on a even keel is the wisdom to avoid inflaming, and to containing, nationalism in both countries over the question of history.

A greater understanding of domestic Japanese politics should make the Chinese leadership less jumpy and shrill in its criticism of

---

then. See Young C. Kim, "Japanese Policy Towards China: Politics of the Imperial Visit to China in 1992," *Pacific Affairs*, Vol. 74, No. 2 (Summer 2001).

[17] For a mainstream Japanese perspective on the apology issue, see Okabe Tatsumi, "Japan–China Relations, Past and Future: Moving Beyond the Misunderstanding," *Gaiko Forum*, Vol. 1, No. 2 (Summer 2001). Okabe, a leading authority and former cochairman of the Japan–China 21st Century Committee, writes: "I cannot help feeling a sense of outrage whenever I hear the accusation that Japanese have never properly apologized to China." Okabe, *Japan–China Relations*, p. 10.

[18] It will certainly help if Japanese politicians especially cabinet ministers were to observe a gag rule and not say anything importune concerning Japan's invasion of Asia including China. Japanese scholars, opinion shapers, and mainstream politicians who argue that Tokyo has sufficiently apologized, and that Japan is a democratic country which permits different opinions no matter how abhorrent, should realize that "revisionist" comments on history by cabinet ministers will naturally create distrust in Asia especially among China and the two Koreas towards Japan. If they are critical of China for overreacting to the apology issue, they should also exercise their democratic rights to roundly criticize cabinet ministers who hold a historical view that is different from the official position of the Japanese government.

its neighbor. The annual ritual by many conservative politicians of visiting Yasukuni Shrine is, in part, motivated by their desire to win important electoral support from right-wing organizations, especially the War Bereaved Family Association, Shinto Shrine Association, and War Pensioners Association. It has everything to do with winning elections and nothing to do with reviving militarism to again conquer China and the rest of Asia. (The harping on Japanese militarism is absurd given the fact that Japan is a democratic country and China has nuclear-tipped missiles.)

Chinese opinion shapers should be more aware that the contemporary Japanese political system is fundamentally different from the xenophobic, Emperor-centric, military-dominated government that collapsed in 1945. Even if neonationalism were to gather strength in Japan, it is but one political tendency; Japan's liberal democratic system is likely to generate countervailing forces from various political parties, the mass media, and citizen groups. Japan, being a stable and affluent society, its politics is unlikely to veer sharply away from the moderate center.

Residing in a post-Maoist authoritarian system, most Chinese elites appear ignorant of the broad spectrum of views and different political tendencies in democratic Japan. This ignorance was revealed over the recent fracas on the Japanese government's approval of a textbook that adopts a neonationalist viewpoint of history. In reality, this infamous textbook is just one among many choices available in the market place; the number of high schools that actually adopted it amounted to less than 1%. Moreover, many civil society organizations (especially those led by intellectuals, parents, and teachers), and most local school boards were adamantly against that neonationalist textbook. In this regard, the Chinese exaggerated the specter of right-wing nationalism and militarism in Japan.

A Milestone: Showing the Flag Beyond Japan

A challenge to the new leadership is Tokyo's desire to play a larger political and military role. Japan's quest to adopt a higher regional profile is prompted by US pressure on its ally to engage in burden sharing and also by Tokyo's desire to avoid the humiliating debacle of the 1991 Gulf War, when it was severely criticized for not participating in the US-led multilateral forces despite contributing $ 13 billion.

Apparently, US Deputy Secretary of State Richard Armitage told Japanese envoy Yanai Shunji on September 15:

> "At a time when their country faces unprecedented difficulties, the American people are closely watching whether their allies and other friendly countries will join hands with the United States. Speaking in my capacity as a friend of Japan, I would like to suggest that Japan should avoid making an issue over its cooperation with the United States as it did during the Gulf War. So as not to repeat the Gulf War blunder, Japan should at the earliest opportunity announce specific measures to cooperate with the United States—or at least its intention to come up with such measures—in a way in which the Japanese flag and the faces of Japanese people will be visible."[19]

Even before the Epoch of Terrorism, Tokyo had the desire to play a larger political, regional, and global role commensurate with its economic superpower status. After the end of the 1991 Gulf War, Japan sent minesweepers to the Gulf region. Subsequently, it dispatched troops abroad for the first time since the end of World War II for the United Nations Peacekeeping Operations in Cambodia, Rwanda, the Golan Heights, and East Timor. During the 1996 Cambodian coup and the 1998 fall of the Suharto regime, Tokyo deployed military transport planes to Bangkok and Singapore, respectively, for the ostensible reason of evacuating Japanese nationals.

The 1996 Clinton–Hashimoto Declaration and the 1997 New Defense Guidelines between Tokyo and Washington oblige Japan to provide logistic support to its US ally in case of "emergencies in

---

[19] Gasku Shibata, "Japan Perspective: Japanese Media Stuck Up the Flagpole," *Daily Yomiuri On-line*, October 30, 2001.

areas surrounding Japan." In 1999, the Japanese Diet passed legislation that permits the country to fulfill its commitments to the US. The geographical scope of the Guidelines is ambiguous, because "areas surrounding Japan" can be interpreted to cover not only the Korean peninsula but also the Taiwan Strait. One plausible interpretation is that the Guidelines act as an insurance policy for the allies against a potential "China threat." In this regard, Tokyo's potential involvement as a supporter of the US in the Taiwan Strait can be viewed as a challenge to the Chinese leadership and its notion of territorial integrity.

In addition, Japan has agreed to preliminary research and development cooperation with its ally in Theater Missile Defense (TMD). If technological advancement in TMD research were to undermine China's small nuclear deterrent capability, Beijing will also view Japanese collaboration with the US as a challenge to its defense posture and credibility. Moreover, Tokyo has also floated trial balloons about multilateral efforts to engage in antipiracy measures in Southeast Asia especially the Straits of Malacca. So far Beijing has not indicated any support for the Japanese proposal to protect the safety of navigation in Southeast Asian waters.

In October 2001, the Diet approved three antiterrorism bills, including one empowering Tokyo's Self-Defense Forces (SDFs) to provide the US antiterror campaign with noncombat logistic support. (The second bill permits the SDF to guard US bases in Japan, while the third allows MSA [Maritime Safety Agency Law] patrol boats to open fire on unidentified foreign intruders in Japanese waters that seek to escape or resist when ordered to halt.) Analysts noted that "under the new law, the government will send the SDF overseas for the first time during an armed conflict, paving the way for a full-scale SDF deployment abroad at a time of military crisis."[20]

The legislation allows the SDF to provide noncombat and humanitarian support to the US forces, such as ferrying supplies to US troops, providing medical care, and collecting intelligence. Other

[20] "Diet Passes Bills for SDF Action," *Daily Yomiuri On-line*, October 30, 2001.

roles include search-and-rescue activities and humanitarian relief to refugees overseas. According to the media, Washington has informally asked Tokyo to transport fuel and other supplies from US bases in Japan and Guam to Diego Garcia in the Indian Ocean, a key British base used by the US for the Afghanistan operation.[21] The Japanese government also considered the dispatch to the Indian Ocean of navy destroyers equipped with the advanced Aegis battle-management system. The bill also has the following features: a two-year time limit, the government must seek Diet approval within 20 days of an SDF dispatch, and current restrictions on the SDFs' use of weapons have been relaxed to allow them to use arms to defend not only themselves but those "under their care."

Predictably, China was concerned about a higher military profile for Japan beyond its immediate vicinity. China has urged Japan to "exercise prudence" when it embarks on its expanded role and not to forget regional sensitivities to a larger military role.[22] Beijing is probably displeased that Tokyo is establishing a precedent in dispatching its sophisticated navy through waters that include the South China Sea, the Straits of Malacca, and the Indian Ocean.

By the time the fourth generation leaders take over, the Japanese flag may still be flying across these waters if the campaign against terrorism turns out to be a long-drawn-out affair. Despite China's instinctive distrust of any expanded military role by Japan, Beijing should realize that its neighbor still is committed to a nonnuclear weapon policy and has no intention to acquire long-range bombers and aircraft carriers that can project offensive power. Moreover,

---

[21] "SDF Antiterrorism Bill Wins Quick Diet Passage," *Japan Time On-line*, October 30, 2001.

[22] During Koizumi's visit to China in October 2001, Jiang Zemin reminded Koizumi about the sensitivities among Asian nations toward Japan's plan to dispatch the SDF to support the US-led strikes against Afghanistan. Zhu Rongji urged Koizumi to be "prudent" about expanding Japan's military role in the US-led anti-terrorism operations. See "Koizumi Says China Leaders 'Understand' SDF Role", *Japan Times On-line*, October 9, 2001.

Tokyo's SDF dovetails into US war-fighting structures and presently cannot operate autonomously in any major conflict. Insofar as the PRC maintains good relations with the US, it has little to fear from Japan. After all, the alliance makes it unnecessary for Tokyo to significantly spend more on armaments and to possess an independent military posture including nuclear capabilities.

In the Epoch of Terrorism, the US will regard China as a friend if it cooperates in the fight against terrorism. Then Beijing and Tokyo will be in the same bandwagon just like the "good, old United Front days" when the US, China, and Japan were on the same side against the Soviet Union. Objectively speaking, any military conflict between China and Japan does not make sense, especially when both countries are emerging as among each other's best customers in trade.

ECONOMIC TIES THAT BIND?

While certain noncompetitive sectors in Japan may be the hurt by the increasing Sino–Japanese trade, the economic relationship is generally a beneficial one. According to the *East Asian Economic Perspectives*, an authoritative Japanese source, Japan's total global exports in 2000 was $ 492.035 billion; mainland China's share was 6.14% while Hong Kong absorbed 5.63%. The US market is still the most important for Japan; it absorbs 29.63% of Japanese exports. In the case of imports, Japan's total was $ 388.664 billion in the same year. China's share of Japan's imports was 14.44%; Hong Kong's share was only 0.44%. The US share of Japan's imports remains the largest: 19.20% (see Figure 1).[23]

In 2000, China's total exports were $ 242.910 billion. Japan's share was 16.44% while the US absorbed 21.14%. The mainland's

---

[23] "Recent Trends and Prospects for Major Asian Economies," *East Asian Economic Perspectives*, Vol. 12 (February 2001), pp. 21–22.

Figure 1. Japan's Exports and Imports (US$ millions)

	Exports				
	1981	1985	1990	1995	2000 (est.)
Total exports	151,500	177,189	287,664	443,047	492,035
China share (%)	3.35	7.11	2.14	4.95	6.14
Hong Kong (%)	3.49	3.70	4.56	6.27	5.63
US (%)	25.67	37.63	34.22	27.54	29.63
	Imports				
	1981	1985	1990	1995	2000 (est.)
Total imports	142,868	136,142	235,289	336,027	338,664
China share (%)	3.70	5.00	5.12	10.69	14.44
Hong Kong (%)	0.47	0.59	0.93	0.81	0.44
US (%)	17.69	19.99	22.46	22.58	19.20

Source: "Recent Trends and Prospects for Major Asian Economies," *East Asian Economic Perspectives*, Vol. 12 (Special issue) (February 2001), pp. 21–22.

total imports were $ 194.574 billion. Japan's share of China's total imports was 18.46% while the US share was 9.86% (see Figure 2). The *East Asian Economic Perspectives* notes that China State Statistical

Figure 2. China's Exports and Imports (US$ millions)

	Exports				
	1981	1985	1990	1995	2000 (est.)
Total exports	21,476	27,329	62,876	148,955	242,910
Japan's share (%)	22.10	22.29	14.65	19.11	16.44
Hong Kong (%)	24.51	26.16	43.20	24.17	17.79
US (%)	7.01	8.55	8.45	16.61	21.14
	Imports				
	1981	1985	1990	1995	2000 (est.)
Total imports	21,631	42,480	53,915	132,163	194,574
Japan's share (%)	28.58	35.73	14.20	21.95	18.46
Hong Kong (%)	5.71	11.21	27.01	6.51	4.19
US (%)	21.64	12.24	12.22	12.20	9.86

Source: "Recent Trends and Prospects for Major Asian Economies," *East Asian Economic Perspectives*, Vol. 12 (Special issue) (February 2001), pp. 35–36.

**Figure 3. Sources of Foreign Direct Investment
to China (1996–2000)**

Total: US$ 214 billion	
Hong Kong	43%
US	9%
Japan	8%
Taiwan	7%
Singapore	6%
South Korea	4%
European Union	4%
Britain	3%
Canada	1%
Others	15%

Source: Asiaweek, October 26, 2001 (Statistics from: UNCTAD, IMF, CEIC, Institute of International Finance).

Bureau's estimates of Japanese FDI in China between 1995 and 1999 was an average of $ 3.5 billion annually. According to the *Asiaweek*, foreign direct investment between 1996 and 2000 to China was a total of $ 214 billion. The US and Japan's shares were 9 and 8% respectively (see Figure 3).

The *East Asian Economic Perspectives* also points out the structure of merchandise trade between Japan and China:

"Japan's exports are dominated by machinery, followed by other manufactures, and more distantly by chemical manufactures. Japan's largest imports are other manufactures, mainly light manufactures such as textiles, apparel, and footwear. Machinery imports have also grown very rapidly in recent years to become the second largest category, rising from 9% in 1994 to 21% in 1999. Resources based in agriculture, crude materials, and mineral fuels were also important in the past but have grown relatively slowly in recent years."[24]

---

[24] "Recent Trends and Prospects for Major Asian Economies," *East Asian Economic Perspectives*, p. 30.

As China modernizes and becomes more economically developed, the trend that machinery becomes a more important component of its exports to Japan will continue.

The Japan External Trade Organization (JETRO) noted that Sino–Japanese trade has been expanding primarily in the form of processing trade by firms that have their production bases in China. Moreover, machinery and equipment comprised 29.3% of total imports to Japan from China (January–June 2001), surpassing textile products for the first time owing to an expansion in trade in IT products.[25]

Besides trade, both countries have also made progress in environmental protection.[26] If they can anchor their relationship not only bilaterally or trilaterally (with the US) but also in regional and multilateral cooperation, then occasional bilateral tensions can be mitigated by progress made and habits of cooperation forged in nascent processes such as APEC (Asia Pacific Economic Cooperation), ARF (ASEAN Regional Forum), United Nations peacekeeping operations, ASEAN plus 3, and the WTO.

CONCLUSION

In the age of globalization, the economies of China, Japan, and the US have become increasingly intertwined. Subjective perceptions about geo-political and economic "threats", emotional issues over history, and domestic politics may ruffle Sino–Japanese relations occasionally, but objectively they have substantial common interests especially in trade. Common interests among the three great powers are also more likely in the Epoch of Terrorism.

If our hypothesis is correct, better Sino–US relations underpinned by a United Front against terrorism will benefit Sino–Japanese relations too, because the Japanese foreign policy is closely aligned to the US. While the structural framework of the international system in the Epoch of Terrorism may favor Sino–Japanese relations,

[25] "Japan–China trade hit record-high in first half," *Japan Time On-line*, August 10, 2001.
[26] See "Japan to Help China Build Ecological Database," *Daily Yomiuri On-line*, October 24, 2001.

perennial irritants like the apology issue, controversy over the Japanese Prime Minister's visit to Yasukuni Shrine, and neonationalist textbooks are unlikely to vanish in the near future.

Hopefully, the habits of cooperation forged among the three great powers should carry over after the terrorist networks are smashed, and by definition the Epoch of Terrorism is over. Will there be sufficient common grounds for good Sino–US relations and improved China–Japan ties after the war against global terrorism is over? Will the US once again raise the specter of the "China threat" especially when the mainland has become even more prosperous and economically powerful? Will Washington label Beijing as a "strategic rival" once again in the post-Epoch of Terrorism? Will things come to a head over Taiwan, and will Japan find itself dragged into a conflict with China because of its alliance with the US? All these indeed are imponderables.

To be sure, there are at least two probable outcomes in East Asia. The first is the inexorable rise of China insofar as it avoids an armed conflict with the US (over Taiwan) and severe domestic instability (like a repeat of the Tiananmen incident). The second is Japan becoming a "normal" state. Given these two trends, how will the two most powerful states in Asia manage their relations?

Within the next decade or two, a political consensus in Japan is likely to emerge over jettisoning Article 9 of the Constitution. Increasingly, the mainstream in public opinion is in favor of a looser interpretation of Article 9 (allowing collective security) or even ridding it altogether. The fourth generation leaders in Beijing should be psychologically prepared to accept the choice of the Japanese people. The knee-jerk response among many Chinese is likely to swiftly condemn Japan for embarking on the path of "militarism." However, they should not be trapped by their own rhetoric. Even if the Japanese were to jettison Article 9, it does not mean that Tokyo is embarking on "militarism." Except for those on the lunatic fringe, even the right-wing neonationalists in Japan do not advocate military confrontation with China. (Why would a nonnuclear Japan take on a nuclear China?) Tokyo will adhere to its nonnuclear weapon policy insofar as the US–Japan alliance remains.

The fourth generation leaders ought to exercise humility towards their neighbors when their country is emerging rich and powerful. To behave otherwise will instil fear in their neighbors. The new leaders should also be mindful that the phenomenon of "China rising, Japan declining" will not last forever. The rise of China is probable but not inevitable. It will depend, to a very large extent, on the political skills and wisdom of the fourth generation leaders to address considerable domestic problems and also to promote a peaceful regional and international environmental that is conducive to China's economic development. Beijing's leaders should be aware that Japan's economy still is the largest in Asia despite a decade of economic doldrums (Figure 4). Even if China were to succeed in narrowing the gap, Japan remains a key economic player in the world.

Japan may suffer from relative decline and painful restructuring for another five to 10 years. However, analysts should not be oblivious to Japan's history of impressive resilience and adaptability in the face of wrenching domestic transformation and international challenges. Over the past century and a half, the nation made two pivotal shifts: the Meiji transformation during the late 19th century and post-World War II systemic change. While the "lost decade" since the burst of the bubble economy may seem a long period, we should be mindful that the two pivotal shifts took more than a decade each before a new system was put in place.

What if Japan recovers? Will Sino–Japanese relations move away from the prickliness of "China rising, Japan declining"? Will the subsequent phenomenon of "China rising, Japan recovering" lead to

Figure 4. China, Japan and US Compared

	Population (millions)	Per-capita GNP (US$)	Reserves (excluding gold) (US$ in billions)
China	1292.3	840	183.9
Japan	127.1	37,950	361.1
US	285.7	35,277	54.7

Source: Asiaweek, September 28, 2001.

less fear and greater confidence among the Japanese elites towards China? A renaissance enjoyed by both China and Japan may well be a positive-sum rather than a zero-sum game. The outcome will be influenced, for the better or worse, by the leadership in both countries. That will also be the task not only for the fourth but also the fifth generation leaders of China.

Index